Clinical Research
Law and Compliance
Handbook

Edited by
John E. Steiner, Jr., Esq.
Chief Compliance Officer and Privacy Official
Cleveland Clinic Health System

JONES AND BARTLETT PUBLISHERS
Sudbury, Massachusetts
BOSTON   TORONTO   LONDON   SINGAPORE

World Headquarters

Jones and Bartlett Publishers
40 Tall Pine Drive
Sudbury, MA 01776
978-443-5000
info@jbpub.com
www.jbpub.com

Jones and Bartlett Publishers
Canada
2406 Nikanna Road
Mississauga, ON L5C 2W6
CANADA

Jones and Bartlett Publishers
International
Barb House, Barb Mews
London W6 7PA
UK

Jones and Bartlett's books and products are available through most bookstores and online book-sellers. To contact Jones and Bartlett Publishers directly, call 800-832-0034, fax 978-443-8000, or visit our website www.jbpub.com.

Substantial discounts on bulk quantities of Jones and Bartlett's publications are available to cor-porations, professional associations, and other qualified organizations. For details and specific discount information, contact the special sales department at Jones and Bartlett via the above contact information or send an email to specialsales@jbpub.com.

Library of Congress Cataloging-in-Publication Data

Steiner, John (John E.)
  Clinical research law and compliance handbook / by John E. Steiner, Jr.—1st ed.
    p. cm.
  Includes bibliographical references and index.
  ISBN 0-7637-4725-4 (alk. paper)
  1. Clinical trials--Law and legislation—United States. 2. Medicine—Research—Law and legislation—United States. I. Title.
  KF3821.S736 2006
  344.7304'1—dc22
                                                                      2005008613

Production Credits
Publisher: Michael Brown
Editorial Assistant: Kylah Goodfellow McNeill
Production Director: Amy Rose
Associate Production Editor: Renée Sekerak
Production Assistant: Rachel Rossi
Senior Marketing Manager: Ed McKenna
Associate Marketing Manager: Marissa Hederson
Manufacturing Buyer: Therese Bräuer
Composition: PawPrint Media
Cover Design: Kristin E. Ohlin
Printing and Binding: Malloy Incorporated
Cover Printing: Malloy Incorporated

Printed in the United States of America
09 08 07 06 05   10 9 8 7 6 5 4 3 2 1

CONTENTS

CHAPTER EIGHT
Key Compliance Issues for Institutional Review Boards   299

Michael J. Meehan and Marleina Thomas Davis

FOREWORD

The Importance of Paying Attention

The issue of fraud and abuse in government programs has always been with us. Before there ever was a Department of Health and Human Services Inspector General, there was an office for fraud and abuse investigations within the Health Care Financing Administration. Before there ever was a Health Care Financing Administration, there was an office for fraud and abuse investigations in the Social Security Administration. The laws, too, are legendary. Even today, one of the key statutes used for fraud investigations goes back to Civil War times when there was a concern about abuse in government contracting for material to support the army. In short, we are dealing with a human condition: If there is something of value to be transacted, there are always legitimate and illegitimate ways of conducting such a transaction, and there is always someone somewhere who is willing to test the limits of legitimacy or even conduct outright fraud. Government has a responsibility to see that funds made available are spent according to the rules and guides it specifies. Congress, in particular, has the responsibility to conduct oversight of the Executive Branch in the enforcement of these rules, and the potential for embarrassment is a strong motive for writing detailed rules to explain, to the extent possible, what is legitimate. However, it is impossible to write rules that cover all situations and Medicare is a highly complex, constantly evolving program with hundreds of thousands of pages of regulations, rules, guidelines, and forms. Additionally, honesty is not assumed. The formula approaches more that of the Cold War, with President Reagan's maxim "Trust, but verify." Translated to Medicare, that means know the requirements and abide by them to the best of your ability, and document, document, and document!

These words to the wise should be sufficient. Enjoy this fine book!

Dan Nickelson
Former Government Relations Director
Cleveland Clinic Foundation

PREFACE

This timely book addresses important issues related to the rapidly expanding enterprise of clinical research. Clinical research is the application of advances in biomedical, social sciences, and behavioral research to human populations. Without clinical research, there can be no progress in promoting health, or in understanding, preventing, or treating disease; medical progress would halt. However, an explosion in basic knowledge and technology has not only resulted in unparalleled opportunities for clinical research, but also in an unprecedented array of regulatory and policy requirements related to good clinical practice, ethical research conduct, human subject protection, and compliance with regulations. Clinical investigators are having difficulty understanding and satisfying the bewildering array of requirements by diverse regulatory and policy agencies. This book is targeted at this issue. Edited by the director of a compliance office at a major American academic medical center, the book clearly and succinctly reviews many important areas.

From an initial overview in Chapter 1, Key Compliance Issues for Academic Medical Organizations through to the last, Clinical Research Trials in the Courtroom, the contributing authors cover a number of important topics. They are all important, since even the most promising clinical protocol can end in a bad outcome if not carefully conceived and executed in the setting of good practice. This book covers research contracts, research budgeting and billing, fraud and abuse in clinical research, protection of private health information, special issues of post marketing studies, issues related to IRBs, conflicts of interest in clinical research, data integrity in clinical trials, the special case of the multinational trial directed from the United States, and the increasingly common issue of research malpractice.

This book is a must-read for clinical investigators and research administrators alike. One could legitimately argue that it should be required reading for every clinical investigator. In addition to providing important background information, this book provides a fundamental basis for addressing important goals: the need to harmonize diverse adverse event reporting requirements; the overlapping and often unclear roles of data safety and monitoring boards vs. institutional review boards; the emerging field of electronic data capture and electronic research records; the need for accreditation standards and credentialing for institutions and individual investigators. Steiner and his colleagues have done a service by providing this timely and important book. I highly recommend it.

Richard A. Rudick, MD
Chairman, Division of Clinical Research
Cleveland Clinic Foundation

INTRODUCTION

This handbook is intended to serve a diverse audience of readers involved in clinical research trials. Each chapter is formatted and written in a practical, readable style to provide easy access to timely material. The Editor envisioned a book that provides timely, practical analyses and advice for those engaged in advancing medical knowledge and its application, those who support such efforts, and the participants in clinical trials. The authors of this book regularly encounter the complex legal and compliance issues associated with clinical trials.

The opinions, analyses, and recommendations of the authors in this handbook do not, unless expressly indicated otherwise, represent the opinions or recommendations of their respective organizations. Moreover, the service of a competent professional should be sought on any matter or analysis addressed if legal advice or expert assistance is required.

The nature and pace of advances in medical knowledge, technology, pharmaceuticals, and medical devices require a sustained effort by those engaged in clinical trials to comply with applicable laws and regulations. The hard work required to conduct compliant clinical trials combines highly motivated and creative medical scientists, the hopes and concerns of trial participants, the business interests of sponsors and clinical trial sites, and a governmental interest in protecting the health and welfare of clinical trial participants. In sum, clinical research is a vital and serious undertaking for all involved.

In his book *The Lives of a Cell*, (1974, The Viking Press, Inc.) Dr. Lewis Thomas describes three levels of technology in medicine. The first level he calls *nontechnology* that can be defined as supportive therapy, or caring for the patient. This level of medicine does not involve measures directed to the underlying mechanism of disease. The next level he labels as *halfway technology* that represents steps taken after the fact to deal with the debilitating effects of certain diseases. This technology is designed to make up for disease, or to postpone death. Examples include solid organ transplants, implantation of artificial organs, cancer treatments, and the like. It is the type of technology that must be offered until a genuine understanding of disease mechanisms is reached. Finally, he suggests a third category *high technology* that reflects clear and coherent understanding of the disease process. In Lewis's words, "This is the genuinely decisive technology of modern medicine…" (pg. 35). Clinical research trials are essential for modern medicine to move from basic research and advance upward, along the lines suggested by Dr. Lewis, to the level of *high technology* in medicine. This handbook was prepared to assist those engaged in clinical trials that strive to reach the level of *high technology*.

The authors were asked to provide practical examples in order to make the information as useful as possible. In addition, each chapter includes relevant legal and regulatory authorities, practical recommendations, and other insights that contribute to effective clinical research compliance. Several chapters include recommendations for specific action steps and provide sample forms or templates to implement those recommendations.

The legal and compliance issues that arise in clinical research trials conducted at academic research organizations are varied and complex. Nonetheless, this handbook also should prove useful to organizations and individuals involved in clinical research in other settings.

The editor is fortunate to be able to include authors from The Cleveland Clinic Foundation. Chapters contributed by colleagues provide interesting and state of the art insights into how clinical research issues arise and are addressed by a nationally and internationally recognized site for clinical trials. In addition, this book includes contributions from lawyers and consultants with significant expertise in structuring and administering clinical trials. The authors cover key compliance and legal issues that are common in clinical trials, including trials conducted internationally. To round out the coverage of the issues addressed in earlier chapters and illustrate what has been alleged to be non-compliant conduct, this handbook closes with a chapter on trends in clinical trial litigation.

Overview of the Chapters

Chapter 1–Key Compliance Issues for Academic Medical Organizations
Both contributors have extensive clinical research experience, particularly in cardiology and cancer trials. Their perspectives are based on 20 years of cumulative experience at The Cleveland Clinic Foundation, often involving ground breaking clinical advances. This chapter includes planning and implementation documents that should be adaptable to a variety of department settings.

Chapter 2–Contract Issues in Clinical Trials
This chapter, written by a member of the Office of General Counsel at The Cleveland Clinic Foundation, is geared toward the internal client, i.e., Principal Investigators and their support personnel. The key points in this chapter provide guidance and recommendations for effective analysis, negotiation, and performance of contract obligations, including topics such as publication rights, intellectual property, and payor requirements.

Chapter 3–Clinical Research Billing: Process and Monitoring Issues
This chapter combines insights and recommendations from a compliance officer for a large, academic research organization and from a consultant with substantial experience with clinical research compliance. The authors describe the clinical research billing processes and monitoring challenges faced by many academic research organizations and discuss methods and techniques for handling those challenges. Detailed appendices for structuring work plans and self-audits are included.

Chapter 4–Clinical Research Trials: Operational and Budget Issues
This chapter provides straightforward, step-by-step advice for analyzing and addressing the recurring operational and budget issues associated with clinical trials.

The authors have extensive experience in assisting health care organizations in various areas, including Charge Description Master projects. As this chapter illustrates, the analysis of clinical research billing processes, and methods to improve those processes, requires a clear understanding of the interrelationships of billing operations, regulatory requirements, and information technology applications.

Chapter 5–Fraud and Abuse in Clinical Research

This handbook often refers to compliance risks that may arise under the Medicare Antikickback Statute and other laws. The authors of this chapter provide thorough analyses of this important federal statute that was initially enacted in 1972 and provides for both civil and criminal penalties. Various fact patterns and compliance risk areas that should be understood by those involved in clinical research are highlighted throughout this chapter. The chapter also addresses how these legal risks are interpreted and addressed by sponsors of clinical trials.

Chapter 6–Uses and Disclosures of Identifiable Information in Clinical Research: National and International Considerations

Individually identifiable information on trial participants must be collected, analyzed, distributed, and reported in the vast majority of clinical research trials. This issue and the regulatory schemes that are in place in the United States and in other countries to deal with this aspect of clinical research are thoroughly addressed in this chapter. The authors have extensive experience with the myriad of statutes, regulations, and guidance authorities that must be understood by those conducting clinical research.

Chapter 7–Identifying Applicable Laws and Reducing Key Risks in Nonregistrational, Postmarketing Studies

This chapter was developed by a large, contract research organization that is active in numerous domestic and international clinical trials. This topic increases in importance as major pharmaceutical companies work diligently to both expand the application of approved drugs and focus on new breakthroughs in pharmaceuticals. The volume of Phase IV clinical trials continues to increase and with that activity both novel and recurring compliance issues continue to arise. Both categories of issues are addressed in this chapter.

Chapter 8–Key Compliance Issues for Institutional Review Boards

Clinical research in America does not proceed without the approval of an Institutional Review Board (IRB). The underlying sources of authority and delegated responsibilities of IRBs are thoroughly covered in this chapter. The authors effectively focus on issues that are central to the IRB and present them in a practical manner. More recent issues, including the Health Insurance Portability and Accountability Act (HIPAA), and the IRB's role in formal, organizational conflicts-of-interest policies are also discussed. The legal rationale and guiding principles for effective IRB oversight of clinical trials should be components of sound compliance training and education for the workforce.

Chapter 9–Conflicts of Interest in Biomedical Research—Avoiding Bias

The need to define conflicts of interest and to describe a clear, coherent method of managing them presents challenges to many professional activities. Conflicts can and do exist in research. This chapter reflects careful study and practical analysis of this subject by a former senior level attorney for the National Institutes of Health who is now a partner with an international law firm. Her co-author is an associate in the same firm.

Chapter 10–Enhancing Data Quality and Patient Safety through the Use of Technology in Clinical Trials

Fundamentally, clinical trials are about data and the integrity of the process to create, analyze, and communicate results of the clinical trial data. In short, an organization's methods and techniques of data management are critical elements of successful trials. This chapter provides state-of-the art advice and practical examples for managing the data requirements of clinical trials, both for purposes of creating reliable data as well as for patient safety.

Chapter 11–Legal Issues in the Conduct of Multinational Clinical Trials by U.S. Entities

What can become a confusing mix of statutes, treaties, regulations, and directives are presented in this chapter orderly and thoroughly. The chapter illustrates some of the significant differences in legal and compliance structures across several countries. The author is involved as a counselor to sponsors, clinical trial sites, and other entities that conduct clinical research domestically and internationally. For those interested in the international aspects of clinical research, this chapter is a valuable resource.

Chapter 12–Clinical Research Trials in the Courtroom

As the author capably demonstrates in this chapter, the cases and underlying theories of liability that are asserted in clinical trial litigation provide valuable lessons. One key point is that a thorough examination of an organization's clinical research processes can provide *early warnings* of compliance risks. These lessons, some of which are described in detail in this chapter, need to be understood from the perspective of compliance process improvement.

John E. Steiner, Jr., Esq.
Chief Compliance Officer
Privacy Official
Cleveland Clinic Health System

CONTRIBUTOR BIOGRAPHIES

M. Peter Adler, JD

Peter Adler is the president of Adler InfoSec & Privacy Group, a consulting company that provides services to organizations on national and international data privacy and security. He also advises companies on handling transborder data flows, data warehousing, and data mining and technology transfer. In his security and privacy practice, he assists organizations with the administrative security and privacy aspects of the Gramm-Leach-Bliley Act (GLBA), the Health Insurance Portability and Accountability Act (HIPAA), the EU Data Protection Directive (including the US "Safe Harbor"), FDA security regulations (21 C.F.R. Part 11), the Canadian Personal Information Protection and Electronic Documents Act (PIPEDA), and various state laws, including the California Law on Notice of Security Breach. He also assists credit card using businesses to be in compliance with the voluntary Payment Card Industry (PCI) Data Security Standard.

He is on the advisory board and is a contributor to three HIPAA-related publications: The Health Information Compliance Insider, the HIPAA Privacy Staff Trainer, and HIPAA Security Compliance Insider. Mr. Adler is a frequent lecturer and author on the subjects establishing business processes and infrastructure leading to compliance with privacy and information security, infrastructure protection, and technology transfer.

He is a member of the New York Electronic Crimes Task Force and has taught the regulatory compliance and corporate governance aspects of information privacy and security to law enforcement agents at the Federal Law Enforcement Training Center (FLETC) in Glynco, GA.

Mr. Adler obtained his Bachelor of Science degree from Ohio University, Juris Doctor degree from William Mitchell College of Law and his Masters of Law (LL.M., International, with distinction) from Georgetown University. In 2002, he received the prestigious Certified Information Systems Security Professional (CISSP) accreditation granted by the International Information Systems Security Certifications Consortium. In 2004, he was included in the inaugural class receiving the Certified Information Privacy Professional (CIPP) accreditation provided by the International Association of Privacy Professionals (IAPP).

Mr. Adler is a member of IAPP, the American Health Lawyers Association, the Computer Security Institute, and the Information Systems Security Association.

Andrew Agati, Esq.
Andrew Agati is an Associate at Squire, Sanders & Dempsey LLP and a member of the litigation practice group. Mr. Agati has represented clients in both federal and state court on a wide range of matters. Mr. Agati has successfully defended a research university and a group of researchers in a clinical trial litigation. He has advised a study sponsor with respect to informed consent language, adverse event reporting, and related issues. Mr. Agati has also lectured on various topics concerning clinical trial litigation. Mr. Agati is admitted to practice before the bars of the states of Ohio and Illinois, is a member of the American, Federal, Ohio State, and Cleveland Bar Associations, the Anthony J. Celebrezze Inn of Court, the Defense Research Institute, and the Justinian Society, and is a former adjunct professor of law at Case Western Reserve University School of Law. Mr. Agati received his JD (*magna cum laude*) from Case Western Reserve University in 1995.

Judith E. Beach, PhD, Esq.

Judith E. Beach is the Vice President and Senior Associate General Counsel for Regulatory Affairs, Chief Privacy Officer, and Coordinator of Government Affairs with Quintiles Transnational Corp., a global private company headquartered near Research Triangle Park, North Carolina. Quintiles helps improve health care worldwide by providing a broad range of professional services, information, and partnering solutions to the pharmaceutical, biotechnology, and healthcare industries. Dr. Beach's responsibilities include providing legal and regulatory advice and guidance to Quintiles' personnel on various international and domestic regulatory issues concerning the pharmaceutical, medical device, and biotechnology industries. In this capacity, she has been involved in providing counsel with respect to good clinical practices in the conduct of clinical trials and the protection of human participants in research with respect to investigators, institutional review boards, sponsors, and clinical research monitors, and good manufacturing practices regarding drug product ownership. She is the Chair of the Company's Council on Research Ethics (CORE), which provides guidance to the company's research personnel on ethical issues related to all stages of research. As the Chief Privacy Officer and Chair of the Council on Data Protection, Quintiles' internal privacy board, she coordinates the monitoring of the company's policies and procedures for protection of individually identifiable information, including the protection of research subjects' confidential health information. In 2002, she served as Assistant Secretary for the new trade association, the Association of Clinical Research Organizations, and currently participates in ACRO's Policies and Practices and Ethics and Clinical Practice Committees. Dr. Beach graduated *cum laude* from Georgetown University Law Center, where she was an associate editor of *The Georgetown Law Journal.* She served as a judicial clerk for the District of Columbia Court of Appeals, and was an associate attorney with two Washington, DC, law firms: Akin, Gump, Strauss, Hauer & Feld and Hyman, Phelps & McNamara, PC, where she specialized in civil litigation and food, drug, and medical device law, respectively. She is admitted to the Bars of the District of Columbia, Virginia, Maryland, and North Carolina and is admitted to practice before the United States Supreme Court. Prior to law school, Judith received her BS degree *summa cum laude* from Clemson University and her PhD in Physiology and Pharmacology from Duke University. She was a Fellow in Reproductive Endocrinology at the University of California San Francisco, and then a clinical investigator at Walter Reed Hospital in Washington, DC. Dr. Beach has numerous publications in the fields of both science and law. Dr. Beach has been elected as a member of the prestigious scientific societies, Sigma Xi and the Endocrine Society.

Joan Booth, RN
Joan Booth has worked in the Department of Cardiovascular Medicine at the Cleveland Clinic Foundation for 25 years. For the past three years she has managed the Cardiovascular Research Department that includes an Academic Research Organization. Prior to her current role she had been a Head Nurse of a Cardiac Telemetry Unit, Departmental Assistant to the Interventional Cardiology Section, and Project Manager for Cardiovascular Studies.

Joseph B. Clamon, Esq.
Joseph B. Clamon is a judicial clerk to Judge Michael J. Melloy of the United States Court of Appeals for the Eighth Circuit. Mr. Clamon is a graduate of the University of Iowa College of Law and the University of Notre Dame. Prior to his clerkship, he worked as a summer associate for Epstein, Becker & Green in Washington, DC, for the University of Iowa Office of the General Counsel, and as a research assistant to professor and president Emeritus Willard L. Boyd. He has published articles on clinical research law and compliance, in particular on issues of conflicts of interest and conflicts of commitment.

Marleina Thomas Davis, Esq.
Marleina Thomas Davis joined The Cleveland Clinic Foundation as associate counsel and a member of the Institutional Review Board in February of 2004. Prior to that, Ms. Davis was in private practice where she specialized in health care law.

Kendra Dimond, Esq.
Kendra Dimond is a partner at the Washington, DC office of Epstein, Becker & Green, PC, where she practices health law. She has extensive experience advising a wide variety of clients on regulatory compliance in connection with biomedical, clinical, and scientific research. Ms. Dimond served as a health care fraud prosecutor for the Pennsylvania Attorney General and subsequently became Investigative Counsel to the US Senate Special Committee on Aging under Senators Heinz and Cohen. She then joined the Office of General Counsel of the Department of Health and Human Services (HHS), National Institutes of Health (NIH), where she advised NIH on matters relating to the investigation of fraud and misconduct in scientific research. Subsequently Ms. Dimond headed the NIH Office of Legislative Policy and Analysis. In that capacity she was directly involved in Congressional and other governmental

investigations and inquiries pertaining to research support and research fraud issues. Ms. Dimond has authored several articles and given presentations throughout the United States on the topic of compliance with law and policy issues in the research setting.

Karen Owen Dunlop, Esq.

Karen Owen Dunlop is a partner in the health law group of Sidley, Austin, Brown & Wood. Ms. Dunlop specializes in compliance counseling, including fraud and abuse, health privacy issues, and other health regulatory issues. Ms. Dunlop works extensively on matters relating to clinical research, representing primarily sponsors and investigators.

Jeffrey A. Green, Pharm.D., FCP

Jeffrey A. Green is founder of DATATRAK International, Inc. and has served as President, Chief Executive Officer, and Director since March 1992. From 1984 to 1992, Dr. Green served as an Assistant Professor of Medicine and Radiology at Case Western Reserve University, Cleveland, OH. During his tenure at Case Western, Dr. Green established and directed the Cardiovascular Clinical Pharmacology Research Program at University Hospitals of Cleveland. In addition, Dr. Green was an established investigator in clinical cardiology and PET scanning, and was responsible for directing over 90 individual investigations.

Katherine Hammerhofer, RN, BSN

Katherine Hammerhofer is the Director at the Center for Clinical Trials, The Division of Clinical Research. She is responsible for the creation of central core resources, such as data management and finance/contracting to support departmental clinical research activity. She serves as lead for the implementation of an electronic clinical trial management system, to allow tracking, benchmarking, and improved budgeting/invoicing for clinical trial activities. Ms. Hammerhofer is a member of the Research Compliance Committee, focusing on standardizing clinical research activity in accordance with Good Clinical Practice guidelines. Her research experience prior to her current position includes Program Manager of the Cancer Center Experimental Therapeutics program, Manager of the CCF - Quintiles Alliance, and Research Nurse Manager for the Department of Colorectal Surgery. Peer review publications include *RN, Diseases of the Colon & Rectum,* and *Oncology.* She received a BS in Nursing (*magna cum laude*) from the University of Toledo.

William A. Hunt

William A. Hunt is the current President and owner of MedCom Solutions, Inc., and is one of the original founders of the company. Mr. Hunt specializes in conceptualizing consulting and software solutions for various Charge Master Review and maintenance processes, as well as pricing solutions for MedCom clients. He is personally involved in each consulting engagement to ensure that project goals are attained and that the client is satisfied. Mr. Hunt has over 20 years of experience in the healthcare industry. He worked as Director of Reimbursement Services for four years before founding MedCom Solutions in 1986. He received a BS in Finance from Robert Morris University. With his years of experience in health care, his depth and breadth of industry knowledge provide clients with unparalleled expertise in many different matters, such as pricing strategies, charge master regulations, Medicare compliance, and registration issues.

Bryan Lee

Bryan Lee graduated *magna cum laude* from Harvard University in 2000 with a degree in biochemistry. He is currently earning an MD/JD at Washington University in St. Louis School of Medicine and Harvard Law School. He co-authored this chapter while a summer associate at Sidley, Austin, Brown & Wood LLP in Washington, DC.

Michael J. Meehan, Esq.

Michael J. Meehan received his bachelor's degree from John Carroll University and his law degree from The University of Toledo. He was licensed to practice law in the states of Michigan in 1981 and Ohio in 1982. Prior to practicing law at the Cleveland Clinic, Mr. Meehan was an Associate Attorney at Dykema & Gossett in Detroit. He also was an accountant at both the Clinic and at Toledo Hospital. He held an active CPA license but that is no longer active.

Mr. Meehan has served as in-house legal counsel for the Clinic for over 20 years and also for Cleveland Clinic Florida. During most of this time he managed the Clinic's medical malpractice docket and handled loss prevention, risk management, and corporate insurance activities for the Clinic in Cleveland and Florida. He has provided legal guidance to the Clinic on a wide range of other issues over the years. He serves on the Clinic's Medical Legal Risk Management Committee, Institutional Review Board, Research Compliance Committee, Research Compliance Audit Committee, Conflict of Interest Committee, Physician Health Committee, HIPAA Privacy Council, HIPAA Steering Committee, and Scientific Misconduct Committee.

He is a member of the Clinic's Ethics Committee and leads the HIPAA Legal Advisory Group of the Cleveland Clinic Health System. He serves as corporate Assistant Secretary and is the Clinic's statutory agent.

Mr. Meehan taught health law as Adjunct Assistant Professor at The Cleveland State University Nance School of Business for eight years and has lectured extensively in-house, locally, and nationally.

Donna J. Meyer, Esq.

Donna J. Meyer is Associate Counsel with the Office of the General Counsel for The Cleveland Clinic Foundation. Ms. Meyer earned her JD from the Case Western Reserve University School of Law, and her BA from The American University, Washington, D.C. Prior to joining the Cleveland Clinic, Ms. Meyer clerked in the chambers of The Honorable Norma Holloway Johnson, United States District Court for the District of Columbia and the Cleveland regional office of the Federal Trade Commission, and practiced with the law firms of Kirkpatrick & Lockhart LLP in Pittsburgh, Pennsylvania and Arter & Hadden LLP in Cleveland, Ohio. Ms. Meyer is admitted to the Pennsylvania and Ohio bars.

Ms. Meyer has focused her law practice in the areas of business and health law, providing counseling on corporate, tax, and antitrust aspects of business transactions and regulatory aspects of the health care industry, including federal and state regulation in the ears of fraud and abuse, provider relations, charitable trust, tax-exemption, and animal and clinical research. For the Cleveland Clinic, Ms. Meyer is primarily responsible for industry sponsorship relationships and coordinates on contracting, compliance and audit matters, and provides training on a variety of issues, including private contracting, fraud and abuse, and sponsored research.

Jeffrey G. Micklos, Esq.

Jeffrey G. Micklos is Vice President and General Counsel of the Federation of American Hospitals, where he is responsible for a variety of federal health care policy and legal matters affecting investor-owned community hospitals. Previously, Mr. Micklos was a partner with the law firm of Foley & Lardner LLP, where he advised various types of health care organizations on reimbursement, regulatory compliance, and administrative law issues related to federal and state health care programs. Mr. Micklos began his legal career with the federal government, where he represented the Department of Health and Human Services in federal court matters and counseled the Health Care Financing Administration on regulatory and policy matters.

Jan E. Murray, Esq.

Jan E. Murray focuses her practice on the health care and life science industries with a specific emphasis on corporate and regulatory compliance, regulation of sponsored clinical trials, commercialization, pricing and marketing of drugs and devices, international transmission of health data, and e-health ventures including licensing, medical privacy, and Web site development. Ms. Murray has lectured and published widely. Recent presentations include "Pediatric Research Issues," Academic Medical Centers Annual Conference sponsored by the American Health Lawyers Association, Washington DC, January 2003, and "Navigating the Clinical Trials Process: US/EU Comparison," First Annual Irish BIO Conference, Dublin, Ireland, November 2002; "Contracting with CROs," BIO 2005 Annual International Conference, San Francisco, June 2005. She is a partner in the law firm of Squire, Sanders & Dempsey L.L.P., a firm with over 700 lawyers located in 26 offices worldwide.

F. Lisa Murtha, JD, CHC

F. Lisa Murtha is a principal in the Philadelphia office of Parente Randolph, LLC and focuses her practice in clinical research compliance, revenue cycle work, billing and coding issues, internal investigations, corporate governance/ethics, and HIPAA work. Prior to joining Parente Randolph she served as the Vice President of Audit, Compliance and Chief Privacy Officer for The Children's Hospital of Philadelphia, the Stokes Research Institute, and The Children's Hospital of Philadelphia Practice Association. Ms. Murtha received her BA (with distinction) from The Pennsylvania State University in 1983 and her JD from the Dickinson School of Law in 1986. Ms. Murtha previously served as a Managing Director for KPMG LLP's New York-based health care fraud and compliance practice and as a Senior Manager for Deloitte and Touche's compliance practice where she assisted her clients with the development and implementation of comprehensive corporate compliance programs, clinical research compliance programs, complex reimbursement, and other internal investigations and in supervising Independent Review Organization projects for clients under Corporate Integrity Agreements with the government. Prior to her consulting career, Ms. Murtha worked as the Chief Compliance Officer for the University of Pennsylvania and University of Pennsylvania Health System, and prior to that as the Corporate Compliance Director for Pennsylvania Blue Shield (focusing primarily on Medicare Carrier Contract Compliance). Ms. Murtha is a Board member of the International Association of Privacy Officers and a Board Member and former officer of the Health Care Compliance Association. She frequently lectures nationally on compliance-related issues, and has published numerous articles on various health care topics, and provides advisory services to BNA and other publications.

Susan M. O'Connell

Susan M. O'Connell is currently employed as a Healthcare Consultant with MedCom Solutions, Inc., where she has worked for the past five years. Ms. O'Connell's expertise lies in the development of technical and professional pricing structures that positively impact net reimbursement, as well as in spearheading Charge Master maintenance projects for various clients. She is involved in all aspects of the consulting division that carry financial ramifications, and assists in quantifying these benefits for the client. In addition, she provides input for software specifications to the IS team at MedCom Solutions, to assist in the development of software products for pricing, budgeting, and Charge Master maintenance projects. Ms. O'Connell received a BS in Mathematics and a BSBA in Finance from the University of Pittsburgh.

William A. Sarraille, Esq.

William A. Sarraille is a Senior Partner in the Health Care Practice of Sidley, Austin, Brown & Wood, LLP. Resident in the firm's Washington, DC office, Mr. Sarraille is a nationally known authority on health care compliance and regulatory issues, including those affecting clinical research. He has represented pharmaceutical manufacturers, device and equipment manufacturers, and other sponsors, medical societies, health care trade associations, academic medical centers, research sites, and clinical researchers in a broad range of regulatory, contracting, compliance, appropriations, legislative, and enforcement matters relating to the conduct of clinical research. He is the co-author of two books on clinical research issues and has served on the editorial board of more than a dozen publications, focusing on health care and Food and Drug Administration issues.

Marc Shlaes, BB

Marc J. Shlaes has served as Vice President of Research and Development and Chief Technology Officer of DATATRAK International, Inc. since October 2000. Mr. Shlaes is responsible for the development of DATATRAK EDC™ and related software offerings. From October 1999 through December 2000, Mr. Shlaes served as Vice President and Managing Director of North America. Prior to both appointments, Mr. Shlaes served as Director of Technology and Services. Prior to joining DATATRAK International, Inc. in 1998, Mr. Shlaes served in a variety of positions in the software development and delivery industry, including as an employee of IBM from 1982 to 1996.

Nancy A. Strehlow, Esq.

Nancy A. Strehlow is a special counsel for Health Law and Policy for Quintiles Transnational Corp., a global company headquartered near Research Triangle Park, North Carolina, and the Antikickback Compliance Officer for the Strategic Research Services Division of Quintiles, Inc. Quintiles helps improve healthcare worldwide by providing a broad range of professional services, information and partnering solutions to the pharmaceutical, biotechnology and healthcare industries. Ms. Strehlow's responsibilities include providing contractual and regulatory advice to Quintiles' personnel on various issues, the including the Antikickback Statute, False Claims Act, electronic records, financial disclosure, and data transfer. Ms. Strehlow is responsible for drafting Quintiles' contract forms and for negotiating customer and site agreements. Ms. Strehlow graduated from Washington University School of Law, where she was a member of the Order of the Coif and a Senior Editor of the Law Review. She served as a judicial clerk for the Honorable Barefoot Sanders of the United States District Court for the Northern District of Texas. Thereafter, she was an associate attorney with the Dallas law firm of Locke, Purnell, Rain, Harrell, where she specialized in civil litigation. She joined Quintiles' Legal Department in 1996.

ABOUT THE EDITOR

John Steiner is the Chief Compliance Officer and Privacy Official for the Cleveland Clinic Health System (CCHS). He is responsible for the design, implementation, and administration of the Compliance and HIPAA Privacy programs for a multi-state, integrated delivery system that includes an academic medical center. The compliance programs include requirements of government and private payors, clinical research, and HIPAA Privacy and Security. He previously served as Senior Counsel for the American Hospital Association where he was a legal liaison with federal agencies, private payers, and health care trade associations to provide compliance guidance, advice, and analyses for 5,000 member hospitals. John was a member of the health law department of a national, full-service law firm headquartered in Chicago where hs specialized in corporate law, healthcare regulatory and administrative issues, Medicare and Medicaid matters, managed care projects, medical staff issues, taxable and tax-exempt financings, joint ventures, and business arrangements with physicians. Mr. Steiner obtained his BA from Johns Hopkins University, his Certificate from the Johns Hopkins University School of Advanced International Studies and his JD, with honors, from Chicago-Kent College of Law in Chicago, Illinois. Mr. Steiner is a Board Member of the Health Care Compliance Association (HCCA) and Chairman of the American Medical Group Association's (AMGA) Council of Compliance Officers. Mr. Steiner is a national speaker on health law and compliance topics including Aspen Publications, *Health Law and Compliance Update*, published annually since 2003 and Health Care Compliance Association, *Auditing & Monitoring Principles for Effective Compliance*.

ONE

Key Compliance Issues for Academic Medical Organizations

Joan Booth and Katherine Hammerhofer

Introduction

The intent of clinical research activity conducted at an academic medical center (AMC) is to demonstrate proof that a therapy will ultimately improve the delivery of human medical care. In order to generate valid results from a clinical trial, it is a critical responsibility of research management and the research team to ensure that trials are conducted according to Good Clinical Practice guidelines. "Good Clinical Practice" (GCP) is a term coined by the pharmaceutical and medical device industry to encompass international and federal regulations, as well as industry-accepted standards, that govern the conduct of clinical trials on humans.[1] In order to ensure GCP compliance from your staff, it is necessary to have developed written standards in three key areas: operational processes, staff training, and regulatory compliance. Structured staff training, which includes formal orientation, assessment, and documented sign-off on key job competencies, are essential for a competent and accountable workforce. A formal approach to key job activities, research

1

processes, and standard operating procedures (SOPs) are critical to achieving standardization in your practice. Finally, establishing a defined approach to assess the effectiveness of your staff training and practice standards, via regularly scheduled quality assurance audits, should provide documentation to support your AMC regulatory compliance efforts.

If you are just beginning to formulate GCP processes for your AMC, the identification of key compliance "risk areas" will facilitate the development of your quality assurance framework, which will be integral to risk management at your institution. The Food and Drug Administration (FDA) site audit findings are a valuable resource for identification of risk areas. Additionally, review of the FDA's Compliance Program Guidance Manuals posted on their web site will give you detail about the standards for the FDA's monitoring program. There are five separate sections in the FDA manual, each addressing the oversight of different areas of practice: clinical investigators; sponsors, monitors, and contract research organizations; laboratory; bioequivalence programs; and institutional review boards. Based on the guidance in these manuals, and over a period of 27 years, the FDA has tabulated violations found upon audit of clinical investigator sites. Of 10,021 violations that are attributed to a specific problem, FDA results identify four major areas as most problematic for clinical sites: inadequacies in the informed consent process (34%), failure to follow the protocol (26%), source documentation issues (22%), and inadequate drug accountability (12%).[2] [Table 1-1] We have found that additional key risk areas include serious adverse event (SAE) reporting, and clinical research billing compliance.

Table 1-1 shows examples of findings related to the informed consent process, including failure to obtain Institutional Review Board (IRB) approval, improper timing of consent (i.e., consent obtained after the patient has been enrolled in the study), or inadequate consent documentation. Protocol violations involve inadequate drug accountability, failure to adhere to the protocol, administration of unapproved concomitant therapy, patients receiving two or more investigational drugs, and the failure to report adverse reactions. Source documentation issues often result from incomplete or absent records or fabrication of clinical data.

In this first chapter, we provide our approach and examples of our processes that illustrate how we conduct clinical research according to GCP. In order to be compliant in clinical research practice, you first must have a clear understanding of your responsibility. As outlined in the Code of Federal Regulations (CFR), a site's responsibilities encompass conducting a study according to the protocol and FDA regulations, and being responsible for the protection of participants' rights and well-being through

TABLE 1-1 *Major Problem Areas at Clinical Sites*

Informed Consent	#	Protocol	#	Records	#
Inadequate IC	2622	Failure to adhere to protocol	2380	Inadequate/incorrect records	1979
Failure to notify IRB of changes	455	Use unapproved concomitant meds	178	Problems with record availability	177
Failure to obtain IRB approval	160	Simultaneous use of investigational drugs	18	Submission of false information	61
Failure to obtain informed consent	129				
	3366		**2576**		**2217**

Source: FDA Clinical Investigator Inspection List, inspections through 4/5/2004.

obtaining informed consent; controlling drug, biologic, or device distribution; retaining adequate and accurate records; and issuing timely reports of adverse events and ensuring that the IRB obtains relevant information for initial and continued review of the study. In contrast, study sponsor responsibility includes selecting and educating qualified sites, ensuring proper oversight of the investigators, maintaining an effective Investigational New Drug (IND) application, ensuring timely and comprehensive notification of new significant risks, ensuring that the study is conducted as outlined in the protocol, ensuring accurate record keeping and retention, and overseeing appropriate disposition of unused study supplies.

Our approach in this chapter is from two perspectives, one as a single clinical site participating in an externally sponsored multi-institutional trial, and the other as the academic coordinating center or IND/Investigational Device Exemption (IDE) holder for such a trial. An important distinction to note between these scenarios is that when an institution holds the IND/IDE or assumes trial coordinating oversight, it is considered the sponsor of the trial, which dramatically increases its GCP responsibilities (21 CFR 312.3, 312.50, 312.60). A clinical trial sponsor is defined as an individual, company, institution, or organization that assumes responsibility for the conduct of the study.[3] As such, there is an increased potential for a loss of GCP oversight, unless established, documented processes are in place that outline accountability.

In what instance does an investigator need to hold an IND/IDE? Such an assignment of responsibility occurs in several situations: (1) when an application is made to the FDA by an individual investigator to study a drug that either has not yet been released by the FDA for marketing and general use, or (2) when a drug is commercially available but (a) is being used for a new indication, (b) is being administered in a new dose or by a new method, (c) is a novel combination of two or more drugs, or (d) varies the proportion of a combination of drugs (42 U.S.C. 201). Similarly, an investigator-held IDE is obtained when an investigator wishes to conduct a study of a device that otherwise would be required to comply with a performance standard or have premarket approval to be shipped lawfully.

Academic medical center project management can vary both in scope and in terms of responsibility for the project. As an example of such management, The Cleveland Clinic Foundation Cardiology Coordinating Center (C5) approaches the project, site, and data management/analysis of cardiology multi-center trials through the rigorous application of scientific method, using the most advanced medical technology available. The involvement of practicing medical physicians, nurse coordinators, biostatisticians, and core laboratory technicians, selected for their expertise in the disease under study, allows C5 to enhance the quality, accuracy, and validity of multicenter trials.

It is critical to understand that when an institution holds investigator INDs or IDEs, the scope of responsibility for the conduct of the investigation lies solely on the shoulders of that investigator. Such responsibility is present even if the study is only being conducted at a single site, or if the investigator's research team only manages part of the coordination of such a trial, such as within The Cleveland Clinic's cardiology research area. The CFR defines individuals who initiate and conduct a clinical investigation as "Sponsor-Investigators" (21 CFR 56.102k), and therefore such individuals are required to fulfill the Federal Regulations for *both* sponsors and investigators, as delineated in 21 CFR 312 (new drugs) or 21 CFR 812 (new devices). Such a role has an important effect on research management at the institution where a sponsor-investigator practices. Specifically, the responsibility to implement and maintain quality assurance and quality control systems for the conduct of such trials rests with the institution (ICH 5.1.1, 6.11).

In this chapter, we will review briefly a few of the key compliance issues that we consider of vital importance for appropriate management of an investigator-initiated trial. Also included are numerous templates and tools that we have found helpful for standardizing our practice, and which have provided us with documentation that demonstrates compliant clinical trial execution.

Operational Interventions to Enhance Compliance

Standard Processes

By definition of the International Conference on Harmonization (ICH), an SOP is "a detailed, written instruction to achieve uniformity of the performance of a specific function" (ICH 1.55). Furthermore, ICH states that "the sponsor of a trial is responsible for implementing and maintaining quality assurance and quality control systems with SOPs, to assure data are generated, documented, and reported in compliance with the protocol, GCPs and applicable regulatory requirements" (ICH 5.1.1). It has been noted that most deficiencies uncovered during audits of clinical research occur because of poor SOPs or a lack of SOPs on specific topics.[4] SOPs should be written for procedures supporting adherence to GCP and any institutional policies related to research. Development of such detailed process standards will provide research management with an adjunct tool for training new employees.

How to implement

Our approach towards formalizing GCP in research areas that did not have existing SOPs was to review that area's practice and list the practice areas that were most critical for patient safety (i.e., informed consent and adverse event submission), as well as those activities that were performed at high volume (i.e., study drug accountability, maintenance of study files). These identified areas became the focus of initial SOPs drafted for the area. Table 1-2 lists examples of SOPs for a site. Table 1-3 lists key SOPS for a sponsor. In order to promote efficiency, we also queried our colleagues practicing in cardiology, who had developed an extensive framework of SOPs for clinical research. Additional library and Internet research uncovered numerous sources of suggested guidance on the development of SOPs. Some of our favorites include The Center for Clinical Research Practice (www.ccrp.com) and various university health system web sites.

The format of SOPs should be uniform, and include SOPs that address the development, approval process, review, and modification of SOPs. That is, there should be an SOP on SOPs. A standard should be written regarding management of situations where trial processes deviate from an SOP. For example, our site selection SOP states we will select sites by using a grading system that includes past performance in recruitment, retention, and clean data submission. We managed one project where the operational team decided that it would be more important to select sites that had experience with a new procedure, and the operational team would provide the support and education for each site concerning recruitment, retention, and data submission. In this case, we wrote a "memo to file" with the supporting documentation for following a project-specific SOP.

SOPs should follow a formal numbering sequence and be compiled in an SOP manual, listed by a table of contents. We have found that electronic management of SOPs is an extremely efficient way of disseminating updated information to members of the research team. All clinical SOPs should include the following minimal information: informative title, effective date, amendment dates, statement of purpose, author and approver names and signatures, and references, if applicable (i.e., section of the CFR, other internal policies/procedures, local law, etc.) Figure 1-1 illustrates an example of a typical format for an SOP. Figure 1-2 illustrates an example of a coordinating center SOP, using an alternative format.

SOPs should be clear, concise, and well-defined to a specific area of practice within the conduct of clinical research, however it is important that they be generic enough to allow for minor, noncritical deviations in practice so that such variations do not interfere with SOP compliance (i.e., use position titles rather than individual names to avoid the necessity of SOP amendments for personnel changes).

Our institution has begun to implement Foundation Standard Operating Guidelines, which state the legal and institutional bases for the conduct of certain research practices. Departmental SOPs also must harmonize with these guidelines as appropriate. We require that someone other than the author approve the SOP, and that this person be an individual with appropriate and relevant management/oversight authority who has an understanding of the research practice and can enforce adherence to the policy. We also require that SOPs be reviewed, at minimum, on an annual basis both by research staff (to ensure compliance) and by management (to assess if any updates/changes are required). Such review is documented in employee personnel training files, and SOP amendments are documented as described above.

In addition to annual SOP review by employees, our institution has begun development of a tiered approach to additional levels of SOP education to include departmental managerial guidelines for assessment of staff understanding, computer-based training to explain the rationale and genesis of the Foundation SOPs, and the addition of SOP review training at our quarterly clinical research coordinator training sessions.

FIGURE 1-1 *Sample Site SOP*

[INSERT INSTITUTION NAME]
[INSERT DEPARTMENT/SECTION NAME]
Standard Operating Procedure Cover Page

Effective Date: March 1, 2001

SOP Title: Regulatory Binder Maintenance, In-House Trials

Author:
Name:
Title: Supervisor
Department: Cancer Center

_____   _____
Signature   Date

Approved By:
Name:
Title: Program Manager
Department: Cancer Center

_____   _____
Signature   Date

Revision #	*Section*	*Pages*	*Initials*	*Date*

(continues)

FIGURE 1-1   *Sample Site SOP (continued)*

[INSERT INSTITUTION NAME]
[INSERT DEPARTMENT/SECTION NAME]
Standard Operating Procedure
SOP Title: Regulatory Binder Maintenance, Investigator Initiated Trials

Effective Date: March 1, 2001

1. **Purpose:** To ensure regulatory documents are maintained for In-House Trials in a consistent manner

2. **Procedures:**

   A. The study coordinator assigned to the trial will prepare and maintain the regulatory binder.

   B. The regulatory binder will contain the following sections, labeled as follows and in the following order:

      i.   Protocol—All versions of the protocol are to be retained.

      ii. IRB correspondence—Include all correspondence with the IRB, including but not limited to, IC approval, SAE submissions, protocol amendment correspondence, and all versions of the approved informed consent forms.

      iii. Patient informed consent forms—File all signed, original consent for each person enrolled on study.

      iv. Regulatory information—Include current/signed CVs and medical license of the principle investigator, CCF laboratory, CLIA, and CAP.

      v.   General trial correspondence—Include all letters, memorandums, emails, and documentation of telephone contacts and conference calls that reference study or conduct of study.

   C. All documentation, per section, will be filed in reverse chronological order.

3. **References:** ICH Section 8; 8.1

4. **Appendices:** None

(continues)

FIGURE 1-1   *Sample Site SOP (continued)*

[INSERT INSTITUTION NAME]
[INSERT DEPARTMENT/SECTION NAME]

Standard Operating Procedure
Regulatory Binder Maintenance, In-House Trials

Effective Date: March 1, 2001

Name (Printed)	Date	Signature— Acknowledgment of Understanding

FIGURE 1-2 *Sample Coordinating Center SOP*

[INSERT INSTITUTION NAME] COORDINATING CENTER
Standard Operating Procedure (SOP)

SOP Title: Breaking the Blind of an Individual Subject's Treatment
SOP Number: PM/SM-059.01 SOP

Approved by: _____ **Date:** _____ **Effective Date:** _____

1. **Purpose:** To describe the circumstances when the unblinding of the treatment of a subject is needed during a clinical trial and the procedures to be followed
2. **Procedures:**
   A. The protocol for any clinical trial where the subject's treatment is blinded must be described in detail: (1) the method of breaking the blind, (2) when the blind can be broken, and (3) who can break the blind. The procedure should apply to all single-, double- or triple-blinded studies.
   B. Breaking the blind of treatment allocation should be done only in situations where subject treatment may differ if the treatment were to be revealed.
   C. In situations where future treatment decisions need to be made quickly, there needs to be a mechanism for breaking the blind 24 hours a day, 7 days a week. This can be done by telephone, with a contact being available round the clock or, in some instances, the Interactive Voice Response System.
   D. Every case of breaking the blind should be documented and immediately reported by site personnel to the sponsor or their designee. Documentation by the site should include:
      i. the name and function of the person who broke the blind
      ii. when the blind was broken
      iii. the names and the functions of additional personnel who had access to the unblinded information
      iv. the reason for breaking the blind
      v. details of the contact with the sponsor regarding the breaking of the blind
      vi. any additional information required by the sponsor

(continues)

FIGURE 1-2 *Sample Coordinating Center SOP (continued)*

    E. The treatment allocation should only be revealed to the site investigator under these conditions:

        i. An effort was made to provide an opportunity where the site investigator or designee could discuss the reason for requesting unblinding with an appropriate person at the sponsor or designee (such as medically qualified staff) or with the trial PI prior to breaking the blind of the subject. Urgency of unblinding and availability of personnel need to be taken into consideration for this condition.

       ii. If it is agreed that there are reasonable grounds for the site investigator to know the treatment allocation in order to decide on the medical management of his or her subject. The overall study PI should remain blinded as to the treatment allocation.

      iii. The reason for breaking the blind should be recorded in the CRF file at the sponsor and, ideally, in the trial database.

    F. All communication with the site regarding potential or actual unblinding should be documented (reference trial communications for consistency of name of trial database reference).

    G. Premature unblinding (defined as unblinding that does not meet the requirements in Ei. and Eii.) must be reported to the sponsor or their designee immediately and should be documented in the sponsor file. The reason for premature unblinding of the treatment allocation should be given, e.g., due to a serious adverse event.

    H. If a blind is broken for reasons outside of those defined in writing by the sponsor, discuss with the site whether a protocol violation needs to be reported to the sponsor, IRB, and possibly the FDA.

    I. Continuing the patient on treatment after unblinding is the decision of the sponsor or as addressed in the protocol.

3. **References:**   ICH 4.7

4. **Appendices:**   None

TABLE 1-2   *Examples of Key SOPs for a Site*

Title	*Purpose*
Obtaining Informed Consent	To ensure all elements of informed consent are met and documentation is complete.
Processing Informed Consent Revisions	Ensure that the current version of informed consent is being utilized.
Protocol Amendment Processing	Ensure accurate, uniform, and timely submission of informed consent revisions.
Study Eligibility Checklist Utilization	Ensure that patients meet all inclusion and exclusion criteria prior to implementation of study testing.
Regulatory Binder Maintenance	Ensure consistent maintenance of regulatory documents.
FDA Inspections	Ensure coordinator understands FDA audit requirements.
Emergency Use of an Investigational Device	Ensure process is in place to meet FDA guidance.
SOP on SOPs	Ensure uniformity of standards formatting.
Deviation from an SOP	Process to document deviation from standard practice.
21 CFR 11 Compliance	Defines computing infrastructure validation and security.
Record Retention	Describe system for long-term maintenance of paper and electronic records.
Monitoring Visits	Ensure key staff are adequately prepared to assist review of the trial.
Orientation and Training	Provide standard training for team.
Adverse Event and Serious Adverse Event Management	Ensure timely and comprehensive communication of AEs and SAEs according to federal regulations.
Monitoring Quality Assurance Review	Describes method to ensure that data on CRF is accurate, complete, and verifiable.
Clinical Trial Budget Development	Define standard process.
Research Billing Compliance Notification Policy	Define process to audit research patient billing to ensure accuracy.

Competencies and Training

Good Clinical Practice guidelines require that the principal investigator and clinical research staff are qualified by education, training, and experience to be responsible for the proper conduct of a clinical trial (ICH 4.1.1, 4.1.5, 4.2.3–4). The first step in developing a competent and skilled work force is to identify key job responsibilities for each unique role within your clinical research team. Responsibility may vary by trial, however the following are examples of key job competencies that we use in various clinical research areas at The Cleveland Clinic Foundation. Such competencies have been developed as we have found that these areas are typically a key focus for FDA inspections and critical for legal compliance. Establishing competency standards must be linked with a mechanism for assessing that personnel have received adequate training to understand the information that is relevant to their role in the conduct of a clinical trial.

Examples of key competencies for management of a clinical trial as a site include:

- Demonstrates accurate and comprehensive knowledge of assigned research protocols. Acts as resource to colleagues for protocol questions/inquires.
- Appropriately recruits, screens, and assigns patients to research protocols.
- Provides appropriate nursing care to patients during studies, including follow-up care. Demonstrates good clinical judgment and appropriate communication of patient status to medical staff.
- Compiles data obtained in studies, including documentation of all required study parameters, and ensures accuracy of data.
- Appropriately documents grade of adverse event and ensures accuracy of data according to departmental SOP.
- Reports SAEs to all appropriate parties in timely manner, in accordance with 21 CFR, institutional IRB policy, and the SOPs of the department.
- Coordinates and schedules tests/procedures to be performed on patients selected to participate in a research study.
- Provides education, information, and support to patient and family regarding research.
- Obtains IC and documents IC teaching according to departmental SOP guidelines, both in chart and in electronic medical record.
- Reviews and evaluates data to ensure patient's eligibility and protocol compliance.
- Accurately abstracts/codes information onto case report forms/computer.

TABLE 1-3 *Key SOPs for a Sponsor*

Title	*Purpose*
Protocol Development	Define required content.
Collection and Review of Regulatory Documents	Develop a plan and review process for document collection.
Project Team Communication	Describe expectations and methods.
Trial Master File Management	Define who will be accountable for the final file and all elements that must be maintained.
Management of Noncompliant Sites	Establish guidelines for addressing noncompliance.
On-Call Services	Ensure provision of clinical resources 24×7.
Site Evaluation and Selection	Describe procedures for site evaluation and selection.
Reports	Define expectations for content, completion, and distribution.
Drug/Device Accountability	Define process.
Serious Adverse Event Reporting	Describe process for receipt, review, and reporting of serious, unexpected, and reasonably related adverse events.
Data Safety and Monitoring Board	Describe membership, format, and attendance of meetings, delineation of data access, assessment of conflict of interest, and reporting requirements.
Database Development	Define creation, implementation, and testing of database.
Systems Validation	Describe process.
Data Processing Flow Plan	Describe process.
Data Validation Process	Ensure data are accurate, consistent, and complete.
Initial New Protocol Case Report Form Formatting	Defines standard development and approval process.
Case Report Form Template Revisions	Ensure CRF accurately reflects protocol, and changes are implemented and communicated in a timely manner.
Data Entry	Ensure timely and concise data entry.
Statistical Analysis Plan	Define content and purpose.

TABLE 1-3 *Key SOPs for a Sponsor (continued)*

Title	Purpose
Data Discrepancy Resolution	Describe process for timely resolution.
Statistical Analysis Plan	Define content and purpose.
Data Back-up and Recovery	Plan for back-up and recovery of critical data including databases, operating systems, and user files.
System Operations	Describe incidence of problems and maintenance of report logs.
Breaking the Study Blind	Define the process for breaking the study blind.
Fraud, Misconduct, or Deception	Procedure for investigating, addressing, and reporting incidents of suspected fraud.

- Accurately registers/randomizes patients to studies.
- Coordinates, schedules, and prepares for monitoring visits as needed. Follows through with monitor's requests, data clarifications, and changes.
- Submits all required data in a timely manner.
- Reads and comprehends (or makes appropriate inquiries regarding protocol) prior to initiation visit.

Examples of key project manager competencies for trial coordination include:

- Oversees site's ability to recruit, screen, and assign patients appropriately.
- Performs ongoing assessment of site/investigator performance. Spearheads initiatives to improve quality or make recommendations to discontinue site if necessary.
- Monitors planned versus actual patient recruitment and implements effective strategies to address deviations from proposed timelines.
- Demonstrates ability to meet all deadlines. Demonstrates appropriate use of resources. Demonstrates ability to use creative strategies and flexibility to meet deadlines and adhere to study timelines.
- Ensures that lab and other medical tests are done in accordance with protocol to maintain patient safety and enhance compliance with protocol endpoints.
- Recommends appropriate interventions, in accordance with the protocol, to address patient scenarios. Assesses the outcomes of such interventions.

- Organizes and attends Investigator/Coordinator meetings.
- Compiles data obtained in studies and ensures accuracy of data.
- Maintains files, site records, and documented correspondence with sites, sponsors, CROs.
- Develops and/or reviews case report forms (CRF) for appropriateness and efficient data collection.
- Provides timely education, information, and support to sites/Clinical Research Associates (CRAs) regarding research study.
- Ensures appropriate project-related training of study site personnel.
- Develops and maintains planned communications with sites of a general study nature (i.e., newsletters, study progress updates, supportive reinforcement of sponsor communications).
- Demonstrates ability to adhere to study budget and provides creative strategies to limit financial resources both at individual site and coordination level.

Once you create specific key responsibilities for each role in your clinical research team, the next step is to develop a specific, documented, and standardized orientation focused on assuring mastery of the appropriate responsibilities and SOPs of your area, beginning with protocol development through study close-out. Figure 1-3 shows a sample orientation schedule. The focus of orientation should always reflect GCP adherence. A preceptor, whose responsibility will be to guide and train the new research employee, should be assigned prior to that individual's start date, to ensure that there is an employee-specific plan in place when they arrive in the department. The manager should maintain close communication and oversight of the orientation process, and provide frequent opportunity for employee and preceptor feedback. Each employee should understand the rationale for each specific process, whether it be internal policy, federal regulation, or industry standard.

Lack of trained, dedicated study and ancillary personnel is the number one reason for GCP noncompliance. You must develop a plan to educate your study personnel on the protocol, disease state, and treatments. We suggest auditing the data collected on the first two patients enrolled in each study to evaluate further educational needs and identify areas where your research processes need to be improved. Plan for retraining of study personnel quarterly on each protocol. Successful training approaches that we have implemented include use of written resources (i.e., research articles, purchase of training manual from established clinical research consultant company), return demonstration of critical tasks (i.e., obtaining IC, following process for drug accountability), providing opportunity for ongoing clinical research operations training,

FIGURE 1-3 *Sample Orientation Schedule*

Name: _____   Start Date: _____   Point Person: _____

[INSERT INSTITUTION] Department of _____ Research
Orientation Schedule

A	Priority 1=high 2=moderate 3=low	General Section	Person Inservicing	Init./ Date	By the completion of line item/task, new hire will be able to:	Inservice Materials
A1		• Introduction • Tour of Key Resources			• Locate 2 research areas within [Department] • Identify location of conference rooms	
A2		• Clinical Trials goals, objectives, work ethic • Dept. Policies • Dress Code • Expectations • Call ins/PTO/Notification			• Identify daily expectations, objectives, and group procedures	• Expectations Contract for review and signature • Dress Code Policy for review and signature • Non-staff Clinical Research Employee Conflict of Interest

A3		• Timekeeping (Hourly Employees)			• Describe/discuss:
					  • What is expected of hourly employees with regard to their timekeeping
					  • Identify who is responsible for timekeeping
					  • Identify forms completion and parameters
					  • Discuss timeframe for any paperwork forwarded to timekeeper	

A4		• Expectations for Communication
		  • Groupwise
		  • Group e-mails
		  • Groupwise Rules
		  • Long distance access codes
		  • Pagers
					• Set up e-mail group(s)
					• Identify expectations for out of office, PTO and meetings
						• Written instructions for rules & tools
						• VMX booklet

(continues)

FIGURE 1-3 *Sample Orientation Schedule*

A	Priority 1=high 2=moderate 3=low	General Section	Person Inservicing	Init./ Date	By the completion of line item/task, new hire will be able to:	Inservice Materials
A5		Meeting Attendance • Application for Meeting Attendance • Travel & Expense forms			• Describe processes required to attend meeting away from campus • Demonstrate proper completion of paperwork required and process of events	• Meeting Attendance and Expense Forms
A6		Offsite Storage • Procedures			• Discuss offsite storage of documents • Describe processes required for proper off-site document storage	
A7		Cost Saving Objectives			• Save money • Become conscious of spending habits • Utilize ___ for ordering of supplies • Obtain overnight courier service account number from sponsor for trial related correspondence • Utilize ___ for domestic shipments	
A8		Review of Org Charts			• Identify organizational structure of ___, Clinical Trials, CEC/ECG, and associated departments	• Overall Org Chart • Clinical Trials Org Chart ___ Org Chart • Biostatistics Org Chart • Contracts/Finance Org Chart
A9		Department Resourcing/Roles & Responsibilities • Department Manager • Department Supervisor • Research Coordinator • Research Assistants • Clerical Assistant			• Identify roles and responsibilities within the department • Verbalize understanding of work flow and scope of work within Clinical Trials	

FIGURE 1-3 *Sample Orientation Schedule*

A	Priority 1=high 2=moderate 3=low	General Section	Person Inservicing	Init./ Date	By the completion of line item/task, new hire will be able to:	Inservice Materials
A10		Proper completion of forms: • Swiping (if applicable) • PTO • Hours Input (if applicable) • Time Tracking (if applicable) • Anecdotal • Schedules • On Call calendars			• Identify documentation expected with scheduling alterations and flexibility	• Samples of all forms
A11		Computer Classes (if applicable) • Word • Excel • PowerPoint • Microsoft Project • Groupwise			• Attend classes as needed	
A12		GCP Materials required for GCP Test • CFR & ICH Guidelines Books • **NOTE**: There will be tests at 45, 90 and 120 days. All hires except for clerical support will take a GCP Evaluation Test • Point Person to decide if new hire is required to take			• Discuss materials and expectations for test • Identify location, purpose and when each would be used • Verbalize understanding of GCPs/ICH guidelines and when to use each • Identify how GCPs/ICH are updated and followed	• 45 Day Test is on CFR 50&56 • 90 Day Test is on CFR 312, 314, 812, 814 and ICH Guidelines • 120 Day Test has no source. It is based on practical application of the GCP/ICH Guidelines • (See GCP binder)

(continues)

FIGURE 1-3 *Sample Orientation Schedule*

A	Priority 1=high 2=moderate 3=low	General Section	Person Inservicing	Init./Date	By the completion of line item/task, new hire will be able to:	Inservice Materials

A13		• JCAHO Compliance
		  • Age Specific Competency Test
		  • Individual Education Record
		  • Education Binder
					• Discuss location and procedures for compliance with JCAHO regulations
					• Complete Age Specific Competency (to be completed annually)
					• Complete Individual Education Record (to be completed and will be turned in to Division of Nursing for all working in each department with direct pt care annually and kept on file in the Education binders)
						• Individual Education Record
						• Education Binder
						• Age Specific Competency reading information and test

A14		• Completion of CVs
		  • CV Template
		  • Where they should be saved
		  • Who needs copies
					• Complete/update CV
					• Forward CV update to _____ within 2 weeks of start date	

A15		• Review of SOP Process and Forms
		  • SOP Binder
		  • Location
		  • Annual Review Process
		  • CV Binder
		  • Job Description
		  • Review of Current SOPs & Sign-off (within 4 weeks of new hire start date)
					• Locate and identify binders
					• Locate and review Clinical Trial and Standard SOPs
					• Verbalize understanding of purpose of SOPs and binders
					  • SOP
					  • CV/Job Descriptions
					• Verbalize understanding of purpose of
					  • Review and revision of SOPs
					  • Current SOPs
					  • Sign off SOP
						• SOP Book
						• Optional review of SOP video

FIGURE 1-3

Sample Orientation Schedule

A	Priority 1=high 2=moderate 3=low	General Section	Person Inservicing	Init./ Date	By the completion of line item/task, new hire will be able to:	Inservice Materials

A16		• Meeting Scheduling
		   • General procedures
		   • Catering
		   • Contacting participants
		   • Meeting agendas
		   • Who will do agenda (if applicable)
		   • Distribution of agenda at least 24 hours prior to meeting
					• Discuss meeting planning
					• Conference room reservation
					• Anticipation of materials, AV
						• Standard Meeting Scheduling SOP
						• Meeting Planning Checklist

A17		• PC Computer Support
		• PC Overview
					• Describe network on call service
					• Discuss:
					   • Version Control
					   • Saving/moving documents
					   • Software support
					• Verbalize basic understanding of
					   • Authorization
					   • Public
					   • Shared
					   • INCR
					   • CEC/ECG
					• Demonstrate basic skills with
					   • Groupwise
					   • Document save/copy
					   • Word
					   • Intranet
					   • Phone/Page access
						• IS Handout

A18		• Clinical Research Orientation Training Sessions — To attend 2 half day sessions • Complete on-line Human Subject Protection training course			• Provide comprehensive review of some of the fundamental elements of the research process	

(continues)

FIGURE 1-3 *Sample Orientation Schedule*

A	Priority 1=high 2=moderate 3=low	General Section	Person Inservicing	Init./ Date	By the completion of line item/task, new hire will be able to:	Inservice Materials
A19		• CRF Part 11 Electronic Records			• Understand CFR Part 11 Electronic Records as it relates to research	
A20		• HIPAA compliance standards			• Understand HIPAA privacy rules as they relate to CCF and research	
A21		• [Therapeutic specialty] Anatomy & Physiology			• At the completion of this presentation, the participant will be able to: • Display a basic understanding of ___ anatomy and physiology as it pertains to [specific disease state] • Identify basic ___ anatomy as it pertains to [certain pathophysiology]	• On-line slide presentation to be reviewed w/ Preceptor
A22		• Equipment			• At the completion of this presentation, the participant will be able to: • Identify standard equipment utilized in ___ • Define equipment used during a ___ • Differentiate between x,y,z	• Hands-on demonstration given by Preceptor
A23		• New Employee Orientation Tour				• See Orientation Tour Calendar
A24		• New Employee Orientation Slide Presentation				• See Slide Presentation Calendar

FIGURE 1-3 *Sample Orientation Schedule*

A	Priority 1=high 2=moderate 3=low	General Section	Person Inservicing	Init./ Date	By the completion of line item/task, new hire will be able to:	Inservice Materials

A25		• Office Equipment
		  • Phone
		  • Fax
		  • Copy Machine(s)
		  • Printer
					• Describe/discuss proper usage of all office
					  equipment:
					• Phone
					  • Etiquette
					  • Call Transfers
					  • Do Not use Hold on conference calls
					  • Mute
					  • Hands Free
					• Fax Machine
					• Copy Machine
					  • Single/2-sided Copies
					  • Collated
					• Printer
					  • Labels
					  • Letterhead	

(continues)

FIGURE 1-3 Sample Orientation Schedule

B	Priority 1=high 2=moderate 3=low	Clinical Trials Section	Person Inservicing	Init./ Date	By the completion of line item/task, new hire will be able to:	Inservice Materials
B1		• Administar/CMS Requirements			• Understand reimbursement issues related to Administration	
B2		• Ethics in Research			• Discuss: • Proper conduct on conference calls • Ownership of articles • Passwords • Confidentiality clauses • Trademarks • Copy Right • Protocol can and cannots • CRF can and cannots	
B3		• Study Overview • Study Name: • Overview of study • Spend _____ (min(s)/hr(s) with each Research Nurse/Coordinator for overview of work			• Describe study background, endpoints, inclusion and exclusion criteria, and all study-related procedures	• Copy of: • 2 Drug Protocols • 1 Device Protocol • 1 Blood Protocol
B4		• Study Overview • Study Name: • Overview of study • Spend _____ (min(s)/hr(s) with each Research Nurse/Coordinator for overview of work			• Describe study background, endpoints, inclusion and exclusion criteria, and all study-related procedures	• Copy of: • 2 Drug Protocols • 1 Device Protocol • 1 Blood Protocol

FIGURE 1-3 *Sample Orientation Schedule*

B	Priority 1=high 2=moderate 3=low	Clinical Trials Section	Person Inservicing	Init./ Date	By the completion of line item/task, new hire will be able to:	Inservice Materials
B5		Study Overview • Study Name: _____ • Overview of study • Spend _____ (min(s)/hr(s)) with each Research Nurse/Coordinator for overview of work			• Describe study background, endpoints, inclusion and exclusion criteria, and all study-related procedures	Copy of: • 2 Drug Protocols • 1 Device Protocol • 1 Blood Protocol
B6		Study Overview • Study Name: _____ • Overview of study • Spend _____ (min(s)/hr(s)) with each Research Nurse/Coordinator for overview of work			• Describe study background, endpoints, inclusion and exclusion criteria, and all study-related procedures	Copy of: • 2 Drug Protocols • 1 Device Protocol • 1 Blood Protocol
B7		Study Overview • Study Name: _____ • Overview of study • Spend _____ (min(s)/hr(s)) with each Research Nurse/Coordinator for overview of work			• Describe study background, endpoints, inclusion and exclusion criteria, and all study-related procedures	Copy of: • 2 Drug Protocols • 1 Device Protocol • 1 Blood Protocol
B8		Study Overview • Study Name: _____ • Overview of study • Spend _____ (min(s)/hr(s)) with each Research Nurse/Coordinator for overview of work			• Describe study background, endpoints, inclusion and exclusion criteria, and all study-related procedures	Copy of: • 2 Drug Protocols • 1 Device Protocol • 1 Blood Protocol

(continues)

FIGURE 1-3 Sample Orientation Schedule

B	Priority 1=high 2=moderate 3=low	Clinical Trials Section	Person Inservicing	Init./ Date	By the completion of line item/task, new hire will be able to:	Inservice Materials

B9		• Study Overview
		  • Study Name: _____
		  • Overview of study
		  • Spend _____ (min(s)/hr(s) with each Research Nurse/Coordinator for overview of work
					• Describe study background, endpoints, inclusion and exclusion criteria, and all study-related procedures	• Copy of:
						  • 2 Drug Protocols
						  • 1 Device Protocol
						  • 1 Blood Protocol

B10		• Study Overview
		  • Study Name: _____
		  • Overview of study
		  • Spend _____ (min(s)/hr(s) with each Research Nurse/Coordinator for overview of work
					• Describe study background, endpoints, inclusion and exclusion criteria, and all study-related procedures	• Copy of:
						  • 2 Drug Protocols
						  • 1 Device Protocol
						  • 1 Blood Protocol

B11		• Study Overview
		  • Study Name: _____
		  • Overview of study
		  • Spend _____ (min(s)/hr(s) with each Research Nurse/Coordinator for overview of work
					• Describe study background, endpoints, inclusion and exclusion criteria, and all study-related procedures	• Copy of:
						  • 2 Drug Protocols
						  • 1 Device Protocol
						  • 1 Blood Protocol

B12		• Study Overview
		  • Study Name: _____
		  • Overview of study
		  • Spend _____ (min(s)/hr(s) with each Research Nurse/Coordinator for overview of work
					• Describe study background, endpoints, inclusion and exclusion criteria, and all study-related procedures	• Copy of:
						  • 2 Drug Protocols
						  • 1 Device Protocol
						  • 1 Blood Protocol

FIGURE 1-3 Sample Orientation Schedule

B	Priority 1=high 2=moderate 3=low	Clinical Trials Section	Person Inservicing	Init./ Date	By the completion of line item/task, new hire will be able to:	Inservice Materials

B13		• Study protocols
		  • What is a protocol
		  • Sponsor development
		  • Internal development
		  • How does a protocol get to Clinical Trials
		  • How is a protocol assigned to a Research Nurse/Research Coordinator
					• Describe the rational, objectives and study population of a protocol
					• Describe the experimental design (i.e. treatment groups, duration of treatment, blind, double–blind, etc.)
						• Clinical protocol
						• 21 CFR 314.126: Adequate and Well-Controlled Studies

B14		• Institutional Review Board (IRB)
		  • Role of IRB
		  • Process of IRB
		  • CCF IRB submission
					• Describe general provisions and organization of the IRB (i.e. scope, full vs. expedited review, exemptions and membership
					• Identify IRB communications and who is responsible to complete
					• Discuss annual updates
					• Discuss adverse events
					• Discuss protocol amendments
					• Complete a CCF IRB submission
					• Describe the step-by-step process of approval
						• IRB website
						• 21 CRF 56: Institutional Review Boards

B15		• Good Clinical Practices (GCP)
		  • 21 CFR 50: Informed Consent
		  • 21 CFR 56: Institutional Review Board
		  • 21 CFR 312: Investigational New Drug
		  • 21 CFR 314: New Drug Application
		  • 21 CFR 812: Investigational Device Exemptions
		  • 21 CFR 814: Pre-Market Approval
					• Explain why we adhere to the GCP in Clinical Trials
					• Explain each GCP
					• Identify, understand and access GCP references when it occurs within a protocol
						• ICH book

(continues)

FIGURE 1-3 *Sample Orientation Schedule*

B	Priority 1=high 2=moderate 3=low	Clinical Trials Section	Person Inservicing	Init./ Date	By the completion of line item/task, new hire will be able to:	Inservice Materials
B16		Study Phases • Phase I—IV • Characteristics • Definition • Data focus • Examples			• Explain the different trial phases • Identify examples of trial phases we do here in Clinical Trials	• Phases of Clinical Trials • 21 CFR 312.21: Phases of an Investigation • 21 CFR 312.23: IND Content and Format • 21 CFR 312.85: Phase IV Studies

B	Priority 1=high 2=moderate 3=low	Clinical Trials Section	Person Inservicing	Init./ Date	By the completion of line item/task, new hire will be able to:	Inservice Materials
B17		• Informed Consent • 8 Requirements of Informed Consent • 6 Additional elements if applicable to Informed Consent • Requirement for obtaining Informed Consent • Documentation • General expectations • Emergency use • CCF Informed Consent requirements • Informed Consent approval			• Identify and incorporate the required elements into a CCF Informed Consent • Identify who is responsible for Informed Consent documentation • Describe the requirements for obtaining Informed Consent • Describe what the IRB stamp means and what do you do with the original	• IRB website • 21 CFR 50: Informed Consent •

FIGURE 1-3 *Sample Orientation Schedule*

B	Priority 1=high 2=moderate 3=low	Clinical Trials Section	Person Inservicing	Init./ Date	By the completion of line item/task, new hire will be able to:	Inservice Materials

B18		• Regulatory Documents
		  • FDA Form 1572
		  • CV of PI & Co-PIs
		  • Signed Investigator Agreement (for device only)
		  • Protocol (All)
		  • Consent Form
		  • Laboratory certification
		  • Normal lab values
		  • Laboratory directors CVs
		  • IRB members
		  • IRB approvals
					• Explain the difference between a Form 1572 and an Investigator Agreement
					• Identify who is responsible for collecting the documents and what do you do with the documents once they are collected
					• Determine which documents need to be updated upon expiration
					• Verbalize understanding that all protocols need to be kept by the Study Coordinator
						• Study Documents
						• 21 CFR 312.60 through 21 CFR 312.70 Responsibilities of Investigators
						• Responsibilities and obligations of Investigators

B19		• IND/IDE
		  • Investigational New Drug (IND)
		  • Investigational Device Exemption (IDE)
					• Describe an IND
					• Describe how the Investigator s Brochure figure in an IND
					• Determine who is responsible for an IND
					• Describe an IDE
					• Describe how an IDE differ from an IND
					• Determine who is responsible for an IDE
						• 21 CFR 312.23: IND Content and Format
						• 21 CFR 312.30: Protocol Amendments
						• 21 CFR 312.31: Information Amendments
						• 21 CFR 312.32: IND Safety Reports
						• 21 CFR 312.33: Annual Reports
						• Investigational New Drug Application
						• 21 CFR 812: Investigational Device Exemptions Device Development

(continues)

FIGURE 1-3 *Sample Orientation Schedule*

B	Priority 1=high 2=moderate 3=low	Clinical Trials Section	Person Inservicing	Init./ Date	By the completion of line item/task, new hire will be able to:	Inservice Materials
B20		Adverse Events • Adverse Events (AE) • Serious Adverse Events (SAE) • Time requirements for reporting (SAE) • Documentation • Communications • FDA MedWatch form			• Define an Adverse Event • Define a Serious Adverse Event • Define the time requirement for the Investigator/Coordinator to report a SAE • Determine who is responsible to notify the sponsor, the IRB and the FDA • Discuss why would you fill out a MedWatch form	• 21 CFR 312.32: IND Safety Report • IRB website
B21		Case Report Forms (CRF) and Source Documentation • CRFs: • How to fill out a CRF • Corrections • Follow-ups • Query resolutions • Source Documents			• Describe how to make a correction on a CRF • Identify what color ink to use on a CRF • Describe what a source document • Give 4 examples and where you would find it • Discuss how you turn a verbal source into a written source • Describe a query and what you do with it	• 21 CFR 312.62: Investigator Record Keeping and Record Retention • Case Report Form • Source Documentation
B22		Screening / Consenting Patients			• Describe screening process, consenting and enrolling patients. • Describe roles, responsibilities, back up, late person, stickers (how stickers are changed and generated)	• 21 CFR 50: Informed Consent
B23		Randomization & Hotline			• Describe randomization and 2 different ways of randomizing a patient • Explain the process of using the randomization hotline	• Randomization worksheet
B24		Study File Maintenance • Regulatory documents • Study binder • Communications • Sponsor screening logs • Patient files			• Explain the process of organizing a study binder • Describe how to fill out sponsor screening logs • Describe documentation of study communication: email and telephone logs • Describe how to organize patient study files	• Screening logs • Facilitator to bring study binder

FIGURE 1-3 *Sample Orientation Schedule*

B	Priority 1=high 2=moderate 3=low	Clinical Trials Section	Person Inservicing	Init./ Date	By the completion of line item/task, new hire will be able to:	Inservice Materials
B25		• Contracts and Budgets • Assessing the budget • Per patient reimbursement • Grant Maintenance form • Reviewing the contract • CCF process			• Determine budget line items • Determine what costs are charged to study budget vs. patient • Complete/discuss Grant Maintenance form • Discuss/verbalize understanding of a contract • Describe the step-by-step process that a contract goes through	• Facilitator to bring sample contract • Grant Maintenance form • Budget Calculator form • Contract Information form
B26		• FDA Audit Talk and SOPs				• FDA Audit Video
B27		• Research Bulletin Board			• Explain types of studies, what each section of bulletin board are for and when & how updated • Describe In Planning, In Progress, Enrollment • Describe the different interventional procedures and medications.	• Bulletin Board Book • Study start-up packet form
B28		• Site Visit (study start-up meeting) • Monitors			• Describe purpose, what is needed, location, who to be in attendance • Locate study folders?	• 21 CFR 312.53: Monitor Responsibilities • 21 CFR 812.43: Monitor
B29		• Research Database (RD)			• Describe RD • Access RD • Explain what it can do? • Discuss how to set up a new study	• Study start-up packet form • How to access instructions

(continues)

FIGURE 1-3 *Sample Orientation Schedule*

B	Priority 1=high 2=moderate 3=low	Clinical Trials Section	Person Inservicing	Init./ Date	By the completion of line item/task, new hire will be able to:	Inservice Materials

B30		• Research Assistant Duties
		  • Nurses, support staff and coordinator s calendars
		  • On Call System
		  • Study folders, blood reqs
		  • Research Info Sheets
		  • Bulletin Boards
		  • Bulletin Board enrollment
		  • Black Books
		  • Charts
		  • Wanding, Ordering
		  • Record Handling
					• Describe responsibilities and materials needed to run a clinical trial as a site	

FIGURE 1-3 Sample Orientation Schedule

C	Priority 1=high 2=moderate 3=low	Overview Section	Person Inservicing	Init/ Date	By the completion of line item/task, new hire will be able to:	Inservice Materials
C1		• Coordinating Center Overview Video			• Discuss areas of ___ and scope of responsibilities	• ___ Video
C2		• CEC/ECG Overview Video			• Discuss CEC/ECG area and scope of responsibilities	• CEC/ECG Video
C3		• Glossary of Terms			• Become with common terminology used in Cardiology and Cardiology Research	• Glossary of Terms handout
C4		• Book & Video Library			• View/review books and/or videos as designated or desired	

(continues)

FIGURE 1-3 Sample Orientation Schedule

D	Priority 1=high 2=moderate 3=low	Other Departments	Person Inservicing	Init./ Date	By the completion of line item/task, new hire will be able to:	Inservice Materials
D1		• Lab			• Discuss role and functions of the Lab	
D2		• Special Studies			• Describe the process for setting up a new study • Review of requisitions	
D3		• Pharmacy (Office & IV Pharmacy)			• Identify how to relay problems to them. • Describe fax drug order system, process for obtaining study drugs and time expectations. • Determine what information pharmacy needs to process drug orders	• Give example of physician s orders
D5		• Emergency Department • CCF • Kaiser • CDU			• Locate both CCF and Kaiser E.D.s • Locate E1-35 and E1-60 conference rooms • Identify key contacts and their role • Locate/describe content of research carts in all areas	
D6		• Graphics/Photography			• Discuss role of graphics specialist and submission requirements	
D7		• _____ Core Lab			• Describe _____ Core Lab and its relationship to Clinical Trials	

FIGURE 1-3   *Sample Orientation Schedule*

D	Priority 1=high 2=moderate 3=low	Other Departments	Person Inservicing	Init./ Date	By the completion of line item/task, new hire will be able to:	Inservice Materials

D9		• Finance
		   • Overview of Finance
		   • Roles and responsibilities
					• Discuss:
					   • Role of Research Finance Department
					 • Define:
					   • Study start-up costs
					   • Study account identification
					   • Scope of work	

D10		• Contracts
		   • Overview of site contracts
		   • Roles and responsibilities (include rationale)
					• Describe:
					   • Site contract process
					   • Execution	

D11		• Stats, Programming and Data Management			• Discuss role of Stats, Programming and Data Management • Describe Data Management process on all trials	

(continues)

FIGURE 1-3 *Sample Orientation Schedule*

E	Priority 1=high 2=moderate 3=low	Meeting Attendance	Person Inservicing	Init./ Date	By the completion of line item/task, new hire will be able to:	Inservice Materials
E2		• Clinical Trials Meeting			• Provide update of specific trial progress, overall department and Foundation updates	• See monthly calendar of meetings
E3		• Monthly Calendar of Meetings			• Attend other meetings as designated	• See monthly calendar of meetings

Orientation Complete

Signature of Employee _____ Date:_____

Signature of Point Person _____ Date:_____

and annual employee review/assessment. All study personnel need evidence of training, including those with more peripheral roles, such as a floor nurse who is administering a study drug on an off-shift.

Furthermore, personnel should not be delegated a research task unless there is evidence of appropriate training. Delegation of responsibility should be captured in writing on the study signature log. Documentation of employee orientation and yearly training should be maintained, preferably within each employee file for easy accessibility in the event of an audit. For those research teams that function in a sponsor/coordinating center capacity, provide standardized training for each site and include the monitoring team. Assist sites with their internal training needs by providing multiple mediums to communicate information (meetings, conference calls, web sites, videos, and CD-ROMS). Have a contact person available for questions 24/7.

Lastly, employee turnover is a critical issue that advanced preparations and well thought-out training guidelines should help reduce. Any site qualification visit should include an assessment of a site's ability to secure additional personnel resources, as well as a back-up plan for turnover. Over the last three years in cardiovascular research, we have seen average site turnover of research nurse coordinators around 30–50%. Standard site training should be available on video or as an archived cybersession, which will ensure that all staff receive the same information in the event of turnover or additional staff assigned to the project.

Quality Assurance

General Overview
You should set up each trial to be prepared for future monitoring, quality assurance assessment, and potential FDA inspection. Quality Assurance (QA) is planned and systematic actions that are established to ensure that a trial is performed and that data are generated, documented, and reported in compliance with GCP and applicable regulatory requirements (ICH 1.46). Audits are performed as a function of QA practice. Information provided in the "FDA Compliance Program Guidance Manual for Clinical Investigator Inspections" may help you define potential areas of deficiencies, which can then be subject to QA. Copies of the manual are available from the FDA.[5]

Audits help ensure that clinical study data is valid and accurate. Audits also enhance subject safety and your site's integrity. Preplanned and executed quality assurance review will help to prevent ongoing errors and deviations in standard practice. Audit results provide a mechanism to demonstrate the quality of your practice, allowing a competitive edge in obtaining research projects/funding. Establishing an audit practice will also ultimately save time and money, as understanding expectations and learning from audit results will help you to develop a competent and content workforce, which in turn will facilitate staff recruitment and retention.

Best Practices

While not mandated by the FDA, quality assurance audits have become an integral and important part of clinical data development processes. It is recommended to use QA audits during the conduct of clinical trials as part of good clinical practice guidelines.[6] These periodic internal audits provide research management staff with an excellent opportunity to review the quality of work that has been done to date, add substance to employee annual review documentation, and generate documentation to support the accuracy and validity of trial data. Frequency of departmental audits should be based on the volume of activities your staff handles, the size and complexity of each trial, the level of staff experience assigned to a project, and the level of risk associated with administering the investigational agent. Frequency parameters should be documented in an SOP addressing quality assurance.

Aspects of clinical research that we assess encompass compliance with Good Clinical Practice guidelines and Code of Federal Regulations (21 CFR) compliance, particularly in regard to proper informed consent process, source documentation, adverse event reporting, data management practice, personnel compliance with site SOPs, and adherence to the protocol. While research management staff can perform the assessment of clinical research activities according to documented standards, we recommend that designated quality assurance personnel, separate from the research group, perform such clinical trial audits. In our institution, such personnel have specialized training in conducting research audits. We plan to develop policies that will require a certain minimal number of years of clinical research experience, as well as attendance and certification of completion at an industry-validated quality assurance seminar. Implementation of such institutional standards has the benefit of validating the competency of the individual performing the audit, as well as strengthening the validity of the accuracy of audit results.

In clinical research practice today, there is a continuum of many types of quality assurance audits that a research site may undergo: departmental ⟶ institutional ⟶ pharmaceutical/device industry ⟶ FDA. As noted previously, it is our recommendation that departments have a mechanism for internal audit within their own area. At The Cleveland Clinic Foundation, we also have institutional audit mechanisms from the following offices that have oversight for, or perform aspects of, clinical research: Office of Internal Audit, Corporate Compliance Office, Office of Clinical Effectiveness and Quality Management, the IRB, and the Pharmacy department.

To demonstrate compliance at a clinical site, whether it is within your own department or if your team is providing oversight of additional clinical areas, the initial step is to designate trial responsibility in writing, at the outset of a trial. Ideally, the trial agreement should define this same accountability, to emphasize that there is a contractual obligation to perform certain duties according to GCP standards. For site-based research, since the scope of responsibility will be similar for most projects, your department should already have a quality assurance plan in place that delineates your audit process. In general, internal departmental audits should assess that processes are carried out in accordance with GCP and SOPs. In addition, audit responsibility when you function as a sponsor will also include site and CRO assessment. You should ensure that sites have sufficient resources in place to perform the responsibilities assigned and that staff are adequately trained to do the job that they are assigned, and you should monitor the adequacy of their performance. One area that is particularly critical to audit for quality assurance is data integrity. In FDA guidance, responsibility is assigned to both the investigator (21 CFR 312.62) and the sponsor (21 CFR 312.50) to ensure accurate data. Furthermore, ICH guidelines 5.1.1–5.1.3 require quality assurance and quality control for data management. Ensure that clear expectations and timelines are communicated at the start of a trial, and review data according to an established schedule. Such rigorous assessment will help you to identify trends or areas of risk for noncompliance.

The following section highlights areas that our Cardiovascular Coordinating Center has identified as "risk areas" in coordinating clinical trials and related steps to address areas of noncompliance.

Specific Areas for QA/GCP
To increase your success in running clinical trials, you must spend time evaluating protocols prior to initiation. You should evaluate your SOPs as they relate to an individual

project, and determine if you have adequately trained resources and monitoring to ensure regulatory compliance. We have discussed specific areas of risk assessment in the training, standard process, and quality assurance sections.

Risk management is the act or practice of dealing with risk, which includes planning for risk, analyzing risk issues, and developing a plan to monitor the risks.[7] Listed below are examples of how you can proactively evaluate risk prior to the initiation of a study and during a "lessons learned" session at the completion of a study.

The first trial was a large international trial with the following expected enrollment timelines:

	Expected	*Actual*
1st patient enrolled	June	July (one month delay)
Months of enrollment	12 months	19 months
Total enrollment	3605 (1.5 pts/site/mo)	2918 (0.5pt site/mo)
Sites with drug	250	297
Sites that enrolled	225	239

Training and Documentation

1. Lack of training and support by other departments (emergency room, internal medicine department, and cardiology department) for enrollment. This protocol required the cooperation of several departments within the institutions.

2. Investigators depended on outside physicians to enroll participants. Many of these outside physicians had adopted the trials treatment strategies as standard of care. We provided educational sessions for the physicians that explained the rationale for the study, study design, and history of the disease process as related to current evidenced-based medicine. Evidence-based medicine is the practice of medicine using randomized clinical trials to guide patient care guidelines.

3. We had a 30% turnover in study coordinators (higher then previous trials). For our current trials, we now have a proactive plan in place to train study team replacement.

Standard Process
Site Selection:

1. Even though small community hospitals had the patient population we needed, they do not always have personnel who are educated and trained on research processes. These sites were very labor intensive to educate and took additional phone calls and visits. We would still consider using these sites in the future, but would set clear expectations up-front and drop the sites if these expectations were not maintained throughout the trial. We would also add additional monitoring visits for these sites.

2. Consider having sites with IRB regulatory approval ready to replace nonperforming sites during study start-up. Consider having Ethics approval in additional countries (during study start-up) in case enrollment falls behind expectations. This would add additional cost up-front, but may be less then the cost of not meeting timelines.

3. For future trials, we are considering presenting the final protocol to all investigators during the site selection process. This could help principal investigators evaluate whether the protocol requirements will fit in with their clinical practice.

4. Communication to other team members from the Operations Team was not always completed. Need to develop a clear communication plan up-front and evaluate the process continuously. Identify key team members in each company that will be responsible for disseminating information and process flows to their internal team.

5. We now realize the importance of developing an atmosphere that encourages open communication and which looks at the task, risks, and global goals (no finger-pointing) among the Operations Team.

6. Did we crisis-manage instead of managing proactively? Many ideas/issues were addressed early but due to budget constraints the recommendations were placed on the "back burner." Once we were behind timelines, we did receive approval for some actions. Was this too late? Should there be a better process for budget approval? Do we need to be more realistic of the up-front costs of a large trial? These are all questions we ask ourselves in the beginning of a trial.

You cannot always evaluate risk with budgets in mind. The cost of trial over-runs are much more expensive.

7. Decrease enrollment projections to 0.5 or 1.5 pts/site per month in future similar trials.

Quality Assurance

1. Screening logs revealed critical exclusion criteria that prevented enrollment. A steering committee of physicians was put together to evaluate these criteria and it was decided that these criteria could not be altered.

2. There was a clear plan to audit 10% of the sites prior to the mid-way enrollment point. The Operational Team evaluated these audit reports and a process improvement plan was immediately put into place.

Data Management Issues:

1. For case report form (CRF) shipments, consider having a place outside the United States shipping these supplies for sites outside the Americas. In future trials, it would be best to have CRFs shipped with the study drug.

2. At first, fax lines going into the data management group were not enough to keep up with the volume. It is important to have enough faxes active from the start of the trial.

3. Not all sites had fax machines that could use the toll-free 800 numbers. We have added this question to our site selection process.

4. We held weekly conference calls discussing issues that needed resolution in order to lock the database. Quick decisions by the Operational team on query resolution were very helpful for on-time database lock. For this trial, the database was locked within six weeks of the last patient visit.

Monitoring/Site Management:

1. Sites that received a weekly call from the Operational Team had better turn-around time with data management issues (CRF, queries).

2. We monitored only the primary endpoints of the trial and, via our audit reports, we found that the we do not need 100% monitoring on all trials.

The next trial was a large trial run within the United States, with the following expected and actual enrollment targets:

	Expected	*Actual*
1st patient enrolled	April 2000	Sept 2000
Months of enrollment	12 months	6 months
Total enrollment	4620	4808 (9 pts/site/mo)
Sites with drug	100	91
Sites that enrolled	90	89

We were not prepared for the fast enrollment. This resulted in both sites and the data management team being unable to keep up with case report forms and query resolution.

In the future, we would have sites stop enrolling to ensure accurate and timely data collection. If a site has more than three case report forms or ten queries behind expectations, they will be given one week to catch up before enrollment would be stopped. If they are unable to catch up, we will block their access to randomization of patients until they have completed their case report forms and queries.

Resources

This section provides concrete examples of some of the tools we have made reference to in the text. We hope that you can use these examples and modify them to help you structure training, develop standard operating procedures, and create quality assurance plans that will suit your clinical research practice. The web site list is a compilation of public sites that house a wealth of information regarding the conduct of clinical trials, as well as sources to obtain educational materials for clinical research education.

Tools

- Orientation schedule—Figure 1-3
- Competency checklist—Figure 1-4
- Study start-up checklist—Figure 1-5
- Signature and delegation form—Figure 1-6
- Site drug accountability form—Figure 1-7

FIGURE 1-4   *Sample Competency Checklist*

[INSERT INSTITUTION NAME HERE]
[INSERT DEPARTMENT NAME HERE]

90-Day Performance Evaluation

Research Nurse

Name:

Performance Dimensions	*Rating*	*Comments*

TECHNICAL EXCELLENCE/
QUALITY CARE

1. Has completed overview of the Federal and ICH guidelines for GCP.
2. Verbalizes understanding of differences between Phase I–Phase IV clinical trials.
3. Describes different types of research studies in regards to blinds and randomizations.
4. Has reviewed all [departmental] SOPs.
5. Has attended an IRB open house meeting.
6. Obtains and documents Informed Consent of a patient meeting all criteria contained in the Informed Consent SOP.
(a) hands out (therapeutic specific) booklet to pt
(b) documents teaching in chart and EMR

(continues)

FIGURE 1-4 *Sample Competency Checklist (continued)*

Performance Dimensions	Rating	Comments

7. Demonstrates adherence to ongoing Informed Consent process; obtaining revised consent appropriately.
8. Has completed and passed "Human Subject Protection" tutorial.
9. Has completed Barnett Clinical Trial self-tutorial, with at least 85% on quiz scores.

CUSTOMER SERVICE ORIENTATION

1. Is oriented to Division departments including [fill in the blank as appropriate].
2. Develops teaching tools and diary sheets for patient education and adherence to protocol documentation requirements.
3. Conducts clinical assessment of patient status, including history, follow-up assessments, and progress reports to physicians.
4. Maintains team approach with support staff and other personnel in the department.
5. Addresses all issues and concerns of the patient through follow-up.
6. Maintains role as patient advocate.

(continues)

FIGURE 1-4   *Sample Competency Checklist (continued)*

Performance Dimensions	Rating	Comments

ADAPTABILITY

1. Includes initiative and flexibility to accept and master changes in function, equipment, technology and/or departmental needs, and the dependability to adhere to attendance and other CCF policies.
2. Demonstrates positive attitude in meeting staffing and protocol needs within the [departmental] research program.

EFFECTIVENESS AND EFFICIENCY

1. Includes the quality and quantity of desired work, as well as the organizational skills necessary to perform successfully.
2. Demonstrates ability to use EMR resources.
3. Identifies key components necessary to open research study for enrollment.
4. Is aware of and utilizes appropriate resource personnel in the department.
5. Reviews CRFs with Study Coordinator prior to opening study for enrollment.
6. Designs appointment schedules and data collection documents as needed, based on protocol requirements.

(continues)

FIGURE 1-4　*Sample Competency Checklist (continued)*

Performance Dimensions	*Rating*	*Comments*

GOALS

1. Actively recruits patients for study enrollment and meets trial recruitment goals.
2. Maintains patient long-term follow-up.
3. Continues to learn federal regulations governing research.
4. Continues to communicate issues regarding projects (problems, trends, etc.)
5. Identifies learning needs and actively seeks mechanism to meet needs.

Performance Evaluation Signature Page

Employee Signature _____　　Date _____

Supervisor Signature _____　　Date _____

FIGURE 1-5 *Sample Study Start-Up Checklist*

STUDY START-UP CHECK LIST

Study Name: _____

Please return a copy to _____when completed.

Review of Protocol

☐ Does the treatment plan outlined in the study coincide with the standard clinical practice?

☐ Is the number of potential candidates appropriate for study requirements?

Contact

☐ Have sponsor contact person's name, phone number, address, and same for the sponsor's 24-hour contact person?

IRB Submission

☐ Complete IRB application packet, provide all information requested.

    ☐ Include all signatures.

☐ Prepare informed consent.

    ☐ Combine information from sample consent provided in protocol along with previously IRB-approved consents from similar trials.

    ☐ All terms must be described in lay language.

    ☐ Pages must have date and page numbers.

    ☐ Patient obligation must be clearly defined.

        ☐ time commitment

        ☐ follow-up

        ☐ patient costs

☐ Have sponsoring company review/approve consent before submitting it to the IRB.

☐ Application packet

    ☐ Protocol

    ☐ Consent

    ☐ Letter of Indemnification

    ☐ Letter of Attestation

    ☐ Consent

☐ Investigator's brochure (if drug study)

☐ Include copies of any questionnaires to be administered to the patient.

(continues)

FIGURE 1-5 *Sample Study Start-Up Checklist (continued)*

FDA Form 1572

☐ Complete all information and have PI sign. Changes can be made by crossing out error and initialing. NO white out.

Budgets

☐ All budget information is to be filed separately from regulatory documents. Include the following charges:

  ☐ Salaries
  ☐ Travel
  ☐ Supplies
  ☐ Equipment
  ☐ Indirect costs (overhead)/to be assessed at ___%
  ☐ Communication (fax, FedEx, etc.)
  ☐ Parking
  ☐ Patient mileage (__/mile)
  ☐ Patient care items (list quantity required of each)
  ☐ Patient hotel accommodation, if any
  ☐ Pharmacy fees
  $___ start-up fee
  $___ dispensing fee for each item (IVs, syringes, and/or piggybacks)
  $___ randomizing fee (for those patients pharmacy is randomizing)

☐ Document negotiated fee discounts in writing. Contact in writing appropriate personnel involved with billing.

☐ Determine mechanism for identifying study patient and appropriate charges.

Contract

☐ Obtain final contract including budget and proposed payment schedule from sponsoring company.

☐ Obtain all required signatures and forward to legal department.

☐ Contract must be approved by Institution and the study sponsor prior to study start-up.

☐ Provide _____ and research accounting with a copy of the budget and payment scale.

(continues)

FIGURE 1-5 *Sample Study Start-Up Checklist (continued)*

Regulatory Documents Required Prior to Starting

- ☐ IRB approved protocol
- ☐ Letter of notification of IRB approval
- ☐ IRB approved consent form
- ☐ List of IRB voting members and positions
- ☐ Signed FDA form 1572 (blank ones in IRB book)
- ☐ Signed Investigator's Agreement
- ☐ Principal investigator's CV
- ☐ Co-investigators' CVs
- ☐ Laboratory certification (from any site obtaining labs)
- ☐ Laboratory normal values (from any site obtaining labs)

Pharmacy

- ☐ Notify pharmacy if study requires pharmacy's assistance.
- ☐ Provide pharmacy with a copy of the protocol.
- ☐ Negotiate amount of time needed to prepare study drug.
- ☐ Provide copy of all study orders pertaining to pharmacy.
- ☐ Obtain copy of pharmacy inservice attendance sheet and keep on file.
- ☐ Obtain study drug information sheet.

Primary Lab

- ☐ Contact primary lab if special study requisitions are required, for example:
  - ☐ Any lab draw that is not part of standard patient care
  - ☐ Special study labs, i.e., drug pharmacokinetics
  - ☐ Labs that are sent to outside lab to be processed
- ☐ Provide lab with a copy of the protocol.
- ☐ Develop lab requisition.
- ☐ Send copy of lab requisition to lab for review prior to study start.

Letter to Physicians Explaining Study

- ☐ Co-investigators should have copy of entire protocol. Include:
  - ☐ Brief overview of study
  - ☐ Number of patients
  - ☐ Study design
  - ☐ Information on the drug/device (risks/benefits)

(continues)

FIGURE 1-5 *Sample Study Start-Up Checklist (continued)*

☐ Primary questions
☐ Endpoints
☐ Follow-up

Inservices
☐ Maintain file of employees at attendance at each of the meetings.
☐ Research nurses/coordinators.
  ☐ Detailed overview
  ☐ Total # of patients, centers
  ☐ Primary objectives
  ☐ Information needed for randomization
  ☐ Information on the study drug/device (risks/benefits/compatabilities)
  ☐ Step-by-step process of enrolling a patient
  ☐ Follow-up
  ☐ What to do in case of adverse event
  ☐ Unblinding
  ☐ Contact person
  ☐ Cost information
  ☐ Review of study orders
☐ Nurses on floors where these patients will be admitted
  ☐ Brief overview
  ☐ Primary questions
  ☐ Information on the study drug/device (risks/benefits/compatabilities)
  ☐ Specific responsibilities of staff on the floor
☐ Staff physicians/Fellows
  ☐ Brief overview
  ☐ Primary questions
  ☐ Information on the study drug/device (risks/benefits)
  ☐ Specific responsibilities of physicians
    At the time of enrollment
    At follow-up
  ☐ ACRONYM study name
  ☐ Additional data field requests

(continues)

FIGURE 1-5 *Sample Study Start-Up Checklist (continued)*

Folders

- ☐ Shrink all of the following for MD pocket books.
- ☐ Cheat sheets—step-by-step enrolling instructions
    - ☐ Study design (purpose, # of patients, follow-up, endpoints)
    - ☐ Inclusion/exclusion criteria (verbatim from protocol)
    - ☐ Baseline information required and acceptable time frame
    - ☐ Study drug information
      Route
      Preparation
      Dosing (include any tables)
      Administration
        separate line required?
        special tubing needed
        filters
        infusion pumps
      Incompatibilities
      Stability of mixed drug
      Duration of administration
      Half-life
      Side effects
      Antidotes
      Unblinding
    - ☐ Directions on enrolling
      Enrollment form
      Site #
      Randomization hotline #
      If randomizing on site—where is information located
    - ☐ Directions on obtaining drug/device (through pharmacy, research cabinet, etc.)
    - ☐ Special requirements (save device packaging, catheter tips, etc.)
    - ☐ Subsequent labs/tests while in house
    - ☐ What to do in case of complications
    - ☐ Follow-up (what time points, what's needed)
    - ☐ Contact person (#_____ pager), what conditions need to be reported immediately

(continues)

FIGURE 1-5 *Sample Study Start-Up Checklist (continued)*

- ☐ 24-hour study contact person/coordinating center
- ☐ Study orders
- ☐ One page pharmacy order for initial preparation
  - Informed consent obtained
  - Body weight
  - How to randomize
  - Study #
  - Kit #
  - Preparation instructions
  - Drug is needed by _____
  - Contact person's number (Research Nurse on Call #_____)
  - Physician's signature line
- ☐ Study drug orders
  - Cath lab
  - Admitting floor
  - Study drug administration
  - Labs—differentiate which are patient charges or memo acct. charges
  - EKGs
  - Nomogram
  - Contact person
  - Notify study RN if...
  - Physician's signature line (on each page)
- ☐ Special study requisitions with time points and specific labs noted
- ☐ Two consent forms
  - ☐ For 24-hour enrolling studies compose a BRIEF explanation (half page or less; use bullets) of study/risks/benefits/alternatives to make the consent process for the person consenting off hours. Will be printed on bright paper and attached to the consent
- ☐ Any other special information (i.e., worksheets, etc.)

FIGURE 1-6 Signature and Delegation Form

Study Site Number: _ _ _ _   Study Site Name: _____

Name, Title	Initials	Signature	ICD Discuss & Sign-off	Decision to enroll patient	Authorized to use IVRS	CRF Complete	CRF Sign-off	DCF Sign-off*	Study Drug Admi	Other	Start/End date of trial involvement	Approval Principal Investigator (Initials & Date)
			yes / no	yes / no	yes / no	yes / no	yes / no	yes / no	yes / no		Start: —/—/— End: —/—/—	
			yes / no	yes / no	yes / no	yes / no	yes / no	yes / no	yes / no		Start: —/—/— End: —/—/—	
			yes / no	yes / no	yes / no	yes / no	yes / no	yes / no	yes / no		Start: —/—/— End: —/—/—	
			yes / no	yes / no	yes / no	yes / no	yes / no	yes / no	yes / no		Start: —/—/— End: —/—/—	
			yes / no	yes / no	yes / no	yes / no	yes / no	yes / no	yes / no		Start: —/—/— End: —/—/—	
			yes / no	yes / no	yes / no	yes / no	yes / no	yes / no	yes / no		Start: —/—/— End: —/—/—	
			yes / no	yes / no	yes / no	yes / no	yes / no	yes / no	yes / no		Start: —/—/— End: —/—/—	
			yes / no	yes / no	yes / no	yes / no	yes / no	yes / no	yes / no		Start: —/—/— End: —/—/—	
			yes / no	yes / no	yes / no	yes / no	yes / no	yes / no	yes / no		Start: —/—/— End: —/—/—	
			yes / no	yes / no	yes / no	yes / no	yes / no	yes / no	yes / no		Start: —/—/— End: —/—/—	
			yes / no	yes / no	yes / no	yes / no	yes / no	yes / no	yes / no		Start: —/—/— End: —/—/—	
			yes / no	yes / no	yes / no	yes / no	yes / no	yes / no	yes / no		Start: —/—/— End: —/—/—	

Responsibilities

FIGURE 1-7 *Site Drug Accountability Form*

[INSERT INSTITUTION NAME]

Site Name: _____   Site Number: _ _

Investigator: _____

Pharmacy Contact: _____   Phone #: ( ) _ - _

Date Received: _/_/_   Signature: _____

Pt. #	Date Dispensed	Pt. Initials	Kit Number Assigned	Assigned by (Signature)
01	_/_/_	_ _ _		
02	_/_/_	_ _ _		
03	_/_/_	_ _ _		
04	_/_/_	_ _ _		
05	_/_/_	_ _ _		
06	_/_/_	_ _ _		
07	_/_/_	_ _ _		
08	_/_/_	_ _ _		
09	_/_/_	_ _ _		
10	_/_/_	_ _ _		

Web Site List

General Clinical Research Web Resources

www.ich.org

International Conference on Harmonization

www.regsource.com

Code of Federal Regulations, guidance documents, ICH, and other regulatory links

www.fda.gov/cdrh/devadvice/351.html

Center for devices and radiological health, medical device reporting and regulations, links to user facility reporting bulletin (assists in complying with reporting requirements), other government links

www.fda.gov/cdrh/devadvice/ide/print/ideall.pdf

IDE overview with links to 21 CFR 812, 50, 56, 54, 820, monitoring of clinical trials, information sheets, debarment, FAQs, other government links

phrp.osophs.ddhhs.gov/g-topics.htm

Office for Human Research Protections, guidance topics by subject

ohsr.od.nih.gov/info

NIH Information sheets, forms, guidelines, IRB approval criteria, research protocol writing, IC document guidance

bioethics.gov

National Bioethics Advisory Commission

www.usaid.gov/pop_health/resource/phncomrule.htm

Interpretive Guide to the Federal Policy for Protection of Human Subjects

grants.nih.gov/grants/oer.htm

Office of Extramural Research

www.fda.gov/medwatch/safety.htm

Safety information and adverse event reporting

www.fda.gov

Home page to the US Food and Drug Administration, links to warning letters, and Code of Federal Regulations.

www.ncehr-cnerh.org/english/gcp/index.htm#TOC

ICH Guidelines

www.saetool.com/intro.htm

Algorithm for determining SAE reporting requirements

www.centerwatch.com

Information on FDA approved clinical trials and research info for families and subjects.

www.irbforum.com

Institutional Review Board discussion and news forum

www.irbtool.com

Applying human subjects rules to research protocols

www.med.upenn.edu/ohrtrain/docs/ProtocolTemp.doc

Protocol template

ovcr.ucdavis.edu/HumanSubjects/HSDefinitions/HSGlossary.htm

Glossary for lay terms for use in preparing consent forms

nursespdr.com/members/database/index.html-drug

Online PDR

www.labtestsonline.org/

A public resource for explanation of specific clinical lab tests

www.fda.gov/ora/inspect_ref/igs/iglist.html#DRUGS

FDA Inspector's Guide

Education Web Resources

www.barnettinternational.com

Information on instructional seminars related to research

www.ama-assn.org/sci-pubs/amnews/pick_02/hlsc0527.htm

Patient education site on clinical trials

www.socra.org

Society of Clinical Research Associates

www.acrpnet.org

Association of Clinical Research Professionals

www.actmagazine.com/appliedclinicaltrials/issue/issueDetail.jsp?id=2503

Back issues of research periodical, *Applied Clinical Trials,* which provides a forum where pharmaceutical product developers can communicate with the medical researchers who test their new products

Notes and References

1   Ott, Mary Bernadette and Yingling, Gary L. *Guide to Good Clinical Practice.* Thompson Publishing Group, 2001.

2   FDA Clinical Investigator Inspection List, Center for Drug Evaluation and Research, Division of Scientific Investigations, web site: www.fda.gov/cder/regulatory/investigators.

3   Nesbit, Lori A. *Clinical Research: What It Is and How It Works.* Jones and Bartlett Publishers, Inc., 2004.

4   Chase, Sue. "Deficiencies in SOPs/GCPs." Lecture at The Cleveland Clinic Foundation, 1998.

5   Ott, Mary Bernadette and Yingling, Gary L. *Guide to Good Clinical Practice.* Thompson Publishing Group, 2001.

6   Kerzner, Harold. *Project Management: A Systems Approach to Planning Scheduling and Controlling.* 7th edition, John Wiley and Sons, 2001.

7   Hammer, Michael. "Deep Change: How Operational Innovation Can Transform Your Company." *Harvard Business Review,* April 2004.

TWO

Contract Issues in Clinical Trials

Donna J. Meyer

Role of the Research Contract

The decision to undertake a clinical research program imposes a variety of legal and regulatory obligations on the involved parties, including the research sponsor, investigators, study coordinators, and the research institution.[1] This chapter will examine the role of the research contract among private parties to address key legal and regulatory concerns for clinical trials.

Regulation of Clinical Research

Clinical research is subject to oversight by a variety of federal authorities, including the Food and Drug Administration (FDA) and the Office for Human Research Protections (OHRP).[2] As part of the regulatory oversight, the research parties are required to develop certain written documents that serve to outline the performance of the research, which may include the clinical protocol, case report form, investigator brochure, and standard operating procedures. These regulatory documents are designed to ensure that there is a standardized method of performing the research, allowing for subsequent duplication of the research to confirm study results.

Do You Need a Research Contract?

Federal regulations require research sponsors to have written agreements with investigators ensuring performance of the research in compliance with applicable laws, such as Good Clinical Practices.[3] The same regulations, however, do not require sponsors to enter into a written contract with the research institution, or that the written agreements with investigators address the allocation of certain rights and obligations between the parties relative to the outcome of the research study, such as publication and intellectual property rights.[4] But the absence of a written agreement relative to certain rights and obligations has a potential legal meaning and impact on the parties and the outcome of the research.

Common Law and Statutory Rights

In addition to the federal regulations governing clinical research, the rights and obligations of the parties involved in the research are shaped by common law duties—which includes obligations shaped by court decisions, also referred to as "case law"—and state statutes and regulations. Contract law and the rights and obligations of parties to a private agreement are shaped by both common law and state law, including whether an implied or oral contract exists, whether the parties have rights or obligations to each other under the Uniform Commercial Code (as codified or revised by state statute), and what remedies parties have against each other in the event of a dispute, including contract damages and equitable remedies, such as quantum meruit or unjust enrichment. Under common law and state law, legal rights and obligations may exist between private parties absent a written agreement.

By entering into a written contract, the involved parties are voluntarily determining how to allocate certain rights and obligations. The contracting parties may even agree to disregard certain default rights and obligations that may be applied under common law or state law; provided, of course, such agreement is not illegal or contrary to public policy. Without a written contract the determination of the parties' rights and obligations is uncertain and dependent on a variety of factors, including the facts and circumstances of the situation, the status of common law, and even the legal forum where the parties may seek to resolve a dispute. Each party may also have the right to challenge certain claims of rights or request remedies under various theories of law and equity. A written contract provides the parties with the opportunity to introduce certainty in the relationship, so that decisions on rights and obligations are made mutually by the parties up front and not left to a judge or jury in the aftermath of a dispute.

Separating Contract Issues from the Clinical Protocol

You may still question the need for a separate written contract. After all, one may easily conclude that these expressions of the rights and obligations of the parties are already part of the clinical protocol or investigational plan for the research. The protocol details the research hypothesis to be examined, the testing procedures to be followed, and the methodologies for analysis and conclusion. Some research sponsors may already include in the protocol other terms relating to the performance of the research, including publication and intellectual property rights.

Despite the ability to include all the scientific terms and business issues in a single integrated document, such as the protocol, there are several disadvantages for both parties in following this method. First, in order to obtain regulatory approval to proceed with the performance of a clinical trial, research sponsors are required to submit a copy of the protocol and other study-related documents to the regulatory authorities, including the FDA and an Institutional Review Board (IRB) and/or Ethics Review Committee. From the perspective of the research sponsors, the sponsor may prefer to segregate the general business terms of the research, including payment terms, in a separate document that will not be distributed to this broad group of reviewers, thereby ensuring a greater degree of protection for their confidential business terms. Second, the inclusion of both scientific and business terms in a single document may delay the review of a protocol because reviewers must understand and discuss a more complex document before deciding whether to approve the research. For the same reason, it is also generally easier from the researcher's perspective to have the business terms in a separate document for review by professional and internal advisers, such as lawyers or accountants, and leave the scientific details for review by appropriate oversight committees, such as the IRB and/or Ethics Review Committee of the research institution. Lastly, there are practical considerations of contract amendment and modification. Contracts require the formality of amendments for all changes and modifications, requiring signature by all of the original contracting parties. Clinical research protocols frequently undergo modification during the course of the study, sometimes in response to IRB concerns; other times procedural or safety changes are made as data is received and analyzed. Protocol amendments often do not require the formality of a contract amendment, and simply require submission to and approval by the IRB. Such amendments become effective immediately upon review and approval by the IRB. Again, separating the business and clinical terms in the contract and protocol, respectively, allows the parties to dedicate personnel and resources to the appropriate task of review and approval within their expertise. The IRB will continue to review modifications to the clinical protocol to protect the safety and welfare of the prospective subjects. Modifications to the business terms of a study should be in the form of contract amendments to ensure review and consideration of the implication of any amendments to the parties' respective rights and obligations, including budgetary concerns or rights in the outcome of the research.

Clearly there is a practical need for a written research contract. The remainder of this chapter will help you identify and examine certain key legal and regulatory issues that should be addressed in private contracts for clinical trials.

Key Issues in Private Research Contracts

Research Objectives

While both the sponsor and researcher usually have the same objective in the performance of a research protocol—proving or disproving the research hypothesis—the objectives of the parties in the research contract are not necessarily the same. Most researchers in clinical trials are health care professionals, e.g., physicians, doctorates, nurses, or other allied health care professionals. Researchers, whether working for private or public institutions, generally have as a primary goal the furtherance of scientific and medical knowledge, which is fostered through the sharing of research results. On the other hand, sponsors generally have as a primary goal the protection of proprietary information and prevention of disclosure to their competitors. Most sponsors adhere to these objectives by imposing strict confidentiality obligations on research partners and obtaining intellectual property protection on the research results, where available. These objectives of the researcher and of the sponsor can be fundamentally at odds. Through the research contract, each party needs to ensure that its objectives are acknowledged and will be protected, either through affirmative statements of rights and privileges or acceptance of restrictions and limitations. It is a tendency of the party preparing the contract to initially draft provisions in its favor; however, through negotiation and mutual respect for the parties' needs, the final contract should represent a compromise that satisfies both parties' objectives.

Protection of Confidential Information

Through the research contract, sponsors should ensure that there is clear identification of their confidential and proprietary information to protect against inadvertent disclosure or unauthorized sharing. Researchers are also advised not to sign confidentiality statements or agreements unless there is clear identification of the information that is subject to nondisclosure and the extent of their obligations of confidentiality. Identification may be accomplished by listing the documents and types of information to be protected in the contract, or by having the contract require that documents will be marked with a stamp or other designation of confidential status. While the tendency of research sponsors may be to define confidential information broadly to include all data and information from the research study, the obligations of confidentiality need to be balanced so as to not interfere with the researcher's right to publish the results of the research and perform future academic research. The contract should be clear that research results are not confidential information for purposes of publication rights, and should also allow publication of study methodology and other supporting information as necessary for publishers and other researchers to evaluate, validate, and confirm the published results.

Protection of Intellectual Property

Research contracts often combine the concepts of confidentiality with a discussion of ownership of intellectual property. Confidentiality is intended to ensure protection of proprietary information that, while necessary to disclose for the performance of the research, needs to be protected against sharing with competitors. Intellectual property, on the other hand, represents a category of property with claims of ownership and rights for use and exploitation. While proprietary information necessary for performance of the research needs to be held in confidence to ensure adequate protection, not all intellectual property should be treated as confidential information that will be subject to restrictions on subsequent use and disclosure. For example, sponsors may consider the research results and data as intellectual property; however, researchers should question whether it is appropriate for research results to be subject to confidentiality. Of course, the question of whether the research results are considered intellectual property and owned by the sponsor is another question that should be addressed in the research contract and depends on the relationship of the parties and their respective roles and obligations in the research.

The most commonly recognized categories of intellectual property are patents, copyrights, and trademarks, each of which is well defined under federal statutory law[5] with commonly accepted methods to protect and prevent against subsequent use and exploitation. If the research sponsor is responsible for the protocol, either as the author through its own employees or as a work made for hire by independent contractors, the sponsor usually will claim ownership of derivative works that represent a reduction to practice of the ideas from the clinical protocol. Because U.S. patent law and/or state law may assign inventorship, and consequently ownership, to the researchers for intellectual property arising from the researchers' performance of the study, sponsors will want to address ownership and assignment of intellectual property in the research contract. To the extent the researcher is the author of the protocol or otherwise responsible for the design and conduct of the research, the researcher may be entitled to claim ownership of the derivative works.

In addition, sponsors that are also manufacturers or licensees of the study product that is tested under the clinical protocol will also want to protect intellectual property rights in the study product. From a researcher's perspective, it is important that sponsors' claims of ownership over the study product do not overreach to interfere with the researcher's exercise of academic rights and dissemination of study results for furtherance of medical knowledge and education. The researcher should also ensure that the sponsor's claims to intellectual property do not overreach to novel ideas or innovations arising outside of the scope of the study or developed in conjunction with information previously existing or partially developed from other research projects. In particular, intellectual property that represents ideas or innovations from one or more research studies could raise a question of ownership by multiple persons.

For example, if a researcher or institution receives funding from the federal government to assist in a research project, the federal government may have rights in the resulting intellectual property. The rights of the federal government vest by virtue of federal regulation under the Bayh-Doyle Act,[6] regardless of whether there is a private contract between the researcher and a sponsor that has rights in the study product. The Bayh-Doyle Act applies to all inventions conceived or first reduced to practice in the performance of a federal grant, contract, or cooperative agreement, even if the federal government is not the sole source of funding. There is an obligation to disclose each new invention to the federal funding agency within two months after the inventor discloses it to the institution. The institution has the right to elect to retain title in the invention, the decision on which must be made within two years after the invention disclosure. If the institution does not elect to retain title then the funding agency has the right to title to the invention. If the institution does elect to retain title, then the government must be provided a nonexclusive, nontransferable, irrevocable, paid-up right to practice or have practiced the invention on behalf of the federal government throughout the world.[7]

Protection of Publication Rights

As already discussed, the right to publish the results of a research project is a primary concern for most researchers. The research contract must balance the interest of the sponsor to protect proprietary information with the objective of the researcher to share the research results through academic publication. In addition to the objectives of the contract parties, the issue of publication is an important issue in the current regulatory environment of clinical research. Not all research projects involve a direct benefit to the research subject. In some cases, the expectation of the oversight committees, including the IRB, and the research participants is that the research will serve a societal benefit by advancing scientific and medical knowledge. Later in this chapter there will be a discussion of publication rights and current industry and regulatory guidelines for control over and disclosure of research results.

Protection against Study-Related Liabilities

Clinical research trials may involve potential liability to third parties, including claims by research subjects. Consequently, the parties involved in the research should understand their legal responsibilities and have adequate resources to cover liabilities. In this regard, evidence of insurance is the best method to ensure the availability of resources by each party involved in the research study. For the sponsor and the clinical trial site, both will need to obtain and maintain throughout the course of the study comprehensive general liability (also referred to as "CGL insurance"). CGL coverage generally applies to injuries and damages resulting from an accident or unexpected occurrence. CGL insurance usually excludes from coverage any injury or damage related to a product liability. The most likely injuries to research subjects from use or administration of an investigational product, such as a biologic, drug, or device, could be excluded from coverage. Therefore, separate insurance coverage may be required specifically for product liability.

Researchers who are health care professionals will need to obtain and maintain professional liability for their role if there is interaction with a research subject that establishes a physician–patient relationship. Generally, state law establishes the minimum amount of professional liability insurance coverage required for licensed health care professionals. Researchers may also need to consider whether the scope of their current professional liability insurance covers the anticipated research activities. For instance, their insurance may exclude experimental therapies, which could include research protocols if the study product has not been approved by the FDA. It may also be advisable for organizations carrying out research studies to maintain directors and officers and/or errors and omissions coverage for decisions made by directors, officers, and other fiduciaries of the organization. Depending on the nature of the study, the parties may want to establish the types and minimum amounts of insurance coverage in the research contract, or the contract may simply require that the parties show proof of insurance.

Protection against Third-Party Claims

Indemnification is a legal means for parties to the research contract to protect themselves from third-party claims and liabilities that may be asserted by, or on behalf of, participants in a research study. In the course of a research study a third party, such as a research subject, may suffer an injury for which he/she may seek recourse against one of the research participants. For instance, a research subject may name a researcher in a lawsuit for injuries sustained from use of the study product. However, the research sponsor, if the manufacturer or licensee of the study product, may be legally responsible for the subject's injury, not the named researcher who was the subject's provider for the duration of the study. Because third-party claims may be asserted without specific reference to who ultimately has legal responsibility, the parties should consider addressing in the research contract how third-party claims will be handled, including which party assumes primary responsibility for defense of the claim and the right to settle the claim. This agreement between the parties to the research contract does not act as an exculpation of liability as it relates to the third party, but rather is a mechanism for the contract parties to decide in advance how to handle these situations without resorting to lengthy and expensive litigation to determine their roles and responsibilities with respect to third-party claims.

The scope of the parties' responsibility will depend on the nature of the study, such as whether the study product is investigational or approved by the FDA for sale for its intended use. Likewise, the parties' roles in the study need to be addressed in the research contract, including who will be responsible for study design. Generally, the research sponsor will agree to indemnify the researchers against third-party claims for study design, use, and administration of the study product in accordance with the clinical protocol. Because of the researcher's role in the study, sponsors may want protection against injuries allegedly due to the researcher's professional malpractice and/or failure to follow the protocol. Both parties also will have responsibility for other injuries or damages that result from their respective negligence, misconduct, and failure to comply with their legal obligations. Once the scope of the indemnification is included in the contract, the parties also should address procedures for seeking indemnification and handling any third-party claims. This should include procedures to notify the other party of a prospective claim for which indemnification may be sought, a determination of who is responsible for selection of legal counsel, and control over the defense or settlement of the claim.

Regulation of Health Care Transactions

In addition to the FDA and OHRP regulations that govern the conduct of clinical research by sponsors and researchers, there are federal and state regulations that apply to the financial relationship between sponsors and researchers for the performance of a research project. The first regulatory scheme we will address is referred to collectively as "fraud and abuse regulations."[8] Fraud and abuse regulations apply to business arrangements between health care professionals and medical vendors that may raise concerns for undue influence over health care decisions. The fraud and abuse regulations are not intended to prevent or hinder legitimate business arrangements between vendors and health care providers. Rather, the regulations are intended to help define elements of legitimate business relationships that do not pose risks of fraud and abuse by the parties. One common recommendation of the regulations for all business relationships is for the parties to enter into a written contract that describes with specificity the intent of the parties and the nature of the business arrangement.

Overview of the Fraud and Abuse Regulations

The health care industry is heavily regulated due to the unique position of health care providers as surrogate decision-makers for the health care consumer. One of the primary objectives of the regulations is to ensure that the financial relationship between the health care provider and medical vendor does not interfere with the health care provider's clinical decision-making. In the context of clinical research, the concern is to ensure that financial relationships between industry sponsors and researchers do not affect the outcome of the research by challenging the legitimacy of the data, the independence of the researcher, or the voluntary nature of subject participation due to undue influences over the researcher.

The Federal Anti-Kickback Statute

The Federal Anti-Kickback Statute (AKS)[9] is a fraud and abuse law that applies to most business arrangements between medical vendors and health care providers. The AKS makes it a felony for any person to receive, give, solicit, or offer any payment or other form of remuneration with the intent to induce or influence the purchase, order, or referral of drugs, devices, products, services, or other items reimbursable under a federal health care program. Both the offeror and recipient in an impermissible transaction may be subject to criminal and civil penalties for violation of the AKS.

In 1994, the Department of Health and Human Services Office of Inspector General (OIG) issued a Special Fraud Alert[10] concerning marketing practices that potentially implicate the AKS. The Special Fraud Alert described practices that the OIG considered suspect and which could trigger enforcement action. Specifically in the area of sponsored research, the OIG indicated that payments made by pharmaceutical companies characterized as research payments, where the recipients were required to perform only *de minimis* ministerial tasks or research with little or no scientific merit, may constitute illegal kickbacks. The government's position was reinforced in its recent issuance of OIG Guidance for Pharmaceutical Companies.[11] The purpose of the arrangement is inferred from the facts and circumstances, but the OIG noted the following factors that make a research arrangement suspect:

- Studies initiated or directed by the marketing departments of the sponsoring companies

- Studies whose results are not shared with the science divisions of the sponsoring companies
- Studies that duplicate existing research or serve no legitimate purpose
- Product promotional activities that are disguised as postmarketing research

Because research sponsors have other financial relationships with the researchers outside the scope of the research being performed, including product purchasing and equipment loan arrangements, it is important to evaluate the totality of the business relationship between the sponsoring company and the researcher when entering into a sponsored research arrangement. As discussed earlier, relationships outside the scope of the research, including honorarium and professional consulting arrangements, may taint the integrity of the research under financial conflict-of-interest regulations. Likewise, sponsored research arrangements may be scrutinized as creating undue influence over health care professionals in their decision-making, including purchasing decisions and prescribing practices, if the financial relationships between the parties are not consistent with the fraud and abuse regulations.

The intent of the AKS and other fraud and abuse regulations are to prevent and prohibit questionable business practices that are used merely as a pretext for an otherwise impermissible purpose. For instance, the provision of an excessive research grant that is disproportionate to the *de minimis* tasks to be performed may constitute illegal remuneration in return for the researcher's agreement to purchase additional sponsor products or to switch from a competitor's products. However, the regulations are not intended to impede clinical trials or research funding from industry sources that support legitimate and bona fide research activities.

The AKS, like other federal fraud and abuse laws, applies only to the extent that there is a cost incurred by, or lack of discount offered to, a federal health care reimbursement program. This may lead to the conclusion that the absence of federal health care reimbursement, such as Medicare billing, negates the application of these regulations. However, the scope of each regulation is slightly different and may be implicated simply by the nature of one of the involved parties, such as a health care provider that has agreed to abide by Conditions of Participation,[12] that is implicitly required to comply with all applicable regulations. In addition, most states have statutes similar in design and purpose to the AKS. These state laws target fraudulent and abusive business practices that potentially affect private health insurers or that pose a risk of increasing health care costs to public consumers. Consequently, because of the complexity of this area of regulation and the high stakes involved for noncompliance, it is recommended to follow the guidelines issued under the federal fraud and abuse regulations for all business transactions, regardless of the source of reimbursement.

Personal Services Safe Harbor

The AKS establishes safe harbors that describe business arrangements between medical vendors and health care providers. Those business arrangements will not be considered suspect if all requirements of the safe harbor are satisfied and the arrangement supports a bona fide business purpose. While there is no specific safe harbor under the AKS for sponsored research, the enforcement agencies have indicated that the personal services safe harbor[13] under the AKS should be followed for sponsored research arrangements. The following requirements of the personal services safe harbor should be satisfied in the research contract for each sponsored research arrangement:

- The research contract must be in writing and signed by the parties.
- The written agreement must cover and specify all services to be provided as part of the research arrangement for the term of the agreement.[14]
- The term of the contract must be for not less than one year.
- The aggregate compensation paid over the term of the contract, or the methodology for compensation, must be set in advance and included in the written contract and must be consistent with fair market value for the services.
- The compensation or methodology for compensation must not be determined in a manner that takes into account the volume or value of any referrals or business otherwise generated between the parties.
- The services performed under the contract must not involve the counseling or promotion of a business arrangement or other activity that violates any state or federal law.
- The aggregate services do not exceed the services that are reasonably necessary to accomplish the commercially reasonable business purpose of the services.

Other Financial Relationships in Sponsored Research

As discussed above, the fraud and abuse regulations concern the nature and intent behind certain financial relationships between sponsors and researchers. In addition to these regulatory requirements, conflict-of-interest regulations also require examination of the financial relationship between the parties, outside the scope of the research to ensure that there is no undue influence over the outcome of the research. Conflict-of-interest regulations[15] may address these concerns by limiting the amount of compensation a researcher may receive from a sponsor outside the scope of the research, or may require disclosure and management of the conflict by an oversight committee or governing body to ensure the independence of the researcher from other proprietary goals and interests. While a discussion of conflict of interest regulations is beyond the scope of this chapter, it is important to consider the potential intersection of the financial terms in the research contract with conflict-of-interest principles to ensure against undue influence in each sponsored research arrangement.

Performance or Outcome Incentives

Research sponsors may offer the possibility of an incentive to a researcher to influence the outcome or performance of the study. An incentive payment that is not intended to compensate researchers for providing services may be perceived as an inducement for an outcome in the research. Incentives may be in the form of increased payment or may be an in-kind bonus, such as a gift certificate or coupon. Incentives may even be structured as an alternative payment to the researcher unrelated to the research, such as an unrestricted educational grant or purchase of equipment. As discussed previously, financial arrangements between the sponsor and researcher outside of the research should be examined to protect against any undue influence on the outcome of the research. Because payment should be made only for the fair market value of bona fide services rendered, an incentive payment to reward performance or outcomes may be considered excessive remuneration, questioning the independence of the researcher. The American Medical Association's position on incentive payments is that "offering or accepting payment for referring patients to research studies is unethical."[16] Many other medical associations and industry associations have issued similar position statements and guidelines on financial arrangements for sponsored research; these should be considered when structuring payment terms as part of the research contract. If the payment is perceived as an inducement for enrollment or product promotion, outside of what normal professional judgment would have recommended in the absence of the possibility of receipt of payment, then the payment may constitute an improper incentive under both conflict-of-interest and fraud and abuse regulations, as well as ethical directives for the protection of human subjects. Due to these concerns, in addition to review by legal advisors, incentive programs should also be reviewed by the IRB or Ethics Review Board overseeing the research project.

Incentive Payment or Payment for Service?

Before offering an incentive payment, sponsors should determine if the payment is actually intended as a performance incentive or if it is more properly described as compensation for increased services or additional expenses that the researcher may incur to satisfy the conditions of the research program. For instance, a sponsor may offer an additional payment for each research subject that is enrolled within 30 days of study initiation. While the payment may be perceived as an incentive for accelerated enrollment, the additional payment may be to cover the costs of an additional study coordinator to be assigned to the study for the first 30 days to meet protocol timelines. If the latter is true, then the payment may be appropriate compensation for additional time and effort. The payment should be properly documented as compensation for personnel time. The amount actually paid by the sponsor for such time and effort should not exceed the fair market value of such service, as may be established in the study budget for personnel for other portions of the research. Accordingly, payment would only be made for services rendered and would not be appropriately paid if the researcher did not in fact add an additional study coordinator during the time period of the incentive program. Incentives that are paid for reaching accelerated enrollment targets or are unrelated to the performance of services, including unrestricted educational grants, should not be offered or accepted as part of the sponsored research arrangement.

Billing for Research Costs

Another important consideration for financial relationships in sponsored research is the allocation of research funding and third-party billing. The following are the general payment principles for sponsored research under federal health care programs and most state health insurance programs:

- You cannot submit a claim to a patient or third-party payor for covered services rendered if the items or services in the claim are covered by another source of funding.
- You cannot submit a claim to a patient or third-party payor for medically unnecessary care, which may be defined to include experimental procedures or use of investigational products.

Allocation of Research Costs

A discussion of the specific requirements for research billing is not covered in this chapter, however, the general principle to keep in mind is that researchers and institutions cannot "double dip" from payment sources. This means that if a researcher is being paid by the sponsor for research costs, the researcher cannot bill a patient, private insurer, or other third-party payor, such as Medicare, for the same costs, even if the service is covered under the applicable payment rules.[17] If you do submit claims for payment for costs already covered, you may be in violation of the False Claims Act and other federal and state fraud statutes, which may subject you to both civil and criminal penalties.

Many sponsored research projects include both standard-of-care procedures that would be covered under payment rules and noncovered services that are for research purposes. Thus, it is imperative that the research contract or budget specify what costs are included under the sponsor compensation and what costs, if any, are not included in the compensation and may be eligible for third-party reimbursement. Keep in mind from the prior discussion of the AKS that compensation must be fair market value for the services rendered in the performance of the research. Consequently, you may not be able to allocate sponsor funding to only noncovered research costs and bill third-party payors for covered standard-of-care costs if this allocation would result in total compensation from the sponsor being considered excessive or not fair market value for the allocated services. Also, because the informed consent document must identify for prospective subjects any costs that they may incur as a result of participating in the research study, the cost allocation in the research contract or budget should be consistent with the informed consent document. This allocation is easy to perform if all costs are itemized in a detailed budget, separating out personnel costs with procedure costs, and costs of products and supplies; however, most research sponsors establish a single per-patient payment amount for all clinical trial sites that may not be easily allocated among the researcher's budget categories.

Despite the sponsor's perspective on the payment terms, researchers should take the time to go through the allocation process, whether or not the payment terms are negotiable with the sponsor, to determine how the payment compares to the researcher's fair market value of its direct and indirect costs for the performance of the research. This process also should account for all administrative and personnel costs for recordkeeping and study administration tasks that are not billable, and then identify the clinical services that are potentially billable.

Avoiding Private Benefit for Use of Public Resources in Sponsored Research

The final regulatory area to be discussed in this chapter is the potential federal tax treatment of financial relationships in sponsored research under the Internal Revenue Code (IRC).[18]

Federal Tax Exemption

Research institutions relying on exempt treatment of income from sponsored research projects, including many hospitals and universities, must ensure that the research activity satisfies the public benefit standards of the IRC and thereby promotes a charitable purpose. Organizations that are organized and operated under IRC 501(c)(3) have represented to the Internal Revenue Service (IRS) as part of their application for federal tax exemption that their primary purpose is to further a public benefit in exchange for exemption from federal income taxation. To qualify for the exemption, the organization must operate primarily for one or more charitable purposes and any incidental benefit conferred to a private person or entity must be secondary to the public benefit and at fair market value.

When activities are performed by a tax exempt organization for the benefit of a private person, such as a research sponsor, the income that the tax-exempt organization receives from the performance of that activity may not be subject to the same exempt treatment from federal income tax. If the revenue from the activity is subject to federal income taxation, the tax treatment may have an adverse effect on the exempt organization. For example, the exempt organization may need to maintain a system to track and report unrelated business income, as well as pay appropriate taxes for income derived from the activity, or may even face a challenge to its exempt status depending on the nature and scope of the unrelated activity.

Purpose of Sponsored Research

The first question for most exempt organizations is whether a sponsored research activity is related to the furtherance of the organization's exempt purposes. If such a relationship does exist, then the income received from the activity would be exempt from federal income tax. Most exempt research institutions are organized and operated for the furtherance of charitable purposes, including the advancement of scientific knowledge. While the performance of a bona fide research project seems, on its face, to support the charitable purpose of an exempt research institution, the IRS distinguishes sponsored research that constitutes "scientific research," which would be in furtherance of a public interest, from "ordinary testing," which may generate unrelated business income and be subject to income tax reporting and/or other tax compliance concerns for the recipient organization. To make this distinction, the IRS directs its examiners to break down the issue into three separate questions: (1) Is the activity scientific? (2) Is the activity research? and (3) Is the activity in the public interest?

Distinguishing Scientific Research from Ordinary Testing

The first two elements require that the activity for which exempt treatment is sought be both scientific and research. An activity is considered to be research if it is "designed to test an hypothesis, permit conclusions to be drawn, and thereby to develop or contribute to generalizable knowledge."[19] The difference between an activity that is scientific versus ordinary testing is dependent upon the specific facts and circumstances of the arrangement. By definition, ordinary testing includes an activity "of a type ordinarily carried on as an incident to commercial or industrial operations, as, for example, the ordinary testing or inspection of materials or products or the designing or construction of equipment, buildings, etc."[20] Accordingly, from the researcher's perspective the IRS is likely to consider routine and repetitive testing that is of a commercial nature to be considered ordinary testing, while testing that requires intellectual contribution or expertise from the researcher is more likely to be perceived as scientific research.[21] From the sponsor's perspective the IRS may look at the research expenditures in making the distinction. IRS regulations define research expenditures as: "[R]esearch and development costs in the experimental or laboratory sense. The term includes generally all such costs incident to the development of ... a product, a formula, an invention, or similar property, and the improvement of already existing property of the type mentioned. The term does not include expenditures such as those for the ordinary testing or inspection of materials or products for quality control or those for efficiency surveys, management studies, consumer surveys, advertising or promotion."[22] If the determination is made that the activity constitutes ordinary testing, the recipient organization must ensure there is a mechanism to track and account for revenues as possible unrelated business income. The recipient organization must also consider the effect of unrelated business income tax treatment on its overall exempt status. Each situation needs to be evaluated separately to ensure compliance with all requirements of the IRC, including any restrictive covenants accepted by an exempt organization regarding the use of any of its facilities financed by tax-exempt bonds.[23]

Public Benefit from Scientific Research

The third prong of the IRS determination is that the activity serves a public interest. The IRS offers three justifications for determining that scientific research is performed in furtherance of a public interest.[24] First, the results of the research are made available to the public on a nondiscriminatory basis. Second, the research is performed for the U.S. government or any of its agencies. Third, the research is directed toward benefiting the public. To satisfy the first or third justification, the research contract should include affirmative statements on the right of the researcher to publish research results as well as access to and use of study data by the exempt organization performing the research.

Defining Publication Rights

Having an affirmative statement in the research contract on the right or freedom to publish is not the same as mandating publication by a researcher. Rather, the intent of such an affirmative statement and publication provisions is to ensure that the researcher has the independence to perform the research and disclose the results as appropriate in the interests of the subjects and public at large. Further, such statements and provisions help demonstrate that the research furthers the public interest by sharing results to contribute to scientific and medical knowledge rather than simply pursuing commercial interests of the sponsoring company.

While there is no specific language or provisions required to satisfy the public benefit standards, there is a breadth of industry guidance on this topic to direct research sponsors and researchers to an appropriate provision for their research contract. The remainder of this chapter discusses several of the industry guidelines on publication and dissemination of research results.

National Institutes of Health (NIH)
Guidelines on Sponsored Research

The NIH has guidelines for recipients of NIH funds,[25] which include guidelines for publication and treatment of research results. The NIH guidelines are not binding on privately funded research projects. However, the NIH guidelines provide a benchmark of reasonableness in structuring private contractual relationships. That benchmark is useful for researchers that have agreed to conduct all sponsored research activities in a consistent manner in accordance with federal regulations, regardless of the identity of research sponsors or source of funding. Specifically, the NIH guidelines recommend the following provisions in research contracts:

- *Prompt publication*—Research contracts should address the timely publication of research results. Researchers should not agree to significant publication delays or interference with full disclosure of research findings, or any undue influence on the interpretation and reporting of the research results. The NIH indicates that a 30–60 day review period is a reasonable delay to allow time for patent filings or review for confidential proprietary information.
- *Definition of materials*—Research contracts should include clear and concise definitions of research materials that are subject to a transfer and claims of title from the performance of the research. For instance, the NIH guidelines indicate that where the research contract requires transfer of title to all materials resulting from the performance of the research to the funding organization, a definition of "materials" that includes all resulting inventions, derivatives, or modifications would be unacceptable because it is too broad. Conversely, the guidelines also indicate that it would be inappropriate for researchers to believe that they gain ownership or title in research material provided by another person by the mere receipt and use of the materials as part of the research. The guidelines offer several examples of acceptable definitions of materials. As previously discussed with respect to protection of intellectual property, it is generally acceptable for a sponsor to claim ownership over research materials provided to the research for the performance of the research, such as the study product, and derivatives of the original material.

International Committee of Medical Journal Editors (ICMJE)

The ICMJE has been leading an initiative in sponsored research. Of primary concern to the ICMJE is ensuring that changes in treatment decisions and standard of care by health care providers continue to be based on scientific clinical investigation and not merely on marketing studies controlled by industry. In this regard, the independence and accountability of the researcher is crucial to the perception of the importance and integrity of the research study. To address these concerns with the objectivity of reported data and research results from industry sponsored research, the ICMJE issued an editorial entitled "Sponsorship, Authorship, and Accountability."[26] In this editorial, the ICMJE commented that as more proprietary research organizations, including contract research organizations (CROs), become involved as part of the research process, academic researchers are exerting less control over the administration of the research. To protect against further loss of control, the ICMJE concluded that the research contract must play a central role in sponsored research to establish the rights and responsibilities of the researcher and the sponsor in the administration of the study. Moreover, the ICMJE members committed to the following principles for review of publications from sponsored research projects:

- Member journals of the ICMJE agree not to accept any submitted publications if there is a contractual agreement between the author and research sponsor that conditions the author's access to data or the right to publish on the prior consent of the sponsor.
- Member journals of the ICMJE agree to require authors to disclose their role and the research sponsor's role in the design and management of the study that is the subject matter of the proposed publication.
- Member journals of the ICMJE will require authors to sign a statement representing that the author accepts responsibility for the conduct of the study, has meaningful access to the research data, and controls the decision to publish the research results.

The Pharmaceutical Research and Manufacturers of America (PhRMA)

PhRMA, which represents member organizations, including pharmaceutical and biotechnology companies, has also responded to the concern of researchers and academic institutions with respect to the role of industry in the control and conduct of the clinical research process. To offer guidance to its members, PhRMA issued the *Principles on Conduct of Clinical Trials and Communication of Clinical Trial Results* (the "PhRMA Principles"),[27] which are intended to clarify existing ethical and legal requirements for the clinical research process and to ensure objectivity in the outcome of the research. In furtherance of these objectives, the PhRMA Principles recommend the following standards of conduct for its member organizations with respect to the disclosure of clinical trial results:

- Companies should ensure timely communication of meaningful results of controlled clinical trials, regardless of the outcome.
- Companies should report study results in an objective, accurate, balanced, and complete manner, with a discussion of the strengths and limitations of the study.
- Appropriate recognition as an author or contributor should be granted for anyone who provides substantial contribution consistent with the ICMJE and major journal guidelines.
- Authors should include a reference to primary presentations of a multisite clinical trial for subsequent or single-site publications.
- Companies should provide access to any investigator who participated in the conduct of a multisite clinical trial to review relevant statistical tables, figures and reports for the entire study.
- Companies should discuss with researchers communication of a summary of the trial results to research participants.
- Companies should demonstrate a commitment to respond in a timely manner to draft publications and to not suppress or veto publications or other communications.
- Differences of opinion or interpretation of study data should be resolved through appropriate scientific debate.
- If requested by medical journals, companies should offer confidential provision of the protocol synopsis or data analysis plan for proposed publications.

Conclusion

The main objective of the legal and regulatory authorities and guidance discussed in this chapter is to ensure the integrity of the research process by reducing or eliminating undue influence in the form of financial and other relationships between the involved parties. Most of the concerns raised by both the regulations and the industry guidelines are intended to protect the independence of the researcher from the research sponsor so that health care and clinical decisions are exercised solely in the professional judgment of the provider, regardless of whether they are favorable to the commercial interests of the research sponsor. As discussed throughout this chapter, with mutual respect for each party's needs and objectives as part of the research process, the negotiation of a research contract should be able to reach a middle ground that satisfies all parties' needs and requirements. In sponsored research there are often competing, yet legitimate, interests between the researcher and research sponsor. For researchers pledging to serve the public interest, the objective is to ensure their ability to use and disclose the research results. For the sponsor, the protection of intellectual property is necessary to encourage and allow future research and development. The elements of a reasonable compromise include:

- Use clear and concise definitions of confidential information and intellectual protection.
- Add affirmative statements of rights to inspect and use research results for publication purposes.
- Protect proprietary information from inadvertent disclosure through advance notice and review requirements prior to publication.

Through constructive negotiation of contractual relationships, the parties can find a compromise that allows each party's objectives to be met and can avoid lengthy negotiations for future sponsored research activities and potential legal challenges in the event of a disagreement due to the lack of a written research contract.

Notes and References

1   This chapter assumes that the research sponsor is the manufacturer or marketer of the study product, such as a pharmaceutical or medical device company or other industry sponsor. References to the research sponsor throughout the chapter are intended to be a reference to a for-profit industry funding source, and references to researchers include, collectively, the investigators, the study coordinators, and the research institution, if any.

2   For additional information on applicable federal regulations, see the Food and Drug Administration web site at http://www.fda.gov, and the Office for Human Research Protections at http://ohrp.osophs.dhhs.gov.

3   *See* "Good Clinical Practice in FDA-Regulated Clinical Trial," available at http://www.fda.gov/oc/gcp.

4   While the FDA regulations require research sponsors to enter into Investigator Agreements with participating investigators on certain IDE studies, this requirement is intended to memorialize the obligation of the principal investigator to abide by and comply with the regulatory obligations of a principal investigator and does not mandate that the parties include general contract provisions that are typical of a private business arrangement. *See* 21 C.F.R. Sections 312.53 and 812.43.

5   Under 35 U.S.C. Section 1 *et. seq.,* patent protection is available to a person who "invents or discovers any new and useful process, machine, manufacturer, or composition of matter, or any new and useful improvement thereof." Copyright protection is available under 17 U.S.C. Section 1 *et. seq.*, for "original works of authorship fixed in any tangible medium of expression." Trademarks can be registered with the U.S. Patent and Trademark Office under 15 U.S.C. 1114 *et. seq.*, but may also receive protection under the Uniform Trade Secrets Act (UTSA), if codified by state statutes, or by other state statutory law or common law.

6 The Bayh-Dole Act is the popular name for The Patent and Trademark Law Amendments Act, P.L. 96-517, amended at P.L. 98-620.

7 *See* "Rights to Inventions Made by Nonprofit Organizations and Small Business Firms," 37 C.F.R. Part 401.

8 There are a variety of federal regulations presiding over health care business transactions and relationships including, by way of illustration only, the following: Federal Prohibition Against Self-Referrals, 63 Fed. Reg. 1659, 66 Fed. Reg. 856, 66 Fed. Reg. 17813; Federal Anti-Assignment Statute, 42 U.S.C. §1395g(c); False Claims Act, 18 U.S.C. § 287, 31. U.S.C. § 3729, 42 C.F.R. §1320a-7a; Prescription Drug Marketing Act 21 U.S.C. §§ 353(c)–(d); Medicaid Drug Rebate Statute 42 U.S.C. §1396r-8; Medicare Civil Monetary Penalty Law 42 C.F.R. §1320a-7a.

9 42 U.S.C. §1320a-7b(b), *et. seq.*

10 *See* OIG Fraud Alert on Prescription Drug Marketing Schemes (December 19, 1994).

11 The OIG Compliance Program Guidance for Pharmaceuticals Manufacturers, published April 2003. The OIG is also currently working on draft guidance for medical device companies, which is expected to be similar in context and scope to the final guidance for pharmaceutical manufacturers.

12 *See* 42 C.F.R. *et. seq.*, including Sections 482 *et. seq.*, for conditions of participation for hospitals.

13 42 C.F.R. §1001.952(d).

14 The second requirement is intended to ensure that the research contract integrates all arrangements between the parties for the same subject matter to avoid potentially having the research tainted by an arrangement that is outside of the research contract and which does not comply with the safe harbor or other statutory requirements. The services only need to be described and do not need to be specifically identified. For instance, it would be sufficient to describe the services as "the conduct of the clinical research program in accordance with the protocol," which is generally attached as an exhibit to the research contract. However, it would be inappropriate to have a research contract for a specific protocol that does not include all arrangements related to that research project, such as performance incentives.

15 *See* FDA regulations at 21 C.F.R. Part 54; Public Health Service regulations at 42 C.F.R. Part 50. *Also see* draft regulations from the Department of Health and Human Services, available at http://ohrp.osophs.dhhs.gov.

16 Opinion 6.03, "Fee Splitting: Referral to Health Care Facilities." *Also see* AMA, Code of Ethics, E-8.0315 "Managing Conflicts of Interest in the Conduct of Clinical Trials," available at http://www.ama-assn.org.

17 The Medicare National Coverage Decision for Clinical Trial Services expanded federal health care reimbursement coverage for routine costs, including items and services, otherwise generally available to Medicare beneficiaries that are provided in either the experimental or the control arms of a qualifying research trial. For additional informational *see* Final National Coverage Decision, Health Care Financing Administration (now known as Centers for Medicare and Medicaid Services), available at http://www.hcfa.gov/quality.

18 Internal Revenue Code, 26 U.S.C. *et. seq.*

19 The Belmont Report, *Ethical Principles and Guidelines for the Protection of Human Subjects of Research*, The National Commission for the Protection of Human Subjects of Biomedical and Behavioral Research, April 18, 1979, available at http://www.hhs.gov/ohrp/humansubjects/guidance.belmont.htm.

20 *See* Treas. Reg. Section 1.501(c)(3)–1(d)(5)(ii). *See also*, Treas. Reg. Section 1.512(b)–1(f)(4).

21 *See* G.C.M. 39196.

22   *See* Treas. Reg. Section 1.174-2.

23   The terms of most tax-exempt bonds require the recipient organization to agree to restrict the use of the bond-financed property to exempt purposes, consistent with the recipient's representations on the intended use of the property. The bond document generally only permits an incidental use of the bond-financed property for private activities. For instance, private use may include leasing space for vending machines or other business machines for the convenience of visitors and guests. Generally the limitation on these private uses is no more than 3–6% of the outstanding amount of the bonds, which is aggregated among all private uses. Because of the complexity of this area and variances among bond requirements, counsel should be advised before undertaking any potential private use in tax-exempt bond financed facilities. *Also see* Revenue Ruling 97-14.

24   *See* Treas. Reg. Section 1.501(c)(3)–1(d)(5)(iii). *See also* IRC Section 512(9).

25   *See* National Institutes of Health, *Guidelines for Acquiring Research Resources for Use in NIH-Funded Research*, Federal Register, Vol. 64., No. 246, December 23, 1999, Page 72095.

26   "Sponsorship, Authorship, and Accountability," *JAMA* Vol. 286, No. 10, September 12, 2001.

27   Pharmaceutical Research Manufacturers of America, *Principles on Conduct of Clinical Trials and Communication of Clinical Trial Results,* issued June 20, 2003, and available at http://www.phrma.org/publications/policy/2002-06-24.430.pdf.

This Agreement is provided for discussion purposes only and should not be relied upon for any purpose without independent legal review.
MASTER CLINICAL TRIAL AGREEMENT

THIS MASTER CLINICAL TRIAL AGREEMENT (the "Agreement") is effective _____ (the "Effective Date") between _____ ("Institution"), and _____ ("Sponsor"), having the respective addresses as set forth below. Each Institution and Sponsor may be referred to individually herein as a "Party," and jointly as the "Parties."

WHEREAS, Institution possesses certain expertise in the field of clinical and related research and evaluation of such research; and

WHEREAS, Sponsor is interested in engaging Institution in order to obtain the benefit of such expertise with respect to certain research and development projects being conducted by Sponsor;

Therefore, in consideration of the premises and undertakings set forth herein, Institution and Sponsor agree as follows:

1. DEFINITIONS

1.1 **"CFR"** means the United States Code of Federal Regulations.

1.2 **"Consent Form"** shall have the meaning ascribed in Section 7.

1.3 **"FDA"** means the United States Food and Drug Administration.

1.4 **"FD&C Act"** means the United States Federal Food, Drug and Cosmetic Act, as may be amended from time to time.

1.5 **"GCP"** means the Guidelines for Good Clinical Practices promulgated by the FDA, including the applicable regulations at 21 CFR.

1.6 **"IRB"** means an Institutional Review Board.

1.7 **"Investigator"** means the principal investigator for a Study, as specified in the applicable Work Order.

1.8 **"Materials"** means all substances, compounds, devices and/or materials provided to Institution by or on behalf of Sponsor for use in the performance of a Study.

1.9 **"Product"** means the study product that is(are) the subject of a Study.

1.10 **"Proprietary Information"** means (a) all confidential information and Materials, including, but not limited to know-how, trade secrets, technology, expertise or other information, whether or not patentable or copyrightable, that is disclosed or provided by Sponsor to Institution in connection with this Agreement, (b) the terms of this Agreement and of any Work Order, and (c) any other information designated as "Proprietary Information" under this Agreement.

1.11 **"Protocol"** means the protocol for the conduct of a Study, as set forth in the relevant Work Order.

1.12 **"Study"** means one or more clinical research studies requested by Sponsor and agreed to be performed by Institution as set forth in the relevant Work Order, which may be referred to collectively as the "Studies."

1.13 **"Study Data"** shall have the meaning ascribed in Section 14.4.

1.14 **"Work Order"** shall have the meaning ascribed in Section 3.1.

2. SCOPE OF THE AGREEMENT

The Parties intend for this Agreement to allow them to contract for multiple Studies through the issuance of Work Orders without having to renegotiate the basic terms and conditions contained herein.

3. WORK ORDERS

3.1 The specific details of each Study under this Agreement shall be separately negotiated by the Parties and specified in writing, on terms and in a form acceptable to the Parties (each such writing, a "Work Order"). Each Work Order will include the Protocol, time line, and payment schedule for such Study. A sample Work Order is attached hereto as Exhibit A.

3.2 Institution shall conduct each Study covered by each executed Work Order in accordance with the terms and conditions of such Work Order. Each executed Work Order shall be deemed to be a part of this Agreement; provided that, to the extent any terms or provisions of a Work Order conflict with the terms and provisions of this Agreement, the terms and provisions of this Agreement shall control, except to the limited extent that the applicable Work Order expressly and specifically states, an intent to supersede this Agreement on a specific matter.

4. INVESTIGATORS' QUALIFICATIONS

4.1   Each Work Order shall identify the Investigator for the Study that is the subject of such Work Order. As requested by Sponsor, the Investigator shall provide to Sponsor a detailed *curriculum vitae*, certificates of training, and, if applicable, a signed investigator statement (Form FDA-1572).

4.2   With respect to each Study, the applicable Investigator shall make the following representations to Sponsor as part of each Work Order:

   (a)   Such Investigator has no financial interests and/or arrangements with Sponsor that will require disclosure to FDA in accordance with 21 CFR Part 54;

   (b)   Such Investigator has not been "debarred" by the FDA under the provisions of the Generic Drug Enforcement Act of 1992, 21 U.S.C. § 335a (a) and (b), nor have debarment proceedings been commenced against him or her;

   (c)   Such Investigator is aware of and agrees to be bound by the terms of this Agreement and of the Work Order covering such Study.

5. FDA AND IRB APPROVAL

For each Study to be conducted hereunder, Sponsor shall provide to the FDA and to the applicable Investigator for submission to the IRB, adequate information (i.e., investigator's brochure, the Protocol, and sample informed consent form) for review and approval to begin such Study. If any modification of such informed consent form is required by the IRB, a copy of the form as modified shall be promptly provided to Sponsor for its approval. Any withdrawal of IRB approval shall be immediately reported to Sponsor.

6. CONDUCT OF STUDIES, GENERALLY

6.1   Investigator shall commence each Study as soon as possible following receipt of FDA and IRB written approval, or as otherwise agreed upon in writing with Sponsor, and shall follow any conditions of approval imposed by the FDA or the IRB.

6.2   Institution and the applicable Investigator shall conduct each Study in accordance with all applicable federal and state laws and regulations for protecting the rights, safety, and welfare of human subjects and for the control of investigational drugs and devices, including GCP.

6.3   Except in the case of a medical emergency or otherwise necessary for patient safety, neither Institution nor any Investigator shall not make any changes in, nor deviate from, the applicable Protocol without Sponsor' prior written approval.

6.4   Sponsor or its designee will provide clinical monitoring for each Study. Institution and the applicable Investigator shall cooperate with Sponsor and/or its designee in the performance of its duties as clinical monitor.

6.5   Any substitutions or replacements of an Investigator during the course of a Study must first be approved in writing by Sponsor. In the event that the Investigator for a Study becomes unable or unwilling to continue to perform his or her responsibilities under such Study, Institution shall use its best efforts to provide a replacement acceptable to Sponsor as promptly as possible. If Institution is unable to replace such Investigator to Sponsor's reasonable satisfaction, Sponsor shall have the right to terminate such Study upon written notice to Institution, as set forth in Section 6.6 below.

6.6   Sponsor reserves the right to terminate any Study at any time, with or without cause, upon written notice to the Institution and the applicable Investigator. Upon receipt of initial notice of termination of a Study from Sponsor, Institution and the applicable Investigator shall cease the clinical investigation of the applicable Product and the enrollment of further subjects into such Study. Institution and the applicable Investigator shall continue to prepare case report forms for subjects who received such Product prior to receipt of the termination notice as directed in writing by Sponsor. Upon termination, Institution will be reimbursed by Sponsor for (a) all fees incurred in its conduct of such Study through the effective date of such termination, and for any further case report form processing as described above, in accordance with the payment schedule set forth in the applicable Work Order, and (b) any reasonable, noncancelable costs resulting from the termination following Sponsor's receipt of an itemized invoice detailing such costs.

7. INFORMED CONSENT

For each Study to be conduced hereunder, and in accordance with 21 CFR Part 50, Investigator shall inform all subjects of such Study or their legal representatives that the applicable Product is being used for clinical investigation, and shall obtain from these subjects or their legal representatives a signed written informed consent form which has been approved by the IRB and Sponsor (a "Consent Form"). Each subject shall be provided a photocopy of his or her signed Consent Form, the original of which shall be placed in the respective subject's investigational file.

8. SUPERVISING USE

Institution shall permit the Product that is the subject of a Study to be used only by subjects under the applicable Investigator's supervision, or under the supervision of the co-investigators, if any, listed on the applicable Form FDA-1572. The Institution shall not supply the Product to any person other than those authorized under this Agreement. No investigative procedures other than those set forth in the corresponding Protocol shall be undertaken with such Product on the enrolled subjects or otherwise without the prior written approval of Sponsor (and the IRB when necessary). Institution will not supply such Product, nor permit such Product to be supplied, to any third party (including, without limitation, any other investigator except the above-referenced associates) or laboratory or any clinic for use in humans or for *in vitro* or *in vivo* laboratory research, or any other use, without the prior written approval of Sponsor.

9. RECORDS

9.1 Investigator and Institution shall make such records available to Sponsor and its authorized representatives promptly upon request:

(a) any and all correspondence with Sponsor, the IRB, and the FDA

(b) records of receipt, use, or disposition of the Product that is the subject of such Study including:

(i) the date of receipt, type, quantity, lot number, batch number and/or code mark, and other identifying marks of such Product

      (ii)   the names of all persons who received, used, or disposed of each unit of such Product

      (iii)   an explanation of the reasons why any Product and how many units of the Product was returned to Sponsor

  (c)   records of each subject's case history and exposure to such Product, including:

      (i)   source records of each subject's case history and exposure to the Product

      (ii)   signed copies of Consent Forms

      (iii)   source records of all relevant observations, including adverse device effects, previous medical history, results of diagnostic tests, and other data and records pertinent to such Study

  (d)   the applicable Protocol, and any amendments thereto, with documents showing the dates of and reasons for each deviation from such Protocol

9.2   Investigator shall review, sign, and date the case report forms for each subject enrolled in a Study. Source documents must be available for copy and review as needed by Sponsor to audit or correct study case report forms or to respond to the FDA. Institution shall make such source documents and records available for inspection and copying at routine clinical monitoring visits. Institution and its staff shall cooperate with Sponsor during monitoring visits or for the resolution of questions regarding records or clinical data generated throughout the performance of this Agreement.

9.3   The parties recognize that the sharing of clinical data with Sponsor in the performance, audit, or monitoring of a Study may involve disclosure of individually identifiable health information, as that term is defined under the privacy rules of the Health Insurance Portability and Accountability Act of 1996. The parties each agree to treat all individually identifiable health information disclosed as part of a Study as confidential and in accordance with the patient's written authorization and all applicable federal, state, or local laws and regulations governing confidentiality and privacy of individually identifiable health information.

10. REPORTS

10.1 Institution shall prepare and submit to Sponsor or its designee the following complete, accurate, and timely reports with respect to each Study:

(a) *Case Report Forms:* Institution shall submit completed case report forms as required in the applicable Protocol or as otherwise requested by Sponsor. In the event subject follow-up is not possible for any reason, Institution shall document this fact and the circumstances thereof on a case report form and promptly submit such form.

(b) *Adverse Events:* Any serious adverse events that occur during such Study shall be reported by Institution to Sponsor, and to the IRB if required by federal regulations, as soon as possible following receipt of such information.

(c) *Withdrawal of IRB Approval:* Institution shall report to Sponsor the IRB's withdrawal of approval of the Institution's or applicable Investigator's participation in a Study immediately following receipt of such notice from the IRB.

(d) *Deviations from the Protocol:* Institution shall promptly notify Sponsor of any deviation from the Protocol, as permitted under Section 6.3.

10.2 Institution shall provide to Sponsor (a) periodic written progress reports for each Study, and (b) a final written report for such Study, in each case as described in the applicable Work Order.

11. COMPENSATION

11.1 Institution will be compensated by Sponsor for its conduct of each Study in accordance with the payment terms and fee schedule set forth in the applicable Work Order.

11.2 Sponsor shall report any payments made to Institution under this Agreement, and shall withhold from such payments any required taxes for remittance to the applicable authority, solely to the extent required by applicable federal, state, or local tax laws or regulations.

11.3 The Parties specifically intend to comply with all applicable laws, rules, and regulations, including (a) the federal anti-kickback statute (42 U.S.C.

1320a-7(b)) and the related safe harbor regulations; and (b) the Limitation on Certain Physician Referrals, also referred to as the "Stark Law" (42 U.S.C. 1395nn). Accordingly, no part of any consideration paid hereunder is a prohibited payment for the recommending or arranging for the referral of business or the ordering of items or services; nor are the payments intended to induce illegal referrals of business.

12. REGULATORY ISSUES; INSPECTIONS

12.1   Each of Sponsor and Institution shall be responsible for obtaining and maintaining, at its respective expense, all permits, licenses, approvals, authorizations, and the like required for its respective performance under this Agreement.

12.2   If any governmental or regulatory authority or any entity representing such an authority (each, a "Regulatory Authority") requests access to Institution's records, facilities, and/or personnel, or conducts an unannounced inspection, in each case relating to a Study, then Institution shall promptly notify the contact set forth in the Work Order covering such Study by telephone.

12.3   Institution will permit Sponsor's representatives to examine or audit the work performed pursuant to any Study and the facilities at which the work is conducted, upon reasonable advance notice during regular business hours, to determine that Institution is conducting Study in accordance with the applicable Work Order and applicable regulatory requirements and that Institution is providing adequate facilities and staffing.

13. DISPOSING OF CLINICAL SUPPLIES [FOR DRUG STUDIES ONLY]

In accordance with 21 CFR 312.59, upon the earlier of completion or termination of each Study or at Sponsor's request, Institution shall return to Sponsor any remaining Product (including investigational devices, if any) and other Materials from such Study, or, if so instructed by Sponsor, destroy any such remaining Product in accordance with the instructions provided by Sponsor and consistent with applicable local, state, and federal guidelines and shall supply Sponsor with a certificate of such destruction.

14. CONFIDENTIALITY/INTELLECTUAL PROPERTY

14.1   Institution hereby agrees:

    (a) not to use any Proprietary Information except for the purpose of conducting the applicable Study or as otherwise expressly authorized in writing by Sponsor, and

    (b) not to disclose or transfer Proprietary Information to any person or entity, other than to those employees or agents (including without limitation Investigators) who reasonably require same for the purpose hereof and who are bound by like written obligations to protect such Proprietary Information, without the express written permission of Sponsor.

    (c) The obligations of this provision shall remain in effect for three (3) years following the disclosure of such Proprietary Information.

14.2 The obligations set forth in Section 14.1 shall not apply to any Proprietary Information that:

    (a) Institution can demonstrate by written records was known to Institution prior to its disclosure hereunder; or

    (b) is now or later becomes publicly available other than by breach of this Agreement; or

    (c) is lawfully disclosed to the recipient on a nonconfidential basis by a third party who is not obligated to Sponsor or any other party to retain such Proprietary Information in confidence.

14.3 Nothing in this Agreement shall prevent Institution from disclosing Proprietary Information that is duly required to be disclosed by order of a court, government agency, or the like having competent jurisdiction, provided that Institution shall promptly notify Sponsor to permit Sponsor to seek a protective order or injunctive relief to protect the confidentiality of the Proprietary Information.

14.4 The case report forms, progress reports, and any other reports prepared in the performance of the Study ("Study Data") shall be the sole and exclusive property of Sponsor. Nothing in this Article 14, however, shall prevent the Institution from maintaining copies of such materials to use for (a) regulatory compliance purposes and evidencing compliance with this Agreement; (b) publishing scientific articles on the Study, as contemplated by Article 15 below; or (c) internal research, education, and patient care purposes, subject to the surviving obligations of Section 14.1.

14.5 The furnishing of Proprietary Information under this Agreement shall not constitute any grant, option, or license to the Institution under any patent or other rights now or hereafter held by Sponsor. This Agreement shall not be deemed or construed to convey or transfer to Institution any rights with respect to any Product, except as insofar as necessary to permit Institution and the applicable Investigator to conduct the Study.

14.6 The sole and exclusive right to any inventions, discoveries, or innovations, whether patentable or not, arising in the direct performance of a Study, and constituting a reduction to practice of an invention, discovery, or innovation previously conceived by or on behalf of Sponsor, including the Protocol or involving any improvements or modifications to the Product that enhances its safety or efficacy in the subject of this Study ("Sponsor Inventions"), shall be the sole and exclusive property of Sponsor.

14.7 "New Invention" shall mean any invention, discovery, or innovation conceived or reduced to practice during and as a part of a Study that is not a Sponsor Invention. The terms "conceived" and "first reduced to practice" shall be given the meaning of those terms as they appear in 35 U.S.C. Section 102(g). The parties will retain title to any patent or other intellectual property rights in New Inventions made solely by their respective employees in the course of the Study. New Inventions made jointly by Institution and Sponsor shall be jointly owned by the parties.

14.8 For New Inventions developed solely by Institution and/or jointly by Institution and Sponsor, the Institution grants to the Sponsor, without fee or charge, the right of first refusal with respect to Institution's rights in any New Invention(s) under the following the terms:

(a) Institution shall notify the Sponsor, in writing, of the New Invention(s) and provide the Sponsor with sufficient detail to evaluate the New Invention(s) in confidence.

(b) The Sponsor shall have sixty (60) days after such notification to evaluate the New Invention(s) and notify Institution, in writing, that the Sponsor desires to license the New Invention(s) pursuant to Sponsor's right of first refusal.

(c) Upon notification by the Sponsor of its desire to license the New Invention(s), the Parties shall negotiate, in good faith, for a period not to exceed one hundred and twenty (120) days, unless extended by mutual written agreement of the Parties, in an effort to arrive at terms and conditions mutually satisfactory for the license by the Sponsor of the New Invention(s).

(d) If the Parties do not reach such agreement within said one hundred-and-twenty-day (120-day) period, or if the Sponsor fails to notify Institution within said sixty-day (60-day) period, or if the Sponsor decides not to license the New Invention, Institution shall be free to deal with the New Invention(s) as Institution may decide, and Institution shall have no further obligations to the Sponsor with respect to the New Invention(s).

14.9 Sponsor shall have the responsibility for filing all applications that may be required by health or regulatory authorities relating to the Product, including, without limitation, filing a Premarket Application ("PMA") with the FDA. All costs and expenses associated with such filings shall be borne by the Sponsor. Sponsor shall own all right, title, and interest in any FDA or other regulatory approvals that are obtained by or on behalf of the Sponsor.

14.10 Institution understands and acknowledges that the United States securities laws prohibit any person who has material nonpublic ("inside") information about a company from purchasing or selling securities of such company, and prohibits communicating such material nonpublic information to any other person under circumstances where it is reasonably foreseeable that such person is likely to purchase or sell securities of such company. Institution further acknowledges that the Proprietary Information can constitute such material nonpublic information.

15. PUBLICATION OF RESULTS

15.1 Sponsor recognizes the importance of communicating medical study or scientific data and, therefore, encourages their publication in reputable scientific journals and at seminars or conferences. Any results of the

Study and publication/lecture manuscripts thereon shall be exchanged and discussed by the Investigator and Sponsor prior to publication. Due regard shall be given to Sponsor's legitimate interests, e.g., ensuring compliance with the statistical analyses for the primary endpoints of the Study according to, and consistent with, the Protocol; obtaining patent protection; coordinating and maintaining the proprietary nature of submissions to health authorities; and protection of confidential information, and so on.

15.2   Any proposed publications that are to make public any findings, data, or results of the Study shall be submitted to Sponsor for Sponsor's review and comment at least thirty (30) days prior to submission of a manuscript for publication, or at least seven (7) days prior to submission for an abstract. If Sponsor reasonably determines that the proposed publication contains patentable subject matters that require protection, Sponsor may require the delay of publication for a period of time not to exceed sixty (60) days for the purpose of filing patent applications. If no written response is received from Sponsor within the applicable review period, it may be conclusively presumed that publication may proceed without delay.

15.3   If a particular Study is a part of a multicenter study, the Institution and Investigator agree that the first publication of the results of such Study shall be made in conjunction with the presentation of a joint, multicenter publication with all appropriate sites. However, if such a multicenter publication is not submitted within twelve (12) months after conclusion, abandonment, or termination of the Study at all sites, or after Sponsor confirms there will be no multicenter Study publication, the Institution and/or Principal Investigator may publish the results from the Institution's site individually in accordance with the procedures above.

15.4   The above procedure also applies to information on prematurely discontinued and other noncompleted studies. Institution shall give Sponsor and/or Sponsor's personnel appropriate credit for any direct contribution made by them, subject to their prior consent.

16. REPRESENTATIONS AND WARRANTIES

16.1   Institution hereby represents and warrants that:

(a)   It is under no obligation to any third party, and will not during the term of this Agreement agree to assume any obligation to any third party, that would conflict with, prohibit, or otherwise interfere with its performance of its obligations under this Agreement;

(b)   It has no financial interests and/or arrangements with Sponsor that will require disclosure to FDA in accordance with 21 CFR Part 54;

(c)   It has not been debarred under 21 U.S.C. § 335(a) or 335(b), and will not use the services of any persons debarred under 21 U.S.C. § 335(a) or 335(b) in any capacity in connection with the performance of its obligations under this Agreement; and

(d)   It has not been debarred, excluded, suspended, or otherwise determined to be ineligible to participate in any federal health care reimbursement programs, including the Medicare and Medicaid programs.

16.2   Sponsor hereby represents and warrants that:

(a)   It is under no obligation to any third party, and will not during the term of this Agreement agree to assume any obligation to any third party, that would conflict with, prohibit, or otherwise interfere with its performance of its obligations under this Agreement.

17. INDEMNIFICATION

17.1   To the extent permitted by law, Sponsor shall indemnify, defend, and hold harmless Institution and its directors, officers, agents, and employees, including Investigators and associated staff (collectively, the "Covered Parties") from any and all liability, loss, or damage including attorneys' fees they may suffer as the result of any third-party claims, demands, costs, or judgments against them that arise as a result of (i) personal injury or death to a participant in a Study caused by the procedures required by the applicable Protocol, (ii) arising from the fault, failure, or negligence of Sponsor under this Agreement, or (iii) arising from any use or administration of a Product that is the subject of a Study in accordance with the applicable Protocol; provided, however, that Sponsor shall have no obligations under this Section 17.1 to the extent that any such liability, loss, or damage arises as a proximate result of (a) a Covered Party's failure to adhere to the terms of such Protocol or Sponsor's other written instructions with respect to the use of such Product, (b) a Covered Party's failure to comply with any applicable FDA or other governmental requirements, or (c) a Covered Party's negligence or willful malfeasance.

17.2   To the extent permitted by law, Institution shall indemnify, defend, and hold harmless Sponsor and its directors, officers, agents, and employees from any and all liability, loss, or damage including attorneys' fees they may suffer as the result of any third-party claims, demands, costs, or judgments against them resulting from (i) a Covered Party's failure to adhere to the terms of a Protocol or Sponsor' other written instructions with respect to the use of a Product in a Study, (ii) a Covered Party's failure to comply with any applicable FDA or other governmental requirements, (iii) a Covered Party's improper or unauthorized usage of computer hardware, software, Product, or Materials provided by Sponsor hereunder, or (iv) negligence or willful malfeasance, by a Covered Party; provided, however, that Institution shall have no obligations under this Section 17.2 to the extent Sponsor is obligated to indemnify Institution under Section 17.1 with respect to any such liability, loss, or damage.

17.3   If a Party (the "Indemnitee") intends to claim indemnification from the other Party (the "Indemnitor") under this Article 17, then the Parties shall proceed as follows:

(a)   The Indemnitee shall promptly notify the Indemnitor in writing of any action, claim, or other matter in respect of which the Indemnitee or any of its directors, officers, employees, or agents intend to claim such indemnification; provided, however, the failure to provide such notice within a reasonable period of time shall not relieve the Indemnitor of any of its obligations hereunder except to the extent the Indemnitor is prejudiced by such failure.

(b)   The Indemnitee shall permit, and shall cause its directors, officers, employees, and agents to permit, the Indemnitor at its discretion to settle any such action, claim, or other matter, and the Indemnitee agrees to the complete control of such defense or settlement by the

Indemnitor. Notwithstanding the foregoing, the Indemnitor shall not enter into any settlement that would adversely affect the Indemnitee's rights hereunder, or impose any obligations on the Indemnitee in addition to those set forth herein in order for it to exercise such rights, without Indemnitee's prior written consent, which shall not be unreasonably withheld or delayed.

(c) No such action, claim, or other matter shall be settled without the prior written consent of the Indemnitor, which shall not be unreasonably withheld or delayed. The Indemnitor shall not be responsible for any attorneys' fees or other costs incurred other than as provided herein. The Indemnitee and its directors, officers, employees, and agents shall cooperate fully with the Indemnitor and its legal representatives in the investigation and defense of any action, claim, or other matter covered by the indemnification obligations of this Article 17. The Indemnitee shall have the right, but not the obligation, to be represented in such defense by counsel of its own selection and at its own expense.

18. SUBJECT INJURY

Sponsor agrees that if a subject enrolled in a Study according to the applicable Protocol suffers an injury as a result of (a) receiving the Product that is the subject of such Study, administered in accordance with such Protocol and this Agreement, or (b) research procedures required and conducted in accordance with such Protocol and the Agreement, and provided in each case that such injury is not caused in any way by an Investigator's or Institution's negligence, gross negligence, or misconduct, in accordance with the requirements of the Institution, then without any admission of wrongdoing on the part of Sponsor, Sponsor shall pay all reasonable medical expenses engendered by the immediate medical treatment of such injury.

19. NOTICES

All notices, requests, consents, and other communications under this Agreement shall be in writing and shall be delivered by hand or mailed by first class, certified, or registered mail, return receipt requested, postage prepaid, as follows (or to such other address as a Party hereto may notify the other in writing):

In the case of Sponsor, addressed to:

_____

_____

_____

Phone: _____

Facsimile: _____

In the case of Institution, addressed to:

_____

_____

_____

Phone: _____

Facsimile:_____

20. TERM AND TERMINATION

20.1   This Agreement shall become effective as of the Effective Date, and shall remain in force until the third (3rd) anniversary of the Effective Date and may be extended by mutual written agreement of the parties, unless and until terminated as set forth in Section 20.2 or by written agreement of the Parties. Upon such termination, all currently ongoing Studies shall remain in effect and be completed in accordance with the terms of this Agreement, unless such Study is terminated in accordance with Section 6.6.

20.2   Either Party may terminate this Agreement if the other Party materially breaches this Agreement and such breaching Party fails to cure such breach within thirty (30) days from the receipt of written notice from the nonbreaching Party of such material breach.

20.3   The following provisions shall survive termination of this Agreement: Sections 6.6, 9.3, and Articles 12, 14, 15, 17, 18, 19, 20.3, and 21.3. Termination of this Agreement shall not relieve either Party of any liability which accrued hereunder prior to the effective date of such termination, nor preclude either Party from pursuing all rights and remedies it may have hereunder or at law or in equity with respect to any breach of this Agreement, nor prejudice either Party's right to obtain performance of any obligation. The remedies provided under this Agreement are cumulative, and are not exclusive of other remedies available to a Party in law or equity.

21. MISCELLANEOUS PROVISIONS

21.1 Institution shall not assign, subcontract, or otherwise transfer any of its rights or obligations hereunder, or any part hereof, without the prior written consent of Sponsor. Any such assignment or transfer made without Sponsor's prior written consent shall be null and void.

21.2 Institution shall, at all times, be an independent contractor, not an agent of Sponsor, and shall have no actual, apparent, or implied authority to act or make representations for, or on behalf of, or to bind or commit Sponsor in any manner or to any obligation whatsoever.

21.3 Except as may be required by law, each Party will obtain prior written permission from the other Party before using the name, symbols, and/or marks of such other Party, or such Party's employees or agents, in any form of publicity.

21.4 Paragraph and section headings are included for convenience of reference only and form no part of the agreement between the parties.

21.5 Any delay in enforcing a Party's rights under this Agreement or any waiver as to a particular default or other matter shall not constitute a waiver of such Party's rights to the future enforcement of its rights under this Agreement, excepting only as to an express written and signed waiver as to a particular matter for a particular period of time.

21.6 A Party shall not be deemed to be in breach or default of any provision of this Agreement by reason of a delay or failure in performance due to acts of God, acts of governments, wars, riots, strikes, accidents in transportation, or other causes beyond the control of the parties. However, if material performance becomes impossible for more than a sixty-day (60-day) period by reason thereof, either Party may terminate this Agreement by giving notice to the other Party.

21.7 If any provision of this Agreement is or becomes or is deemed to be invalid, illegal, or unenforceable in any jurisdiction, then such provision will be deemed amended to conform to applicable laws of such jurisdiction so as to be valid and enforceable. If such provision cannot be so amended without materially altering the intention of the Parties, then it will be stricken. The validity, legality, and enforceability of such provision will not in any way be affected or impaired thereby in any other jurisdiction, and the remainder of this Agreement will remain in full force and effect.

21.8 This Agreement, and any Work Orders executed in connection herewith, set forth the complete, final, and exclusive agreement between the Parties with respect to the subject matter hereof, and all of the covenants, promises, agreements, warranties, representations, conditions, and understandings between the Parties hereto with respect to such subject matter, and supersedes and terminates all prior agreements and understandings between the Parties with respect to such subject matter. There are no covenants, promises, agreements, warranties, representations, conditions, or understandings, either oral or written, between the Parties with respect to such subject matter other than as are set forth herein and therein. No subsequent alteration, amendment, change, or addition to this Agreement shall be binding upon the Parties unless reduced to writing and signed by an authorized officer of each Party.

[Signature Lines Follow on Next Page]

IN WITNESS THEREOF, the parties have executed this Agreement as of the Effective Date.

Sponsor _____ **Institution**

By _____ By _____

Print Name_____ Print Name _____

Title _____ Title _____

Date _____ Date _____

EXHIBIT A
FORM OF WORK ORDER

WORK ORDER # _____

This Work Order is issued pursuant to the Master Clinical Studies Agreement, dated as of _____, between _____ ("Sponsor") and _____ ("Institution") (the "Agreement").

Any capitalized terms not otherwise defined herein shall have the same meaning ascribed to them in the Agreement.

Protocol Title and Number: _____ (the "Study"). A copy of the Protocol is attached hereto as Schedule 1 and incorporated herein by this reference.

Principal Investigator(s) Name: _____ ("Investigator(s)"). Correspondence to Investigator can be addressed to the following:

_____

_____

_____

Phone: _____

Facsimile:_____

E-mail: _____

A copy of the Investigator's Certification is attached hereto as Schedule 2, and is incorporated herein by this reference.

Sponsor's Clinical Leader: _____. Correspondence to Sponsor' Clinical Leader can be addressed to the following:

_____

_____

_____

Phone: _____

Facsimile:_____

E-mail: _____

Study Schedule:

1.   Study Initiation and Completion

    (a)   All contractual and regulatory documentation must be completed, executed, and received by Sponsor no later than _____ .

    (b)   The Study shall be initiated no later than _____ ("Initiation Date") and shall be completed no later than _____ ("Completion Date").

2.   Enrollment

    (a)   It is anticipated that the Principal Investigator(s) may enroll _____ patients into the Study (the "Site Maximum"). Patient enrollment shall be completed on or before _____ . Enrollment of each patient over the Site Maximum requires the agreement of Sponsor.

    (b)   Notwithstanding whether the Site Maximum has been reached, the Investigator(s) agrees to immediately cease enrolling patients upon notice from Sponsor that Sponsor' target enrollment for the Study has been achieved.

Study Budget. All payments will be made in accordance with the Study Budget, which is attached hereto as Schedule 3 and incorporated herein by this reference.

All payments will be made payable to:

_____

_____

_____

Federal Tax Identification Number:_____

This Work Order is entered into and made effective as of _____ .

Accepted and Agreed to by:

SPONSOR   INSTITUTION

_____   _____
Signature   Signature

_____   _____
Typed Name and Title   Typed Name and Title

Date: _____   Date: _____

Schedule 1 to Work Order # _____

PROTOCOL

Schedule 2 to Work Order # _____

PRINCIPAL INVESTIGATOR'S CERTIFICATION

I acknowledge that I have read this Work Order # _____ and am aware of and understand its terms and conditions and the terms and conditions of the Agreement referred to therein. I agree to and will comply with all the terms and conditions of the Work Order and the Agreement, both as an individual and as an employee of Institution.

I represent and warrant that I have no financial interests and/or arrangements with Sponsor that will require disclosure to FDA in accordance with 21 CFR Part 54, and that I will promptly notify Sponsor if any such interests or arrangements later arise.

I represent and warrant that I have not been disqualified by the federal Food and Drug Administration or otherwise disqualified from serving as a Principal Investigator for this Study.

I represent and warrant that I have not been debarred under the provisions of the Generic Drug Enforcement Act of 1992, 21 U.S.C. § 335a(a) and (b). In the event that I (i) become debarred; or (ii) receive notice of an action or threat of an action with respect to my debarment, during the term of this Study, I agree to immediately notify Sponsor and Institution. I also agree that in the event that I become debarred, I shall immediately cease all activities relating to this Agreement.

I understand that in the event Sponsor receives notice or otherwise becomes aware that (i) I have been debarred, (ii) a debarment action has been brought against me, or (iii) I have been threatened with a debarment action, Sponsor shall have the right, at its sole discretion, to (a) terminate immediately my participation in the Study, or (b) agree with Institution to a substitute Principal Investigator who will assume full responsibility and perform all the remaining activities under this Study.

PRINCIPAL INVESTIGATOR

_____

Print Name

_____

Signature

Date: _____

Schedule 3 to Work Order # _____
STUDY BUDGET

THREE

Clinical Research Billing: Process and Monitoring Issues

John E. Steiner, Jr. and F. Lisa Murtha*

Introduction

While clinical trials have been a staple of the U.S. health care industry for decades, the techniques and methods for conducting these trials are varied and increasingly complex. This chapter does not address issues related to the science of clinical trials or to related patient care or patient consent matters. This chapter focuses on the billing process and monitoring issues related to clinical trials.

The difficulties clinical trial sites experience with the proper creation and submission of claims for clinical trials are similar to other health care billing situations. That is, the diversity of coverage and payment rules, coupled with the sheer volume of claims, present numerous challenges for health care organizations.[1] Those challenges include attracting, training, and retaining skilled

*The authors wish to acknowledge the assistance of Heidi Carrol, Esq., of The Cleveland Clinic Health System, in the preparation of this chapter.

clinical research personnel; providing continuous training and education on clinical trial budgeting, documentation, and billing requirements; and providing the workforce with appropriate tools to perform their jobs (including standardized templates, software support, clinical trial management systems, and the like). The sections in this chapter are presented in a practical, issue focused format to assist the reader in identifying clinical research compliance risks and includes suggestions to reduce those risks. At the time of the publication of this book, the authors are unaware of a single set of best practices at health care research organizations that fully addresses all of the complexities of clinical research billing. However, the points covered in this chapter and other chapters in this book should provide useful guidance in this area.

Clinical Research Billing Process Issues

Why Is Clinical Trial Billing a Significant Compliance Concern?

Most organizations that conduct a high volume of clinical research, sometimes referred to as academic research organizations (AROs), were created and are operated to focus on the treatment aspects of clinical research trials. The attention of Principal Investigators (PIs) still is primarily focused on advancing medical knowledge and improving patient care. Thus, AROs rarely design or implement clinical trial billing systems at the outset, either as stand-alone systems or integrated systems within the organization's core billing system. Yet most AROs provide a mix of "standard-of-care" patient treatment modalities and "research-related" health care services. In nearly every case, the mission critical work for the organization is providing standard-of-care services to patients. Thus, those who oversee and support clinical trials have had to work within the organization's core billing system and/or develop work-arounds to ensure that clinical trial billing can occur.

From both a business and a compliance perspective, there should be advance planning, adequate checks and balances, self-monitoring, independent auditing, and internal controls to achieve compliant clinical trial billing. Although this is easier said than done, the industry is working diligently to improve its training, procedures, monitoring, and its billing systems in this area. There are external pressures as well to do so, not the least of which is patient satisfaction levels among those who participate in trials and receive bills from the AROs.

The main task facing AROs that attempt to address these compliance concerns is to design and implement a process to ensure that tests or services performed are identified in a timely manner as either "standard of care " or "research" and that those tests and/or procedures are budgeted appropriately. The next major task is to ensure that standard-of-care charges are billed to the insurer, grant source, or patient and that research charges are billed against the clinical trial budget. Billing a payor for standard-of-care charges and then charging those items against a clinical trial budget is an example of improper double billing. Thus, it is essential to differentiate standard of care and research. As discussed later in this chapter, there also are compliance issues that may arise with residual balances in clinical trials.[2]

What Are AROs Doing about Clinical Trial Billing?

Over the past few years, leading AROs have intensified their efforts to examine the sources and possible solutions to problems that arise in clinical trial billing. Some organizations have implemented dual departments to minimize double billing risks. These organizations have a research laboratory or a research radiology department to serve clinical trial participants who receive tests related to a research protocol. However, most AROs are not structured or staffed to handle dual departments that allow for segregation of patient encounters. Thus, many organizations developed systems or methods to work around the organization's core billing systems.

More recently, AROs are adopting processes to capture research tests, services, or procedures at the time of patient registration. This usually is an effective process but presents challenges that require a team approach for adequate design and implementation. For example, what happens when a patient presents to receive both a standard-of-care clinical service and a research-only type of service? Currently, most registration systems do not have the capability to segregate these types of services on the same date of service. Services designated as research-only are suspended or held in the billing system. Later in the process, a clinical trial coordinator or the PI on the trial may perform a reconciliation to ensure that only research charges are charged against the clinical trial budget.

Other organizations track clinical trial billing charges through the medical record process. Research related charges are flagged in the medical record, then an individual in the medical records department or a related support department will forward a batch of research charges to the billing department. At this point, there is no generally accepted process for handling clinical trial billing. The important task at hand is to perform a compliance assessment and work diligently toward addressing any identified problems.

Challenges in Clinical Trial Billing

The major obstacles for most AROs are segregating, tracking, posting, and billing standard-of-care versus research charges. Thus, it is important to create a strong systems link between the research accounting systems and billing systems. However, such links often do not exist. One suggested approach for building such links is presented in Chapter 00 and includes sample computer screen shots to illustrate the type of information captured.

Another major obstacle to administering compliant clinical research billing is the decentralized nature of clinical trials in AROs. Principal investigators and clinical trial coordinators often create work-arounds within the core billing system. Even then, the work-arounds may be highly variable and tailored to work only for a specific PI or a department. At a minimum, it is recommended that the presence and extent of these work-arounds be assessed and discussed by a designated committee. Simply knowing, with precision, what is going on in your organization is a solid step forward.

Financial Management Considerations

From a financial management perspective, the starting point is the clinical trial budget. These budgets often are incomplete and may not consistently account for standard-of-care and research-related items or services. A primary consideration is whether the budget is adequate to cover the expected costs of the trial. Some of the questions to ask are as follows:

- From an accounts receivable perspective, are bills sent and payments collected from sponsors in an accurate and timely manner?
- Are research discounts correctly reflected in the research budget?
- Are professional fees budgeted and billed correctly?
- Are research study participants identifiable in the registration and billing systems?
- Does the Charge Description Master (CDM) permit segregation of charges for research (e.g., an "R" designation) that then allows costs to be charged to the proper place?
- Is there a way to reconcile or scrub the charges before billing?

The points addressed by these questions are not all inclusive, but illustrate the importance of the process of clinical trial billing. It is a useful exercise to assemble a multidisciplinary workgroup and diagram or flow-chart the multiple steps in this process. In particular, it is useful to focus on a linear flow, i.e., one step following another, from patient registration through to billing. The discipline of flow-charting the process usually results in a clinical research billing cycle that can then be explained to key members of executive administration and the ARO workforce. Often, that explanation helps the appropriate personnel understand the complexities of clinical research billing and the resources required for process improvement.

Critical Areas of the Clinical Trial Billing Process

As previously mentioned, the steps involved in administering compliant clinical research billing lend themselves to a diagram or flow chart, which may be used for each clinical trial protocol. Thus, the main effort requires description of the relevant steps for financial, compliance, and operational purposes.

Many organizations identify and assess these factors by reviewing current policies and procedures and walking through a sample of active clinical trials. Such an analysis usually provides insights into specific gaps that need to be addressed from the clinical, budgeting, registration, information systems, and billing perspectives. In some departments, clinical research personnel may have engineered a compliant work-around process that might be feasible to implement across the entire organization. While this practice may be a step in the right direction, it is not a recommended enterprise-wide solution. Thus, most organizations need to revisit clinical research billing from the start and create new procedures and processes.

Many organizations have been diligently educating and training their workforce on clinical research regulatory requirements, but struggle to effectively implement policies and procedures to fully address those requirements. The personnel and process areas responsible for the clinical research billing process will vary based on the structure and size of the institution. In general, the key personnel and function areas responsible for clinical trial billing processes are as follows:

- Principal Investigators (ultimately responsible for the terms and conditions of the research agreement, including the research budget)
- Office of Contracting and/or Technology Transfer
- Research Finance and/or Research Billing and/or Research Accounting (approving research budgets, establishing research accounts, billing sponsors, monitoring research budgets)
- Clinical Trial Coordinators and/or Research Nurses (responsible for creating patient schedules and notifying registration staff)

- Reimbursement Specialist (assisting in the creation of a research budget, correcting all billing variances)
- Registration Staff (inpatient and outpatient)
- Information Systems Staff (providing the necessary ITD support)
- Clinical Trials Office (if one exists; assisting with the development and/or approval of study budgets)
- Health Information Management Staff
- Pharmacy and Laboratory Support (creating standard operating procedures, billing procedures, and registration and notification)
- Compliance Officer and Legal Resources (educating, monitoring, and establishing standard operating procedures)
- Hospital Administrators (tracking research activity in their division/department, approving use of departmental funds, establishing a research monitor Hospital/Physician Practice Billing Office

In addition to outlining the key responsibilities of team members, the critical process steps—from establishment of a budget to enrollment of a patient to the close-out of a trial—should be reviewed. Each of these topics is briefly discussed in the following sections.

- Preparation and approval of study budget
- Preparation of a clinical research billing plan
- Enrollment of clinical trial participant
- Arrival of research participant for the first exam/test/procedure
- Completion of exam/test/procedure and charge entry
- Billing process review
- Budget reconciliation and grant closure/treatment of residuals
- Related billing issues

Preparation and Approval of Study Budget

Proper preparation of a study budget assists an organization in identifying and providing the resources necessary to conduct the clinical trial, and is an essential component of the billing process. To assist research personnel in the establishment of a research budget, standardized budget templates and related, detailed instructions should be created. The standardized budget template should include the following items:

- Compensation/personnel costs (salaries, fringe benefits, professional fees, etc.)
- Supplies
- Travel
- Per-patient costs
- Ancillary services (research pharmacy, lab, radiology)
- Equipment
- Administrative costs (IRB fee, clinical trial office fee)
- Start-up fees (screening costs)
- Other (phone, fax, shipping, subject payments, records retention)
- Overhead costs
- Contingencies cost (e.g., IRB Amendments, adverse event costs: It is important to consider who will be responsible for costs of items or services that are provided as a result of complications or adverse events associated with the clinical trial. Will the sponsor pay for such items and services, if needed?)

An essential part of the clinical research billing process is identifying prior to the initiation of a trial the individual patient costs and the source of funding (e.g., sponsor, patient, patient's insurance) for each item or service. Individual patient costs can be identified by thoroughly reviewing the protocol and then creating a research participant's schedule outlining all the items or services per visit. If the study sponsor has not agreed to cover all the participant's care costs, the study budget should specifically document the items or services that the sponsor will cover. Next to each item or service listed on the study budget, three columns should be listed: (1) research charges, (2) standard of care, and (3) noncovered standard of care. ("Monitoring of Clinical Research Participant Billing," *Compliance Today* Vol. 7, No. 1, page 20, January 2005, John Steiner, Esq., Heidi Carroll, Esq.)

Research Charges: nonroutine costs, noncovered charges (collectively "research charges"). Examples of research charges from the Center for Medicare and Medicaid Services (CMS) National Coverage Decision (NCD) of September 19, 2000, include:

- Items or services (a) for which there is no Medicare benefit category; (b) that are statutorily excluded from coverage; or (c) that fall under a national noncoverage policy;

- Items or services provided solely to satisfy data collection and analysis needs and that are not used in the direct management of the patient (e.g., a monthly CT scan for a condition that usually requires only a single CT scan);
- Items or services provided for free by the sponsor;
- Items or services provided solely to determine trial eligibility;
- The investigational item or service itself;
- Research charges may be covered by external or internal sponsors:
  a. Government funded (e.g., NIH, DOD, CDC, VA, CMS)
  b. Nongovernment sponsored research
  c. Internally funded research

Standard-of-Care or Routine Costs: items or services that are typically provided absent a clinical trial (e.g., medically necessary conventional care). Under CMS's NCD of September 19, 2000, routine costs for "Qualifying Trials" may also include:

- Items and services required for the provision of the investigational item or service (e.g., administration of a noncovered chemotherapeutic agent),
- Items and services required for the clinically appropriate monitoring of the effects of the item or service, or the prevention of complications; and
- Items and services that are medically necessary for the diagnosis or treatment of complications arising from the provision of an investigational item or service.

Noncovered Standard-of-Care: an item or service that may be considered standard of care, but for which coverage is limited. The item or service may not be covered because it is statutorily excluded or provided more frequently than allowed under a National Coverage Decision (NCD), or Local Coverage Decision (LCD) from Medicare or a clinically accepted standard of practice.

...The Principal Investigator (PI), nurse coordinator, and reimbursement specialist should coordinate . . . and determine whether or not each item or service is either standard-of-care or a research charge. The reimbursement specialist should then review those items identified as standard of care and determine whether coverage is limited because the item or service is provided more frequently than allowed under a National Coverage Decision (NCD) or Local Coverage Decision (LCD) from Medicare or a clinically accepted standard of practice. The reimbursement specialist should be responsible for reviewing all NCDs and LCDs in order to accurately complete the third column titled noncovered standard of care. The reimbursement specialist also should provide the appropriate ICD-9 code and applicable CPT codes, as well as the current prices listed on the institutional charge master description. These steps should be completed before budget negotiations are finalized, in order to determine who will be responsible for noncovered standard-of-care costs. ("Monitoring of Clinical Research Participant Billing," *Compliance Today* Vol. 7, No. 1, pages 20–21, January 2005, John Steiner, Heidi Carroll)

In general, the sponsor should pay for all research charges and costs associated with conducting the trial. However, if a sponsor does not cover all research-related costs, the PI's clinical department should be responsible for the costs. An administrator or the Division Chair of the PI should provide a Memo of Understanding to the appropriate office (Research Finance and/or Research Billing and/or Research Accounting) stating that certain items or services are not funded and/or that reimbursement for those charges will not be available, and that departmental funds should be used to cover these items or services.

All budgets should be approved by appropriate personnel, such as the PI, the clinical trial coordinator, and, if one exists, the Research Department finance executive.

Preparation of a Clinical Research Billing Plan

After the final budget is approved, a billing plan should be developed for each clinical research trial. The plan should clearly describe who will be responsible for what costs. It also should include timelines or deliverables to promote timely and accurate billing of trial costs. The billing plan should outline in detail the costs that are borne by the sponsor and those borne by other parties, including payors, patients, and, if applicable, the clinical department that is conducting the clinical trial.

The plan should also outline how the department will communicate with other affected departments and provide them with relevant study information, including patient calendars and, if necessary, the budget. This step requires the research personnel to outline how they will actively communicate with affected departments that support the clinical trial, particularly Laboratory, Pharmacy, Radiology, and those clinical specialty areas that are integral to the clinical trial. All ancillary department personnel must be informed that a clinical trial is ongoing, and what is chargeable to payors and what is covered in the clinical trial budget must be clarified.

The plan should describe how the clinical research participant's visit will be scheduled and identify what information should be provided to the registration area by the department that is conducting the clinical trial. To facilitate identification of a research participant, at the time of registration some organizations use a "research prescription" form that patients use during registration to identify the type of test, visit, or procedure for the specific clinical trial, and provide participants with documentation (e.g., prescriptions, ancillary tests schedule, etc.) to bring with them to the registration area at the time of their first clinical trial appointment.

Enrollment of Clinical Trial Participant

Part of the clinical research billing process is ensuring that trial participants have a complete understanding of their potential financial obligations. Research studies that involve human subjects require a thorough informed consent form that is signed by the research participant or legal representative, as discussed at more length in Chapter 6. At a minimum, the consent must address the financial responsibility of the participant and what the clinical trial site will cover. Therefore, as part of the informed consent process, participants should be informed of their financial obligations associated with participating in the study.

Arrival of Research Participant for the First Exam/Test/Procedure

Upon arrival at the registration area for the first exam, test, or procedure, the participant should be registered in accordance with information previously provided to the registration area by the department that is conducting the clinical trial. These procedures likely will differ for inpatients and outpatients because, in most organizations, the information systems for inpatients and outpatients are different.

The information collected at the time of registration must be sufficient to ensure that the proper account is charged for trial-related procedures or research costs. The most important step is to designate in the registration system when a patient is receiving "research" services as a participant in a clinical trial. Many registration systems can accept edits that will hold charges related to these participants. Later, billing reconciliation can be completed by clinical trial coordinators or finance personnel. An effective way to improve the accuracy of clinical trial billing is to pre-register clinical trial participants.

Many billing information systems have the potential to create research accounts and patient accounts. Therefore, it is essential to involve your Information Technology personnel in the discussion and design of these recommended processes.

Completion of Exam/Test/Procedure and Charge Entry

Charges are entered into the billing system after the health care service or item is furnished, along with the appropriate billing account number for that patient. If the health care service is billable to an insurance company as "standard of care," the charge should be entered accordingly. Likewise, if the service is "research only," the research billing account number should be used.

Ensuring that research charges are identified and posted to a research account is one of the most complicated steps of the clinical trial billing process. It is possible to program a Charge Description Master (CDM) to designate research charges with an "R" or other symbol that will direct the charge correctly within the billing system. If this capability exists, it is critical to educate and train ancillary departments on this functionality and help them understand and identify what will be paid for by the research sponsor. If this part of the billing process does not occur, productivity and utilization data may be inaccurate because the overall volume of clinical activity may not be entered into the order entry and billing systems. Thus, all ancillary department personnel must be informed that a clinical trial is ongoing, and what is chargeable to payors and what is covered in the clinical trial budget must be stipulated.

Billing Process Review

Periodic billing reports should be generated for active clinical trials. Those reports should be shared with the clinical trial coordinator, the PI, a research accountant, and other clinical trial support personnel. Weekly or monthly reports will help ensure close monitoring of the trials and that research and standard-of-care charges have been posted to the appropriate account.

Budget Reconciliation and Grant Closure/Treatment of Residuals

Briefly, a step that may be overlooked due to time pressures, staffing, or other reasons is final reconciliation and grant closure. This step provides a final check and balance that the study budget is reconciled against billing information created during the trial. During this phase, if discrepancies are identified they should be corrected before the grant is closed. Also, policies should be developed to properly address situations in which residual balances remain in the research account even after a budget reconciliation. Completion of the study budget review ensures that the research personnel acted in compliance with the approved study budget, contractual terms, as well as applicable laws and regulations, and is a valuable learning experience.

Budgets, even those based on sound careful planning, are really no more than operational plans expressed in financial terms. To continue to produce meaningful budgets, the research organization must review each and every budget upon study completion. If you do not know if you are successful, how can you successfully budget the next project? Track your performance statistics. You should always be able to present them by therapeutic area, type of patient (e.g., children), sponsor, and CRO. Prepare internal reports of site's performance for each study in a clear and concise format that can be reviewed each time you consider a similar study (cite "Six Phases of a Research Site Budget" CCRC and John T. Wilson, M.D., *Monitor,* Summer 2002, page 34)

These steps are fairly straightforward to state, yet for those involved in clinical research the effective implementation of processes to accomplish these steps may require significant changes in behavior and use of information systems tailored to these specific requirements. Typically, the organization will have to develop training and education programs for the PIs, clinical trial coordinators, registration staff, and billing staff. The principal emphasis, both in terms of process improvement and training, should be on development of standardized budgeting templates. Those templates should include costs associated with administration and other overhead expenses that might otherwise not be included in the budgeting process. As mentioned earlier, it is imperative that all clinical trials have clearly identified funding sources, which may include the PI's clinical department. The PI should maintain a current list of hospital charges that can be consulted for entering associated charges for each exam, test, or procedure that is performed during the trial. This step is essential to minimize the likelihood of under-budgeting, which occurs periodically. Billing milestones should be designated to ensure timely and complete billing to the sponsor, payor, or patient.

Related Billing Issues
As the clinical research billing process is implemented and, hopefully, becomes part of the organization's standard operations, errors and mistakes will still occur. Thus, it is important to develop policies and procedures to handle disputed charges and discounts for research-related costs. In addition, the organization should have formal policies for handling patient complaints about research bills.

Clinical Trial Monitoring Issues

The previous section addressed major challenges associated with billing for clinical research trials. It also described key personnel and practical steps that are necessary for developing a sound clinical research billing program. Most academic research organizations are examining their processes and the need for conducting compliant clinical research trials. Those efforts are timely and important, even though there is not a commonly accepted approach to clinical trial billing in the industry.

Given the number and variety of legal, administrative, contractual, and accounting requirements that relate to clinical trials, some monitoring should be undertaken. In addition, the monitoring should be complemented by ongoing training and education of the workforce. Monitoring, for purposes of effective compliance, can be a delegated responsibility based on specific tasks assigned to those with responsibility for conducting the clinical trial, and their support staff. Likewise, there are external oversight bodies that expect the ARO to have adopted standard operating procedures that include some level of self-monitoring or periodic internal auditing of clinical trials. For example, the FDA, commercial sponsors of clinical trials, the National Institutes of Health, and other third parties have a variety of methods for assessing the quality of an organization's monitoring efforts.

Independent of these external auditing or review authorities, some type of self-monitoring should be implemented. There are sound management reasons as well as legal risk management reasons to do so. The most prominent example of potential exposure to legal risks is presented by the civil False Claims Act (FCA).

Under the FCA, a whistleblower or a federal prosecutor can bring suit and allege that an organization "knowingly" submitted claims for payment to an agency of the federal government and that the claims were "false." Briefly, a "knowing" submission of a false claim may result if the organization:

- Has "actual knowledge" that it submitted a false or fraudulent claim for payment; or
- "Deliberately ignored" the truth or falsity of the claim; or
- "Recklessly disregarded" the truth or falsity of the claim.

Each of the above categories of the intent element of the FCA has been litigated in the health care enforcement arena. A critical component of an organization's defense of an FCA allegation is to attempt, in good faith, to design and implement an effective compliance program.

To that end, a delegated monitoring program is an important part of an effective compliance program. There usually are several components to a compliance monitoring program, including summary reports on workforce training and education related to clinical research issues, including the billing issues. The following sections and Appendices provide suggestions and guidance for a clinical research monitoring program. For the most part, these sections are based on the underlying laws and regulations that apply to clinical trials, as opposed to specific accounting principles or auditing standards.

Clinical Trial Monitoring Tasks

Recommended items to delegate to departmental personnel involved in clinical trials include the tasks listed in Appendix A, "Clinical Trial Billing Assessment Workplan."

Further, the duties delegated to departments should include the responsibility to write a departmental clinical trial billing protocol. An evaluation of each department's clinical trial billing protocol may be conducted either by the department, based on various objective criteria, or by the organization's Internal Audit department, using the same or comparable criteria. This basic approach at the outset should help ensure some measure of consistency across many departments that conduct clinical trials.

Constructing a clinical trial monitoring protocol can vary, depending on the depth of review desired. Appendix B, for example, lists many items that can be used to construct a Grants Assessments Audit Program Plan. The distinction between monitoring and auditing is addressed in this chapter, but, in brief, an audit should be based on generally accepted auditing standards, as opposed to the less formal steps that are associated with monitoring. From a compliance perspective, the Office of Inspector General and other oversight authorities are interested in knowing that some level of monitoring is regularly conducted by the health care organization.

When monitoring is sustained, even for a relatively short period, common findings likely will result across an organization. These include:

- The addition of early attention and planning steps to determine whether the item or service is "research" or "standard of care;"
- More attention will be given to the status of devices or drugs to be used in a trial;

- Efforts to educate patients about their financial responsibilities will be increased;
- Improved communication between departments conducting clinical trials and the ancillary departments that provide services in support of the trial.

Notes and References

1   The Food, Drug, and Cosmetic Act probably was the most important catalyst for the expansion of clinical trials in America. The FDC Act, among other things, requires manufacturers to provide proof of the "safety and efficacy" of a drug or biological for indications specified on a label. Such proof usually is obtained through research involving human subjects, i.e., clinical trials. *See* 21 U.S.C. Section 355.

2   *See* http://www.oig.hhs.gov/publications/workplan.html#1.

Appendix A

Clinical Trial Billing Assessment Workplan

Task	Date Commenced	Date Completed	Responsible Party	Purpose/ Comments	Audit Hours
1. Review existing clinical trial policies and procedures:					
a. Clinical trial budgeting					
b. Registration of research patients					
c. Documentation of care					
d. Standard-of-care *vs.* Research only					
e. Residual balances					
f. Negotiation of sponsor agreements					
g. Gifts and payments from sponsors					
h. Shortfalls—who pays?					
i. Payments to subjects?					
j. Advertising studies					
k. Review research related injury billing					
2. Conduct interviews:					
a. 4–5 key investigations					
b. 4–5 clinical trial coordinators					
c. Budget office staff/tech transfer					
d. Research Finance staff					
e. V.P. Research Administration					
f. Registration Director & Registrars					
g. Internal Audit staff					
h. Compliance Officer					

Task	Date Commenced	Date Completed	Responsible Party	Purpose/Comments	Audit Hours
i. Billing Director					
j. Billing staff					
k. HR staff					
l. Pharmacies & Lab staff					
3. Select 4–5 Clinical Trial Studies and review:					
a. Protocol/Informed Consent					
b. IRB Minutes					
c. Sponsor Contract					
d. Budgets					
e. Sit in on Informed Consent Process					
f. Review Translations of Documents					
g. Review Registration Documents of all Subjects in Studies					
h. Review face sheet company coverage with budget					
i. Review medical records for all subjects and review order entry process					
j. Review adverse event documents					
k. Review bills sent to payors					
l. Review charge back to clinical trial contract					
m. Review budget vs. actual cost					
n. Review residual balances for studies reviewed					
o. Review segregation of research costs & standard of care					

(continues)

Task	Date Commenced	Date Completed	Responsible Party	Purpose/ Comments	Audit Hours
p. Review sponsor charging process & collections process					
q. Review COI forms for all studies					
r. Review CDM & research "charges"					
s. Review commercial payor contracts to see what is paid and what is NOT					
t. Review encounter slips for key departments					
4. Prepare Assessment Report					
5. Review Report with Client					
6. Perform training including NCD					
7. Assist client in selection process improvement teams					
8. Develop PI Workplan with teams					
9. Review clinical trial billing "models" with teams					
10. Select key studies/pilot					
11. Review all processes with key investigators					
12. Pilot new processes					
13. Revise processes as necessary					
14. Create necessary policies and procedures and document new processes					
15. Conduct training with all research staff					
16. Six to twelve months later, select sample of trials to audit					

Appendix B
Grant Assessments Audit Program Plan

Task	Responsible Party	Date Commenced	Date Completed	Comments
1. Purpose To determine whether contract/grant activity is administered in compliance with sponsor agreements and/or applicable governing regulations such as NIH Grants Policy Statement and OMB Circulars A-21 and A-110				
2. Grant Selection Method To be discussed				
3. Notification After discussion with the Vice President for Research Administration, notification of the review will be made to the Principal Investigator, Director of Research Finance, and other staff as may be required				
4. Obtain Data a. Obtain the following general data: • Grant proposal including budget submission • Notice of Grant Award (NGA). • Grant budgeting correspondence				

(continues)

Task	Responsible Party	Date Commenced	Date Completed	Comments
• Any approval notices or other pertinent correspondence from granting agency				
• Current grant budget to actual analysis (activity in general ledger account)				
• Detailed list of grant transactions (including budget transactions)				
• Due dates for progress report submissions				
b. Obtain salary data:				
• Summary of salary expenditures/transactions on the grant, including employee name, title and role on the grant, percent of effort and amount of salary charged to the grant by pay period				
• All time and effort reports pertaining to the period under review				
c. Obtain transaction testing supporting documentation:				
• All supporting documentation of nonsalary transactions, including journal entries (transfers,				

Task	Responsible Party	Date Commenced	Date Completed	Comments
corrections, and budget adjustments), purchase requisitions, invoices, approvals, and any other relevant documentation necessary to validate grant expenditures				
5. Grant Review Plan				
a. General				
• Review the NGA to identify any special terms and conditions that could impact the costs charged to the grant or RESEARCH SITE's responsibilities under the award (e.g., cost sharing and program income). Note the Activity Code for any restrictions or specific policy guidance (PO1, R35 – SNAP exclusions, T32).				
• Review the grant proposal and application to identify any planned cost-sharing use of program income or other special provisions.				
• Review budget correspondence to identify any special terms, agreements, or clarification between				

(continues)

Task	Responsible Party	Date Commenced	Date Completed	Comments
RESEARCH SITE and the funding agency.				
• Review budget transactions to identify significant rebudgeting. This occurs when expenditures in a single direct-cost budget category deviate (increase or decrease) from the categorical commitment level established for the budget period by more than 25 percent of the total costs awarded. For example, if the award budget for total costs is $200,000, any rebudgeting that would result in an increase or decrease of more than $50,000 in a budget category is to be considered "significant rebudgeting." The base used for determining significant rebudgeting excludes the effects of prior year carryover balances but includes competing and noncompeting supplements. Significant rebudgeting may be considered a change in scope and				

Task	Responsible Party	Date Commenced	Date Completed	Comments
could require prior approval. If identified, determine whether prior NIH approval was obtained.				
• Review significant variations of actual grant charges from budget.				
6. Personnel Charges				
a. Agree summary of salary expenditures/ transactions to general ledger salary amount in the grant account. If amounts do not agree, request grant financial staff to reconcile and explain the difference.				
b. Compare personnel data per summary to the grant proposal budget and inquire as to any significant variances. Compare percentage/amount of budgeted effort and salary to actual. (NIH prior approval may be been required for changes in key personnel or levels of effort of key personnel.)				
c. Review effort reports for all periods under review. Note any missing reports.				
d. Determine whether reports are appropriately signed.				

(continues)

Task	Responsible Party	Date Commenced	Date Completed	Comments
e. Determine if reports are being completed and signed in a timely manner. If there are RESEARCH SITE policies requiring a turnaround time for signed effort reports, review if there is compliance with the policy.				
f. Recalculate employee benefits (fringe benefit rate). If grant indicates a different fringe benefit rate than RESEARCH SITE's rate, request grant financial staff to reconcile/explain the variance.				
7. Other Direct Cost Charges				
a. Review supporting documentation to determine if the goods or services are allowable (ref. NIH Grants Policy Manual, A-21, RESEARCH SITE policies, etc.). Note any unallowable costs charged against the grant for reporting purposes.				
b. Determine that the cost passes all four tests of allowability per A-21 (Section C): • **Reasonableness**—"the nature of the goods or services acquired or applied, and the amount involved,				

Task	Responsible Party	Date Commenced	Date Completed	Comments
therefore, reflect the action that a prudent person would have taken under the circumstances prevailing at the time the decision to incur the cost was made." Major considerations are: (a) Is the cost of a type generally recognized as necessary for the operation of the institution or the performance of the sponsored agreement? (b) Was the cost incurred under restraints and requirements imposed by such factors as arm's-length bargaining, federal and state laws, and regulations and sponsored agreement terms and conditions; (c) Did individuals incurring the cost act with due prudence, considering their responsibilities to the institution, its employees, its students, the federal government, and the public at large? and (d) Were the actions taken to incur the cost consistent with the established institution policies and				

(continues)

Task	Responsible Party	Date Commenced	Date Completed	Comments
practices applicable to the work of the institution generally, including sponsored agreements? • **Allocable**—"A cost is allocable to a particular cost objective if the goods or services involved are chargeable or assignable to such cost objective in accordance with relative benefits received or other equitable relationship. Subject to the foregoing, a cost is allocable to a sponsored agreement if (1) it is incurred solely to advance the work under the sponsored agreement; (2) it benefits both the sponsored agreement and other work of the institution in proportions that can be approximated through use of reasonable methods, or (3) it is necessary to the overall operation of the institution and, in light of the principles provided in this Circular, is deemed to be assignable in part to sponsored projects." See A-21 for further guidance.				

Task	Responsible Party	Date Commenced	Date Completed	Comments
• **Consistency of Treatment**—"Costs must be given consistent treatment through the application of those generally accepted accounting principles appropriate to the circumstances." Have costs charged to the sponsored project been treated in the same manner as would costs charged to other RESEARCH SITE activities? Has the department applied consistent accounting treatment within and between accounting periods? Has the department allocated a cost as a direct cost of a federal program when the same or similar costs are allocable to the federal program as an indirect cost?				
• **Conformance to any limitations or exclusions set forth in A-21 or the sponsored agreement as to types or amounts of cost items**—A cost may pass the first three tests but remain unallowable simply because the sponsored agreement specifies it as such. (See #1 above.)				

(continues)

Task	Responsible Party	Date Commenced	Date Completed	Comments
8. **Specific Direct Costs—Travel** (See A-21, Section J, Item 48, and NIH Grants Policy Manual—Allowability of Costs, Selected Items of Cost.)				
a. For travel expenses, determine if the charge is in accordance with RESEARCH SITE's travel policy (2350–2368, 2367 = Sponsored Agreements). Supporting documentation should include the employee's name, title, conference name, purpose of travel, city, state, and country traveled to, dates of travel, and total cost.				
b. Determine that travel charges are related to activities supported by the sponsored project and are not expressly prohibited by the sponsor.				
c. Per the NIH Grants Policy Manual, travel must provide direct benefit to the project, expenses are limited to those allowed by formal organizational policy, and in the case of air travel the lowest reasonable commercial airfares must be used.				

Task	Responsible Party	Date Commenced	Date Completed	Comments
d. Per A-21, travel costs shall be considered reasonable and allowable only to the extent that such costs do not exceed charges normally allowed by the institution in its regular operations as a result of an institutional policy. Airfare costs in excess of the lowest available commercial discount airfare or customary standard airfare are unallowable except when accommodations would require circuitous routing, require travel during unreasonable hours, excessively prolong travel, greatly increase duration of the flight, result in increased costs that would offset transportation savings, or offer accommodation not reasonably adequate for the medical needs of the traveler.				
e. Ensure that the salary of the employee to whom the travel charges relate was being charged to the project during the time of the travel.				

(continues)

Task	Responsible Party	Date Commenced	Date Completed	Comments
9. **Specific Direct Costs—Equipment** (See A-21, Section J, Item 16, A-110, Sections .40–.47, and NIH Grants Policy Statement—Allowability of Costs, Selected Items of Cost.) a. Determine whether equipment is related to the specific activities supported by the sponsored project and is not expressly prohibited by the sponsor. b. For equipment purchases over the small purchase threshold of $25,000, determine that the following A-110 requirements were adhered to: procurement records and files for purchases in excess of the small purchase threshold shall include the following at a minimum: (a) basis for contractor selection, (b) justification for lack of competition when competitive bids or offers are not obtained, and (c) basis for award cost or price. Also consider the requirements of University purchasing policies.				

Task	Responsible Party	Date Commenced	Date Completed	Comments
c. Determine if any equipment purchases were not included in the proposal budget and/or award. If such items exist, determine whether the purchase required prior approval and if approval was received prior to purchase.				
d. Inquire about the department's efforts to secure the equipment and whether they perform physical inventories of departmental grant equipment.				
e. Observe major equipment over $50,000 to verify its existence.				
f. Confirm where ownership of equipment will reside when grant is over.				
10. Cost Transfer Journal Entries (including salary)				
a. Determine whether the cost transfer is related to the specific activities supported by the sponsored project and is not expressly prohibited by the sponsor.				
b. Review documentation of cost transfers to determine if they appear valid.				

(continues)

Task	Responsible Party	Date Commenced	Date Completed	Comments
Transfers of cost from one project to another or budget prior to the next solely to cover cost overruns are not allowable.				
c. Determine adequacy of the supporting documentation and justification for the transfer. Transfers must be supported by documentation that fully explains how the error occurred and a certification of the correctness of the new charge by a responsible organizational official of the grantee. An explanation merely stating that the transfer was made "to correct an error" or "to transfer to correct project" is not sufficient.				
d. Timing—Transfers should be made within 90 days of when the error is discovered (NIH GPS). Transfers that are not made promptly, due to extenuating circumstances, must include an adequate explanation of why there was a delay in correcting the error				

Task	Responsible Party	Date Commenced	Date Completed	Comments
e. Verify that the costs transferred meet the requirements of the sponsoring agency of the project receiving the transfer.				
11. Cost Allocation Journal Entries				
a. Review documentation to determine that the cost allocation is related to the specific activities supported by the sponsored project and is not expressly prohibited by the sponsor.				
b. Review the allocation methodology for reasonableness, documenting the methodology used. Per NIH Grants Policy Manual, costs that benefit two or more projects in proportions that can be easily determined should be allocated on the basis of proportional benefit. If the proportions cannot be easily determined because of the interrelationship of the work involved, it may be allocated on any reasonable basis.				
12. Subcontracts				
a. Determine that invoices were properly prepared to effect timely payment, the costs were reviewed and approved by the				

(continues)

Task	Responsible Party	Date Commenced	Date Completed	Comments
PI as allowable expenditures and were properly prepared to effect timely payment.				
13. Reporting and Close-out				
a. Review award document and identify due dates for technical progress reports and other financial reporting requirements. Confirm that these submission requirements were made in a timely manner and after discussion with the PI and review of documents as necessary.				
b. Ensure that financial report reconciles to accounting records.				
c. Verify that the reports are reviewed and signed by appropriate personnel.				
d. Was the grant closed in a timely manner?				
14. Cost Sharing				
a. Review grant proposals and awards to determine whether the sponsored agreement includes mandatory or voluntary cost sharing.				

Task	Responsible Party	Date Commenced	Date Completed	Comments
b. Review expenses included in the cost sharing to ensure that they: • are allowable under A-21 cost principles; • are necessary and reasonable for the accomplishment of the project; • were incurred during the effective dates of the project; • cannot be used as cost sharing for any other sponsored program; and • meet the terms and conditions of the award.				
15. Program Income (See NIH Grants Policy Statement, page 130, and Table II-3, Requirements for Program Income Accountability.) a. Review grant proposals and awards to determine whether the sponsored activity is expected to generate program income. b. Determine the treatment method applied: • Additive Alternative: Income is used to supplement the awarding agency's fund to continue program objectives.				

(continues)

Task	Responsible Party	Date Commenced	Date Completed	Comments
• Deductive Alternative: Income is used to reduce the agency's share of total allowable program costs.				
• Combination Alternative: Uses all program income up to (and including) $25,000 as specified under the additive method and any amount of program income exceeding $25,000 under the deductive alternative.				
• Matching Alternative: Income is used to finance the nonfederal portion of the program; to satisfy all or part of a matching requirement.				
c. Review accounting records to ensure that program income is being properly recorded and utilized according to the specified treatment method.				
d. Review program income-supported costs to ensure that they: • are allowable under A-21 cost principles; • are necessary and reasonable for the accomplishment of the project;				

Task	Responsible Party	Date Commenced	Date Completed	Comments
• were incurred during the effective dates of the project; and				
• meet the terms and conditions of the award.				
e. Reporting of program income (on FSR)?				
16. Human Subjects Issues				
a. If grant involves human subjects' study, were all policies followed?				
b. What informed consent procedures were followed? Were they appropriate?				
c. Who keeps records of the consent forms?				
d. Review IRB meeting minutes for studies reviewed				
• How much time spent on each protocol				
• Quorum present?				
e. Review Common Rule/HIPAA informed consent/authorization documents				
f. Review composition of IRB members, frequency of meetings, and resources allocated to IRB				

(*continues*)

Task	Responsible Party	Date Commenced	Date Completed	Comments
g. Perform concurrent (real time) review of informed consent process on studies reviewed				
h. Interview IRB member(s)				
17. Financial Conflict of Interest				
a. Verify whether conflicts of interest forms (as required by policy) were completed by the PI and staff working on the grant.				
b. Review the forms to ascertain any conflict of interest.				
c. Analyze policies and procedures re: acceptance of consulting fees from sponsors, etc.				

FOUR

Clinical Research Trials: Operational and Budget Issues

Bill Hunt and Sue O'Connell

Clinical research trials offer opportunities for medical institutions to affect the development and advancement of important medical procedures and treatments. In addition, clinical research trials can create a recognizable name for institutions and physicians, and these marketing benefits should not be taken for granted. The well-known medical institutions around the world do have the ability to attract a strong patient base, especially in their most respected treatment specialties. However, clinical research trials, while rewarding, also require extensive internal process development and the establishment of critical control mechanisms in order to successfully ensure that medical science can be advanced, without requiring your facility to provide all the needed financial support.

A solid institutional budgeting process for clinical research trials can help your organization maximize the opportunities presented in conducting clinical trials. In addition to initial budget preparation, sound operational and data gathering processes maintained throughout the course of the trial can facilitate accurate and timely reimbursement. To help you begin evaluating these processes within your own facility, this chapter addresses key components of clinical research trials.

Control Mechanisms

The groundwork for successful study budgeting and operational practices related to clinical research trials conducted at medical institutions includes several key documentation and control mechanisms.

Principal Investigator (PI)

For any given clinical research trial involving human subjects, a PI will be designated. The PI should have appropriate expertise in the specialty of medical care involved in the trial. This individual should be intimately aware of the details of the study protocol as well as the routine treatments required, sometimes referred to as "standard of care," even if the patients were *not* enrolled in the clinical research trial. This knowledge will make the PI invaluable in helping to properly structure the details of the study budget. The PI should be someone with enough time, energy, skills, and experience to devote to the trial in order to make it a successful and compliant endeavor for the participating department(s) as well as a beneficial trial for the sponsor and the enrolled patients. Once the study budget has been developed, the PI will take the lead in treating the enrolled patients according to the study protocol and, in conjunction with support personnel, ensuring that treatments are provided within the guidelines of the study budget. A PI who is well informed of possible compliance pitfalls and budgeting constraints before clinical trial treatment will help minimize compliance risks and financial exposure related to the clinical research trial.

Study/Research Coordinator

The study coordinator (sometimes also called the research coordinator or research nurse) plays a supporting role to the PI and performs supporting tasks associated with the clinical research trial. This individual will most likely assume the administrative role in implementing the research study budget. During the course of the study, he/she will act as the study manager, fielding study- and patient-related issues and questions. This person, in addition to being knowledgeable in the clinical aspects of the treatments, should also be familiar with your facility's processes for registration, charge entry, and billing. Without knowledge of these systems, it will be very difficult for the study coordinator to institute a sound process for enrolling patients, tracking visits throughout ancillary departments, and properly billing for study-related services as they occur.

The study coordinator may also need to work with an information services representative at your institution to create methods to properly capture patient information related to the clinical research trial, if such methods are not already in place facility-wide. However the process is managed (and we will offer some suggestions later in this chapter), the study coordinator must create a fiscally responsible research budget, develop sound patient tracking mechanisms for the study, and have access to all systems related to the registration and billing of patient visits in order to monitor services that relate to the study. While the PI is responsible for the clinical aspects of the trial, the study coordinator usually is responsible for all financial and record-keeping aspects of the trial.

Institutional Review Board (IRB)

It is the responsibility of the Institutional Review Board (IRB) to ensure that the laws and regulations governing research are adhered to by the medical center. The IRB's duties are set forth in federal regulations, i.e., 45 C.F.R. Part 46 and 21 C.F.R. Part 56. Noncompliance with these regulations may cause injury to clinical trial participants, which may result in legal action being brought against both the IRB and the study site. Therefore, it is critical that the IRB be well informed as to regulatory requirements.

Each clinical research trial that is presented to an institution should be approved by the IRB prior to acceptance and enrollment of study participants. The IRB may approve a clinical trial after taking into consideration the following factors:

1. Assuring minimal risk to human subjects using sound research procedures
2. Balancing risk to anticipated benefits
3. Practicing equitable subject selection from cross-population factors
4. Obtaining informed consent from each prospective subject
5. Providing and developing research data to ensure the safety of human subjects
6. Providing privacy and confidentiality measures for clinical trial subjects

Furthermore, the IRB must follow state laws, which may require human research review committees to be established within the study site.

Charge Description Master (CDM)

Every hospital facility maintains a database enumerating all billable services available to patients, known as the Charge Description Master, or CDM. This database, no matter which system is actually used, contains basic charge information: service/item description, price, applicable CPT/HCPCS codes (i.e., the common procedural terminology codes), modifiers, revenue codes, place of service information, etc. Often in addition to these basic fields, the database may contain much more detailed information related to coverage under various insurance plans, system- and facility-specific insurance and service description codes, department and revenue mappings to the general ledger, etc.

With yearly and quarterly national updates, as well as local fiscal intermediary directives, staying current with Medicare policy alone can be difficult, not to mention the other third-party payors and their specific rules and billing regulations. With so many various data fields, the CDM can quickly become an overwhelming dynamic data warehouse. Maintenance of the CDM requires skilled knowledge of billing and coding regulations, reimbursement methodologies regarding pricing of services, as well as a clear understanding of information systems, in order to ensure that accurate information in the CDM can flow to other software systems and arrive on the claim form. This can be a daunting task for normal hospital services, not to mention trying to appropriately bill for clinical research trials.

Given the challenges in maintaining the CDM, we recommend centralization as the best approach for managing this billing data. In other words, any and all additions and updates to the CDM master files should flow through a centralized review. Rather than giving each department manager, administrator, finance person, and reimbursement specialist access to the CDM to make updates, it is suggested that the hospital establish a protocol that requires all update requests to be sent through a person or group who is solely dedicated to ensuring accuracy in the CDM. This person or group may be internal to the organization, or an outside entity, such as a consulting firm.

The benefits of hiring an external firm to perform CDM maintenance lie in eliminating competing incentives, or "agency" problems, that some internal organization personnel may face. For example, if department administrators are compensated based on the revenue numbers they post for the organization, giving them access to make changes to prices for services/procedures performed at the hospital opens the door for conflicts of interest. Additionally, if reimbursement personnel have to handle calls from patients related to medical bills, they may be less likely to bill all applicable services at an appropriate charge if emotions are involved after experiencing direct contact with the patient. Centralizing the CDM with an outside firm can help to eliminate these issues, as well as offer levels of expertise in billing regulations that may be impossible to get internally, based on the many and varied duties required of internal hospital personnel.

No matter who performs the centralized review, you should ensure that proper training in the information system requirements has been provided to the appropriate personnel. You may wonder how centralization of the CDM correlates to success in organizing clinical research trials. As explained this chapter, a centralized CDM can assist in creating a viable study budget, in negotiating with study sponsors for reimbursement, and in tracking appropriate billing of services.

To highlight some of the complexities that can arise within the CDM master file, Tables 4-1 and 4-2 show instances where various data fields may require specific population of codes depending on the insurance carrier, in order to bill appropriately for the same service.

On the technical side, to bill Medicare for a magnetic resonance angiography of the abdomen, without contrast, you must bill C8901, while third-party carriers will accept 74185. Also, to bill for the professional component only, a -26 modifier must

TABLE 4-1 *Technical CDM Information*

Item Number	123456
Department	CT15
Description	MRA ABDOMEN W/O CONTRAST
Medicare CPT/HCPCS	C8901
Commercial CPT/HCPCS	74185
Medicare Revenue Code	618
Commercial Revenue Code	618
Price	$1,800
General Ledger Key	150

TABLE 4-2 *Professional CDM Information*

Item Number	654321
Department	RAD219
Description	MRA ABDOMEN W/O CONTRAST-PRO
Medicare CPT/HCPCS	74185-26
Commercial CPT/HCPCS	74185-26
Place of Service	22
Type of Service	4
Price	$700
GL Key	102

be used on the professional side, while the hospital side will not require a modifier. Different prices will be assigned to both components, and various other codes including Place of Service, Type of Service, Revenue Codes, and General Ledger Keys (which drive the revenue to the appropriate cost center on the general ledger) must all be populated appropriately. This example highlights some of the complexities that can arise in healthcare billing.

IDE Numbers

Billing for Investigational Device Exemptions (IDEs) used in clinical trials involves providing the Medicare fiscal intermediary (FI) with the proper HCPCS and revenue codes, and the associated IDE numbers in the appropriate fields on the claim form. Without the IDE numbers there will be no additional reimbursement for these items, although your organization may indeed incur a cost for these items. Therefore, IDEs should be specific line items within the CDM that include the pertinent billing information. If this step is taken on the front end, all required elements to support payment are more likely to appear on the claim form.

A recommended control measure to ensure that IDE items are billed properly is to mandate a process for adding these items to the CDM. For example, whenever a department wishes to add a device to the CDM, they could be required to submit to the CDM review person/firm the approval letter received from the Medicare FI so that the line item can be structured appropriately with the correct description, IDE number, HCPCS and revenue codes, and price consistent with the amount costed to your institution. The facility should ensure that a centralized process, such as that described previously, is developed and implemented for all clinical research trials. The centralized control of the CDM described in the previous section will offer a framework to support such a facility-wide policy. This policy also will ensure that supportive documentation is in place in case of an audit.

Budget Preparation

Once your facility has established the control mechanisms discussed, and all of the appropriate processes are in place to conduct a clinical research study, several tools will be required to develop a fiscally responsible study budget. Appropriate software tools can aid the PI and the research coordinator in creating a research study budget. Preliminary recommendations are outlined below.

Budget Software Package

In order to create a successful study budget, you should purchase or develop a software package that incorporates all of the needed information elements to create a research budget. A research coordinator will need a clear template to begin building a study budget. Keep in mind that this person often does not have a finance background and may not think of all the applicable elements that should be considered. A budget package can be as simple as a spreadsheet or as in-depth as a stand-alone software product. At the very least, it should have been well thought-out and created by individuals with experience in budgeting, and specifically in research budgeting. If there are individuals within your organization who are familiar with these processes, it is suggested that a committee be formed to explore purchasing or developing study budget "tools" that can be used regularly for clinical research studies. Specific ideas to assist you in developing study budget software or evaluating a purchase of budget templates are presented below.

Classification of Patient Clinical Services

The premise for clinical trials is to test a device or drug based on a planned number of patients (sometimes referred to as "trial participants") and a specific protocol. The level of detail to be spelled out in the study budget should reflect not only the number of patients in the study but also the following charge detail related to each enrolled patient:

- Anticipated number of visits
- All clinical services provided for each visit, including ancillary services
- Specific CDM number to be charged for each service provided

Using the research study protocol as a guide, the research coordinator, with the help of the PI, should identify and classify each service/procedure that will be included as either "standard of care" or "nonstandard of care." Standard-of-care services would be those services that you would be providing to the patients even if they were *not* enrolled in the clinical research trial. These services may be billed as would any other patient procedures that were outside of the research project. While you should enumerate these services on the research study budget, you may not need to include the charges from these services as part of your needed funding. Medicare and other payors may reimburse the standard of care items to the facility, just as they would under normal, nonresearch study circumstances. Refer to your facility's managed care contracts for direction on how your commercial payors handle such charges and adjust your budgeting process accordingly.

Nonstandard of care services will not be paid by Medicare or third-party payors in most cases, and therefore these services need to be accounted for and reimbursed through internal or outside funding, such as grants or commercial sponsors. It is especially critical to identify these services during the study budget development phase, and to associate with a specific expense. If your facility underestimates the expenses associated with these nonstandard-of-care services on the study budget, these expenses could end up not being reimbursed.

Figure 4-1 provides a simplified example of how your facility could set up the basics of a clinical research trial study budget. The example highlights the use of visit-level detail, separating out each visit procedure as either standard of care (SOC) or nonstandard of care (RSCH). The CDM price and units are then totaled to come up with the gross revenue figures associated with standard billing, under the S of C Gross Revenue column, and the figures associated with the research trial, under the Rsch Gross Revenue column. The Rsch Gross Revenue column represents the starting point for any sponsor negotiations of total funds needed to cover the nonstandard-of-care procedures associated with each patient in the trial.

FIGURE 4-1 *Academic Medical Center Patient Level Budgeting Detail*

Clinical Research Trial IRB-1234, September 1, 2005

Item #	Description	Dept	CPT	Visit #1 Gross		Visit #2 Revenue		Visit #3		Tot Vol	Price	S of C Revenue	Rsch Gross Revenue
				SOC	Rsch	SOC	Rsch	SOC	Rsch				
123456	MRI abdomen w/o con	CT15	C8901 74185	1					1	2	$1,800	$1,800	$1,800
894561	CBC, automated	LA49	85027	1		1	1			3	$50	$100	$50
678912	Venipuncture 36415	LA12	G0001	1	1	1	1			3	$25	$50	$25
											Totals	$1,950	$1,875

Detailed CDM Data

In classifying all clinical services that will be provided as part of the research study, provide as much detailed information as possible in the study budget, such as:

- Detailed description of each service (A good rule of thumb to follow would be to provide to the CPT level of detail.)
- Ancillary department providing each service
- CPT/HCPCS codes associated with each service (by payor)
- Modifiers associated with each service
- Diagnosis codes associated with each service
- Price for each service from the CDM

Gathering all of this information before scheduling patients will help develop a sound fiscal basis for services to be provided as well as the billing protocol for the patient's insurance or the research grant/sponsor funding. Addressing the services to be provided before the start of the study will provide a level of detail that will allow you to determine the price of each service in the CDM, frequency of each service for the trial, and ultimately the gross and net revenue anticipated. Additionally, reviewing the CPT/HCPCS and diagnosis codes during budget preparation will help you to assess whether Medicare or a third-party payor will cover the standard-of-care services. In Figure 4-1, we have shown the detailed CDM data that will be needed for the budgeting process, with the exception of the ICD-9 codes, which, as we have mentioned, will also prove helpful.

Identifying the CDM line items to be charged during the clinical research trial also affords the research coordinator the opportunity to create a unique charge ticket specific to the individual study, which can be used by all departments performing services as part of the study protocol. This process would require systematic publishing of the charge tickets and distribution to all ancillary departments involved in the study. Using one centralized charge ticket would provide a consistent billing mechanism for all ancillary departments, so that they could use the same line items in the CDM that have been verified to be structured appropriately to charge all study patients in the same way. This process can aid in a seamless billing process as well as a verifiable audit trail in the CDM showing the study activity. While this sounds very simple, however, it is still incumbent upon all performing departments to first identify each patient as being involved in the research study, in order to use the charge ticket at the appropriate time. This is, of course, not a simple task and it is one we will address in greater detail later on in the chapter.

The trial site should accurately bill services to the responsible third party (e.g., sponsor, Medicare program, grant source, or trial participant). The potential consequences for a medical center's inability to track and distinguish between research and standard-of-care services may present serious compliance risks. Lack of a "good information system," lack of experience, or lack of a sufficient study budget do not constitute a solid defense of billing problems. Conducting clinical research trials calls for revenue controls in the budget, CDM, and billing systems. Once all of the charges for a particular study-related visit have been entered, it may be necessary for the research coordinator to manually intervene before the charges arrive on the claim form. The purpose of that intervention is to ensure that the items that are nonstandard of care get posted to the research trial rather than inadvertently billed to Medicare or other third-party payor. It is important to take all appropriate action at your institution to ensure that the correct information is being charged and credited in the billing and accounting systems.

Tracking and Control of "Actuals"

In addition to laying out the visit and CDM details for patient management and billing, the budgeting software also should be structured to provide tracking and control mechanisms on the back end. These mechanisms are needed to report and summarize actual statistics from the trial. By importing the actual patient visit activity and posting this against the budget estimates, you will have at your fingertips crucial information to provide sponsors, to improve future budgeting efforts, account for revenue across various departments, etc.

The budget software, in addition to showing the "big picture" of the overall progress of the clinical research trial, should also provide a breakdown of each patient's charges as budgeted and as actually incurred, such as that shown in Figure 4-2. This screen should provide specific visit information and actual billed charges by individual patient. This step serves to verify that the services on the protocol were performed and that the planned services were charged and accounted for properly.

The following is a simplified example of what such a module might show.

Each individual patient's activity summaries could then be combined into a format that could give a snapshot of the overall progress of the trial, such as that shown in Figure 4-3. Budget variances are then easily identifiable, and adjustments can be made, as needed, if it becomes evident that budget shortfalls will require additional grant money to be secured for the research trial expenses.

FIGURE 4-2 Academic Medical Center Patient #1 Budgeted versus Actuals Detail

Clinical Research Trial IRB-1234

Description	Budgeted Visit #1		Budgeted Visit #2		Budgeted Visit #3		Budgeted $ of C Gross Revenue	Budgeted Rsch Gross Revenue
	SOC	Rsch	SOC	Rsch	SOC	Rsch		
MRI abdomen w/o con	1					1	$ 1,800	$ 1,800
CBC, automated	1			1			$ 100	$ 50
Venipuncture		1	1		1		$ 50	$ 25

Description	Actual Visit #1		Actual Visit #2		Actual Visit #3		Actual $ of C Gross Revenue	Actual Rsch Gross Revenue
	SOC	Rsch	SOC	Rsch	SOC	Rsch		
MRI abdomen w/o con	1					1	$ 1,800	$ 1,800
CBC, automated				1			—	$ 50
Venipuncture		1	1		1		$ 50	$ 25
					Budget Variance		$ (100)	$ —

| FIGURE 4-3 | *Academic Medical Center* |

Budgeted versus Actuals Summary, Clinical Research Trial IRB-1234

	Budgeted SOC Charges	Actual SOC Charges	Budgeted RSCH Charges	Actual RSCH Charges
Patient No. 1	$ 1,950	$ 1,850	$ 1,875	$ 1,875
Patient No. 2	$ 1,950	$ 1,950	$ 1,875	$ 1,850
Patient No. 3	$ 1,950	$ 1,950	$ 1,875	$ 1,875
Patient No. 4	$ 1,950	$ 1,925	$ 1,875	$ 1,875
Patient No. 5	$ 1,950	$ 1,950	$ 1,875	$ 1,825
Patient No. 6	$ 1,950	$ 1,950	$ 1,875	$ 1,875
Patient No. 7	$ 1,950	$ 1,950	$ 1,875	$ 1,875
Patient No. 8	$ 1,950	$ 1,950	$ 1,875	$ 1,875
Patient No. 9	$ 1,950	$ 1,950	$ 1,875	$ 1,875
Patient No. 10	$ 1,950	$ 1,950	$ 1,875	$ 1,875
Budget Variance		**$ (125)**		**$ (75)**

Electronic CDM Viewing Access

In order to use the budget software package described above, there is a great deal of information from the CDM that will be required to describe the clinical services. In a large institution, it may not be easy to know which departments are providing the ancillary services needed, and prices and codes may not be readily accessible to a research coordinator who may be trying to construct a budget that includes services outside of the main department conducting the research study.

The CDM has become an exceptionally important component of charging for services, including services associated with clinical research trials. When the research coordinator builds the clinical trial budget, it is crucial that the expected treatments, supplies, and devices are specifically listed in the budget section for patient care services, with detailed information from the CDM as described in the previous section. However, in order to obtain this information, there must be a user-friendly search capability for the CDM master file available to the research coordinator.

Providing an entry port to electronically view the medical center's CDM and even to possibly import the selected CDM line items into the budget software would provide an invaluable tool to the research coordinator in attempting to complete the

FIGURE 4-4

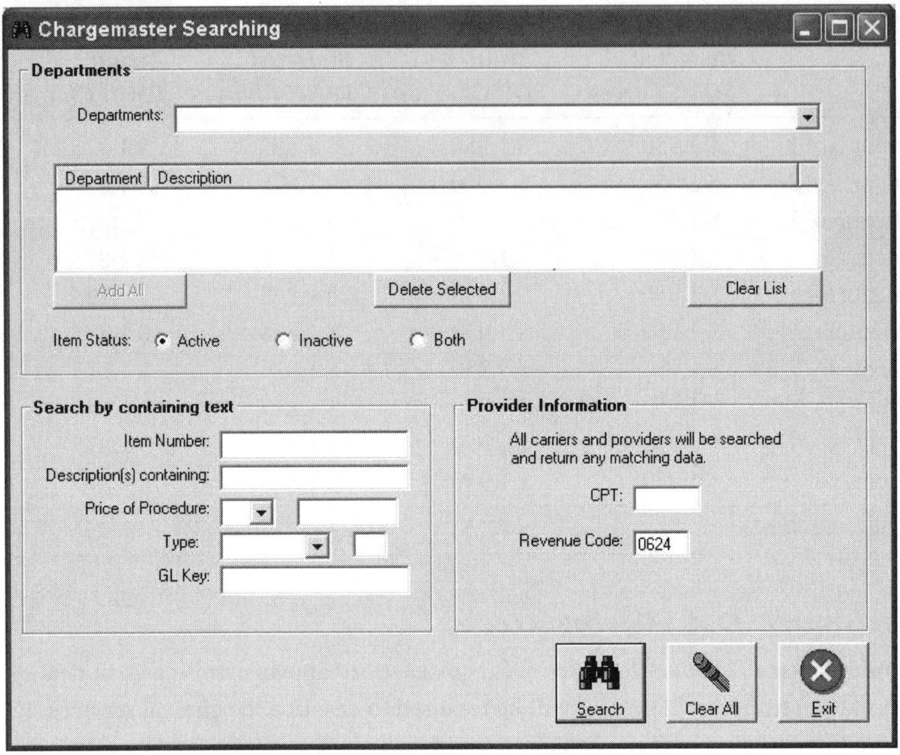

Source: MedCom Solutions, Inc.

study budget, and eliminate the potential for human error in transmitting data manually from one program to another. This would help ensure that the proper line item information, such as item number, department code, IDE number, CPT/HCPCS code, revenue code, and price, are correctly identified in the budget. Having an interface between the budgeting software and the CDM may require specialized expertise.

A basic query, such as the example shown in Figures 4-4 and 4-5, can be used to identify any number of groups of line items, which may be of assistance to the research coordinator in constructing the study budget. This example identifies active line items with Revenue Code of 624 (looking for active IDE items.)

This software could be an invaluable tool for various staff members to assist in running queries of the system to obtain information on usage, coding, pricing, and

| FIGURE 4-5 | *Academic Medical Center, CDM Search Results* |

Criteria: Active Line Items with Revenue Code of 624
CDM Data Date: September 1, 2005
YTD Volume Data: 8 Months

Item #	Dept	Description	CPT Code	Revenue Code	Price	YTD Volume
789654	NA45	IDE G000123 Stent	A4649	624	$ -	15
456532	FG56	IDE G1452 Catheter	L8601	624	$ 150	92
456321	NA45	IDE G896513 Balloon	L1843	624	$ 250	2
984563	NA45	IDE G19825 Vascular Stent	L9040	624	$ -	31

more. This decision support tool would assist staff members in developing queries from the CDM and revenue and usage databases, in order to track charge information throughout the course of a clinical research trial, as well as assisting in the initial phases of budgeting.

Medical Necessity Software

When preparing the clinical research trial study budget, it is beneficial to examine the correlation between the ICD-9 procedure and CPT codes. Many combinations of ICD-9 to CPT codes are not deemed medically necessary by payors and may not be eligible for reimbursement under a standard of care classification. Looking at code links during the budgeting process will enable you to evaluate, based on the CPT code of the rendered service and the applicable ICD-9 diagnosis code, whether the service will pass medical necessity tests or edits and be eligible for reimbursement. If there are services that will not be considered medically necessary, these services can be factored into the study budget as either patient responsibility or can be negotiated with the sponsor for additional payment. Either way, identifying these services and how they will be reimbursed allows you to answer these important questions before you begin treatment. Planning ahead to inform the patients in advance about which portions of the study will be covered and not covered is a key step in the screening and enrollment process.

There are outside vendors who offer medical necessity screening software, which may be beneficial to incorporate into the budgeting process. An example screenshot

FIGURE 4-6

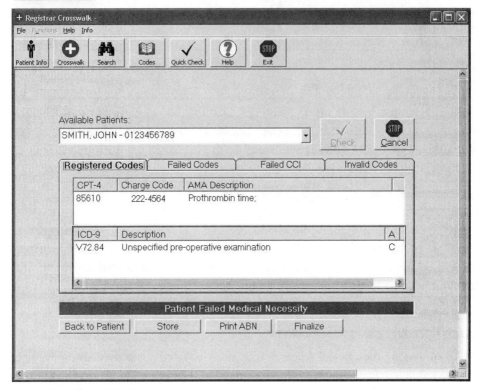

Source: MedCom Solutions, Inc.

of one such software program is shown in Figure 4-6. A database of code links that will pass or fail medical necessity is stored behind the scenes in the software, and by inputting any number of code combinations, the software will indicate if the services pass or fail medical necessity edits. This is one possible solution for incorporating medical necessity checks into the budgeting process with a user-friendly software product.

Correct Coding Software

The Correct Coding Initiative (CCI) edits are defined on the CMS web site to be "pairs of CPT or HCPCS Level II codes that are not separately payable except under certain circumstances. The edits are applied to services billed by the same provider for the same beneficiary on the same date of service. All claims are processed against the CCI tables." CCI, therefore, compares CPT code to CPT code to determine if one service or procedure is inherent in another procedure. Medicare updates this initiative quarterly throughout the year with additional code combinations that cannot be billed together as a standard practice. Consequently, when preparing the clinical trial budget it is beneficial to determine if there are any conflicting codes before those are submitted for payment.

Again, there are outside vendors who offer CCI screening software, which may be beneficial to incorporate into the budgeting process. An example screenshot of one such software program is shown below in Figure 4-7. Stored behind the scenes is an

FIGURE 4-7

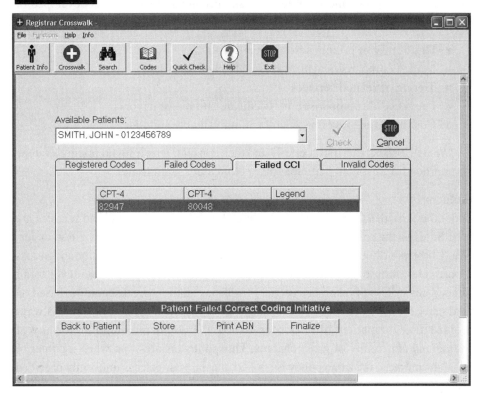

Source: MedCom Solutions, Inc.

updated database of CCI code combinations that cannot be billed simultaneously. By inputting groups of two CPT codes, the software will indicate whether the services are subject to a CCI edit. This is one possible solution for incorporating CCI information into the budgeting process with an easy-to-use software program.

Pricing Software with Current Market Data

In general, it is good business practice to have a well-defined pricing strategy for your facility's services. It becomes especially critical for hospitals participating in clinical research trials to have this pricing strategy in place prior to the start of the research trial. One important tool in that process is a pricing software package that can assist in periodic pricing reviews and updates to the entire hospital's CDM. Several important elements should be considered when performing pricing reviews, all of which should be incorporated into any pricing software that is developed or purchased.

- Uniformity of pricing across departments
- Market comparison against reasonable benchmarks
- Tiering of related services
- Fee schedule comparison for Medicare and major payors
- Cost-based metrics for general and implantable supplies

We will discuss each point briefly and then consider why a sound pricing strategy is important for hospitals participating in clinical research trials.

Uniformity

Under the Provider Reimbursement Manual, Part I § 2202.4, items and services are to be billed to the responsible party at the same price for the respective item or service. Correspondingly, each item and service provided by your facility and across departments should be priced and charged respectively, at the same level to all patients, regardless of insurance carrier or self-pay status. Any discounting based on third-party contracts, charity policies, or special corporate negotiations should always be done after the patient bill has been issued, thereby maintaining uniformity of pricing and uniformity of gross charges. This policy ensures that when it comes to research contracts, the same policy is applied, that is, your price is uniformly provided to all payors.

Market Comparison

A pricing comparison of services by CPT code against appropriate benchmarks can be accomplished by first purchasing market data from a health care data vendor. Generally, market data can be purchased for a minimal fee, can be chosen by region or facility depending on the vendor, and is readily available for CPT-coded services. This data provides useful insights about market competition and gives your facility a benchmark in pricing your services. Using a market-based approach to pricing also offers a defensible pricing strategy that is critical in defending a pricing structure as reasonable. This is a key point in negotiating payments with third-party payors as well as with clinical research trial sponsors, which are discussed in more depth in the next section.

Tiering of Related Services

Tiered pricing for related CPT coded services provides a common-sense approach for pricing your services, particularly from the patient's perspective. Examples of related CPT-coded services would be radiology services offered "with contrast" versus "without contrast," or surgical procedures offered "with biopsy" or "without biopsy." Additionally, many CPT code ranges specify wound lengths, or classify procedures as "simple" versus "complex," or "single" versus "multiple." All of these key phrases, which are found in the CPT definitions, can be a basis for a tiered pricing approach that offers common-sense charging throughout the range of services that your facility provides.

Fee Schedule Comparison

CDM prices also should be compared to any and all applicable payor fee schedules (generally listed by CPT code) to ensure that the price charged is higher than the reimbursement amounts applicable to the given service/procedure. Many payor contracts will stipulate that the actual payment amount will be based on the lesser of the fee schedule payment posted or the billed amount, placing the responsibility on your facility to ensure that your prices sufficiently cover all posted fee schedule amounts in order to obtain reimbursement levels available for services provided.

Cost-based Review for Supplies

CDM prices are determined in a variety of ways as we have highlighted above. However, for supply items, often the best and only way to determine pricing is based on cost. Since no market data or fee schedule information is available for noncodable supply items in most instances, using invoice cost with multiple markup schedules, or using your facility's "Ratio of Charges as Costs Associate to Charges" (RCCAC) factor as a basis, are generally the best approaches. (The RCCAC factor is determined on the Medicare cost report.) Supplies should be reviewed on a periodic basis, so that when invoice costs or RCCAC factors are adjusted, gross charges can be adjusted correspondingly. Keep in mind that no markups should be applied to IDE items, however, which should be reported at cost.

Having a common-sense, competitive approach to pricing, which includes the five tenets we have suggested, can assist your facility in achieving appropriate reimbursement, as well as assisting in sponsor negotiations, which are addressed below.

Negotiating Services with a Sponsor

When negotiating the medical center fees for conducting a clinical research trial with a sponsor, it is important to recognize all of the factors that relate to this effort. Preparing a thorough study budget prior to finalizing sponsor negotiations is a critical step toward ensuring that all incurred costs are negotiated for reimbursement on the front-end. It also is imperative to be ready to negotiate for appropriate grant amounts using a variety of strategies. To support adequate reimbursement for procedures performed on study subjects, rely on your sound pricing strategy that incorporates market data to support your facility's charges as being reasonable. Do not blindly accept Medicare payment rates as sufficient reimbursement for these procedures. Medicare is generally the lowest of all payors, and at times does not cover the facility's cost of operating and providing the service. Be ready to support and defend the reimbursement that will be fair and reasonable, considering the following:

- *Prices for Services:* The medical center's prices for all services or supplies must be supportable either in terms of cost or comparable market data, as discussed previously.
- *Fee Schedules:* Every facility has various fee schedules from payors, including Medicare. Negotiated prices should always remain at a higher or comparable level than the best third-party fee schedule amounts.
- *Actual Costs:* It is advisable to have supporting work papers that can be shared with a sponsor to illustrate these costs. Overhead calculations should be supported in a summary fashion.
- *Ratio of Charges as Costs Associate to Charges (RCCAC):* This is a Medicare cost report derivative that is historically determined and used for payment

purposes for NIH grants. This information may be used for supplementing or augmenting actual cost documentation.

In addition to the costs associated with actual patient work that is done as part of the study, do not forget to include administrative expenses, supplies, and overhead in negotiating contracts with sponsors. Furthermore, the cost of accurate budgeting and billing should be part of the negotiating effort. Without these budgeting and billing control mechanisms, the clinical trial is unlikely to be conducted in a fiscally responsible manner. If you get in the habit of incorporating these items into the study budgets, it should become natural to request funding for these items during the clinical trial negotiation process.

Research Charging Operations

Once the clinical research trial is underway, the difficulty comes with the operational details of handling patient visits and billing properly for them, while staying within the framework set out by the study budget. We will now address some of the main pitfalls associated with this aspect of running the clinical research trial. Figure 4-8 shows a branch diagram of key steps in research charging.

Patient Identification and Tracking

One of the most difficult tasks when handling billing for a research patient is to identify the procedures that are nonstandard-of-care and those that are considered standard-of-care. For many medical centers, it is difficult to clarify the distinction between these two classes of service. The consequence of confusing these services could result in over-billing a payor for nonstandard-of-care services, or under-billing a payor for standard of care services. Both are undesirable scenarios for your institution. Since we have recommended a budgeting approach that addresses these scenarios before any actual patient visits, you should be well-equipped to make these distinctions in service classification based on the study budget that has been laid out, but only if you can identify the patient as "research."

Clinic trial participants somehow must be identified as being part of the research study at the time of treatment in the main department performing the study, or in any of the ancillary departments providing services in the protocol. For those research

FIGURE 4-8 *Key Steps in Research Charging*

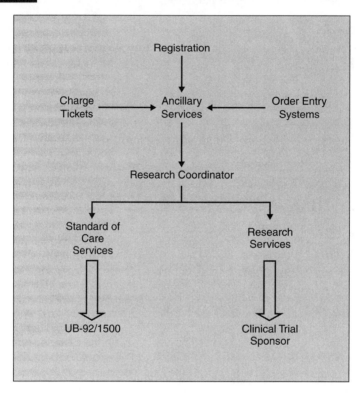

procedures that are scheduled, having the registration process interfaced to your clinical trial budgeting software is an ideal process that would automate the identification of research patients at the time of registration. However, this process would require two basic software functions in addition to your registration and budgeting software: first, a scheduling program that would contain each patient's research schedule by procedure and date of visit, and second, a registration system that would be able to electronically match the patient's research schedule for a given visit to determine if the patient is part of the research protocol. If the patient were found to be in the study protocol, the system would somehow "flag" the patient's records as part of the research trial, which would hold all billing until a manual review had been done. This manual review would be the responsibility of the study coordinator, or other named party, who could then process the bill to account for standard of care and nonstandard of care services. Standard of care services would pass on to the payor as usual, while other nonstandard of care services would be posted to the research grant as appropriate.

To provide a sound basis for delivering accurate bills to both the sponsor and the patient's payor, it is imperative that this registration process correctly identifies the research patient at the time of registration, so that all procedures are held and accounted for on the back end. Each department can then bill through normal channels, such as charge tickets or order entry systems, without worrying about whether the patient is part of the research study or not. The research coordinator then must segregate the research study's nonstandard of care charges from standard of care charges and bill each to the appropriate payor.

However, if the patient receives extended services during the course of treatment that were not scheduled, or reschedules an appointment for any reason, it is incumbent upon the research coordinator to recognize these changes and update the scheduling software, so that the patient is appropriately identified as research, and services do not get charged inappropriately to payors.

While the scenario described above would be a great solution to the patient tracking problem, it is well known that most medical centers are not currently equipped with registration software that has interface capabilities to accept research patients' schedules. Therefore, without the benefits of this software solution, registration staff must be educated in terms of identifying research patients in lieu of electronically importing an individual research patient's schedule. Furthermore, the patient billing area arguably should have established practices that are capable of identifying research patients throughout the course of treatment. Adding to the difficulty of this problem, many research participants are not "scheduled" through the study coordinator ahead of time, but rather brought into the study at a point during the treatment process when it becomes apparent that they are a good candidate for the protocol. This scenario presents a whole host of other issues, not the least of which is identifying and properly billing the patient's procedures. Again, it is the responsibility of the study site to identify research services and bill these services to the proper party. Consequently, in many medical centers, a myriad of patchwork efforts have been instituted to capture research procedures and attempt to bill them properly. Evaluation of best practices will need to be specific to your facility and the capabilities of the current software programs.

Billing Cycle

Billing for clinical research trials is a major undertaking, as we have discussed throughout the chapter. Principal Investigators are obligated to provide sponsors with accurate and sufficient financial information so that the sponsor may complete necessary disclosure statements. Furthermore, the PI must monitor and update the financial information to report any significant changes for up to one year following the study's completion (21 C.F.R. § 54.4(b)). To further underscore the importance of billing and maintaining accurate financial data, the 2004 edition of the Department of Health and Human Services, Office of Inspector General Work Plan focuses on auditing efforts in clinical trial billing.

That being said, the actual billing cycle becomes a critical juncture of the clinical research trial process. The study coordinator, as noted previously, must ensure a sound basis for delivering accurate bills to both the sponsor and the patient's payor. Therefore, it is imperative that the registration process correctly identifies each research patient at the time of registration or during the course of treatment. The research coordinator must then segregate the research study's nonstandard-of-care charges from the standard-of-care charges and bill each to the appropriate payor. This is the ultimate goal of appropriate research billing.

It is apparent that in addition to the PI and study coordinator, your facility's electronic data coordination team should be intimately involved in the clinical research trial process. They can help to ensure a smooth data flow between charge tickets, order entry systems, billing systems, and separation of claims to the appropriate party.

The cost reporting staff must identify the appropriate cost-to-charge ratios (RCCAC factors) that should be used when billing to certain sponsors, such as the National Institute of Health (NIH). Failure to accurately bill services based on the RCCAC could result in compliance problems. However, knowing the RCCAC is also beneficial when negotiating with a private sponsor to ensure the negotiated payment will be above cost, as noted previously. Routinely accepting sponsor reimbursements below facility costs undermines the fiscal strength of the medical center.

Finally, under the Civil False Claims Act, (31 U.S.C. § 3729 *et. seq.*) study sites must be mindful of regulatory requirements when submitting claims to the government. Billing payors erroneously for clinical research services, which may occur if "standard of care" charges are not distinguished from "research" services, may present compliance risks. This fact makes the billing cycle a critical phase in the process of successfully administering a clinical research trial. The conduct of clinical research trials requires disciplined people and actions along with excellent technology.

FIVE

Fraud and Abuse in Clinical Research

Karen Owen Dunlop, William A. Sarraille, and Bryan Lee

Introduction

In recent years, regulatory and law enforcement officials have focused increased attention and resources on reducing fraud and abuse in health care, with one of the areas of particular emphasis being clinical research.[1] "Fraud" refers to intentional acts of deception, while "abuse" describes a significant or repeated deviation from accepted practices.[2] The most significant fraud and abuse statutes are the federal Antikickback Statute and the federal False Claims Act (FCA).[3] The Antikickback Statute and related guidance from the Department of Health and Human Services' Office of Inspector General (OIG) attack improper inducements that lead to referrals or the purchase, lease, or ordering of an item or service reimbursable by the federal health care programs. Although the OIG has carved out regulatory safe harbors to counter the extremely broad scope of the Antikickback Statute, certain research arrangements may increase the likelihood that the government will challenge a relationship as a kickback that fraudulently drains public funds. For example, minimal research-related activities, sham consulting arrangements, and fees for the mere referral of patients to clinical studies raise suspicion. Potentially problematic issues in the research context also may include side arrangements to avoid government pricing obligations and improper payments to patients.

The second statute, the FCA, provides even greater leeway for the government to challenge research-related activities. The FCA allows a *qui tam* relator (often referred to as a "whistleblower") to bring suit, which greatly increases the incentive for whistleblowers to bring actions under the FCA. Furthermore, the certification theory has expanded the scope of the FCA's applicability. Essentially, whenever a clinical researcher applies for and receives a research grant, submits a claim for reimbursement for research-related care, or submits an application to the U.S. Food and Drug Administration (FDA), the government requires multiple certifications of compliance. Some of these certifications involve the protection of human subjects, managing conflicts of interest, research misconduct, and manufacturer observance of all laws and regulations applicable to a new drug application. Whenever a clinical researcher makes a certification (and, increasingly, even if the certification is only implied) and then fails to satisfy the underlying requirement, the FCA becomes an enforcement vehicle. The certification theory maintains that the government dispensed funds relying on the false certification, and any deviation from a legal or regulatory requirement can therefore lead to a whistleblower FCA suit. In fact, multiple suits have employed the FCA to attack various fraudulent research arrangements, including ones involving the payment of kickbacks, misuse of grant funds, and making false statements to obtain and maintain grants. The certification theory reaches far enough to implicate failure to protect human subjects adequately. In fact, it even extends to the argument that false or missing disclosures to the FDA were a but-for cause of FDA approval, so the drug or device manufacturer obtained any federal funds used to purchase the product fraudulently.

As the number and value of fraud and abuse cases in clinical research have increased, so has the creativity of the *qui tam* (or whistleblower's) bar and the U.S. government. More than ever, the quality of clinical research matters. Sham researchers and authors, inadequate oversight, faulty safety precautions, and study misdesign now are considered fraud and abuse issues in much the same way as a straightforward kickback or inappropriate claim for government grant or research money. This chapter examines the Antikickback Statute and the FCA, first setting out the statutory background and the relevant regulatory guidance. It also discusses industry guidance that may not have binding legal authority but which informs the clinical research process. Finally, each section contains a summary of significant cases that illustrate some problematic clinical research arrangements and reinforce the legal framework surrounding the Antikickback Statute and FCA.

The Antikickback Statute

Relevant Statutory Provisions and Safe Harbors

The Antikickback Statute makes it a criminal offense to knowingly and willfully offer, pay, solicit, or receive any remuneration in exchange for referring an individual for items or services reimbursable by a federal health care program.[4] It also prohibits purchasing, leasing, or ordering a good, facility, service, or item reimbursable by a federal health care program in return for remuneration.[5] Penalties for violations of the Antikickback Statute include a fine of not more than $25,000 or imprisonment for up to five years, or both.[6] Additionally, violations can lead to exclusion from federal health care programs, including Medicare, as well as state health care programs, including Medicaid.[7] The Department of Health and Human Services (HHS) also may seek a civil monetary penalty for a defendant who "commits an act described" in the Antikickback Statute.[8] This establishes a $50,000 penalty for each act that violates the Antikickback Statute plus damages up to three times the prohibited remuneration.[9] The civil monetary penalty statute gives prosecutors a powerful weapon because a preponderance of the evidence suffices, lowering the hurdle from the Antikickback Statute's "beyond a reasonable doubt" standard, applicable in criminal matters.

As a practical matter, exclusion from federal health care programs would mean the end of business for almost all individual providers. The effect may be less dramatic for manufacturers or institutional providers, such as hospitals. In one prominent case, however, the OIG asserted that the exclusion may run to an institutional provider. The OIG planned to exclude Tenet Healthcare Corporation's Redding Medical Center (Redding, California) from Medicare, Medicaid, and other federal health care programs because of alleged unnecessary cardiac catheterizations and open heart surgeries.[10] The OIG relented and agreed not to issue a formal notice of exclusion after Tenet promised to sell the hospital.[11]

A line of cases interpreting the Antikickback Statute holds that if just one purpose of the remuneration is prohibited, then the statute has been violated.[12] In the leading case, Cardio-Med's president, Dr. Greber, argued that the Antikickback Statute required that "the only purpose behind a fee was to improperly induce future services."[13] Cardio-Med provided cardiology services for patients of referring physicians. However, a panel of the Third Circuit rejected that argument and affirmed Greber's conviction. Cardio-Med had claimed that it paid referring doctors a fixed percentage of the Medicare payment it received up to $65 per patient. The court said that the evidence suggested payment from Cardio-Med to its consulting physicians even when Cardio-Med did the actual data analysis.[14] This violated the Antikickback Statute because the statute targeted "the inducement factor" by using the word "'any remuneration'" instead of "kickback."[15] Therefore, the Third Circuit upheld the trial court's instruction: "even if the physician interpreting the test did so as a consultant to Cardio-Med, that fact was immaterial if *a purpose* of the fee was to induce the ordering of services from Cardio-Med."[16] Another court confirmed the "one purpose" test, finding that "the issue of the sole-versus-primary reason for payments is irrelevant since *any* amount of inducement is illegal."[17] The court also rejected the argument that a defendant avoids liability as long as its actions do not induce a new drain on public funds because the money would have been spent anyway, or because the funds were not used directly to make the illegal payment.[18] Obviously, this "one purpose" test greatly expands the scope of the Antikickback Statute and calls many behaviors into question.

The government must, however, prove intent in order to prevail in an Antikickback action.[19] Therefore, remuneration only violates the statute if it is knowingly and willfully intended to induce a referral.[20] In the clinical research context, this may occur, for example, when a manufacturer provides a research grant to a current or potential customer or referral source if one purpose of the grant is to induce the customer to buy or recommend that manufacturer's products, which are reimbursable by a federal health care program.[21] Another potential violation of the Antikickback Statute is payment of excessive fees to an investigator for performing studies.[22] Again, the motive behind the excessive fees could be to induce referrals for the sponsor's products.

The reach of the Antikickback Statute is very broad. To protect legitimate payments from potential scrutiny, the law contains a number of exceptions. Additionally, the OIG, which is charged with enforcing various laws relating to the federal Medicare program,[23] has issued regulatory "safe harbors." Several of these safe harbors protect relationships between clinical research sponsors, investigators, health care institutions, and others. These include the safe harbors for personal services and management contracts, space and equipment leases, employee relationships, and the managed care exception. No liability for violating the Antikickback Statute attaches as long as a transaction fits completely within a safe harbor.

The most relevant safe harbor in the clinical research context protects personal services. The safe harbor excludes from the definition of "remuneration" a payment that satisfies all seven requirements. The agreement must

1. be in writing and signed;
2. cover all the services the agent provides and specify those services;
3. specify the exact time, length, and charge for services rendered part time;
4. last for at least one year;
5. set out the aggregate compensation in advance, make the compensation consistent with fair market value, and avoid compensation that takes into account the volume or value of any referrals or business otherwise generated between the parties for which payment may be made in whole or part by Medicare, Medicaid, or other federal health care programs;
6. not include services involving the counseling or promotion of a business arrangement or other activity that violates any state or federal law; and
7. not call for aggregate services that exceed those reasonably necessary to accomplish the commercially reasonable business purpose of the services.[24]

The personal-services safe harbor essentially allows a physician rendering personal services to have independent contractor status. However, it is very difficult to comply with all seven requirements for clinical research. For instance, the safe harbor requires that the aggregate compensation be set out in advance. Clinical research contributors usually receive a set dollar value per patient, and it is impossible to know the exact number of patients at each research site in advance. Also, a contract for part-time service must specify the exact times for performance, which remains unfeasible for a year-long contract.

Although the personal-services safe harbor rarely applies, failure to fit squarely within a safe harbor does not necessarily mean that the Antikickback Statute is violated. In comments published with the first safe harbors, OIG acknowledged that the regulations do "not expand the scope of activities that the statute prohibits."[25] According to the OIG, the failure of a specific transaction to comply with the strict terms of the regulation could "mean one of three things":

1. that the arrangement did not violate the Antikickback Statute because it "is not intended to induce" reimbursable referrals;
2. that the arrangement clearly violated the statute; or
3. that the arrangement violates the statute in a less serious manner so that "there is no way to predict the degree of risk."[26]

To minimize the degree of risk, clinical research collaborators should structure their personal services transactions to adhere as closely to the safe harbor provisions as possible. Parties should emphasize the degree of necessity of the services provided, explain why they selected the particular investigator and/or site, and calculate fair market value as objectively as possible. Evidence of other arrangements for similar services or any third-party data on similar contracts would bring the transaction nearer the safe harbor. The OIG Compliance Program Guidance for Pharmaceutical Manufacturers, discussed in detail below, also gives advice on how to structure arrangements between manufacturers and physicians when the relationship falls outside the personal-services safe harbor.

Administrative Guidance

1994 OIG Special Fraud Alert

OIG periodically issues special fraud alerts to publicize concerns about the possibility of widespread abusive practices in the health care industry.[27] OIG uses the fraud alert as a vehicle to single out fraudulent and abusive practices within the health care system and to disseminate this information directly to health care providers.[28] Fraud alerts provide guidance to the health care industry about what constitutes a violation of federal law, most often the Antikickback Statute.[29]

OIG identified several problematic arrangements in the clinical research context in the August 1994 special fraud alert.[30] Many of the problematic arrangements stem from an increase in research funded by the pharmaceutical industry, which OIG asserted can create a conflict between the patient and the physician.[31] OIG indicated its suspicion that physicians' interest in treating the patients may compete with loyalty to the pharmaceutical industry because of outside compensation from pharmaceutical manufacturers.[32]

In the clinical research context, OIG cited as a problematic example a research grant program where investigators were given "substantial payments for *de minimis* recordkeeping tasks."[33] OIG alleged that, in a typical arrangement, a pharmaceutical manufacturer would pay a physician for administering its drug to a patient and recording a minimal amount of data about the outcome, sometimes as little as a single word.[34] Where there is no safe harbor protection for this arrangement, the manufacturer and the physician could be subject to liability under the Antikickback Statute if just one purpose of the pharmaceutical manufacturer's payment is to induce the referral or purchase of a prescription drug reimbursable by a federal health care program.[35] The personal-services safe harbor might apply here, but this arrangement likely does not meet all of the safe harbor requirements, especially those for length of contract and fair market value of service.

OIG listed three ways by which payment from a pharmaceutical manufacturer to a physician could lead to a violation of the Antikickback Statute.[36] First, the physician may be in a position to generate business for the pharmaceutical manufacturer.[37] As a practical matter, however, this criterion would affect nearly every arrangement. Second, if the payment is related to the volume of business the physician generates for the manufacturer, the payment may be suspect.[38] As a result, extensive research support to high-volume prescribers may be problematic. Third, if the payment to the physician exceeds the fair market value of any legitimate service that was performed, or if the payment is unrelated to any service other than referral of patients, the payment would be suspect.[39]

Manufacturers as well as clinical investigators are at risk for violating the Antikickback Statute if the sponsor provides too much, or improper, funding to the investigator for the services actually performed. The Fraud Alert warns that if research grants are awarded as a guise for paying extra compensation to investigators, then both the sponsor and the investigator may be subject to criminal prosecution for violating the Antikickback Statute.[40]

2003 OIG Compliance Program Guidance for Pharmaceutical Manufacturers

In April of 2003, the OIG issued its Compliance Program Guidance for Pharmaceutical Manufacturers ("Guidance") to assist pharmaceutical manufacturers in developing a compliance program that conforms to applicable federal statutes.[41] The Guidance instructs manufacturers to engage in a two-step analysis to determine if a given arrangement violates the Antikickback Statute.[42] First, the manufacturer should identify any possible remunerative relationships between the manufacturer and those in a position to generate federal health care business for the manufacturer.[43] After making this initial determination, the manufacturer should determine if any purpose of the remuneration could be unlawful; if so, then the Antikickback Statute may have been violated.[44] OIG also listed some aggravating factors that increase the risk of prosecution. It advised manufacturers to ask whether the arrangement has the potential to interfere with clinical decision-making or a formulary process, or to affect the accuracy of information distribution.[45] Manufacturers also should consider the potential of increased costs to federal health care programs or beneficiaries, and the possibility of a disguised discount aimed at circumventing the Medicaid Best Price calculation.[46] Furthermore, manufacturers should judge whether the practice will increase over or inappropriate utilization, and whether patient safety or quality of care concerns will increase.[47] OIG recommends structuring arrangements "to fit in a safe harbor whenever possible."[48]

The Guidance also highlights certain practices involving educational grants and research funding that have historically led to enforcement action. It acknowledges the value of educational funding but warns that funding conditioned "in whole or in part, on the purchase of product implicates the statute, even if the educational or research purpose is legitimate."[49] This essentially applies the "one purpose" test to the educational setting. A manufacturer's influence over an educational program leads to an increased risk of inappropriate marketing. OIG offers as risk-reducing practices the separation of grant making and marketing or sales, establishment of objective grant making criteria, severing control over speaker selection or educational content, and documentation and monitoring of compliance with these procedures.[50]

Purchasers and manufacturers often make research arrangements as well, and the personal-services safe harbor may apply.[51] Payments "for research services should be fair market value for legitimate, reasonable, and necessary services."[52] Postmarketing research activities receive special scrutiny "to ensure that they are legitimate and not simply a pretext to generate prescriptions of a drug."[53] Manufacturers should establish practices that separate research contracting from marketing because research contracts "that originate through the sales or marketing functions—or that are offered to purchasers in connection with sales contacts—are particularly suspect."[54] Again, research grants "can be misused to induce the purchase of business without triggering Medicaid Best Price obligations," so manufacturers are wise to segregate sales activity and research grant making.[55]

Other parts of the guidance suggest additional areas that manufacturers should scrutinize. Any remuneration "directly or indirectly to person [sic] in a position to influence formulary decisions related to the manufacturer's products [is] suspect and should be carefully scrutinized."[56] Because formulary decision-makers frequently engage in research activities, segregation of sales and research activities may be critical here. Furthermore, arrangements with physicians "for services connected directly or indirectly to a manufacturer's marketing and sales activities, such as speaking, certain research, or preceptor or 'shadowing' services . . . also pose a risk of fraud and abuse. In particular, the use of health care professionals for marketing purposes—including, for example, ghost-written papers or speeches—implicates the anti-kickback statute."[57] Disclosure does not eliminate this risk. Arrangements that take the guise of research, such as the time physicians spend accessing web sites in the detailing context, are "highly susceptible to fraud and abuse."[58]

OIG's recommendations extend to research arrangements between manufacturers and physicians as well as manufacturers and purchasers.[59] Payments should be fair market value, and research initiated by sales or marketing personnel is "particularly suspect."[60] Other indications of questionable "research" include research not transmitted to or reviewed by a manufacturer's science division, unnecessary or duplicative research, and postmarketing research used as a pretense for product promotion.[61]

OIG listed several factors to evaluate the appropriateness of arrangements between pharmaceutical companies and physicians that do not fit squarely in a safe harbor. The guidance recommends examining

1. the nature of the relationship between the parties, including the degree to which the physician influences the generation of business for the manufacturer and the relationships the manufacturer has with the physician or members of his or her group;
2. whether remuneration takes into account the volume or value of business generated directly or indirectly, to what extent it does so, and whether there are services in addition to referrals;
3. the value of the remuneration, especially in comparison to fair market value;
4. the remuneration's potential to affect the costs of federal health care programs; and
5. potential conflicts of interest, such as the objectivity of professional judgment, patient safety, quality of care, and the impact on information dissemination.[62]

The Guidance also references the Pharmaceutical Research and Manufacturers of America (PhRMA) Code on Interactions with Healthcare Professionals (the

"PhRMA Code") as a valuable resource, although code compliance does not guarantee compliance with the Antikickback Statute.

Industry Guidance

Pharmaceutical Research and Manufacturers of America Principles on Conduct of Clinical Trials and Communication of Clinical Trial Results

The Pharmaceutical Research and Manufacturers of America adopted guidelines on appropriate relationships between manufacturers and clinical researchers both to record already-existing good practices and to attempt to restore confidence in the clinical trials process after several highly-publicized incidents.[63] PhRMA's Principles on Conduct of Clinical Trials and Communication of Clinical Trial Results ("PhRMA Principles") apply to all clinical research trials begun after October 1, 2002. Several of the PhRMA Principles' recommendations directly address Antikickback Statute issues in clinical research. First, a legitimate scientific relationship must motivate the sponsor's interactions with clinical research collaborators. Therefore, sponsors should select investigators "based on qualifications, training, research, or clinical expertise in relevant fields, the potential to recruit research participants and ability to conduct clinical trials in accordance with good clinical practices, and applicable legal requirements."[64] The investigators' value as referrers and prescribers or their influence on formularies should not come into consideration.

Furthermore, only some considerations are legitimate when sponsors and investigators make compensation arrangements. The parties should have a "written contract or budgetary agreement" that specifies "the nature of the research services to be provided and the basis for payment of those services."[65] Manufacturers should structure this contract to fall within the personal-services safe harbor whenever possible. Additionally, investigator compensation "should not be tied to the outcome of clinical trials."[66] Instead, payment should be "reasonable and based on work performed by the investigator and the investigator's staff, not on any other considerations."[67] The form of payment also matters, so the principles prohibit compensation "in company stock or stock options."[68] Manufacturers are allowed to pay investigators extra compensation if enrollment for the study is unusually difficult and if the investigator had to expend more time and effort than usual.[69] Manufacturers also may pay for reasonable travel expenses, lodging, meals, and time if investigators must travel to meetings associated with the clinical trial.[70] Sponsors should not offer the rewards associated with authorship as compensation, either. The principles state that "anyone who provides substantial contributions into the conception or design of a study, or data acquisition, or data analysis and interpretation; and writing or revising of the manuscript; and has final approval" should receive appropriate recognition.[71] Conversely, someone who did not contribute at this level does not deserve authorship. The principles encourage clinical investigators to disclose to patients that they or their research institution receive payment for conducting the clinical trial.[72]

Sponsors and investigators should also make sure that they avoid other entangling arrangements that decrease the independence and discretion of investigators. Clinical researchers investigating a pharmaceutical product should not serve on the Data and Safety Monitoring Board or Committee that performs ongoing safety monitoring for that trial, nor should a Board or Committee member "have significant financial interests or other conflicts of interest that would preclude objective determinations."[73] Additionally, investigators "or their immediate family should not have a direct ownership interest in the specific pharmaceutical product being studied," which includes arrangements such as royalty fees or patents.[74] Prior-held stock—as opposed to stock provided as compensation—"does not disqualify the investigator from participating in clinical research for the company."[75] Moreover, there is an OIG safe harbor for investment interests that may apply, especially if the sponsor has over $50 million in assets or if less than a predetermined percentage of the sponsor's investors can make or induce referrals to the sponsor.[76]

The PhRMA Principles also issue guidelines for appropriate compensation arrangements between sponsors of clinical research and research participants. The principles propose institutional review board (IRB) review of any payment, and research participants should receive payment based on their time and/or reasonable expenses.[77] Any benefit to a research participant should "be consistent with the principle of voluntary informed consent," which includes a participant's right to withdraw from a trial at any time.[78] Therefore, any compensation to a research participant should not be wholly contingent on completion of the study protocol, although "payment of a small portion as an incentive" is acceptable.[79]

PhRMA Code on Interactions with Health Care Professionals

In response to highly-publicized government investigations into promotional practices and the accompanying public outcry, PhRMA issued a voluntary Code on Interactions with Healthcare Professionals in 2002. Although the code does not have any explicit legal effect, OIG declared that it "provides useful and practical advice for reviewing and structuring" relationships between manufacturers and providers.[80] Therefore, although "compliance with the PhRMA Code will not protect a manufacturer as a matter of law under the Antikickback Statute, it will substantially reduce the risk of fraud and abuse and help demonstrate a good faith effort to comply with the applicable federal health care program requirements."[81] Because several of the code provisions apply to clinical research relationships, manufacturers should structure their interactions with physicians accordingly.

The PhRMA Code opposes arrangements that would clearly violate the Antikickback Statute. It declares that "[n]o grants, scholarships, subsidies, support, consulting contracts, or educational or practice-related items should be provided or offered to a healthcare professional in exchange for prescribing products or for a commitment to continue prescribing products."[82] The code also lists factors tending to prove a *bona fide* consulting relationship between a provider and a manufacturer. Manufacturers decrease the probability of having "[t]oken consulting or advisory arrangements" if they have

1. a written contract specifying the services and the basis for payment of those services;
2. a clearly-identified legitimate need for services;
3. criteria for selecting consultants that are directly related to the purpose;
4. assurance that the persons selecting consultants have the required expertise;
5. a number of retained health care professionals that is reasonably necessary;
6. maintained records; and
7. a venue and circumstances conducive to the consulting services, and made activities related to the consulting services the primary focus of the meeting.[83]

Therefore, when manufacturers arrange for physicians to collaborate in clinical research, they should make sure that these *bona fide* consultant factors apply to the greatest extent possible. As the PhRMA Principles suggest, the best practice is for the manufacturer to document thoroughly the services to be rendered and why the consultants are qualified and necessary. A provider's participation should be based on the research contribution he or she can make and not operate as a backdoor way to provide compensation. As an illustration, the PhRMA Code allows a company to retain "15 nationally known physicians" to advise it on "general medical and business issues and provide guidance on product development and research programs."[84] The company also could fly the physicians—but not their spouses—to resorts once or twice a year "to discuss the latest product data, research programs and Company plans."[85]

AdvaMed Code of Ethics

Although the same general principles apply to both pharmaceutical products and medical devices, the Advanced Medical Technology Association ("AdvaMed") has promulgated its own Code of Ethics for interactions between device manufacturers and physicians. The AdvaMed Code also sets out a set of factors to determine *bona fide* consulting services, which can include research and product collaboration.[86] The factors closely adhere to the PhRMA Principles and PhRMA Code. Arrangements must be written, consistent with fair market value for the services provided, and entered into only where the need is legitimate and the purpose identified in advance.[87] Manufacturers should select consultants "on the basis of the consultant's qualifications and expertise to address the identified purpose, and should not be on the basis of volume or value of business generated by the consultant."[88] The other factors involving device manufacturer meetings with consultants, hospitality, and payment for expenses incurred also are identical.[89] AdvaMed includes as another factor the presence of a "written research protocol" when an AdvaMed member contracts with a consultant for research services.[90]

The AdvaMed Code specifically requires that a clinical investigator be treated as a consultant and emphasizes that manufacturers should restrict the number of consultants to what is "legitimate and appropriate to provide *bona fide* services; moreover, the requirements of Section V [on legitimate consulting arrangements] must be satisfied for each consultant."[91] The AdvaMed Code also specifies factors for an appropriate venue and circumstances for a consultant meeting, such as a *bona fide* business justification for the meeting, a venue conducive to the exchange of information, the value of the lodging and hospitality, the subordination of hospitality to the business focus of the meeting, and "whether the overall meeting has a genuine business purpose and tenor and does not represent improper inducement of the Health Care Professional."[92]

Both pharmaceutical and device manufacturers should take advantage of the recommendations contained in the applicable industry guidelines and should conform

their research relationships to maximize compliance with the guidelines. This does not guarantee immunity from Antikickback Statute enforcement, but the government would likely have a favorable view of the manufacturer's commitment to current best practice.

Application of Antikickback Principles to Clinical Research

Remuneration to Investigators and Research Institutions

The Antikickback Statute governs all circumstances in which an investigator or research institution receives research funds, which are "remuneration," from a manufacturer that also sells products reimbursable by the federal health programs. In that circumstance, the statute could be violated if the researcher or institution solicited the funding, even in part, as a *qui pro quo* for purchasing additional products, or if the manufacturer offered the funding to induce the researcher or institution to buy more products. The purpose of the research grant is inferred from the facts and circumstances surrounding it.[93] The statute, therefore, is not violated in cases in which, as in most instances, manufacturers support *bona fide* research efforts.

On the other hand, improper payments from pharmaceutical manufacturers to clinical investigators can occur in a variety of ways. The OIG fraud alert warns manufacturers that payments to investigators cannot exceed the fair market value of the work performed.[94] The statute may be implicated by free travel, highly remunerative consulting arrangements, or other personal services arrangements. Finally, it is important to note that transfers of equipment raise the same issues as cash payments. The Antikickback Statute makes any remuneration illegal, whether in cash or kind.[95] The OIG has provided guidance on this issue as well. The OIG has stated that if a free personal computer is provided to the investigator, the investigator may be able to use it for a variety of purposes, including ones not connected with the clinical study.[96] The OIG cautions that, depending on the specific circumstances, this could qualify as illegal remuneration under the Antikickback Statute.[97] The OIG counsels that the substance, not the form, of the transaction controls in determining if there is a reasonably foreseeable misuse of the free goods.[98] "[I]f the equipment is used by the recipient for any purpose other than in connection with the ordered service, there is potential illegal remuneration and potential liability for both parties to the transaction."[99] Therefore, although sponsors may certainly provide equipment to investigators where the sole possible use of the equipment relates to the study, sponsors should make a more careful inquiry if the equipment has additional uses.

In 1996, Caremark International settled an Antikickback suit against stockholders and the U.S. government for approximately $250 million.[100] Caremark allegedly awarded physicians research grants in exchange for those physicians' prescribing Caremark's products.[101] Warner-Lambert settled a prominent case in 2004 for $430 million because of its off-label promotion of Neurontin after allegations of widespread kickback arrangements.[102] The relator alleged that false claims arose from a network of kickbacks that included sham consulting agreements where Parke-Davis flew physicians to various locations to promote off-label uses instead of to receive consulting services.[103] Parke-Davis also used highly-controlled continuing medical education seminars and distributed educational grants out of the marketing budget based solely on an individual's support of Neurontin or willingness to host a program with a known Neurontin supporter.[104] The Neurontin promotion allegedly included bad faith "research" grants, where the defendant funded research that "had no scientific value."[105] One protocol called on over 1,200 physicians "to enroll only a few patients each."[106] Parke-Davis also allegedly paid doctors honoraria for lending their names to ghost-written scientific articles and paid physicians "far in excess of the fair value of the work they performed" to belong to a speakers' bureau.[107] The relator concluded that Medicaid conditioned payment on compliance with relevant statutes and regulations, including the Medicaid antikickback provisions, resulting in hundreds of thousands of false claims.[108]

Drug samples also may draw enforcement action as part of a kickback arrangement. For instance, in the TAP Pharmaceuticals litigation, which settled for a record $290 million criminal fine and $585 million in civil fines, a relator who sued under the FCA for standing reasons alleged a kickback scheme under which TAP encouraged urologists to bill Medicare for Lupron that TAP provided either as free samples or "at a significantly discounted price because of volume."[109] Another relator alleged that TAP offered him a $20,000 "'educational grant,' with no restrictions on how the money could be spent" for each of the next three years as part of its plan to promote Lupron.[110] The grant increased to $25,000 a year if Tufts Associated Health Maintenance Organization agreed to reimburse for Lupron exclusively. Although the fraudulent grant was "educational" rather than for "research," the same fraud and abuse analysis would apply to the clinical research context.

Excessive Enrollment and De Minimis *Activity*

Investigator activities associated with enrolling patients in clinical trials have the potential to be problematic as well. As a general rule, manufacturers should not pay investigators finders' fees for only enrolling patients in a clinical trial.[111] Such payments could result in the investigator having a financial conflict of interest. If the investigator receives payment for each patient he or she merely enrolls in a clinical study without performing additional work, the investigator may refer some patients to the study even if it is not in the patients' best interest.[112] The American Medical Association Council on Ethical and Judicial Affairs has stated that "obtaining a fee simply for referral of a patient to a research study . . . is unethical."[113] Additionally, the 1994 Fraud Alert made it clear that this type of arrangement raises Antikickback Statute concerns.[114] When setting compensation arrangements for referring physicians, research sponsors should first make sure that the clinician is offering legitimate services other than referral. Second, they can increase the probability that the compensation arrangement is reasonable by looking at similar arrangements in studies of comparable scope.

Entertainment

Potentially problematic situations can arise when manufacturers provide investigators with fringe benefits. These benefits include meals, honoraria, conference travel, and continuing medical education courses.[115] In addition to influencing physicians' treatment decisions, such interactions with pharmaceutical manufacturers can also implicate the Antikickback Statute.[116] The Fraud Alert states that "any prize, gift, or cash payment . . . offered to physicians . . . in exchange for, or based on, prescribing or providing specific prescription products" is suspect and may warrant further investigation.[117] Therefore, investigators who are receiving fringe benefits from a manufacturer when they increase their prescription rates of the manufacturer's products may run afoul of the Antikickback Statute.[118]

Although the Antikickback Statute does not contain a *de minimis* limitation, some pharmaceutical companies have looked to other authority and imposed per-episode limits on themselves. For instance, HIPAA instituted civil monetary penalties for offering inducements to beneficiaries ("Anti-Beneficiary Inducement provision"). Remuneration now includes waiver of all or part of deductible and coinsurance amounts as well as transfer of items and services for free or less than fair market value.[119] The statute exempts some waivers, but OIG may impose a civil monetary penalty for arrangements that fall outside these exceptions.[120] OIG has proposed a local transportation benefit exemption of no more than $50 aggregate and a general definition of a "nominal" inducement as being less than $10 per item and $50 annually.[121] In the same solicitation of public comments, OIG expressed interest in examining inducements to enroll after the 2000 National Coverage Decision to determine if any exemptions to the civil monetary penalty are appropriate. It has asked for comment on the threshold level of Medicare reimbursement, limiting the exception to trials of "clear potential public benefit" instead of "chiefly commercial value," the type and amount of permissible inducements, and sources of benefits.[122]

False Claims Act

Relevant Statutory Provisions

The FCA occupies an even more prominent place than the Antikickback Statute in the government's arsenal against fraud and abuse in research.[123] The FCA dates back to the Civil War era and prohibits the knowing submission of false or fraudulent claims and false statements to the government.[124] "Knowing" is a statutorily defined term, which includes not only actual knowledge but also deliberate ignorance or reckless disregard of the truth or falsity of a claim.[125] Notably, the FCA does not proscribe the innocent, inadvertent, or even negligent filing of false reimbursement claims.[126] Penalties for violating the FCA include treble damages plus up to a $11,000 penalty for each false claim submitted.[127] If the suit is brought by a private whistleblower, known as a *qui tam* relator, the whistleblower may receive as much as 30 percent of the reward if the government does not intervene.[128] The FCA is a civil statute but has a closely-corresponding criminal equivalent that also punishes knowingly making or presenting a claim that is false, fictitious, or fraudulent to a department or agency of the United States.[129] Therefore, research sponsors and clinicians should bear in mind throughout this discussion that violation of the FCA likely has criminal repercussions.

Several different behaviors may constitute submission of a false claim, such as presenting a false claim to receive payment, making or using a false statement to get a claim paid, participating in a conspiracy involving a false claim, government contractor embezzlement, false certification of delivery, black market purchases of public property, and "reverse false claims," which are false statements intended to reduce an obligation owed to the government.[130]

FCA violations may occur when research institutions improperly report costs, inflate costs, or incur costs in a manner inconsistent with the grant documents.[131] Additionally, the government may also allege violations of the FCA when applications for federal grants and certifications required for federally funded research grants are false.[132] Some courts have held that filing a claim in violation of the Antikickback Statute, standing alone, will provide the basis for an FCA suit.[133]

Within the clinical research context, an investigator's submission of reimbursement claim to a federal health care program for items or services that are either not reimbursable or are covered by other resources, such as research grants, also violates the FCA.[134] Clinical investigators are at risk for FCA violations if they seek reimbursement from federal health care programs for services that should not be covered by those federal programs, or if they accept federal grant money based on fraudulent grant applications. Moreover, when calculating the total cost of a clinical trial, the sponsor must identify all clinical and research services that will be provided by investigators, and should clarify whether government programs or private insurance will provide reimbursement. Billing the government for services that are not covered under government health plans or are otherwise reimbursable by either private insurance or a private research grant implicates the FCA.[135] The sponsor should calculate the total of all costs that will not be covered by a third-party payer and should provide research funding sufficient to cover those costs. Finally, in order to avoid possible legal consequences, the sponsor agreement should clearly identify which clinical services are covered by the research grant and which services are not covered. Sponsors should carefully tailor the amount of funding given to investigators in order to ensure that compensation does not exceed the fair market value of services provided.

Certifications and FCA Liability

The Intersection between the Antikickback Statute and FCA

Although the Antikickback Statute does not have a *qui tam* provision, relators have found a way to pursue kickbacks through the FCA. Whenever a provider submits a claim for reimbursement and certifies compliance with a given statute, violation of that underlying statute becomes grounds for a false claims case. In one critical case, a panel of the Fifth Circuit allowed a relator to survive a motion for summary judgment for his claim that the defendant violated the FCA. The case survived because the relator did not merely allege that the claims were "for services rendered in violation of a statute" but instead involved claims "where the government has conditioned payment of a claim upon a claimant's certification of compliance."[136] The Fifth Circuit remanded the question of whether Medicare's requirement that the defendant certify in annual cost reports that it was complying with the laws and regulations on provision of health care services rendered violations of the Antikickback Statute and the "Stark" law (i.e., Limitation on Certain Physician Referrals, 42 U.S.C. 1395 nn. Section 1877 of the Social Security Act) into false claims pursuable by a *qui tam* relator.[137] On remand, the district court held that antikickback violations can support a suit under the FCA, largely because a Center for Medicare and Medicaid Services (CMS) representative stated that CMS understood the cost report certification to include a representation that a kickback had not "'infected'" the services.[138] The Parke-Davis and TAP cases, discussed previously, clearly have allowed *qui tam* relators to assert FCA violations based on kickbacks.

Grant Certifications

Research sponsors must make multiple certifications of compliance with various rules and norms in clinical research to receive grants from the government. If any of these certifications is false, then the government may take the position that the entity submitting the certification has knowingly made a false claim to a government agency, violating the FCA. Because the clinical investigator must make certifications for essentially every part of the research process, the certification theory has become a powerful weapon in suits brought over clinical research fraud.

The NIH grant application process requires many certifications—each application to the Public Health Service requires assurances and certifications for the following:

- Human Subjects
- Research on Transplantation of Human Fetal Tissue
- Women and Minority Inclusion Policy
- Inclusion of Children Policy
- Research Using Human Embryonic Stem Cells
- Vertebrate Animals
- Debarment and Suspension
- Drug-Free Workplace
- Lobbying
- Non-Delinquency on Federal Debt

- Research Misconduct
- Civil Rights
- Handicapped Individuals
- Sex Discrimination
- Age Discrimination
- Recombinant DNA and Human Gene Transfer Research
- Financial Conflict of Interest
- Certification of Research Institution Participation[139]

Some of these certifications clearly relate to clinical research, such as the requirement that investigators certify that they will include women and minorities as subjects in clinical research unless there are clear and compelling reasons not to.[140] Other certifications potentially will implicate clinical research as science and technology progress. For instance, grant applicants must certify that they will make physician statements and informed consents available for audit if they research human fetal tissue transplantation.[141] The NIH Grants Policy Statement warns, "Even if a grant is not awarded, the applicant may be subject to penalties if the information contained in or submitted as part of an application, including its certifications and assurances, is found to be false, fictitious, or fraudulent."[142] Moreover, grants for multiyear projects require a continuation grant application, which reiterates the original certifications.[143]

Human Subject Protection

Three grant certifications present a significant current threat of FCA litigation. The NIH grant applicant must take responsibility "for safeguarding the rights and welfare of human subjects in HHS-supported research activities."[144] This requires compliance with HHS's Office for Human Research Protections (OHRP), which has issued regulations for appropriate protection of human subjects. Seventeen executive branch departments and agencies have adopted the "Common Rule," the Federal Policy for the Protection of Human Subjects. The Common Rule "applies to all research involving human subjects" except for a few exempt categories.[145] The Common Rule states, "Each institute engaged in research which is covered by this policy and which is conducted or supported by a Federal Department or Agency shall provide assurance satisfactory to the Department or Agency head that it will comply with the requirements set forth in this policy."[146] This certification requirement also compels the research institution to certify "to the Department or Agency head that the research has been reviewed and approved by an IRB provided for in the assurance, and will be subject to continuing review by the IRB [Institutional Review Board]."[147]

The certification must include a statement of principles governing the institution in the discharge of its responsibilities, "[d]esignation of one or more IRBs established in accordance with the requirements of this policy," and a "list of IRB members" that includes their qualifications and any employment or other relationship with the research institution."[148] Furthermore, the institution must provide written procedures that the IRB will follow in both its initial and continuing review of research as well as its "[w]ritten procedures for ensuring prompt reporting to the IRB."[149] The government agency then may evaluate these certifications and "the adequacy of the proposed IRB."[150] After the agency approves a research institution's assurance, that institution "shall certify that each application or proposal for research covered by the assurance and by § 46.103 of this policy has been reviewed and approved by the IRB."[151] Certification of compliance with the Common Rule is a requirement for beginning human subject research.

An IRB must make sure that the "[r]isks to subjects are minimized" and "reasonable."[152] It also must make sure that subject selection is "equitable" and that the researcher will seek "informed consent" that "will be appropriately documented."[153] The IRB also should make sure that the research plan adequately will monitor "the data collected to ensure the safety of subjects" and will protect "the privacy of subjects" and "confidentiality of data."[154]

The Common Rule requires a certain number of IRB members and requires different backgrounds and nondiscriminatory selection.[155] The IRB shall review informed consent to make sure that the requirements for "legally effective informed consent" are fulfilled.[156] The IRB acts as a backstop as a research project changes to make sure that human subject protections persist, and it may have an increased role for certain vulnerable populations, such as pregnant women, human fetuses, neonates, prisoners, and children.[157] The regulations prohibit the use of federal funds when the Common Rule requirements are not satisfied, and it allows the granting department or agency to terminate or suspend support of research that fails to protect human subjects adequately.[158] Therefore, failure by a clinical researcher to comply with all of the Common Rule's requirements for human subject protection through IRBs actually can lead to FCA liability, because the researcher certified compliance with the relevant regulations as a condition of receiving federal research grant money.

Financial Conflicts of Interest

The second certification implicating the FCA that the grant applicant must make is compliance with financial conflict of interest regulations. HHS considers "anything of monetary value" to be a significant financial interest, with important exceptions such as salary or other remuneration from the applicant research institution and an equity interest that does not exceed $10,000 or five percent ownership.[159] Each grant institution must have an appropriate written and enforced conflict of interest and should require each investigator to list "his/her known Significant Financial Interests (and those of his/her spouse and dependent children)" that the research reasonably appears to affect.[160] The research institution must require updates of financial interests as well.[161] The institution then must designate an official and have him or her identify conflicting interests and manage, reduce, or eliminate them.[162] Institutions need to maintain records for at least three years and establish adequate enforcement and sanctions.[163] Each application for funding to which the regulations apply requires the institution to certify that it has a written, enforced administrative process for conflicts of interests and that it will report and manage, reduce, or eliminate conflicts of interest.[164] Possible methods of dealing with conflicts of interest include public disclosure, monitoring by an independent reviewer, modification of the research plan, disqualification, divestiture of significant financial interests, or severance of relationships.[165]

HHS has released a final guidance on financial relationships and interests in research involving human subjects. This guidance does not bind HHS or change any existing regulations or requirements.[166] However, it combines multiple suggestions to assist in evaluating the presence of possible financial conflicts of interest, such as having institutions segregate responsibility for research activities from management of financial interests and establish conflict of interest committees that communicate clearly with IRBs.[167] It also recommends that investigators consider how to disclose their financial interests to research participants as part of the informed consent process.[168] Avoiding conflicts of interest intersects with the certification of adequate human subject protection because the Common Rule requires IRBs to disallow IRB members to participate if they have "a conflicting interest."[169]

Research Misconduct

Third, the grant applicant must certify that it is complying with the regulations governing research misconduct. The NIH grant requires certification that the institution will comply with the research misconduct regulations, establish policies and procedures incorporating the provisions, and submit an annual report on possible misconduct.[170] The Office of Science and Technology Policy (OSTP) of the Public Health Service published a finalized definition of research misconduct stating that it is "fabrication, falsification, or plagiarism in proposing, performing, or reviewing research, or in reporting research results."[171] This definition has not become effective yet, but it substantially resembles the former version, which is still in effect, and HHS has proposed adopting and incorporating this government-wide definition in its proposed rule on Public Health Service policies on research misconduct.[172] OSTP specifies that honest error or differences of opinion do not constitute research misconduct and that research misconduct requires "intentionally, knowingly, or recklessly" making a "significant departure from accepted practices."[173] Again, the result of these certifications is that the government may take the position that the research misconduct is worse than merely being bad science—that it is a false claim under a government research grant.

Certifications for Use of Grant Funds

Even after the government awards a research grant, the investigator must continue to make certifications throughout the research process. For instance, the investigator has to certify eligibility to receive an award,[174] and the Public Health Service emphasizes that the certifications made during the application process still apply.[175] A successful grant applicant must comply with grant program legislation, program regulations, and the NIH Grants Policy statement.[176]

By accepting federal monies subject to the NIH's standard grant application and notice of grant award, recipients of federal research funds contractually agree to perform certain tasks in exchange for the government's commitment to cover both direct and specific indirect (or facilities and administrative) costs associated with these tasks. Direct costs, including salaries, travel, equipment, and supplies directly benefiting grant-supported projects or activities, are those that "can be identified specifically with a particular sponsored project, an instructional activity, or any other institutional activity."[177] Examples include depreciation and use allowances, operation and maintenance expenses, and certain administration expenses.[178]

In seeking reimbursement for these costs, researchers or their institutions must certify the truth and accuracy of various aspects of their claims in much the same manner that hospitals and other providers of clinical care must generally certify the accuracy of claims for clinical services.[179] Thus, for example, recipients of NIH funds are obligated to certify that "all disbursements have been made for the purpose and conditions of the grant" and that "all outlays and unliquidated obligations are for the purposes set forth in the award documents."[180] They also must certify that indirect costs have been calculated in a manner consistent with federal guidelines and do not include unallowable costs such as the costs of advertising, public relations, entertainment, contributions and donations, fines, penalties, or lobbying.[181] Federal payers generally do not prepay audit and merely process claims. Grant and other federal fund recipients should not assume that federal payment represents a stamp of approval from the government.

Using an awarded grant itself necessitates dozens more certifications, such as the requirement that nonprofit organizations affirm that "the distribution of activity represents a reasonable estimate of the actual work performed by the employee during the period covered by the report" for the purposes of a payroll distribution system for salaries and wages.[182] Another form requires certification "to the best of my knowledge and belief that this report is correct and complete and that all outlays and unliquidated obligations are for the purposes set forth in the award documents."[183] Research institutes receive funds through the NIH Payment Management System and annually reconcile costs and receipts with Financial Status Reports.[184] At the termination of their project, researchers must submit final Financial Status Reports, Final Invention Statements, and certified facilities and administration costs.[185]

NIH has provisions for administrative recovery of misspent grant funds, and much of the enforcement in this area has come from administrative agencies.[186] However, there is no conceptual limitation to whistleblowers who may use a certification FCA theory to go after research fraud.[187]

Administrative Guidance: The National Coverage Decision

CMS and OIG have produced relatively little administrative guidance for compliance with the FCA. Instead, much of the scope of the FCA's impact on clinical research comes from the results of litigation. The most relevant administrative guidance deals with national coverage decisions and payment for health services during the course of a clinical trial.

Clinical Research on Pharmaceuticals

The Antikickback Statute prohibits providers from knowingly and willfully paying for referral of patients covered by federal health care programs. Additionally, the

Civil Monetary Penalty Act disallows "remuneration to any individual eligible for benefits" if the person offering remuneration "knows or should know" that the payment "is likely to influence such individual to order or receive from a particular provider, practitioner, or supplier any item or service for which payment may be made."[188]

The possibility of remuneration to patients leading to prosecution appeared mostly theoretical until September 2000, when the Clinton administration issued a national coverage decision (NCD) that extended Medicare coverage for many items and services to patients in clinical trials.[189] Before the NCD, Medicare's Research Costs Regulation provided that Medicare would not cover medical services provided *solely* as a result of a patient's participation in a research protocol but said that the costs of "usual patient care" were reimbursable where research was conducted in connection with and as a part of the care of patients.[190] The *Medicare Carriers Manual* (MCM) took a somewhat more restrictive view, stating that hospital and medical services "related to and required as a result of services which are not covered under Medicare" are not themselves covered services.[191] Some carriers and intermediaries, in turn, interpreted this instruction to prohibit *any* reimbursement for services related to uncovered—e.g., research—services, regardless of the independent medical necessity of the otherwise covered services. Under these rules, providers were required to identify services, such as laboratory tests, procedures, and physician services that were provided to patients solely because the patients were involved in the research study, and their billing systems had to be configured to exclude these research-only charges from bills to Medicare.[192]

President Clinton directed HHS to "explicitly authorize [Medicare] payment for routine patient care costs . . . and costs due to medical complications associated with participation in clinical trials."[193] Soon after, the Health Care Financing Administration (now CMS) issued a proposed NCD, which was finalized in September 2000. The NCD extends Medicare coverage to routine costs of qualifying clinical trials and then sets out criteria for determining whether different expenses are covered.[194]

The improper provision of remuneration to research subjects may take any number of forms, including the waiver of copayments or deductibles. Generally, it is inappropriate to waive Medicare copayments and deductibles unless the patient has a legitimate financial need. In an advisory opinion issued in July 2000, OIG stated that waivers of Medicare copayments and deductibles in clinical studies "would potentially generate prohibited remuneration under the Antikickback Statute if the requisite intent-to-induce referrals were present."[195] OIG stated, however, that the parties requesting the advisory opinion (clinics and physicians involved in the National Emphysema Treatment Trial sponsored by the Health Care Financing Administration and the National Heart, Lung, and Blood Institute) would not be subject to sanctions because the particular arrangement at issue "reasonably accommodate[d] the needs of an important scientific study sponsored by the Health Care Financing Administration without posing a significant risk of fraud and abuse of the Medicare program."[196] OIG made clear that this opinion addressed "unique circumstances" and that it was not endorsing waivers of Part A or Part B copayments and deductibles in the context of clinical studies generally.[197]

The NCD defines as routine costs "all items and services that are otherwise generally available to Medicare beneficiaries (i.e., there exists a benefit category, it is not statutorily excluded, and there is not a national noncoverage decision) that are provided in either the experimental or the control arms."[198] Routine costs do not include the investigational item or service itself, "items and services provided solely to satisfy data collection and analysis needs and that are not used in the direct clinical management,"[199] and items and services "customarily provided by the research sponsors free of charge for any enrollee in the trial."[200] Therefore, the NCD extends Medicare coverage to "items or services that are typically provided absent a clinical trial (e.g., conventional care), . . . items or services required solely for the provision of the investigational item or service," and "items or services needed for reasonable and necessary care arising from the provision of an investigational item or service—in particular, for the diagnosis or treatment of complications."[201]

To be a qualifying clinical trial, the trial must be evaluating an item or service in a Medicare benefit category. The trial should not test only toxicity or pathophysiology and "must enroll patients with diagnosed disease rather than healthy volunteers."[202] In addition to these necessary factors, clinical trials should have certain desirable characteristics. The trial should test improvement of health outcomes, be scientifically well-supported, be intended to clarify commonly-used interventions, not unjustifiably duplicate other studies, be designed appropriately for the research question, be sponsored by a credible organization or individual, comply with protection of human subject regulations, and adhere to the standards of scientific integrity.[203] CMS presumes that certain trials automatically meet these criteria, such as trials funded by the National Institutes of Health, Centers for Disease Control and Prevention, Agency for Healthcare Research and Quality, CMS, Department of Defense, or the Department of Veterans Affairs.[204] Trials by centers or cooperative groups that these agencies fund also qualify, as do trials conducted under an investigational new drug application to FDA or subject to 21 C.F.R. 312.2(b)(1).[205] Having Medicare cover costs associated with clinical trials while failing to meet the criteria of the NCD opens the door to potential FCA liability. A whistleblower accused New York University of underreporting money received from trial participants' insurers and fraudulently billing Medicare for extended 40- to 60-minute visits instead of the actual 10-minute simple patient visits.[206] Providers were and are prohibited from billing Medicare for the costs of items or services that are already reimbursed by other sources.[207]

An underlying policy concern causes the tension in the rules for compensating patients for their participation. Compensation may undermine autonomous decision making and concern for the dignity of the human body and protection of human subjects. Furthermore, research participants may view the study as having therapeutic value. On the other hand, clinical research provides an indisputable value to society at large, and studies sometimes run into problems with recruitment. OIG is trying to balance these competing concerns with its rules in this area.

Clinical Research on Devices

The Medicare Modernization Act also opens up the door to Antikickback Statute and FCA liability in device research because it covers routine costs associated with certain clinical trials of Category A devices. Specifically, if an individual eligible for Medicare Part A or B enrolls in a Category A clinical trial, Medicare will cover "routine costs of care" in the trial.[208] A Category A clinical trial tests an experimental or investigational medical device for which "initial questions of safety and effectiveness have not been resolved and the FDA is unsure whether the device type can be safe and effective."[209] In a proposed rule, CMS said that for payment of routine costs, the trial must conform to "appropriate scientific and ethical standards."[210] CMS also promised to discuss in a later NCD the requirement that the devices in pre-2000 trials "be intended for use in the diagnosis, monitoring, or treatment of an immediately life-threatening disease or condition."[211] Medicare will cover services "to treat a condition or complication that arises due to the use of a noncovered device or a non-covered device-related service" and "[r]outine care services related to experimental/investigational (Category A) devices. . . and furnished in conjunction with an FDA-approved clinical trial."[212]

Medicare has long covered Category B devices and associated costs as well. CMS defined Category B devices as a nonexperimental/investigational "device believed to be in Class I or Class II, or a device believed to be in Class III for which the incremental risk is the primary risk in question (i.e., underlying questions of safety and effectiveness of that device type have been resolved), or it is known that the device type can be safe and effective because, for example, other manufacturers have obtained FDA approval for that device type."[213] CMS relies on FDA's determination of which category a device falls into, and it provides coverage of a device that falls in Category B and is furnished in a trial in accordance with FDA-approved protocols.[214] However, Medicare will not pay for hospital and medical services related to use of the device that is not covered because CMS "determines the device is not 'reasonable' and 'necessary'. . . or because it is excluded from coverage for other reasons."[215] This includes services in preparation for use of the device, contemporaneous services and services necessary to use of the device, and necessary aftercare. Medicare will pay for service "ordinarily covered by Medicare, to treat a condition or complication that arises because of the use of a noncovered device or from the furnishing of related noncovered services."[216] Therefore, the same Antikickback Statute and FCA considerations raised by the NCD for payments to beneficiaries apply to devices.

Industry Guidance

PhRMA Principles

Several parts of the PhRMA Principles suggest best practices that are relevant to areas of potential FCA liability, especially in light of the false certification theory. The Principles commit to "conduct clinical research in a manner that recognizes the importance of protecting the safety of and respecting research participants."[217] The Principles also affirm the importance of review by an IRB, true informed consent, and open disclosure of the investigator or institution's financial interest in the clinical trial.[218] The research sponsor commits to "receipt and verification of data from all research sites" and says it will "ensure the accuracy and integrity of the entire study database."[219]

The PhRMA Principles deal at length with the issue of conflicts of interest, which they define as a situation where "an investigator's professional judgment could be influenced by a secondary interest, such as a potential financial gain, publication opportunity, career advancement, outside employment, personal considerations or relationships, investments, gifts, payment for services, and board memberships."[220] Although this definition means that there is almost always at least some degree of conflict of interest, physicians should "put patient care above all other concerns."[221] To

avoid conflicts, sponsors "may not use investigators if investigators or their immediate family have a direct ownership interest in the investigational product, and sponsors may not compensate investigators in company stock or stock options."[222]
Sponsors must collect and disclose information on investigators' financial interests
above a certain threshold, but investigators also must meet local standards.[223] Medical journals also may review financial interests, then require disclosure or even reject
publications.[224] Sponsors may manage bias by using double-blind study designs
where neither physician nor patient knows who is receiving which drug.[225] Other
parts of the principles that deal with conflicts of interest overlap with the discussion
for the Antikickback Statute, such as the principle that payment to clinical investigators should not correspond to the outcome of the trial and the requirement that the
investigator and immediate family should not have a direct ownership interest in the
product being researched.[225]

Disclosure Requirements by Journals

Publication in medical journals occupies central importance in any manufacturer's
business strategy. The research process itself makes a few physicians and researchers
aware of the product, but publication to a larger audience disseminates information
about the product and provides legitimacy. Furthermore, journal reprints provide a
crucial means for detailing and disclosing off-label use. Journals have become increasingly concerned about improper relationships between researchers and research sponsors. An article in *The Journal of the American Medical Association* found that over
80 percent of authors involved in writing clinical practice guidelines had some tie to
the pharmaceutical industry.[227] Another area of concern involves conflicts of interest
at medical schools, which often have weaker conflict policies than industry.[228]

Journals have accordingly changed their policies on financial conflicts of interests for authors. For instance, the editors of 11 major journals, including *The Journal
of the American Medical Association* and *The New England Journal of Medicine,*
issued a joint editorial "decrying the diminishing independence of medical
research."[229] The journals now require authors to "reveal details of their own roles
in the clinical research, [explain] the study sponsor's role in the study, and disclose
any conflicts of interest."[230] They also vowed not to publish articles based on studies
where sponsors possessed sole control over data and the power to withhold publication.[231] Additionally, the Nature Publishing Group, which includes the prestigious journal *Nature*, requires contributors of primary research papers, editorials,

commentaries, and review articles to declare their competing financial interests, such as research support and other corporate financing, employment, stock holdings, consultant fees, and patents.[232]

American Medical Association on Conflicts of Interest

In December 2001, the Association of American Medical Colleges issued principles for creating institutional policies regarding financial interests in research conducted by a facility. It recommended that there be a "rebuttable presumption that an individual who holds a significant financial interest in research involving human subjects may not conduct such research . . . whether the research is funded by a public agency, a nonprofit entity, or a commercial sponsor, and wherever the research may be carried out."[233] A conflicted researcher may participate if circumstances are "compelling," but the risk is greatest if the "financial interest is directly related to the research."[234] Institutions should require prior reporting of financial interests and have the IRB review those interests before final approval of the project.[235]

Arrangements Prosecuted under the FCA

Misuse of Grant Funds

A false claim in the clinical research context may be as simple as lying about the use of government funds. For instance, the University of Connecticut settled an FCA suit in 1997 for $1.3 million because it allegedly falsely represented to the federal government that it operated a joint medical and dental fellowship program when in fact there were no joint rotations.[236] The Beth Israel Deaconess Medical Center in Boston agreed to pay $920,000 to settle a FCA suit in 1999 for allegedly accepting fraudulent federal research grants for three years.[237] The principal investigator listed on the grant application left the country before the initial grant was made, and the Medical Center allegedly accepted grant money after that time and used it for other research projects.[238] Thomas Jefferson University agreed in 2000 to pay $2.6 million to settle a whistleblower's false claim allegations. One of the allegations stated that the University applied for NIH funding under the name of a prominent researcher, promising a certain percentage of effort over three years.[239] However, the named investigator had moved to Italy and did not do the research, and the University failed to inform the government and also allegedly charged salaries on the grant for postdoctoral fellows who did not work on the related research.[240]

In 1997, New York University Medical Center settled a FCA suit for $15.5 million.[241] The *qui tam* relator, a former employee, alleged that the Medical Center submitted fraudulent information to the federal government in connection with indirect costs relating to a federal research grant.[242] Among the allegedly fraudulent claims submitted were dollar amounts for voluntary cost sharing, which were much lower than amounts found in the Medical Center's internal documents.[243] Additionally, the Medical Center allegedly submitted duplicate claims for the same utility costs and for certain environmental service costs.[244] The complaint also alleged that the Medical Center sought federal reimbursement for noncovered expenses, including entertainment.[245] That same year, the University of Chicago settled FCA charges because it allegedly misapplied grant funds by "improperly charging salaries, computer maintenance, telephone calls, and equipment to the grant account."[246]

In 1998, the University of Minnesota agreed to pay the federal government $32 million to settle a FCA suit.[247] The government alleged that the University illegally profited from the sale of an unlicensed drug, failed to report those earnings to the National Institutes of Health, and misused federal grant money.[248] The University allegedly inflated billing to 29 federal grants by charging salaries and supplies to the grants for employees who did not work on those projects and by charging for supplies not used by those projects.[249] Similarly, Northwestern agreed to pay $5.5 million in 2003 to settle charges that "the university knowingly failed to comply with federal government requirements that a specified percentage of the researchers' effort be devoted to a grant."[250] This wrongful "effort reporting" took place both during the grant proposal and implementation stages.[251]

In 2004, Johns Hopkins University agreed to pay the federal government $2.6 million to settle an FCA action.[252] The government alleged that Johns Hopkins Bayview Medical Center fraudulently obtained federal grant money by overstating the percentage of work effort researchers would devote to the project and the percentage of effort that personnel actually did devote to the project.[253] It also alleged that Johns Hopkins applied various fringe benefit rates against the grants erroneously.[254]

Notably, some of the aforementioned settlement agreements contain provisions requiring the research institution to implement a compliance program or to make necessary corrective changes to an existing compliance program.[255] In other cases, the research institutions voluntarily implemented changes in their compliance and oversight programs.[256]

Breakdowns in Human Subject Protection

Prominent cases have highlighted the dangers associated with clinical research trials and have spurred litigation on failure to protect human subjects. The media attention over certain breakdowns in protection has given this issue great political significance as well. A House panel scolded the FDA for breakdowns in protections for human research participants in 1998, the same year that OIG found "'disturbing inadequacies" in IRB oversight.[257] HHS found only minimal progress in 2000.[258]

Several well-known clinical research mishaps have shown that FCA allegations over false certification of appropriate research protections or conflict of interest screening could engender a significant amount of litigation. In 1999, a teenager died in a gene therapy clinical trial at the University of Pennsylvania. The hospital settled the case after the plaintiffs charged failure "to provide proper care," failure "to obtain his informed consent," strict product liability, infliction of emotional distress, fraud, and fraudulent representations to the FDA.[259] The Gelsinger complaint used a tort cause of action, intentional assault and battery with lack of informed consent.[260] It also alleged common law fraud because of failure to disclose risks and misrepresentation of the possible benefits of participation.[261] Furthermore, the hospital and physicians conducting the study had various financial interests that they failed to disclose; these interests included stock in a company, a research grant from that company to the university, and patents.[262] The complaint alleged that despite all of these interests, the university allowed the experiment to continue, and the IRB approved the protocol.[263] A whistleblower faced with the same set of facts would lack standing for these causes of action and would have to resort to an FCA theory.

A second high-profile case occurred at Johns Hopkins when a healthy young volunteer died after inhaling hexamethonium. OHRP found that the IRB failed to investigate hexamethonium before approving the research and did not review changes to the research protocol.[264] The IRB also approved an inadequate informed consent document, allowed IRB members to participate in review of protocols in which they had a conflicting interest, and was overburdened.[265] As a result, OHRP ordered Johns Hopkins to suspend all federally-supported research projects.[266] Johns Hopkins settled with the research participant's family outside of court.[267]

Another illustrative case involved melanoma vaccine research at the University of Oklahoma in Tulsa. OHRP halted all human trials at the center, alleging problems with the vaccine tested, overenrollment of participants, failure to follow protocol, improper substitution of nonphysicians, enrollment subjects who failed IRB criteria, failure to attain informed consent, and lack of oversight by the IRB.[268] Even studies conducted by the federal government have raised issues of patient protection, such as a suit against Veterans Affairs researchers who allegedly altered medical records and tests to enroll patients "in drug studies for which they would not otherwise have qualified."[269] The study resulted in manslaughter charges against a research assistant.[270]

Fraud in Obtaining and Continuing Grants

A few cases have examined the possibility that false statements intended to secure approval of a grant application could support an FCA claim for false certification. The first scientific fraud case settled under federal whistleblower laws involved the accusation that various defendants "made false statements on grant applications and status reports to the National Institutes of Health."[271] Eventually, the University of California system and the University of Utah agreed to pay almost $1.6 million to settle the charges.[272] Another relator won in district court but lost on appeal after alleging research misconduct. She alleged that the defendants had made false statements in their annual progress report by claiming her work as theirs, misrepresenting the amount of data that had been computerized, and including plagiarized work.[273] In the Thomas Jefferson University case, the University allegedly falsely claimed during the application process that one investigator would be doing the work, falsely promised a percentage of time he would devote to the project, and submitted false or fabricated data to obtain funding.[274]

A top obesity researcher at the University of Vermont, Eric T. Poehlman, recently admitted to fabricating results in 17 federal grant applications. As a result of his plea agreement with federal prosecutors for criminal fraud, Poehlman "will be barred for life from receiving funding, pay back $180,000, and plead guilty to a criminal charge of fraud that could bring jail time. He agreed to ask scientific journals to retract and correct 10 articles they published by him." The director of the Office of Research Integrity described Poehlman's conduct as "the most serious case of research fraud since a mid-1980s investigation." As a result of his grant applications, Poehlman received almost $3 million in federal funding.[275]

The Supreme Court upheld a whistleblower's right to sue a county as a "person" under the FCA when she accused the research institute of submitting "false statements to obtain grant funds in violation of § 3729(a)(1)."[276] The relator also accused the defendants of violating "the grant's express conditions," failure "to comply with the regulations on human-subject research," and false submission of reports on "'ghost'" research subjects.[277]

In addition to charges associated with payments made by government entities, physicians who create false research data to receive payments from private pharmaceutical companies have faced criminal charges of mail fraud and false statements.[278] If the data the physician falsified will ultimately be submitted to the FDA as part of the drug approval process, the physician could also face charges for defrauding the government.

In 2000, OIG entered into its first "Institutional Integrity Agreement" (akin to a "Corporate Integrity Agreement") with an institution accused of research-related fraud.[279] The core of the agreement involves a requirement that the institution implement a compliance program "to prevent fraud, false statements or misspending of funds related to HHS grants, contracts and cooperative agreements."[280] Among other obligations, the institution must maintain or establish policies and procedures concerning the submission of accurate and appropriate claims and data retention, and must provide training on various aspects of grants management.[281]

Certifications for Drug Approval

Manufacturers who submit an application for drug approval to the FDA make multiple certifications as well. In fact, there is substantial overlap for FDA and federal grant certifications, with the difference being how the FCA applies. Under fraud-on-the-FDA theories, plaintiffs argue that false statements to the FDA result in a drug being approved when it should not have. The result of that approval is inevitably the use of federal funds to pay for the product, resulting in a potential indirect application of the FCA.

FDA requires certification of financial disclosure by anyone submitting a marketing application.[282] The applicant must list "all clinical investigators who conducted covered clinical studies" and identify any who are employees.[283] The applicant also must "completely and accurately disclose or certify information concerning the financial interests of a clinical investigator" who is not an employee.[284] Furthermore, clinical investigators subject to the investigational new drug or device exemptions must provide the study sponsor with enough information to allow subsequent disclosure.[285] For each clinical investigator, the applicant must submit a form and disclose or, if appropriate, certify the absence of certain financial arrangements, including compensation affected by study outcome, significant equity interest, proprietary interest in the product, or a significant payment of greater than $25,000 exclusive of study costs.[286]

In addition to these financial disclosures, a manufacturer submitting a new drug application must certify that if the FDA approves the application, it will comply with "all applicable laws and regulations."[287] These may include good manufacturing practices, biological establishment standards, labeling regulations, prescription drug advertising regulations, regulations for making changes in application, regulations on reports, and local, state, and federal environmental impact laws.[288] Furthermore, the data and information in the application must be "reviewed" and "certified to be true and accurate."[289]

A manufacturer who wants to disseminate information on unapproved and new uses and has not submitted a supplemental application for the new use must certify that it "has completed the studies needed for the submission of a supplemental application for [insert new use] and will submit a supplemental application."[290] Alternatively, if those studies are in the planning stage, the manufacturer must certify that it "will exercise due diligence to complete the clinical studies necessary."[291] A manufacturer filing an application for FDA approval to market a new drug must certify patent information and the relevant financial disclosures.[292] Device manufacturers also have certifications related to their application process.[293] An investigational drug exemption application must contain a certification that all the participating investigators have signed agreements and a certification for each IRB asked to review the investigation.[294]

An investigator filing in compliance with an investigational new drug application must commit to conducting the study in accordance with protocol, personally conducting or supervising the investigation, obtaining informed consent, and reporting adverse events.[295] The investigator also promises to understand information about the drug, inform others of their obligations, and maintain accurate records.[296] The clinical investigator must ensure that an IRB compliant with FDA regulations reviews the investigation and pledges to report all changes in research activity and unanticipated problems.[297]

Fraud-on-the-FDA theories represent an emerging field in fraud and abuse law, with some early cases already providing some precedent. Because certifications to the FDA mirror those made in other fraud and abuse areas, whistleblowers have an incentive to report noncompliant submissions. Lifescan, a device manufacturing subsidiary of Johnson & Johnson, pleaded guilty to misdemeanor charges and paid $60 million in civil and criminal penalties in 2000.[298] In settling the *qui tam* suit, Lifescan admitted to "introducing into interstate commerce a misbranded medical device, failing to furnish appropriate notifications and information to the Food and Drug

Administration, and submitting false and misleading reports to the FDA."[299] Lifescan also conceded that it failed to tell customers of two defects in a device, failed to file reports of the illnesses and injuries with the FDA, and filed reports with "false, incomplete, or misleading information in that they failed to disclose the existence of either the error-message defect or incomplete strip insertion problem."[300] In a similar whistleblower case, a dental product manufacturer paid $600,000 to settle allegations that it failed to report complaints about one of its devices to the FDA.[301] This case proceeded on a certification theory because failure to report complaints as required under the Food, Drug and Cosmetic Act and implementing regulations "resulted in the submission of false claims to the Veterans Administration and Defense Department because [the company's] government contracts required it to comply with all FDA statutes and regulations."[302]

Endovascular Technologies, a subsidiary of Guidant, entered a guilty plea and agreed to pay $92.4 million in criminal fees and a civil settlement because of multiple FDA violations in its sale of a medical device.[303] The civil agreement settled allegations that Endovascular's actions "caused Medicare, Medicaid, and the Veterans Affairs Program to pay millions of dollars for the adulterated and misbranded devices."[304] Endovascular admitted to one felony count of false statements to a federal agency and nine felony counts of shipping misbranded medical devices in interstate commerce.[305] The defendant knew that its representatives were encouraging use of the device in an off-label manner and failed to inform the FDA and file a Pre-market Approval Application supplement.[306] Instead, the company continued to discuss with doctors a technique that had not been tested and that doctors had not been trained on. The company failed to train its sales representatives on the technique and alter the instructions for use.[307] Only a letter from seven anonymous employees alerted the FDA to investigate, and Endovascular eventually admitted that it had failed to file over 2,600 medical device reports.[308] Another recent case focuses on a different FDA regulatory violation, with a relator alleging that 28 pharmaceutical companies "defrauded the United States government by selling products to the United States and its instrumentalities that were not manufactured in full compliance with FDA Current Good Manufacturing Process, and were therefore adulterated."[309]

Several allegations in the Neurontin case also discuss fraud on the FDA in off-label promotional practices. The relator claimed that Parke-Davis "knew or should have known that pharmacists and physicians would routinely and necessarily file false claims with the government when they sought federal reimbursement for Neurontin prescriptions."[310] The FDA permitted discussion of off-label uses only through distribution of published articles, objective continuing medical education meetings, and in response to physician requests. Parke-Davis allegedly implemented a scheme to undermine this regulatory regime at every level. It hired "nonphysician technical writers to create articles for medical journals and then paid actual specialists to be the articles' 'authors.'"[311] Parke-Davis allegedly had ghostwriters prepare at least twenty articles on "off-label usage of Neurontin" as evidence of "independent research."[312] Furthermore, Parke-Davis submitted to the FDA a list of studies on pain, pain syndromes, and psychiatric disorders that failed to include the research from grants alleged to be kickbacks because it knew the research "had no scientific value and would not be deemed to be studies by the FDA."[313]

The manufacturer also "provided written abstracts of the presentations that detailed off-label use of Neurontin to each of its 'consultants' despite "the FDA's prohibition regarding the provision of promotional materials on off-label uses."[314] Furthermore, Parke-Davis trained its liaisons "to aggressively solicit requests for off-label information from physicians."[315] All of these deceptive practices may implicate the FCA because fooling the FDA into thinking that promotion of off-label use is appropriate and enjoys significant scientific support is a prerequisite for claims paid out by Medicare and Medicaid: "deliberate disregard of FDA regulations concerning off-label promotion" was part of a system "to cause ineligible claims to be submitted to Medicaid."[316]

In a case where the plaintiff has standing, he or she may utilize the fraud on the FDA theory that appears in the Gelsinger complaint.[317] The complaint did not focus on the false claims nature of the fraud but instead applied a tort cause of action, alleging that the violations of FDA guidelines and fraudulent misrepresentations led to the FDA's approval of the experiment.[318] Gelsinger accused the defendants of removing mention of prior bad results and falsely promising to report adverse events to the FDA.[319] Gelsinger then alleged that the fraud was a prerequisite for FDA approval, which was a critical step that triggered a chain of causation leading to the research subject's death.[320]

Future Enforcement Areas

Fraud and abuse in clinical research will remain an active area in the law for the foreseeable future. States may look to fraud and abuse cases to recoup health care costs during budget shortfalls, and state actions under various consumer protection, state false claims acts, and state antikickback statutes may increase.[321] James Sheehan, the Associate U.S. Attorney for the Eastern District of Pennsylvania and one of the most active prosecutors in health care fraud and abuse, said that areas of concern include improper recruitment, "false or forged consent forms, failure to disclose to patients the risks of a study, and false statements to subjects to induce them to participate."[322] Sheehan also warned that secret payments for recruitment and investigators' failure to inform patients of their conflicts of interest will draw scrutiny.[323] Other areas of emphasis include fraudulent billing and "ghostwriting, gag clauses, and prior approval clauses."[324]

HIPAA compliance also may become an issue in fraud and abuse cases related to clinical research. The Office of Human Research Protections (OHRP) and FDA require IRBs to make "adequate provisions to protect the privacy of subjects and to maintain the confidentiality of data."[325] The HIPAA rules are different because they involve disclosure of information, not participation in a trial. Furthermore, the HIPAA privacy regulations apply to all providers of health care, meaning that clinical research that does not involve federal grants or submission to the FDA must still satisfy the regulations. Patients must authorize the full use or disclosure of the protected health information for clinical research that involves provision of care,[326] but IRBs or privacy boards may waive that authorization for "minimal risk" studies.[327] Furthermore, information that has been de-identified may always be used for research.[328] The FCA could become a tool for HIPAA enforcement depending on the certifications that apply to a provider submitting a claim for reimbursement. In fact, class action suits involving groups of patients who suffered improper disclosure of their protected health information may be on the horizon.

Conclusion

Fraud and abuse issues in clinical research are an important and still-growing field, especially with the possibility of large awards to relators. At almost every stage of the research process, sponsors and investigators must recognize and obey the relevant statutory and regulatory requirements. As use of the Antikickback Statute and FCA has evolved, an increasing number of aspects of research have fallen under their reach. The potentially devastating impact of the damages under these statutes has contributed to the large number of settlements in this area, which emphasizes the necessity for sponsors and investigators to carefully plan and monitor their research projects from start to finish.

Notes and References

1   *See generally* "Federal Research Grant Fraud a Growing Issue for Federal Enforcers, Researchers," 9 *Health L. Rep.* (BNA) 1695 (Nov. 7, 2000); "Prosecutor Details Potential Concerns for Sponsors of Clinical Studies of Drugs," 8 *Health Care Fraud Rep.* (BNA) 11 (Jan. 7, 2004); Paul E. Kalb & Kristin Graham Koehler, "Legal Issues in Scientific Research," 287 *JAMA* 85 (2002).

2   Kalb & Koehler, *supra* note 1 at 86, *citing* US General Accounting Office, "Health Insurance: Vulnerable Payors Lose Billions to Fraud and Abuse," Washington, D.C.: U.S. General Accounting Office (1992).

3   42 U.S.C. § 1320a-7b (2004); 31 U.S.C. §§ 3729 et seq. (2004).

4   42 U.S.C. § 1320a-7b(b) (2004).

5   See *id.* This includes recommending to purchase, lease, or order an item or service.

6   *Id.*

7   *Id.*

8   Pub. L. No. 105-33, 111 Stat. 384, § 4304(b)(1)(c) (Aug. 5, 1997).

9   *Id.*

10 Press Release, Office of Inspector General, "OIG and Tenet Healthcare Corporation Reach Divestiture Agreement to Address Exclusion of Redding Medical Center" (Dec. 11, 2003), *at* http://oig.hhs.gov/publications/docs/press/2003/121103release.pdf.

11 See *id.*

12 *United States v. Kats,* 871 F.2d 105, 108 (9th Cir. 1989); *United States v. Greber,* 760 F.2d 68, 71 (3rd Cir. 1985).

13 Greber, 760 F.2d at 71.

14 See *id.* at 70.

15 *Id.* at 71.

16 *Id.* at 71.

17 *United States v. Bay State Ambulance and Hospital Rental Service, Inc.,* 874 F.2d 20, 30 (1st Cir. 1989) (emphasis in original).

18 See *id.* at 33 n.21, 33–34.

19 42 U.S.C. § 1320a-7b (b) (2004); Health Law & Business Portfolio: Fraud & Abuse, § 1500.01(C) *at* http://healthlaw.bna.com.

20 42 U.S.C. § 1320a-7b (b) (2004); Health Law & Business Portfolio: Fraud & Abuse, § 1500.01(C) *at* http://healthlaw.bna.com.

21 Paul E. Kalb & Scott Bass, "Government Investigations in the Pharmaceutical Industry: Off-Label Promotion, Fraud and Abuse, and False Claims," 53 *Food and Drug L.J.* 63 (1998).

22 Jill Wechsler, "Fraud, Abuse, and Consent: Federal Prosecutors Target Sponsors and Clinical Investigators . . ." 5 *Applied Clinical Trials* 1 (May 1, 2002).

23 56 Fed. Reg. 35,954, 35,958 (1991) ("Because the statute is so broad, the payment practices described in these safe harbor provisions would be prohibited by the statute but for their inclusion here.").

24 See 45 C.F.R. § 1001.952(d).

25 56 Fed. Reg. 35,954.

26 *Id.*

27 Publication of OIG Special Fraud Alerts, 59 Fed. Reg. 65,372 (Dec. 19, 1994).

28 *Id.* at 65,373.

29 *Id.*

30 Publication of OIG Special Fraud Alerts, 59 Fed. Reg. 65,372, 65,376 (Dec. 19, 1994).

31 *Id.*

32 *Id.*

33 *Id.*

34 *Id.*

35 *Id.* See also Mark Barnes & Sara Krauss, "Conflicts of Interest in Human Research: Risks and Pitfalls of 'Easy Money' in Research Funding," 9 *Health L. Rep.* (BNA) 1378 (Aug. 31, 2000) (stating that the Antikickback Statute prohibits compensation from sponsors who provide health care services or products to investigators for their research, if the compensation is intended to induce the investigator to buy drugs or services from the sponsor which will be reimbursed by a federal health care program).

36 Publication of OIG Special Fraud Alerts, 59 Fed. Reg. 65,372, 65,376 (Dec. 19, 1994).

37 *Id.*

38 *Id.*

39 *Id.* See also Karine Morin et al., "Managing Conflicts of Interest in the Conduct of Clinical Trials," 287 *JAMA* 78, 81 (2002) (stating that receiving a fee simply for referring a patient to a research study is unethical according to the American Medical Association Council on Ethical and Judicial Affairs).

40 Publication of OIG Special Fraud Alerts, 59 Fed. Reg. 65,376 (Dec. 19, 1994).

41 OIG Compliance Program Guidance for Pharmaceutical Manufacturers, 68 Fed. Reg. 23,731 (May 5, 2003).

42 OIG Compliance Program Guidance for Pharmaceutical Manufacturers, 68 Fed. Reg. at 23,734.

43 *Id.*

44 *Id.*

45 See *id.*

46 See *id.*

47 See *id.*

48 *Id.*

49 *Id.* at 23,735.

50 *Id.*

51 *Id.* at 23,735.

52 *Id.*

53 *Id.*

54 *Id.* at 23,736.

55 *Id.* at 23,736.

56 *Id.* at 23,736.

57 *Id.* at 23,738.

58 *Id.*

59 See *id.*

60 *Id.* at 23,738.

61 See *id.*

62 OIG Compliance Program Guidance for Pharmaceutical Manufacturers, 68 Fed. Reg. 23,731, 23,737 (May 5, 2003).

63 See Press Release, PhRMA, "Quick Facts: A Q&A on PhRMA's Principles on Conduct of Clinical Trials and Communication of Clinical Trial Results" (June 30, 2004), *at* http://www.phrma.org/publications/quickfacts/24.06.2002.429.cfm.

64 PhRMA, "PhRMA Principles on Conduct of Clinical Trials and Communication of Clinical Trial Results" 7 (revised June 30, 2004) [hereinafter "PhRMA Principles"], *at* http://www.phrma.org/publications/publications//2004-06-30.1035.pdf.

65 PhRMA Principles at 15.

66 PhRMA Principles at 15.

67 PhRMA Principles at 15.

68 PhRMA Principles at 16.

69 PhRMA Principles at 17.

70 PhRMA Principles at 17.

71 PhRMA Principles at 20.

72 PhRMA Principles at 9.

73 PhRMA Principles at 13–14.

74 PhRMA Principles at 15.

75 Appendix, PhRMA Principles at 25.

76 See 45 C.F.R. § 1001.952(a).

77 PhRMA Principles at 15.

78 hRMA Principles at 9, 15.

79 Appendix, PhRMA Principles at 43.

80 OIG Compliance Program Guidance for Pharmaceutical Manufacturers, 68 Fed. Reg. 23,731, 23,737 (May 5, 2003).

81 68 Fed. Reg. 23,737.

82 PhRMA Code on Interactions with Healthcare Professionals 19 (Apr. 19, 2002) [hereinafter "PhRMA Code"], *at* http://www.phrma.org/publications/policy//2004-01-19.391.pdf.

83 PhRMA Code at 11. Not all of these factors may be relevant for all arrangements.

84 PhRMA Code at 38.

85 *Id.*

86 AdvaMed, Code of Ethics on Interactions with Health Care Professionals 3 (Sept. 5, 2003), *at* http://www.advamed.org/publicdocs/code_of_ethics.pdf.

87 AdvaMed, Code of Ethics on Interactions with Health Care Professionals 4.

88 AdvaMed, Code of Ethics on Interactions with Health Care Professionals 4.

89 AdvaMed, Code of Ethics on Interactions with Health Care Professionals 4.

90 AdvaMed, Code of Ethics on Interactions with Health Care Professionals 4.

91 AdvaMed, Code of Ethics on Interactions with Health Care Professionals 10–11.

92 AdvaMed, Code of Ethics on Interactions with Health Care Professionals 11.

93 See Kalb & Kohler, *supra* note 1, at 89.

94 *Id.* (stating that a payment is improper under the Antikickback Statute if it does not reflect the actual value of a legitimate service rendered by the investigator).

95 42 U.S.C. § 1320a-7b (b)(1) (2004).

96   56 Fed. Reg. 35,978 (July 29, 1991).

97   56 Fed. Reg. 35,978 (July 29, 1991).

98   Free Computers, Facsimile Machines and Other Goods (July 3, 1997) *at* www.oig.hhs.gov/fraud/docs/safeharborregulations/freecomputers.htm (last visited June 23, 2004).

99   *Id.* The OIG goes on to state that they believe that many of these types of arrangements are merely shams, where there is no substantial business need for the equipment as well as no attempt to ensure that equipment is used solely for business purposes. *Id.*

100   *In re Caremark Int'l Inc.,* 698 A.2d 959, 960 (Del. Ch. 1996).

101   *Id.* at 964.

102   Press Release, Department of Justice, "Warner-Lambert to Pay $430 Million to Resolve Criminal & Civil Health Care Liability Relating to Off-label Promotion" (May 13, 2004), *at* http://www.usdoj.gov/opa/pr/2004/May/04_civ_322.htm.

103   Complaint ¶¶ 24–31, *United States ex rel. Franklin v. Parke-Davis,* No. 96-11651-PBS (D. Mass. filed July 31, 2001).

104   See *id.* at ¶¶ 33, 37–38.

105   *Id.* at ¶ 40.

106   *Id.* at ¶ 41.

107   *Id.* at ¶¶ 43, 47.

108   See *id.* at ¶ 70.

109   Complaint ¶¶ 10-12, *United States ex. rel. Durand v. TAP Holdings, Inc.* (May 6, 1996).

110   Complaint ¶¶ 38-39, *United States of America ex rel. Gerstein v. TAP Holdings, Inc.* (Mar. 26, 1998).

111   HCFA, Medicare and Medicaid Programs: Physicians' Referrals to Health Care Entities with Which They Have Financial Relationships, 66 Fed. Reg. 856, 917 (2001) ("All money paid to a referring physician for research must be used solely to support *bona fide* research. We are concerned that research funding could be used to disguise additional payments for referrals."); see also Morin et al., *supra* note 38 at 79 (stating that "even if recruiting physicians were not involved in conducting the trials, they were offered financial incentives simply to refer patients to investigators.").

112   *Id.* The authors note that finder's fees can reach several thousand dollars per patient, an amount that has the potential to sway a physician's judgment. See Morin, *supra* note 39, at 79. One recent report claims that a pharmaceutical manufacturer paid investigators $1,610 for each patient enrolled in the study, part of which covered the study expenses and part of which would go to the investigators as profit. Kurt Eichenwald & Gina Kolata, "Drug Trials Hide Conflicts for Doctors," *N.Y. Times,* May 16, 1999, at A1.

113   Morin, *supra* note 39, at 81 (citation omitted).

114   Publication of OIG Special Fraud Alerts, 59 Fed. Reg. 65,376 (Dec. 19, 1994) (stating that payment may be improper under the Antikickback Statute if it is "unrelated to any service at all other than referral of patients").

115   Ashley Wazana, "Physicians and Pharmaceutical Industry: Is a Gift Ever Just a Gift?", 283 *JAMA* 373, 375 (2000) (concluding that gifts from pharmaceutical manufacturers do correlate with increased rates of prescription of the manufacturer's products).

116   Studies have shown that if an investigator has a financial interest in a sponsor company, the research is of lower quality, the results are more likely to favor the sponsor's product and are less likely to be published. Catherine D. DeAngelis, "Conflict of Interest and the Public Trust," 284 *JAMA* 2237, 2238 (2000).

117 Publication of OIG Special Fraud Alerts, 59 Fed. Reg. 65,376 (Dec. 19, 1994). In the Fraud Alert, the OIG discussed a "frequent flier" campaign as an example of problematic activity. *Id*. In that case, physicians were given credit for airline frequent flier miles every time they completed a survey for a new patient for which they had prescribed the manufacturer's product. *Id*. Another commentator has noted that "gifts or travel offered to those in a position to decide whether or not a particular product will be used in a research protocol and perhaps billed to Medicare or Medicaid" may violate the Antikickback Statute. "Federal Research Grant Fraud a Growing Issue for Federal Enforcers, Researchers," 9 *Health L. Rep.* (BNA) 1695 (Nov. 7, 2000).

118 42 U.S.C. § 1320a-7b (b)(1)(B) (2004); *see also* Barnes, *supra* note 35.

119 OIG, Revised OIG Civil Money Penalties Resulting from Public Law 104-191, 65 Fed. Reg. 24400, 24401 (2000).

120 65 Fed. Reg. 24415. One exception is waiver of co-insurance and deductible if the waiver is not part of any advertisement or solicitation. This type of waiver is not routine, and there is a good faith determination that the individual cannot pay or payment cannot be collected after a good faith effort. It is also permissible to have a waiver of co-insurance and deductible that complies with a safe harbor to the Antikickback Statute. Disclosed differentials in co-insurance and deductibles may be part of a plan design, and proportional, noncash incentives for preventative care also are exempted.

121 OIG, Solicitation of Public Comments on Exceptions Under Section 1128A(a)(5) of the Social Security Act, 67 Fed. Reg. 72892, 72893–72894 (2002).

122 67 Fed. Reg. 72893.

123 Kalb & Koehler, *supra* note 1 at 86.

124 31 U.S.C. § 3729(a) (2004).

125 31 U.S.C. § 3729(b) (2004).

126 *Id.*; see also Paul E. Kalb, "Health Care Fraud and Abuse," 282 *JAMA* 1163, 1164 (1999).

127 31 U.S.C. § 3729(a) (2004); 28 C.F.R. § 85.3(a)(9) (2001).

128 31 U.S.C. § 3730(d)(2) (2004). If the government chooses to intervene in the action, then the relator's recovery is limited to 25 percent. 31 U.S.C. § 3730(d)(1) (2004).

129 *See United States v. Nazon,* 940 F.2d 255, 260 (7th Cir. 1991), interpreting 18 U.S.C. § 287.

130 *See* Robert Fabrikant et al., Health Care Fraud: Enforcement and Compliance § 4.01[2] (2004).

131 Kalb & Koehler, *supra* note 1 at 85.

132 *See* "Johns Hopkins to Pay $2.6 Million to Settle Claims on Research Grants," 8 *Health Care Fraud Rep.* (BNA) 191 (Mar. 3, 2004).

133 Kalb, *supra* note 19 at 1164; *Barrett v. Columbia/HCA Healthcare Corp.*, 251 F.Supp.2d 28, 32 (D.D.C. 2003).

134 Wechsler, *supra* note 14 at 1; Mark Barnes & Sara Krauss, "Research Issues Take Center Stage in Compliance Process," 8 *Health Care Fraud Rep.* (BNA) 1344 (Aug. 12, 1999). Generally, "reimbursement" deals with payment for treatment and services, while "grants" cover research and related administration costs.

135 See Barnes, *supra* note 35.

136 *United States ex rel. Thompson v. Columbia/HCA Healthcare Corp.,* 125 F.3d 899, 902 (5th Cir. 1997).

137 See *id.*

138 *United States ex rel. Thompson v. Columbia/HCA Healthcare Corp.,* 20 F.Supp.2d 1017, 1041-42 (S.D. Tex. 1998).

139 HHS, Public Health Service Grant Application (PHS 398), OMB No. 0925-0001, 9-10 (2004), *at* ftp://ftp.grants.nih.gov/forms/phs398.pdf.

140 *Id.* at 46–47.

141 *Id.* at 46.

142 NIH, NIH Grants Policy Statement 24 (2003), *at* http://grants.nih.gov/grants/policy/nihgps_2003/nihgps_2003.pdf.

143 See PHS Form 2590, *at* http://grants.nih.gov/grants/funding/2590/2590.htm.

144 HHS, Public Health Service Grant Application (PHS 398) at 46.

145 45 C.F.R. § 46.101(a) (2001). The exempt categories include research conducted in established or commonly accepted educational settings; research involving the use of educational tests, survey procedures, interviews, or observation of public behavior; research involving the collection or study of existing data or specimens; research conducted by or subject to the approval of Department or Agency heads to evaluate public benefit or service programs; and taste and food quality evaluation and consumer acceptance studies. See 45 C.F.R. § 46.101(b).

146 45 C.F.R. § 46.103(a).

147 45 C.F.R. § 46.103(b).

148 45 C.F.R. § 46.103(b)(1)–(3).

149 45 C.F.R. § 46.103(b)(4)–(5).

150 45 C.F.R. § 46.103(d).

151 45 C.F.R. § 46.103(f).

152 45 C.F.R. § 46.111(a)(1)–(2).

153 45 C.F.R. § 46.111(a)(3)–(5).

154 45 C.F.R. § 46.111(a)(6)–(7).

155 45 C.F.R. § 46.107(a)–(b).

156 45 C.F.R. § 46.109(b); see 45 C.F.R. § 46.116 for the general requirements for informed consent.

157 See 45 C.F.R. § 46.118–19, 45 C.F.R. §§ 46.201–46.409.

158 See 45 C.F.R. §§ 46.122–23.

159 HHS, Responsibility of Applicants for Promoting Objectivity in Research for Which PHS Funding Is Sought, 42 C.F.R. § 50.603 (2000). Those exceptions include salary or other remuneration from the applicant institution; an ownership interest in the institution if it is applying under the Small Business Innovation Research Program; income from seminars, lectures, teaching engagements, or service on advisory committees or review panels for public or nonprofit entities; an equity interest that does not exceed $10,000 or a five percent interest for the investigator and his or her immediate family; and other payments for the investigator and immediate family that do not exceed $10,000 for the year.

160 42 C.F.R. § 50.604(a)–(c).

161 42 C.F.R. § 50.604(c).

162 42 C.F.R. § 50.604(b)–(d).

163 42 C.F.R. § 50.604(e)–(f).

164 42 C.F.R. § 50.604(g).

165 42 C.F.R. § 50.605.

166 HHS, Final Guidance, Financial Relationships and Interests in Research Involving Human Subjects: Guidance for Human Subject Protection 2, May 5, 2004, *at* http://www.hhs.gov/ohrp/humansubjects/finreltn/fguid.pdf.

167 *Id.* at 7.

168 *Id.* at 9.

169 45 C.F.R. § 46.107(e).

170 Grant Application PHS 398 at 51.

171 OSTP, Notification of Final Policy, 65 Fed. Reg. 76260, 76262 (Dec. 6, 2000).

172 HHS, Public Health Service Policies on Research Misconduct, 69 Fed. Reg. 20777, 20779 (Apr. 16, 2004).

173 65 Fed. Reg. 76262. Fabrication is "making up data or results and recording or reporting them," falsification is "manipulating research materials, equipment, or processes, or changing or omitting data or results such that the research is not accurately represented," and plagiarism is "appropriation of another person's ideas, processes, results, or words without giving appropriate credit." *Id.*

174 NIH, NIH Grants Policy Statement 34 (2003), *at* http://grants.nih.gov/grants/policy/nihgps_2003/nihgps_2003.pdf.

175 *Id.* at 37–38.

176 NIH, NIH Grants Policy Statement at 35–36.

177 See Office of Management and Budget, Cost Principles for Educational Institutions, Circular A-21 (2000), *at* http://www.whitehouse.gov/omb/circulars/a021/a021.html.

178 See *id.*

179 See Fabrikant, *supra* note 130, at § 2.04[1].

180 HHS, Federal Cash Transactions Report (PMS 272), *Manual for Recipients Financed Under the Payment Management System* Appendix C (1994), *at* http://www.dpm.psc.gov/doc/ch4.pdf; OMB, Financial Status Report (Standard Form 269) 1, *at* http://www.whitehouse.gov//omb/grants/sf269.pdf.

181 HHS, Application for Continuation Grant (PHS 2590): Certificate of F&A Costs (2001), *at* http://grants.nih.gov/grants/funding/2590/2590.htm.

182 NIH, NIH Grants Policy Statement at 97.

183 OMB, Financial Status Report (Standard Form 269) 1.

184 See HHS, Program Support Center Financial Management Service, DHHS Manual for Recipients Financed Under the Payment Management System (PMS) (Jan. 1994), *at* http://www.dpm.psc.gov/doc/hhsrecmanual.pdf; OMB, Financial Status Report 1, Standard Form 269, *at* http://www.whitehouse.gov/omb/grants/sf269.pdf.

185 See HHS, Final Invention Statement and Certification (HHS 568), *at* http://grants.nih.gov/grants/hhs568.pdf; National Business Center, Certificate of F&A Costs, *at* http://www.nbc.gov/Cert_School.doc.

186 See 45 C.F.R. Parts 74, 92.

187 See, e.g., *United States ex rel. Mikes v. Straus,* 274 F.3d 687 (2d Cir. 2001); *United States ex rel. Siewick v. Jamieson Science & Engineering, Inc.,* 214 F.3d 1372 (D.C. Cir. 2000). Some courts also have begun to accept a theory of implied certification, where the FCA applies even when the claims form does not require an express certification of compliance with a regulatory scheme. Most courts allow a plaintiff to invoke implied certification only when the government's payment is explicitly conditioned on certifications of compliance. A panel of the Second Circuit cautioned that the implied certification rationale does not fit comfortably into the health care context because the False Claims Act was not designed for use as a blunt instrument to enforce compliance with all medical regulations—but rather only those regulations that are a precondition to payment—and to construe the impliedly false certification theory in an expansive fashion would improperly broaden the Act's reach.

United States ex rel. Mikes v. Straus, 274 F.3d 687, 699 (2d Cir. 2001). Mikes allows implied certification "only when the underlying statute or regulation upon which the plaintiff relies expressly states the provider must comply in order to be paid." *Id.* at 700. The Fifth, Ninth, and D.C. Circuits all appear to have adopted this rule. *See United States ex rel. Thompson v. Columbia/HCA Healthcare Corp.,* 125 F.3d 899, 902 (5th Cir. 1997) (applying false certification "where the government has conditioned payment of a claim upon a claimant's certification of compliance"); *United States ex rel. Hopper v. Anton,* 91 F.3d 1261, 1266 (9th Cir. 1996), cert. denied, 519 U.S. 1115 (1997) (saying that false certification creates liability "when certification is a prerequisite to obtaining a government benefit"); *United States ex rel. Siewick v. Jamieson Sci. and Eng'g, Inc.,* 214 F.3d 1372, 1376 (D.C. Cir. 2000) (stating that the rule is "adopted by all courts of appeals to have addressed the matter"); *Luckey v. Baxter Healthcare Corp.,* 2 F.Supp.2d 1034, 1044-45 (N.D. Ill. 1998) (applying this general rule).

The Tenth Circuit held that "a false implied certification may constitute a 'false or fraudulent claim' . . . even absent an affirmative or express false statement by the government contractor." *Shaw v. AAA Eng'g & Drafting, Inc.,* 213 F.3d 519, 531-32 (10th Cir. 2000); *see also United States ex rel. Augustine v. Century Health Servs.,* 289 F.3d 409 (6th Cir. 2002). A few courts have approached the implied certification theory skeptically. *See United States ex rel. Joslin v. Cmty. Home Health of Maryland, Inc.,* 984 F. Supp. 374 (D. Md. 1997). The Fourth Circuit also expressed its concern. It cited Joslin and said its own "decision in Berge [*United States ex rel. Berge v. Bd. of Trustees of Univ. of Ala.,* 104 F.3d 1453 (4th Cir. 1997)], holding, in part, that there can be no False Claims Act liability for an omission without an obligation to disclose, also makes questionable an implied certification claim in the Fourth Circuit." *Harrison v. Westinghouse Savannah River Co.,* 176 F.3d 776, 786 n.8. However, the Fourth Circuit decided not to address "the validity and problems of an implied certification theory" at that time.

188 Civil Monetary Penalties Act, 42 U.S.C. § 1320(a)-7(a)(5) (2001).

189 CMS, Medicare Coverage—Clinical Trials: Final National Coverage Determination, *at* www.cms.hhs.gov/coverage/8d2.htm.

190 42 C.F.R. §§ 413.90(a)-(b)(2).

191 MCM Part 3, § 2300.1(A).

192 The question of how to bill for services provided to persons involved in clinical trials at hospitals reimbursed under a prospective payment mechanism (e.g., DRG) was even more complicated. In that context, most providers refrained from billing the Medicare program for the services provided to the patient where the services were provided solely on the basis of the patient's enrollment in the research protocol. Instead, prudent providers billed Medicare only where the admission and services were adequately documented to support the medical necessity and which were not traceable solely to the patient's participation in the research study.

193 President's Memorandum to the Secretary of Health and Human Services, "Increasing Participation of Medicare Beneficiaries in Clinical Trials" (June 7, 2000).

194 For the routine costs of trial participants to fall within the National Coverage Decision, the trial itself must meet certain designated requirements:

(1) The trial must evaluate an item or service that falls within a Medicare benefit category (e.g., physicians' services, durable medical equipment, diagnostic tests) and is not statutorily excluded from coverage (e.g., cosmetic surgery, hearing aids);

(2) trials that are designed exclusively to test general subjects such as toxicity or basic disease biology are excluded from coverage; and

(3) trials of therapeutic interventions must enroll patients with a diagnosed disease rather than healthy volunteers. *Id.* at 2.

Federally funded trials conducted under an Investigational New Drug Application are automatically deemed to receive Medicare coverage of associated routine costs. *Id.* at 3. A federal multi-agency group will develop qualifying criteria to determine if other trials meet the requirements. *Id.*

195 Department of Health and Human Services, Office of Inspector General. *National Emphysema Treatment Trial (NETT) Advisory Opinion No. 00-5.* Washington, D.C.: Dept. of Health and Human Services, Office of Inspector General; 2000.

196 Department of Health and Human Services, Office of Inspector General. *National Emphysema Treatment Trial (NETT) Advisory Opinion No. 00-5.* Washington, D.C.: Dept. of Health and Human Services, Office of Inspector General; 2000.

197 *Id.*

198 CMS, Medicare Coverage—Clinical Trials: Final National Coverage Determination, *at* www.cms.hhs.gov/coverage/8d2.htm.

199 HCFA has stated that, for the purposes of the NCD, protocol-induced costs are patient costs incurred in a clinical trial for items and services necessary solely to satisfy the data collection needs of the clinical trial, such as monthly CT scans for a condition usually requiring only a single scan. Care that would otherwise be required (e.g., conventional care)—even if it is also required by the trial protocol—is not considered protocol-induced.

200 CMS, Medicare Coverage—Clinical Trials: Final National Coverage Determination.

201 *Id.*

202 *Id.*

203 *Id.*

204 See *id.*

205 *Id.* Clinical research that does not meet these criteria require certification by the trial's lead principal investigator to obtain Medicare coverage. See *id.*

206 "Each Fraudulent Financial Report, Invoice Could Constitute Violation, Trial Court Rules," 8 *Health Care Fraud Rep.* (BNA) 575 (July 7, 2004). Underreporting money owed to the government, such as money received from private insurers, is known as a "reverse false claim."

207 This includes free drug samples that have been provided by the manufacturer during a research study. For example, in May 2002, Fresenius Medical Care North America agreed to pay $1.67 million to settle False Claims Act charges that one of its subsidiaries obtained free samples from the manufacturer of the drug under study and then billed Medicare and other federal health care programs for the drugs provided as part of the study. "Dialysis Services Company Agrees to Pay $1.6 Million to Settle Health Care Fraud Case," *Health Care Fraud Rep.* (BNA) 408 (May 15, 2002).

208 Medicare Modernization Act of 2003, Pub. L. 108-173, § 731(b) (2003).

209 42 C.F.R. 405.201(b) (2004).

210 Proposed Fee Sched, 277 (printed form?), citing the National Coverage Determination Manual, CMS Pub. 100-3, Manual § 310.1.

211 Same thing.

212 Same thing: Proposed rule 42 C.F.R. § 405.207(b) (2004).

213 42 C.F.R. 405.201(b) (2004). A Class I device is considered reasonably safe based on the general controls of the Food, Drug, and Cosmetic Act, while Class II refers to devices that require additional special controls, such as performance standards or postmarket surveillance. Class III devices cannot be categorized into Class I or II.

214 42 C.F.R. § 411.15(o)(2) (2000).

215 42 C.F.R. § 405.207 (a) (2001).

216 42 C.F.R. § 405.207(b) (2001).

217 PhRMA Principles at 5.

218 PhRMA Principles at 8–9.

219 PhRMA Principles at 19.

220 PhRMA Principles at 49.

221 PhRMA Principles at 49.

222 PhRMA Principles at 50.

223 See PhRMA Principles at 50.

224 See PhRMA Principles at 50.

225 See PhRMA Principles at 50.

226 See, e.g., PhRMA Principles at 16.

227 "Pharmaceutical Industry Relationships with Guideline Authors Raising Concerns," 6 *Health Care Fraud Rep.* (BNA) 131, Feb. 20, 2002.

228 "Medical Schools Need Tighter Rules to Avoid Conflicts of Interest, Journal Says," 4 *Health Care Fraud Rep.* (BNA) 875 (Dec. 13, 2000).

229 "Authors Must Reveal Conflicts of Interest, Medical Journals Say in New Guidelines," 10 *Health L. Rep.* (BNA) 1443 (Sept. 20, 2001).

230 *Id.*

231 See *id.*

232 "Financial Disclosure Review for Authors," 6 *Nature Neuroscience* 997 (Oct. 2003). Authors may decline to disclose their financial interests or may state that they are bound not to by a confidentiality agreement. In either of those cases, the journal will publish a notice.

233 AAMC Task Force on Financial Conflicts of Interest in Clinical Research, Protecting Subjects, Preserving Trust, Promoting Progress—Policy and Guidelines for the Oversight of Individual Financial Interests in Human Subjects Research 7 (2001), *at* http://www.aamc.org/members/coitf/firstreport.pdf.

234 Id. at 7.

235 See id. at 8.

236 "UConn Agrees to Pay $1.3 Million to Settle Alleged Health Care Grant Fraud," 1 *Health Care Fraud Rep.* (BNA) (Oct. 22, 1997) *citing U.S. v. University of Connecticut Health Center,* D.C. Conn., No. 3:96CV000288 PCD (1997).

237 "Boston Hospital Pays $920,000 to Settle Dispute Over Grant Fund," 3 *Health Care Fraud Rep.* (BNA) (Apr. 21, 1999) *citing United States ex rel. Boerrigter v. Beth Israel Deaconess Medical Center,* D. Mass., No. 97-11858, (1997).

238 *Id.*

239 Taxpayers Against Fraud, 19 False Claims Act and Qui Tam Quarterly Review 53 (July 2000), *at* http://www.taf.org/publications/PDF/jul00qr.pdf.

240 See *id.*

241 "NYU to Pay $15.5 Million to Settle Federal False Research Grant Charges," 1 *Health Care Fraud Rep.* (BNA) (Apr. 9, 1997) *citing Ex rel Emmanuel Roco v. NYU Medical Center,* D.C. SNY, No. 93-8012 (1997).

242 *Id.*

243 *Id.*

244 *Id.*

245 *Id.*

246 "University of Chicago, Providers Agree to Pay to Settle FCA Charges," 2 *Health Care Fraud Rep.* (BNA) 4 (Feb. 25, 1998).

247 "University of Minnesota to Pay $32 Million to Settle Illegal Drug Profit Charges," 2 *Health Care Fraud Rep.* (BNA) (Dec. 2, 1998) *citing United States ex rel. Zissler v. Regents of University of Minnesota,* D. Minn., No. 3-95-168 (1995).

248 *Id.*

249 *Id.*

250 "Northwestern University to Pay $5.5 Million to Settle Government False Claims Charges," 8 *Health Care Daily Rep.* (BNA) 27 (Feb. 10, 2003).

251 *Id.*

252 "Johns Hopkins to Pay $2.6 Million to Settle Claims on Research Grants," 8 *Health Care Fraud Rep.* (BNA) 191 (Mar. 3, 2004) *citing United States ex rel. Grau v. Johns Hopkins University,* D. Md., No. 99-1448 (1999).

253 *Id.*

254 *Id.*

255 *See* id.; "Boston Hospital Pays $920,000 to Settle Dispute Over Grant Fund," 3 *Health Care Fraud Rep.* (BNA) (Apr. 21, 1999).

256 *See* "University of Minnesota to Pay $32 Million to Settle Illegal Drug Profit Charges," 2 *Health Care Fraud Rep.* (BNA) (Dec. 2, 1998); "UConn Agrees to Pay $1.3 Million to Settle Alleged Health Care Grant Fraud," 1 *Health Care Fraud Rep.* (BNA) (Oct. 22, 1997).

257 "HHS IG Finds Only 'Minimal Progress' in Protections for Research Subjects," 5 *Health Care Daily Rep.* (BNA) 74 (Apr. 17, 2000).

258 See *id.* The report found that continuing review after research receives initial approval remains a low priority, IRBs had not been shielded from conflicts of interest, and IRB workload remained too high. Furthermore, IRBs still had not installed educational requirements for their members.

259 "Federal Research Grant Fraud a Growing Issue for Federal Enforcers, Researchers," 9 *Health L. Rep.* (BNA) 1695 (Nov. 9, 2000).

260 Complaint, *Gelsinger v. Trustees of the University of Pennsylvania, at* http://www.sskr-plaw.com/links/healthcare2.html.

261 See *id.*

262 See *id.*

263 See *id.*

264 Letter from OHRP to Johns Hopkins University 4–8 (July 19, 2001), *at* http://www.hhs.gov/ohrp/detrm_letrs/jul01a.pdf.

265 See *id.*

266 See *id.* at 10.

267 See Roche Settlement, *Hopkins Medical News,* Winter 2002, *at* http://www.hopkinsmedicine.org/hmn/W02/cnews.html.

268 "Human Trials Halted at University Center After Flaws in Skin-Cancer Study Found," 5 *Health Care Daily Rep.* (BNA) 134 (July 12, 2000).

269 "VA Researchers Sued for Alleged Patient Deaths; Class Action Against Feds Planned," 8 *Health Care Daily Rep.* (BNA) 53, Mar. 19, 2003).

270 "Research Assistant at VA Hospital Indicted on Manslaughter Charges," 7 *Health Care Fraud Rep.* (BNA) 840 (Nov. 12, 2003).

271 *United States ex rel. Condie v. Board of Regents of the University of California,* 1993 WL 740185, at 1 (N.D. Cal. Sept. 7, 1993).

272 Ralph Frammolino, "Scientific Fraud Suit to Be Settled for $1.6 Million," *L.A. Times,* July 23, 1994, at A23.

273 *United States ex rel. Berge v. Board of Trustees of the University of Alabama,* 104 F.3d 1453, 1456 (4th Cir. 1997) (overturning jury verdict in favor of plaintiff who alleged that defendants had misrepresented her work as their own in grant applications and progress reports to the NIH).

274 *United States v. Thomas Jefferson University* (university allegedly submitted false or fabricated data to obtain funding for AIDS research), discussed in "Hospitals and Health Systems HIV/AIDS: Thomas Jefferson University Settles Fraud Case," 6 *Amer. Political Network* 9: 10 (May 23, 2000).

275 Goldberg, Carey & Scott Allen, "Researcher Admits Fraud in Grant Data," *Boston Globe,* Mar. 18, 2005, at A1.

276 *Cook County v. United States ex rel. Chandler,* 538 U.S. 119, 124 (2003).

277 *Id.*

278 *See* "Physician Charged with Falsifying Drug Study Data," Press Release, U.S. Attorney for N.D. Ala. (Aug. 29, 2003).

279 Institutional Integrity Agreement between the United States Department of Health and Human Services and Thomas Jefferson University (May 19, 2000).

280 *Id.* at 1.

281 *Id.* at 3-5.

282 21 C.F.R. § 54.3 (2004).

283 21 C.F.R. § 54.4 (2004).

284 21 C.F.R. § 54.4 (2004).

285 21 C.F.R. § 54.4 (2004).

286 See Disclosure: Financial Interest and Arrangements of Clinical Investigators (FDA 3455), *at* http://www.fda.gov/opacom/morechoices/fdaforms/FDA-3455.pdf; 21 C.F.R. §§ 54.2-54.4 (2004). A significant equity interest is one whose value "cannot readily be determined through reference to public prices" or one that exceeds $50,000 in a publicly traded corporation during the study or one year following. A proprietary interest includes a patent, trademark, copyright, or licensing agreement. See 21 C.F.R. § 54.2.

287 Application to Market a New Drug, Biologic or an Antibiotic Drug for Human Use (FDA 356h), *at* http://www.fda.gov/opacom/morechoices/fdaforms/FDA-356h.pdf.

288 See *id.*

289 *Id.*

290 21 C.F.R. § 99.201 (a)(4)(i) (2004).

291 21 C.F.R. § 99.201 (a)(4)(ii).

292 21 C.F.R. § 314.50(h) (2004).

293 21 C.F.R. §§ 807.87(i)–(j) (2004).

294 21 C.F.R. §§ 812.20(b)–812.25(h) (2004). The regulations also require IRB approval for new facilities. See 21 C.F.R. § 812.35(b) (2004).

295 Statement of Investigator (FDA 1572), *at* http://www.fda.gov/opacom/morechoices/fdaforms/FDA-1572.pdf.

296 See *id.*

297 See *id.*

298 See "J&J Unit Pleads Guilty to Charges Stemming From Defective Medical Device," 5 *Health Care Daily Rep.* (BNA) 244 (Dec. 19, 2000); *United States ex rel. Konrad v. Lifescan, Inc.,* No. C-00-20478-JF (N.D. Cal.).

299 *Id.*

300 *Id.*

301 See Settlement Agreement, *United States ex rel. Kazimiroff v. Dentsply International Inc.,* No. 99-0423 (E.D. Pa. settlement announced Mar. 6, 2003), *at* http://www.usdoj.gov/usao/pae/News/Pr/2003/mar/dentsply.pdf.

302 Press Release, U.S. Attorney's Office for the Eastern District of Pennsylvania, "Whistleblower Triggers Civil Action That Leads to Settlement with World's Largest Dental Supply Manufacturer" (Mar. 6, 2003), *at* http://www.usdoj.gov/usao/pae/News/Pr/2003/mar/mar03.html.

303 Press Release, U.S. Attorney's Office for the Northern District of California (June 12, 2003), *at* http://www.usdoj.gov/usao/can/press/html/2003_06_12_endovascular.html.

304 *Id.*

305 Plea Agreement 2, *United States v. Endovascular Technologies,* No. CR 02-0179 SI (N.D. Cal. filed June 12, 2003), *at* http://www.usdoj.gov/usao/can/press/assets/applets/2003_06_12_Endovascular_plea.pdf.

306 See *id.* at 4.

307 See *id.* at 6.

308 Press Release, U.S. Attorney's Office for the Northern District of California (June 12, 2003), *at* http://www.usdoj.gov/usao/can/press/html/2003_06_12_endovascular.html.

309 United States ex rel. King v. Alcon Laboratories, Inc., discussed in Teva Pharmaceutical Industries Limited, Form 6-K 8, Securities and Exchange Commission, Aug. 2003, *at* http://www.tevapharm.com/pdf/teva6kq22003_isa.pdf.

310 Complaint ¶ 13, *United States ex rel. Franklin v. Parke-Davis,* No. 96-111651-PBS (D. Mass. filed July 31, 2001).

311 *Id.* at ¶ 21.

312 *Id.* at ¶¶ 43, 46.

313 *Id.* at ¶¶ 39-40.

314 *Id.* at ¶ 29.

315 *Id.* at ¶ 51.

316 *Id.* at ¶ 71.

317 See Complaint, *Gelsinger v. Trustees of the University of Pennsylvania, at* http://www.sskr-plaw.com/links/healthcare2.html.

318 See *id.*

319 See *id.*

320 See *id.*

321 See "States Upgrade Enforcement of Medicaid Drug Cases, Target Best Pricing Issues," 7 *Health Care Fraud Rep.* (BNA) 222 (Mar. 19, 2003).

322 "Prosecutor Details Potential Concerns For sponsors of Clinical Studies of Drugs," 8 *Health Care Fraud Rep.* (BNA) 11 (Jan. 7, 2004).

323 See *id.*

324 *Id.*

325 45 C.F.R. § 46.111(a)(7) (2001); 21 C.F.R. § 56.111(a)(7) (2000).

326 45 C.F.R. § 164.508(f) (2002).

327 See 45 C.F.R. § 164.512(i) (2002).

328 45 C.F.R. §§ 164.502(d), 164.514(a)–(c) (2002).

SIX

Uses and Disclosures of Identifiable Information in Clinical Research: National and International Considerations

M. Peter Adler and Jeffrey G. Micklos

Introduction: The Challenge of Protecting Health Information in the Clinical Trial Process

The high speed in which private health care information can be used and shared leaves open the possibility that confidential patient information will be used inappropriately or even criminally by an unauthorized recipient. This has led to the need for increased privacy protections for that health care information. Initially, there was hope in the United States and other countries that the market would regulate itself, creating little need for the passage of laws. Over time, the market failed to regulate itself, resulting in an upsurge of state, federal, and international information privacy laws and regulations. Unfortunately, there has been very little coordination between governments as they have moved to mandate information privacy protection and little regard shown to how affected industries are to comply with various regulations.

The privacy laws increasingly impact U.S. pharmaceutical companies and other health care research organizations involved in international clinical trials. These laws and regulations are aimed at how personal information, including health information, is stored, transmitted, used, and disclosed. Failure to protect this type of information under U.S. and foreign laws may result in fines and other penalties. In addition, some international laws actually prohibit companies located in countries that lack adequate privacy protections from importing personal information unless additional steps are taken.

The increased regulation of privacy is certain to collide with a pharmaceutical company's strategic plans that not only call for increased international business operations, but also an increase in international clinical trials to test their developing products. In 2001, the Office of Inspector General of the U.S. Department of Health and Human Services (HHS) issued a report noting the swift increase in international clinical trials subject to the jurisdiction of the U.S. Food and Drug Administration (FDA), which it reported as increasing 16-fold in the previous decade.[1]

Clinical trials are crossing borders for various reasons, including the general high quality of trials conducted in other countries, the potential mitigation of liability, and the availability of an understandable and harmonized legal framework. The most common locations for these trials has been the European countries subject to European Union (EU) Directives. An increasing number of clinical trials are also conducted in Canada and other countries. As a result, clinical trial data, including personal information, may flow from the United States to these countries and back. It is also possible that data will flow between non-U.S. countries before returning home to the original source.

Companies subject to the myriad of privacy laws and regulations are often perplexed on how to comply. Many entities do not approach information privacy compliance in an organized, integrated, and centralized fashion. Many organizations have permitted privacy compliance to be handled by more than one department, depending on whether the activities of the department fit the focus of the regulation. For example, the human resources department of an international corporation may be tasked with complying with the national laws passed under the EU Data Protection Directive and the Health Insurance Portability and Accountability Act of 1996 (HIPAA), while the finance department may focus on compliance with the Gramm-Leach-Bliley Act. Complicating the efforts are regulatory requirements affecting legal, human resources, executive management, and information technology departments within an organization, as well as business and trading partners.

Even though these laws and regulations are very similar with regard to privacy, an organization often faces several separate privacy initiatives. To address each of these, companies will also hire several consultants or law firms to assess the organization's compliance and provide consulting services. As a result, efforts to comply can be incomplete, redundant, inadequate, and expensive.

This chapter reviews the impact of U.S., Canadian, and European privacy laws on uses and disclosures of personal information used in the clinical trial process. It then discusses a unified approach to privacy that pharmaceutical companies and other organizations involved in international clinical research may follow to efficiently and effectively comply with the myriad of laws and regulations.

Data Management and Data Flows during Clinical Trials

Management of Data during Clinical Trials

Recent years have produced a movement toward harmonizing standard rules for governing clinical trials. For example, the International Conference on Harmonization (ICH) of Technical Requirements for Regulation of Human Use published clinical practice guidelines that provide standards that are accepted by the FDA, as well by as European regulatory authorities.[2]

The ICH Guideline for Good Clinical Practice (GCP) is highly specific with regard to data collection, data handling, documentation, and retention of records.[3] While the main purpose of the ICH GCP is to promote best practices in clinical trials and not to provide privacy guidelines, it nonetheless contains standards on record access and patient subject consent, audit procedures, and sponsor access to source data, such as medical records, and similar personal information.[4]

The EU has also enacted a directive on clinical trials ("Clinical Trials Directive"), which required member states to implement by May 1, 2004, national laws regulating clinical trials.[5] The Clinical Trials Directive is designed to impose new administrative requirements for clinical trials administration rather than further regulate privacy, and is unlikely that national legislation regarding data privacy itself will change.[6]

The Flows of Data in Clinical Trials

Understanding the basic stages of the clinical trial is important to anticipate the use of personal data during the research lifecycle. In most clinical trials emanating in the United States, there are four key players: the sponsor, the Institutional Review Board (IRB), the Clinical Research Organization (CRO), and the principal investigator. Sponsors are the entities or persons that fund the clinical trial, including physicians, medical institutions, foundations, and pharmaceutical and medical device companies. A sponsor can also be a federal agency such as the National Institutes of Health (NIH), the Department of Defense (DOD), and the Department of Veterans Affairs (VA).

Sponsors intending to conduct U.S.-based clinical studies *must* submit an Investigational New Drug Application (IND) to the FDA before beginning research.[7] The FDA then reviews the study design and procedures and suggests changes as appropriate. Sponsors must also obtain a signed attestation form, known as a 1572 form, from each clinical investigator certifying that they will conduct research in an ethical manner and according to FDA regulations.

To commence the clinical trial, the principal investigator submits to the affiliated IRB related documents including a detailed protocol, a proposed informed consent form and related information, investigational drug brochure, recruitment materials, any associated federal grant application, and a description of his or her research qualifications (collectively, referred to as "IRB Materials").

While the IRB Materials do not include personally identifiable information, investigators usually address access and privacy protections related to personally identifiable study data. The ICH GCP includes standards for data handling and record-keeping, record access and subject consent, audit procedures, and sponsor access to source data such as medical records and similar information.[8] The IRB-approved protocol identifies the personal data that will be collected and created, the period of personal identification, coding and/or de-identification measures, and a description of available access to study data.

Research may be performed entirely within a single organization or through collaborations with other researchers and data analysis specialists located in other organizations. The protocol should describe whether existing data (including medical records and stored samples) will be acquired and, if so, from whom. As mentioned later in this chapter, a covered entity participating in the research study is required to comply with the HIPAA privacy regulations when releasing identifiable medical records and other protected health information to outside researchers.

Personal information may be masked when the identity of a clinical trial participant is totally irrelevant. Usually, this is accomplished by assigning a subject identification code (SIC) to each individual participating in the trial. ICH GCP defines the SIC as a unique identifier assigned by the investigator to each trial subject as a means to protect the subject's identity. The SIC is used for reporting trial related data; case report forms (CRFs) from clinical trials carry only the SIC rather than individual identifiers.[9]

Under most privacy laws, the use and disclosure of data designated by a SIC without a decipher code renders the data de-identified and not subject to privacy controls. Nevertheless, researchers must be diligent in identifying situations in which personal information is used and disclosed even when marked with an SIC. In other cases, the trial may require some form of participant identifier in order to track the data over time (e.g., disease progression), to link multiple sources of data related to the participant, or to collect or validate information. These include parties with access to this regulatory information, monitors or auditors of clinical research organizations, or the clinical trial sponsor.

Any person that has direct access will be deemed to be working with individually identifiable health information when the information contains identifiers. As a practical matter, all research-related informed consents should include an authorization permitting the use and disclosure of protected health information (PHI) that will comply with the privacy laws of other countries. A written agreement should also be included in the IRB materials to allow access to all study-related information as required by the protocol, by law, to conduct authorized monitoring, or to facilitate access by the sponsor and the FDA. A comprehensive package of informed consents, HIPAA authorizations, and use and disclosure agreements will not only comply with FDA regulations, but also permit the flow of PHI and other personal information controlled by U.S. and other national laws.

Formal written reports detailing the progress of research are provided to the IRB, the commercial sponsor, and the FDA. These reports do not typically include identified or readily identifiable patient information. Unanticipated problems involving risk to subjects must be reported to the approving IRB, the sponsor, and the FDA. Additional "adverse events" are reported to the FDA and others as required by regulation.[10] These reports should not include identified information, but even if they do, such disclosures are permitted under HIPAA.

U.S. Privacy Protections Affecting the Clinical Trial Process

The Health Insurance Portability and Accountability Act of 1996 (HIPAA)

The privacy of certain health information in the United States is protected by the Health Insurance Portability and Accountability Act, which was enacted in 1996. HIPAA authorized the U.S. Department of Health and Human Services (HHS) to promulgate regulations aimed at safeguarding identifiable health information, which were contained in an August 14, 2002, Final Rule (the "Privacy Rule"). In general, the Privacy Rule establishes a federal floor for privacy protections for an individual's identifiable health information (referred to as "protected health information" or PHI). Covered entities such as health care providers, health plans, and health care clearinghouses were required to comply with the Privacy Rule starting April 15, 2003.[11]

Entities That Must Comply with HIPAA

The Privacy Rule expressly applies to three groups that are collectively referred to as "covered entities:" (1) health plans; (2) health care clearinghouses; and (3) health care providers[12] that electronically transmit health information in connection with certain transactions.[13]

Because of HIPAA's limited scope, researchers are required to comply with HIPAA only if they are a covered entity. In some instances, a researcher may be a health care provider and subject to the Privacy Rule. Researchers employed by, or that contract with, a covered entity are also covered. Researchers and covered entities must follow the Privacy Rule requirements for uses and disclosures of the PHI. These provisions, which are discussed below, dictate the conditions under which a covered entity can use PHI or disclose it to sponsors, CROs, and/or other third parties.

Researchers and research organizations that are not covered entities are not required to comply with the Privacy Rule even if they create or handle PHI. For instance, entities that sponsor health research or create or maintain health information databases may not themselves be covered entities, and thus may not directly be subject to the Privacy Rule.

Even though not required by the law itself, a covered entity may require researchers by contract to comply with all or part of the HIPAA Privacy Rule. For example, researchers may be asked to enter into contracts with covered entities that contain terms requiring the researcher to post a notice of privacy practices and implement policies and procedures to protect the use and disclosure of PHI in the same manner required by the Rule itself. In this way, the Privacy Rule's mandate may be passed through to a researcher that relies on covered entities for research support or as a source of clinical trial medical data.

Type of Information Being Protected

The Privacy Rule applies only to HIPAA and defines PHI as all "individually identifiable health information" that is maintained or transmitted through electronic devices or other media.[14] "Individually identifiable health information" is further defined to include all information "relat[ing] to the past, present, or future physical or mental health or condition" of an individual that can potentially be used to identify such individual.[15]

All individually identifiable information held by an educational institution subject to the Family Educational Right and Privacy Act[16] is excluded from the definition of PHI. Similarly excluded is the employee health information held by covered entities in their capacity as employers.[17]

Uses and Disclosures of PHI under HIPAA

The Privacy Rule permits a covered entity to use or disclose PHI for research under the following circumstances and conditions:

- *Authorization:* If the subject of the PHI has granted his or her specific written permission for use or disclosure through an authorization[18]
- *Reviews Preparatory to Research:* For reviews preparatory to research with representations obtained from the researcher[19]
- *Research on Decedents' Information:* For research solely on decedents' information with certain representations and, if requested, documentation obtained from the researcher[20]
- *De-Identified Health Information:* If the PHI has been de-identified in accordance with the Privacy Rule's standards[21]
- *Limited Data Sets:* If the information is released in the form of a limited data set, with certain identifiers removed and with a data use agreement between the researcher and the covered entity[22]
- *Previously Obtained Authorizations or Consents:* Under the "grandfather" provisions which permit use or disclosure of the information for research pursuant to an executed informed consent to participate in the research, an IRB waiver of such informed consent, an authorization, or other express legal permission[23]

- *IRB Authorization Waiver:* If the covered entity receives appropriate documentation that an IRB or a Privacy Board has granted a waiver of the authorization requirement[24]
- *IRB Alteration of Authorization:* If the covered entity obtains documentation of an IRB or Privacy Board's alteration of the authorization requirement[25]

The foregoing are the primary methods of disclosing PHI to researchers and the focus of this discussion. However, HIPAA permits other uses and disclosures without authorizations that are worth mentioning briefly.

First, the Privacy Rule permits covered entities to use and disclose PHI for purposes of treatment, payment, and health care operations without authorization. This is usually pertinent in the clinical setting but will have little impact on disclosures of PHI from covered entities to noncovered entities such as sponsors and CROs.

Second, the Privacy Rule also permits disclosures to "business associates." Business associates are persons or entities that perform certain functions or services on behalf of the covered entity. Disclosures from a covered entity to a researcher for research purposes do not require a business associate contract, even in those instances where the covered entity has hired the researcher to perform research on the covered entity's own behalf. Notably, a business associate agreement is required only where a person or entity is conducting a function or activity regulated by the administrative simplification rules on behalf of a covered entity, such as payment or health care operations, or providing one of the services listed in the "business associate" definition.[26] Significantly, the Privacy Rule does not *prohibit* a covered entity from entering into a business associate contract with a researcher, and many of them have such agreements. When such a contract is in place, the covered entity will only be permitted to disclose PHI to a researcher as permitted by the Privacy Rule.

Third, the Privacy Rule also permits, without authorization, covered entities to make other disclosures of PHI that are required by law to public health authorities authorized by law to collect such information for public health activities and for adverse event reporting to certain persons subject to the jurisdiction of the FDA (e.g., clinical trial drug sponsors).[27]

Authorization for Research Uses and Disclosures

The primary method used by covered entities to disclose PHI is to obtain an authorization from the individual (which is similar to the term "data subject" used in international privacy laws). The written HIPAA authorization is in addition to the informed consent to participate in research required by the Federal Protection of Human Subjects

Regulations and the FDA regulations, both of which are discussed later in this chapter. Since an authorization can be combined with an informed consent document or other permission to participate in research, researchers are able to comply with both requirements using one document. A covered entity or researcher may present an authorization to an individual for execution.

To be valid under HIPAA, an authorization must be written in plain English and contain core elements and required statements stipulated in the Privacy Rule.[28] The core elements include:

- A description of the PHI to be used or disclosed, which identifies the information in a specific and meaningful manner
- The names or other specific identification of the person(s) (or class of persons) authorized to engage in the requested use or disclosure
- The names or other specific identification of the person(s) (or class of persons) to whom the covered entity may make the requested disclosure
- A description of each purpose of the requested use or disclosure
- Authorization expiration date or event relating to the individual or to the use or disclosure ("end of the research study" or "none" are permissible for research, including for the creation and maintenance of a research database or repository)
- The individual's signature and date of signature. If the individual's legally authorized representative signs the Authorization, the representative's authority to act for the individual must be described in writing

Specific statements must be included in addition to the core elements. These required statements include:

- A statement of the individual's right to revoke the authorization, how to do so, and, if applicable, the exceptions to the right to revoke his/her authorization. Reference to the relevant section of the covered entity's notice of privacy practice is sufficient.
- Whether treatment, payment, enrollment, or eligibility of benefits can be conditioned on authorization, including research-related treatment and the consequences of refusing to sign the authorization, if applicable.
- A statement of the potential risk that PHI will be redisclosed by the recipient and no longer protected by the Privacy Rule. A general statement that the Privacy Rule may no longer protect health information disclosed to the recipient is sufficient.

A research subject has the right to revoke, in writing, a previously provided authorization at any time. The revocation is effective when the covered entity receives the written revocation; however, under the "reliance exception" a covered entity is not required to honor a revocation when it has taken action in reliance upon the authorization. This exception protects a covered entity from the nearly impossible task of locating and retrieving patient information that it disclosed to a researcher under a valid authorization. The reliance exception also permits the continued use and disclosure of PHI already disclosed under the authorization when the information is necessary to protect the integrity of the research. Examples of such protection include reporting adverse events, accounting for a subject's withdrawal from the research study, and conducting investigations of scientific misconduct.

Obtaining an individual authorization is the key method for obtaining PHI from covered entities. Since an authorization for research uses and disclosures need not expire and can be combined with an informed consent, it could be obtained for most research projects involving living recruited subjects.

Reviews Preparatory to Research
Reviews of PHI for research preparation permit researchers to determine whether the information held by a covered entity will support the proposed research protocols. This analysis may help researchers determine whether sufficient records exist (in terms of category, quality, or quantity) to conduct a particular area of research. To assist researchers in this information gathering, a covered entity may permit a review of the PHI it holds without first obtaining an individual authorization, as long as the researcher represents and adheres to the following:

- The use or disclosure is sought solely to review PHI as necessary to prepare the research protocol or for other related purposes;
- No PHI will be removed from the covered entity during the review; and
- The PHI that the researcher seeks to use or access is necessary for the researcher's purposes.

Covered entities may also use or disclose PHI to researchers to aid in study recruitment. However, under this provision, the researcher may identify, but not contact, potential study participants. In order to contact potential study participants, a researcher may do so only under the following circumstances:

- *Researcher as Work Force Member:* If the researcher is a workforce member of a covered entity, the researcher may contact the potential study participant, as part of the covered entity's health care operations, for the purposes of seeking Authorization.

- *Contact by Health Care Provider as Part of Treatment:* A covered health care provider may discuss treatment alternatives, including possible participation in a clinical trial, with the patient as part of the patient's treatment or the covered entity's health care operations.

- *Contact by Business Associate of Covered Entity:* The covered entity may enter into a business associate contract with a researcher, which would permit the researcher to contact individuals on behalf of the covered entity to obtain their authorizations.

- *Waiver of Authorization:* If the covered entity obtains documentation that an IRB has partially waived the authorization requirement to disclose PHI to a researcher for recruitment purposes. If so, the covered entity could disclose that PHI, which is necessary for the researcher to contact the individual.

Research on Decedent's PHI

Covered entities are not required to obtain an authorization from a decedent's next of kin or obtain any other approvals in order to release a decedent's PHI for research. However, before the covered entity may disclose the PHI to the researcher, the covered entity must receive from the researcher:

- oral or written representations that the use and disclosure is sought solely for research on the decedent's PHI;
- oral or written representations that the PHI sought to be used or disclosed is necessary for research purposes; and
- documentation, at the request of the covered entity, of the death for those individuals whose PHI is sought by the researchers.

De-identification of Health Information

Covered entities may use or disclose health information that is de-identified without restriction under the Privacy Rule. De-identifying PHI is the most common method to enable many research activities to operate without first obtaining an authorization. However, recognizing that researchers may need to access and generate identifiable health information for certain types of research, the authorization discussed above and waiver (or alteration of waiver) discussed next provide other viable means to obtain, use, and disclose PHI to support research activities.

Two methods are used to de-identify health information. The first is by removing certain pieces of information from each record as specified in the Privacy Rule ("safe harbor de-identification"). The second is by obtaining from a qualified individual certification that information is de-identified based on statistical analysis ("statistical verification of de-identification").

Safe Harbor Principles De-Identification
The Privacy Rule allows a covered entity to de-identify data by removing all 18 elements enumerated in the Privacy Rule that could be used to identify the individual or the individual's relatives, employers, or household members. Even with removal of the identifiers, the covered entity also must have no actual knowledge that the remaining information could be used alone or in combination with other information to identify the individual who is the subject of the information. The identifiers listed in Table 6-1 must be removed for de-identification purposes.

Under this method, unique identifying numbers, characteristics, or codes must be removed for the health information to be considered de-identified. To assist in clinical trial record identification, the Privacy Rule permits a covered entity to assign to, and retain with, the health information a code or other means of record identification if two criteria are met. First, the code is not derived from, or related to, the information about the individual. For example, a code that uses the last four digits of a Social Security Number is derived from information about that individual and cannot be used. Second, the code cannot be translated to identify the individual. For example, the covered entity may not use or disclose the key to the code or its method of identifying the information. Given this constraint, it is best to use a randomly assigned code that permits identification through a secured key to that code. In the clinical trials context, a randomly assigned SIC without the key for deciphering the information would render the information de-identified and no longer subject to the HIPAA Privacy Rule.

A covered entity is permitted to de-identify PHI or engage a business associate to de-identify PHI. When a researcher is also a covered entity, it may obtain PHI and de-identify it. A researcher may also enter into a business associate contract with a covered entity for the purposes of obtaining and de-identifying PHI. In addition, a covered entity that is a hybrid entity, such as an academic medical center, could designate in its health care component(s) portions of the entity that conduct business associate-like functions, such as de-identification.

TABLE 6-1

1. Names
2. All geographic subdivisions smaller than a state, including street address, city, county, precinct, ZIP Code, and their equivalent geographical codes, except for the initial three digits of a ZIP Code if, according to the current publicly available data from the Bureau of the Census:
   a. The geographic unit formed by combining all ZIP Codes with the same three initial digits contains more than 20,000 people.
   b. The initial three digits of a ZIP Code for all such geographic units containing 20,000 or fewer people are changed to 000.
3. All elements of dates (except year) for dates directly related to an individual, including birth date, admission date, discharge date, date of death; and all ages over 89 and all elements of dates (including year) indicative of such age, except that such ages and elements may be aggregated into a single category of age 90 or older.
4. Telephone numbers
5. Facsimile numbers
6. Electronic mail addresses
7. Social security numbers
8. Medical record numbers
9. Health plan beneficiary numbers
10. Account numbers
11. Certificate/license numbers
12. Vehicle identifiers and serial numbers, including license plate numbers
13. Device identifiers and serial numbers
14. Web universal resource locators (URLs)
15. Internet protocol (IP) address numbers
16. Biometric identifiers, including fingerprints and voiceprints
17. Full-face photographic images and any comparable images
18. Any other unique identifying number, characteristic, or code, unless otherwise permitted by the Privacy Rule for de-identification

Statistical Verification of De-Identification

When a qualified individual certifies that information is not identifiable, fewer identifiers need to be removed for health information to be de-identified. To meet this standard, the Privacy Rule requires four criteria:

- First, the certification is to be provided only by a person with appropriate knowledge of, and experience with, generally accepted statistical and scientific principles and methods for rendering information not individually identifiable.
- Second, the certifying person must apply the statistical and scientific principles.
- Third, the certifying person must find a very small risk that the information could be used, alone or in combination with other reasonably available information, by an anticipated recipient to identify an individual who is a subject of the information.
- Fourth, the certifying person must document the methods and results of the analysis that justify the determination.[29]

A covered entity is required to keep such certification, in written or electronic format, for at least six years from the creation date or the latest effective date, whichever is later.

Limited Data Sets

The Privacy Rule permits a covered entity to use and disclose PHI included in a limited data set. Although a limited data set excludes direct identifiers, limited data sets may be helpful in certain types of longitudinal or geographic studies since the following indirect identifiers may be included:

- any dates related to the individual, including age (expressed in years or in months, days, or hours), dates of admission, service and discharge, and dates of birth and death, or
- five-digit ZIP codes or any other geographic subdivision, such as state, county, city, precinct, and their equivalent geocodes, except for street address.

A covered entity may disclose a limited data set in support of its own research activities or to other covered entities or researchers for their research activities. The only requirement is that the disclosing covered entity and the data recipient enter into a data use agreement, which is a contract that that sets forth permissible uses and disclosures as provided by the Privacy Rule. Limited data sets may be used or disclosed only for purposes of research, public health, or health care operations. Because limited data sets may contain identifiable information, they still represent PHI.

Previously Obtained Authorizations or Consents

The Privacy Rule includes a limited provision that "grandfathers" the following permissions obtained for research obtained prior to the compliance:

- an authorization or other express legal permission from an individual to use or disclose PHI for the research;[30]
- the informed consent of the individual to participate in the research;[31] or
- a waiver of informed consent by an IRB.[32]

The Privacy Rule allows covered entities to rely on express legal permission, informed consent, or IRB-approved waiver of informed consent obtained before the compliance date to use and disclose PHI for research studies, as well as for any future research that may be included in such permission.[33]

If the IRB-approved waiver of informed consent was obtained prior to the compliance date, but informed consent is sought from the research subject after the compliance date, the covered entity must obtain the individual's authorization as required under the Privacy Rule, unless such use or disclosure is permitted without authorization.

IRB and Privacy Board Alteration or Waiver of Authorization

Many health research projects and protocols cannot be undertaken using health information that has been de-identified. Also, it may not be feasible for a researcher to obtain a signed authorization for all PHI the researcher needs to obtain for the research study. In other cases, consents obtained prior to April 14, 2003, that permit the use and disclosure of information obtained from research subjects may be found to be inadequate, insufficient, or restrict a particular research protocol. Recognizing some of these limitations, the HIPAA regulations provide for a waiver or alteration of authorization, which must be obtained from an IRB or Privacy Board. The waiver (or alteration) provides researchers with additional options for access to PHI when the other methods provided by HIPAA are impossible or impractical.

The Role of the IRB under HIPAA

Much of the biomedical and behavioral research conducted in the United States is governed by two rules. The first is entitled the Federal Policy for the Protection of Human Subjects (known as the "Common Rule").[34] While 17 different agencies have their own Common Rule regulations, most federal government-funded human-subject research is subject to the Common Rule regulations of the HHS.[35] The second rule is the Protection of Human Subjects Regulations of the Food and Drug Administration.[36] While the FDA is a component of HHS, the human-subject protection regulations provide additional standards applicable to research involving FDA-regulated products.

Both the Common Rule and the FDA regulations specify when researchers must submit protocols for IRB review and approval and must obtain informed consent documents. The Privacy Rule does not change any of these requirements, but imposes a few additional responsibilities on the IRB. First, since the IRB is required to review research participants' informed consents, it will also review HIPAA authorizations to use and disclose PHI when the Authorization is combined with the informed consent. Second, the IRB is responsible for reviewing requests to waive or alter authorizations.

The Role of the Privacy Board under HIPAA
A Privacy Board is an internal review board authorized by the Privacy Rule to review requests for waiver (or alteration) of authorizations used for research. The regulations specify that Privacy Boards must meet the following criteria:

- Members must have varying backgrounds and appropriate professional competencies as necessary to review the effect of the research protocol on individuals' privacy rights and related interests.
- Each Board must have at least one member who is not affiliated with the covered entity or with any entity conducting or sponsoring the research and who is not related to any person who is affiliated with such entities.
- Members may not have conflicts of interest regarding the projects they review.

Obtaining a Waiver or Alteration of Authorization
Typically, a waiver or alteration is available when a research protocol requires PHI pertaining to individuals, but contact information for purposes of obtaining authorization is not available. In circumstances where research cannot practically be conducted without the PHI and obtaining authorizations is not feasible, the IRB or Privacy Board has the power to permit the use and disclosure of PHI through a waiver (or alteration) authorization.

Under this authority, the IRB may completely waive the authorization requirement or provide a partial waiver. A partial waiver might be requested, for instance, to allow a researcher to obtain PHI as necessary to recruit potential research subjects. As the name suggests, an alteration of authorization simply alters the Privacy Rule requirements for an authorization if certain regulatory criteria are met.

Finally, an IRB or Privacy Board may also approve a request that removes some PHI, but not all, necessary for a research protocol. For instance, for a longitudinal research study, an IRB or Privacy Board may approve the use and disclosure of diagnoses, birth date, and treatment dates but no other identifiers.

For a waiver or alteration to occur, the IRB or Privacy Board must determine that the authorization may be waived or altered to permit the covered entity to use and disclose PHI for a particular research project. However, before the covered entity may use or disclose PHI under a waiver or an alteration, it must receive documentation of the IRB or Privacy Board's determination that the following alteration or waiver criteria have been met:

- The PHI use or disclosure involves no more than minimal risk to the privacy of individuals based on:
  - an adequate plan presented to the IRB to protect PHI identifiers from improper use and disclosure;
  - an adequate plan to destroy those identifiers at the earliest opportunity, consistent with the research, absent a health or research justification for retaining the identifiers or if retention is otherwise required by law; and
  - adequate written assurances that the PHI will not be reused or disclosed to any other person or entity except (a) as required by law, (b) for authorized oversight of the research study, or (c) for other research for which the use or disclosure of the PHI is permitted by the Privacy Rule.
- The research could not practicably be conducted without the requested waiver or alteration.
- The research could not practicably be conducted without access to and use of the PHI.

A waiver alteration of authorization will only be applicable to a particular research protocol. Any subsequent use or disclosure of PHI by a covered entity for a different research study would require an additional authorization or waiver or alteration of authorization, or is permitted under the limited data set provisions of the privacy regulations.

The covered entity must retain documentation of an IRB or Privacy Board approval of waiver or alteration of Authorization for six years from the creation or the last effective date, whichever is later.

Potential Impact of HIPAA on International Research
Since HIPAA applies to covered entities only, it will have mostly an indirect impact on international research. A researcher that works for a covered entity or is a covered

health care provider and provides health care as part of the research will be subject to the full panoply of use and disclosure controls. Nevertheless, researchers and researcher organizations that are not health care providers will be required to know and understand the HIPAA since they are dependent on obtaining personal health information from covered entities.

However, with proper planning, HIPAA should not impose insurmountable obstacles on international research. HIPAA permits researchers to review PHI in preparation for research. Informed consents may include a HIPAA authorization allowing researchers to access the PHI necessary to carry out research protocols and, when all else fails, researchers may request IRBs to waive the authorization altogether. In conducting international research, corporate researchers and sponsors should carefully consider HIPAA compliance requirements as well as the privacy laws and regulations of each country in which the clinical trial is to be conducted.

Canadian Law

On April 13, 2000, the Canadian Parliament enacted by Royal Assent the Personal Information Protection and Electronic Documents Act (PIPEDA), which requires private entities to comply with a statutory code of conduct that mandates individual consent for the collection, use, and/or disclosure of personal information.[37] Prior to the enactment of PIPEDA, Canada's Federal Privacy Act (FPA), which was adopted in 1983, was the only national Canadian privacy law protecting personal information.[38] However, the FPA's proscriptions only apply to over 150 designated public agencies and institutions, and prohibit collection of personal information not related directly to their operating programs or activities, and from making unrelated uses or disclosures of such information without the individual's consent.

To develop privacy guidelines for private entities, the Canadian Standards Association (CSA) approved in 1996 a Model Code for the Protection of Personal Information ("Model Code").[39] At that time, the Model Code was not made part of Canadian law, but was widely viewed as establishing sound parameters for effective data privacy management for private entities. The Model Code was codified into Canadian statutes as part of PIPEDA.[40] The Model Code's ten key guidelines, which serve as PIPEDA's bedrock principles, include:

1. *Accountability:* An organization is responsible for personal information under its control through a designated privacy official.[41]

2. *Identified Purpose(s):* An organization must disclose the purposes for which personal information will be collected at or before the time the information is collected.[42]

3. *Consent:* Generally, the knowledge and consent of the individual are required for collection, use, and/or disclosure of personal information.[43]

4. *Limited Collection:* Personal information shall be collected by fair and lawful means and the collection shall be limited to that which is necessary for the organization's identified purposes.[44]

5. *Limited Use, Disclosure, and Retention:* Personal information shall not be used or disclosed for purposes other than for which it was collected.[45]

6. *Accuracy:* Personal information should be as accurate, complete, and up-to-date as is necessary for the identified purpose.[46]

7. *Security:* Personal information should be protected by security safeguards appropriate to the sensitivity of the information.[47]

8. *Openness:* An organization shall make readily available specific information about its privacy policies and procedures.[48]

9. *Right of Access:* Upon request, individuals shall be informed of the existence, use, and disclosure of, and given access to, such personal information.[49]

10. *Compliance:* an individual shall be able to address any concerns regarding an organization's compliance with the aforementioned principles with the organization's designated privacy official.[50]

While the PIPEDA legislation was being considered, health care organizations expressed concern that the Model Code and resulting legislation did not address important issues unique to the health care industry. Because the health care sector was not involved with the Model Code's development, the Code's design was focused on encouraging electronic commerce and did not focus on unique health care related privacy issues. Notably, the Canadian Medical Association (CMA) adopted its own version of the Model Code in 1998, which addressed health care related issues in greater detail.[51] However, CMA's version of the Model Code was not incorporated into the final PIPEDA legislation. Instead, the Canadian legislature delayed the legislation's application to personal health information for one year (until January 1, 2002) to allow the health care industry sufficient time to implement appropriate policies and procedures. As a practical matter, the Privacy Commissioner may rely upon the CMA version of the Model Code when interpreting PIPEDA privacy issues in a health care context.

Overview of PIPEDA

PIPEDA requires every private person or organization that collects, uses, and/or discloses personal information in the course of commercial activities to take steps to protect the privacy of individual information. This basic rule encompasses four key principles. First, PIPEDA applies to "every organization" including associations, partnerships, persons, or trade unions and to both traditional bricks-and-mortar and e-commerce businesses.[52] In the health care context, physicians, providers, and pharmaceutical and medical device manufacturers are clearly subject to PIPEDA.

Second, PIPEDA applies to the "collection, use, and disclosure" of personal information.[53] "Use" is defined as the "treatment and handling of personal information within an organization" and, based on the Model Code, occurs any time data about an identifiable individual is "assessed, manipulated, altered, deleted, or destroyed within the organization."[54]

Third, PIPEDA applies to "personal information," including personal health information, which is "information about an identifiable individual."[55] Personal information may come in many forms and the ultimate scope of the definition will be determined through interpretations by the Canadian Privacy Commissioner. Notably, personal information includes both factual data about an individual (e.g., name, age, demographics, and identification numbers) as well as subjective data (e.g., an individual's opinion, evaluations, and comments). Also, personal information must be linked to an identifiable individual (living or deceased); data that has been made anonymous is exempt from PIPEDA and may be used freely within an organization or furnished through outside disclosures.

Fourth and finally, PIPEDA applies to "commercial activity," which is defined to include "any particular transaction, act or conduct or any regular course of conduct that is of commercial character."[56] This standard is clearly broad and will encompass most if not all purposes for which pharmaceutical and medical device manufacturers, as well as health care providers and physicians, will collect, analyze, and use personal health information during clinical research.

PIPEDA also contains several express exceptions where the privacy protections do not apply. The exceptions include: (1) government entities, which are subject to the FPA and not PIPEDA; (2) the collection and/or use of personal information for domestic purposes;[57] (3) the collection, use, or disclosure of personal information for journalistic, artistic, or literary purposes;[58] and (4) collection, use, or disclosure of personal information for statistical or scholarly study or research.[59]

Obligations Imposed on Covered Organizations

PIPEDA imposes four main obligations on organizations governed thereunder, which are referred to as "covered organizations." First, a covered organization must identify the appropriate purpose(s) for which it collects, uses, and discloses personal information.[60] The purposes must be identified to the individuals before the information is collected. The scope of permissible data gathering is limited to that which is necessary to fulfill the purposes identified.[61] Once the stated need for certain information ends, that information should be "destroyed, erased, or made anonymous."[62]

Second, as of January 1, 2004, no private organization governed by PIPEDA will be permitted to collect, use, or disclose personal information about someone without that person's consent.[63] The statute requires meaningful consent, which means the person providing consent must understand how the organization intends to use his or her information.[64] Consent must be freely given, and an organization may not make a consent a condition of supplying a good or service. A covered organization should not construe a consent for a given purpose beyond what are the reasonable expectations of the individual. In certain specified instances, a legal guardian may provide consent on behalf of an individual.

PIPEDA permits express and implied consent and recognizes both oral and written consent.[65] An organization should seek express consent, either oral or written, for information considered to be sensitive which, although not expressly defined by statute, is likely to encompass all personal health information. Notably, PIPEDA also contains several specific exceptions to the individual consent requirement for which public policy supports direct and immediate disclosure.[66]

Third, an organization is required to maintain personal information that is accurate and current as appropriate "to minimize the possibility that inappropriate information may be used to make a decision about the individual."[67] The focus in this regard is to ensure that personal information is updated or amended, or erroneous information is corrected as expeditiously as possible.

Finally, PIPEDA imposes a series of administrative requirements intended to ensure that organizations maintain appropriate privacy protection programs. The administrative requirements include developing policies and procedures to address

PIPEDA obligations, designating an individual or individuals responsible for the organization's compliance with PIPEDA, making public the organization's privacy policies and procedures and identifying the persons responsible for implementing them, and adopting security safeguards that are appropriate for the sensitivity of the information.[68] These administrative requirements are essential to ensuring the privacy protections are met.

PIPEDA and Other Applicable Privacy Laws

Within Canada, PIPEDA works in conjunction with the FPA, with the demarcation line drawn based upon whether an organization is private or public. While seemingly complementary in this way, the two privacy laws are not identical in their scope. For example, the FPA does not require individuals to consent to collect personal information when it relates to an activity of the collecting institution. However, because PIPEDA requires consent in most every case, this discrepancy may complicate data transfers of personal health information from the public sector to the private sector.

Privacy issues in Canada also raise federalism concerns similar to those existing in the United States. Prior to the enactment of PIPEDA, several Canadian provinces had already enacted sector-specific privacy laws affecting personal information, including personal health care information.[69] Recognizing that provinces may have perfectly suitable rules to govern the privacy of health information, the PIPEDA provides authority to exempt the organizations from PIPEDA's rules for activities carried on within that province when the province has its own rules that are deemed to be "substantially similar" to PIPEDA. Otherwise, PIPEDA will apply to data collection, use, or disclosure occurring within a particular province.

With regard to international law, Canadian law is consistent with the United States and the EU's Data Directive in that all three recognize generally-accepted principles of privacy law, which include notice, individual choice and consent, access, security, and organization accountability. However, PIPEDA differs from the EU Data Directive and the HIPAA Privacy Rule in certain key respects. For example, the EU clearly distinguishes between sensitive and nonsensitive data and requires express consent for collection, use, or disclosure of sensitive information. In contrast, while Canada also follows an express consent standard for sensitive data, PIPEDA does not define sensitive information leaving open to question whether certain data types qualify.

Another example of a key policy difference is that the U.S. HIPAA requirements specifically list many personal health information identifiers that can be de-identified and therefore fall outside the scope of the HIPAA requirements. Comparatively, the EU Data Directive and PIPEDA do not provide a specific list of personal identifiers and therefore may take different views on whether eliminating a certain element renders the data subject nonidentifiable.

While the international privacy protection schemes differ, it appears unlikely that an organization operating in one of those jurisdictions that is faced with transferring covered data to another jurisdiction will encounter conflicting obligations. Notably, the European Commissioner determined soon after PIPEDA's enactment that the Canadian statute provides "adequate protection" for privacy of data and, therefore, permits transfer of data between European organizations and Canadian organizations. While the different international privacy protection programs can be found generally to fit together, organizations engaged in international commerce must be cognizant of all applicable laws and the nuances between the various requirements.

European Law

EU Data Protection Directive and National Laws

The genesis for comprehensive privacy protection in Europe is the EU Data Directive 95/46/EC (the "EU Data Protection Directive").[70] The EU Data Protection Directive requires the countries that make up the European Economic Area (EEA) [71] to pass national legislation covering the collection and use of personally identifiable information. However, a directive is binding only on the results to be achieved (i.e., the protection of personal information) but leaves the details of how it is to be achieved to national authorities of member states.

This has resulted in slight differences in the wording and substance of each national law. For this reason, it is not sufficient to rely on the Directive for definitive guidance. In addition to applying the concepts found in the EU Data Protection Directive, research organizations are advised to review the domestic privacy laws in each member state in which data will be processed when implementing a comprehensive compliance program.

For example, entities that process data for clinical trials conducted in Germany must comply with the German Federal Data Protection Act.[72] If the clinical trials are conducted in United Kingdom and data is processed there, the entity must comply with the Data Protection Act 1998.[73] The Personal Data Protection Code of Italy, which entered into force on January 1, 2004, harmonizes Italian law with the EU Data Protection Directive.[74] At the time of this writing, France still has not passed the legislation necessary to bring the French Act fully into line with the Directive, although a new law that will do this is imminent. The current law in France is the Act on Data Processing Data Files and Individual Liberties, which contains many, but not all, of the protections provided by the EU Data Protection Directive.[75] Due to the large number of domestic European privacy laws and their sometimes disparate content, this chapter will concentrate on the EU Data Protection Directive. This will provide the reader with a starting point in understanding the framework followed wholly or partially by member states.

The key to knowing which of the national laws apply is where the data is actually processed. Article 4 of the EU Data Protection Directive stipulates that each member state apply its national provisions only if the processing is carried out by a data controller's establishment (offices and other facilities) in the respective member country.[76] This means that the data controller primarily must observe the national laws of those member countries in which it is located.[77]

Type of Information Protected

The EU Data Protection Directive and the related national laws protect a natural person's "right to privacy with respect to the processing of personal data."[78] Personal data means "any information relating to an identified or identifiable natural person ("data subject")."[79] The Directive defines "identifiable person" to mean "one who can be identified directly or indirectly, in particular by reference to an identification number or to one or more factors specific to physical, physiological, mental, economic, cultural or social identity."[80]

"Processing" is a broad term that means "any operation or set of operations which is performed upon personal data whether or not by automatic means."[81] Processing includes any collection, recording, use, or storage of personal information. "Personal data" means any information relating to an identified or identifiable person, also known as the data subject.[82] The inclusion of the term "identifiable" means the

Directive applies even when a person's name is not listed, but can be identified by reference to an identification number or by other means.

Affected Entities

The EU Data Protection Directive refers to regulated persons or entities as "data controllers." These are natural or legal persons who alone or jointly with others "determines the purposes and means of the processing of personal data."[83] The data controller is required to comply with principles relating to data quality, the information furnished to the data subject, the data subject's right of access to data, and the data subject's right to object. The sponsor will be a data controller under the Directive, since it is responsible for designing the clinical trial and determining the purpose of the data processing. In instances where the CRO determines the means of processing the information gathered during a clinical trial, using its own computer systems, it will also be a data controller. The investigator may or may not be a data controller, depending on the facts surrounding his or her activities. In some cases, the investigator merely collects or processes personal data on behalf of the CRO or sponsor. In other situations, the investigator collects or processes data in a manner that makes it a data controller independent of the CRO or sponsor.

Framework and Compliance Requirements

Protections within Europe

The EU Data Protection Directive contains a number of basic privacy protections. Article 6 of the Directive sets forth the principles relating to data quality. This article limits secondary uses of data, meaning that the data collected must be "adequate, relevant and not excessive in relation to the purposes for which they are collected and/or further process."[84] Article 6 also states that data must be processed "fairly and lawfully," must be "accurate and, where necessary, kept up-to-date," and must be kept in an identifiable form no longer than necessary.

Additionally, Article 10 provides that when collecting information from the data subject, controllers and their representatives must make certain disclosures regarding the collection, use, and further disclosure of the collected information. This includes the identities of the controller (or its representative), the purposes for the data processing, and any recipients or categories of recipients of the data.[85] To guarantee fair processing, the controller must also disclose the recipient or category of recipients of the data, as well as whether the replies to questions are mandatory or permissive and the consequences for failure to reply, and existence of the data subject's rights to access their data and rectify any incorrect data.[86]

Similar rules apply when personal data is not obtained from the data subject except that notice must be provided at the time the obtained information is recorded or disclosed to a third party.[87] However, when the data is not directly collected from the individual and the purpose of processing is historical and scientific research, notice will not be required if obtaining it would be impossible or unduly burdensome.[88]

Perhaps most importantly, data subjects are granted extensive rights to discover how data about them are used and can object to some categories of data processing. Under Article 12, the data subject can require the controller to disclose the following to him or her:

- whether personal data is being processed;
- the purposes of the processing;
- the categories of data concerned; and
- the recipients or categories of recipients to whom the data are disclosed.

This information is to be provided to the data subject in an intelligible form. The data subject also has a right to know about any available information as to the source of the data. These rights apply "without constraint or reasonable intervals" and "without delay or excessive expense."[89]

Data subjects also have the right to correct information when it is inaccurate or incomplete. If processing fails to comply with the directive, the data subject has a right to rectify, erase, or block processing.[90] Individuals have the right to be informed by the controller before personal data is disclosed for the first time to third parties for purposes of direct marketing.[91] If the processing is for direct marketing, the data subject has a right to object free of charge to such uses.[92]

Additional rules apply to processing of sensitive data. [93] The processing of sensitive data (including health-related data) is generally prohibited, subject to a number of exceptions.[94] For example, if the obligation of professional secrecy[95] does not exist, health information may be processed when the data subject gives explicit consent.[96] Such consent is usually included in consent forms used for clinical trials in Europe.

Under Article 19, the data controller must notify the responsible supervisory authorities of its processing procedures in the member state in which data collection occurs.[97] The applicable process is determined by the member state and differs from country to country. For example, in the United Kingdom or France, the notification is centralized under the Information Commissioner's Office, which is the

Data Processing Authority (DPA) responsible for regulating the entire country. In France, the Commission National de l'Informatique et des Libertes (CNIL) is the central DPA to which notice is to be given. In other countries, such as Germany, a regional approach has been adopted under competent supervisory authority in each territory or state is responsible for this function. While identifying the DPA may provide some challenges, the actual notification is fairly straightforward and inexpensive. In the United Kingdom, for instance, the annual notification can be completed online for a reasonable fee.[98]

While the controls on the processing of data within Europe are generally more stringent than those found in the United States, the concepts are very similar to those found in HIPAA. In many ways, the existence of harmonized rules within the EU makes transfers between member states fairly predictable and understandable. To conduct a clinical trial entirely in Europe will require knowledge of the EU Directive framework, as well as the terms and nuances contained in the laws of the pertinent EU member states. Overall, the movement of personal data within and between member states is contemplated and promoted by the directive.

Third Country Transfers: Data from Europe to the United States.
Potential problems arise when this information is to be transferred from the EEA to "third countries," which are countries other than countries included in the EAA. Article 25 of the Directive requires member states to allow transfers of personal data to a third country only if the country "insures an adequate level protection."[99] When the EU Commission (the "Commission") finds that a third country does not ensure adequate protection, member states are required to "take the measures necessary to prevent any transfer of data of the same type to third country in question."[100] Instead of listing countries that have been deemed adequate, the Directive provides criteria for determining the adequacy of the privacy protection, which are evaluated based on all facts and circumstances surrounding a data transfer operation. These criteria include the purpose in duration of the proposed processing operation(s), the country of origin and of final destination, the third country's rules of law, both general and sectoral, as well as professional rules and security members that are compiled in the third country.[101]

Using these criteria the commission has so far recognized Argentina,[102] Canada,[203] Guernsey,[104] Hungary,[105] and Switzerland[106] as providing adequate protection. Since the United States lacks a single, comprehensive privacy law, the EU has determined that the United States *does not* have adequate privacy protections. Since the HIPAA Privacy Rule only applies to narrowly defined covered entities, it is unlikely that these new regulations will be deemed adequate by the Commission for transfers of research data to sponsors and other entities that are not covered entities.

Since the EU views U.S. laws as providing inadequate protection of privacy, the only options available for U.S. pharmaceutical companies that wish to receive personal information for their clinical trials conducted in EU countries are as follows:

- *Certification with U.S. Safe Harbor Principles:* The U.S. company certifies its adherence to the Safe Harbor Principles administered by the U.S. Department of Commerce.
- *Data Transfer Agreement:* The EU data exporter and the U.S. company receiving the data enter into a private contract which binds the U.S. company to protect the information at the same level required by the EU Data Protection Directive.
- *Code of Conduct:* The Directive permits trade associations to draft codes of conduct that provide adequate levels of protection of personal information transferred to third countries. This code must be approved by the DPA in the transferring country.
- *De-Identification of Data:* The EU Data Directive only applies to identifiable personal information. Clinical trial data that has been de-identified will not be subject to the third-country transfers prohibition.
- *Unambiguous Informed Consent:* The EU company may transfer data if it obtains an unambiguous informed consent from every data subject before each transfer is made.
- *Binding Corporate Rules:* A recently published nonbinding working document has considered whether binding corporate rules provide adequate protections for international data transfers. To qualify for this method of transborder data flows of personal information, a company must document how identifiable information is used and disclosed and how privacy is managed and protected. This would include internal policy rules, procedures, and mechanisms to ensure the rights of data subjects.

Certification under the Safe Harbor Principles

The Commission issued the Safe Harbor Principles on July 21, 2003, after extensive negotiations with the United States. As a result, U.S. companies or organizations that are regulated by the Federal Trade Commission (FTC) or the Department of Transportation (DOT) may certify their compliance with the Safe Harbor Principles and thereafter be permitted to import personal information from EU Member States. Two conditions must be met before Safe Harbor status can be attained: First, the company must publicly disclose its commitment to comply with the Safe Harbor Principles, and second, the organization must be subject to the statutory authority of a U.S. government body. The seven Safe Harbor Principles are:

- *Notice:* Organizations must notify individuals about the purposes for which they collect and use information about them. They must provide information about how individuals can contact the organization with any inquiries or complaints, the types of third parties to which the information will be disclosed, and the choices and means the organization offers for limiting data use and disclosure.

- *Choice:* Organizations must give individuals the opportunity to determine whether their personal information can be disclosed to a third party or used for a purpose incompatible with the reason the original collection or subsequently authorized by the individual. For sensitive information,[107] the individual must give affirmative or explicit acceptance (opt in) if the information is to be disclosed to a third party or used for a purpose other than its original purpose or the purpose subsequently authorized by the individual.

- *Onward Transfer* (Transfers to Third Parties): To disclose information to a third party, organizations must apply the notice and choice principles. Where an organization wishes to transfer information to a third party that is acting as an agent, it may do so if the third party subscribes to the Safe Harbor Principles or is subject to the EU Directive or another adequacy finding. As an alternative, the organization can enter into a written agreement with such third party, requiring that party to provide at least the same level of privacy protection as is required by the Safe Harbor.

- *Security:* Organizations must take reasonable precautions to protect personal information from loss, misuse, and unauthorized access, disclosure, alteration, and destruction. Unlike HIPAA, the EU Data Protection Directive does not include detailed regulations or guidelines on methods to protect the security of this information. Because the EU Directive and most national laws are silent on how this is to be achieved, many organizations looking to comply with the Safe Harbor Principles will comply with established international security standards such as those provided by the National Institute of Standards and Technology (NIST)[108] or the International Standards Organization (ISO).[109]

■ *Data Integrity:* Personal information must be relevant for the purposes for which it is to be used. An organization should take reasonable steps to ensure that data is reliable for its intended use, accurate, complete, and current.

■ *Access:* Individuals must have access to personal information about them held by an organization and be able to correct, amend, or delete that information where it is inaccurate, except where the burden or expense of providing access would be disproportionate to the risks to the individual's privacy in the case in question, or where the rights of persons other than the individual would be violated.

■ *Enforcement:* In order to ensure compliance with the Safe Harbor Principles, there must be: (a) readily available and affordable independent grievance processes so that each individual's complaints and disputes can be investigated and resolved and damages awarded where appropriate; (b) procedures for verifying that a company's commitment to adhere to the Safe Harbor Principles has been properly implemented; and (c) penalties to remedy problems for failing to comply with the Principles. Sanctions must be sufficiently rigorous to ensure organizational compliance. Organizations that fail to provide annual self-certification letters will no longer appear on the list of participants and, thus, Safe Harbor Principles benefits will no longer be assured.

Once the Safe Harbor Principles certification is accepted by the U.S. Department of Commerce, all member states of the EU will be bound by the European Commission's finding of adequacy. Therefore, companies participating in the Safe Harbor Principles are deemed to have adequate protections and data flows to those companies will continue. Claims brought by European citizens against U.S. companies will be heard in the United States subject to limited exceptions.

Today, over 400 U.S. companies have certified to adhere to the Safe Harbor Principles. However, many other companies continue to deliberate on whether it is a viable option for their operations. One concern is the significant costs and resources required for Safe Harbor Principles implementation and ongoing compliance, as there are significant policies, procedures, and safeguards that must be implemented to promote compliance. However, as state and federal controls on privacy and security continue to rise, most of the Safe Harbor Principles requirements can be met while also complying with U.S. law. The continued growth of privacy and security regulation would suggest that companies reconsider whether Safe Harbor compliance is a reasonable trade-off for receiving personal data from European clinical trials.

Another concern is that by certifying that it is Safe Harbor Principles compliant, the company will become subject to the U.S. Federal Trade Commission's (FTC) enforcement jurisdiction. An organization that develops its own self-regulatory program under the Safe Harbor Principles may find itself subject to scrutiny by the FTC for potential unfair and deceptive trade practices. As recently demonstrated, the FTC will prosecute U.S. companies that fail to adequately protect the privacy and security of personal information in accordance with their notices of privacy practices.[110] These five recent FTC matters were resolved by consent decrees.

Preparing a U.S.-based program for Safe Harbor Principles certification offers many advantages to international corporations. Used in conjunction with other privacy compliance efforts, the Safe Harbor Principles provide a methodology for insuring that privacy is protected throughout the organization. Since the Safe Harbor Principles also include information security safeguards, many of the steps in attaining certification will also improve information security practices within the organization. Most important, the U.S. company that is required (or decides) to comply with HIPAA can combine these mandatory compliance efforts with the voluntary efforts under the Safe Harbor Principles to attain compliance simultaneously with all of the requirements.

The Data Transfer Agreement

The second option for making a U.S. company eligible to receive personally identifiable information from an EEA country is through an individual contract called a Data Transfer Agreement (DTA). DTAs are permitted by the EU Data Protection Directive and enable a data controller to transfer data to third countries if adequate safeguards are also in place through the use of "appropriate contractual clauses."[111] The term "appropriate" is not defined, but the Commission is permitted to determine that certain "standard" contractual clauses are appropriate.[112]

Using this authority, the Commission has promoted a standard DTA.[113] According to the standard agreement, the data importer (e.g., a U.S.-based sponsor) has several obligations. The data importer must warrant to process data in accordance with the data protection principles, which are incorporated by reference into an appendix to the agreement. These terms include obligations regarding the

- purpose of the processing;
- quality and proportionality of the data processed;

- transparency and security of processing; and
- data subjects' rights of access, rectification, and erasure and blocking of data uses.

There is a presumption that the protection is adequate when the model DTA is used. When it is not, the DPA in the EU country exporting the information must approve the alternate DTA.

A major downside of the DTA approach for international data transfers is that large corporations may find themselves managing numerous complicated and inconsistent contracts. Failure to adequately limit actual data flows to those permitted by contract could result in liability for the company. Keeping the contracts valid and enforceable will also be a major problem, unless a person is specifically assigned to this contract management role. The penalty for noncompliance can be significant, as breaches to the DTA could render a U.S. corporation jointly and severally liable for privacy breaches related to personal information it imports. In such way, a U.S. corporation may find itself subject to the jurisdiction of the country from which the information is imported.

Codes of Conduct

Another method that can be used to establish adequate safeguards to permit transfers of personal information from EU member countries are "codes of conduct." The codes must be authorized by the DPA when they are initially established and whenever revised. The EU Data Protection Directive directs member states to require trade associations or other bodies representing other categories of data controllers to draft national codes of privacy protection and submit them to the DPA for approval.[114]

For example, using this option, a trade association comprised of pharmaceutical companies would prepare a code of conduct governing the transfer for personal data to the U.S. for clinical trials. The Code of Conduct would be presented to the DPA in the country of transfer and, if approved, would permit the transfers to occur, even to countries deemed not to have adequate privacy protections. At the present time, this option has not been used to transfer personal information from the EU to the United States for clinical trials.

The De-identification of Information

Like HIPAA, the EU Data Protection Directive and the U.S. Safe Harbor Principles provisions apply only to personal information that is identifiable. If the records used are not identifiable, privacy or security concerns are not present. Therefore, the fourth option is to de-identify information before it is exported from an EEA country.[115]

A couple of concerns are worth mentioning about de-identification. First, member states have not clearly and consistently articulated a harmonized approach to de-identifying personal information. No standard methods for de-identifying information exist that are similar to the "safe harbor" or the "statistician's certification" methods found under HIPAA.[116] While this option may be a viable alternative for a company conducting research that does not require personally identifiable information, contract provisions stating that the international clinical trial data must be de-identified needs to define acceptable de-identification standards. In some situations, this option will not be adequate if the clinical trial requires personally identifiable information.

Unambiguous Informed Consent

Data subjects often consent to data transfers to inadequate third countries, under a principle known as the unambiguous informed consent exception. The EU Data Protection Directive permits the transfer of personal data to third countries without adequate privacy protections when the "data subject has given his consent unambiguously to the proposed transfer."[117]

The consent given must comply with all of the EU Data Protection Directive's consent requirements. The term "the data subject's consent" is defined as "any freely given specific informed indication of his wishes by which the data subject signifies his agreement to personal data relating to him being processed."[118] To give consent "freely" under the Directive, the subject must know the subject matter of the consent and must be capable of giving consent.

To provide informed consent, the data subject must be given all relevant and necessary information before the consent is obtained. The data controller should provide the subject with a contact name and address, the purpose of the collection and processing, and the purpose of the data transfer. Because the consent should be specific, the purpose should be carefully described in terms that ensure clarity and are not overly broad or general. However, as with HIPAA, any change of purpose requires a new consent or waiver. Therefore, care must be taken to ensure that the scope of the consent covers all current and anticipated uses of the data.

The data subject protections provided in Articles 10 and 11 must be included in the informed consent. As discussed earlier, these include notice about the category of data to be transferred (e.g., clinical medical records for clinical trials) and the identity of the recipients in the third country (e.g., regulatory authorities, the CRO, or the sponsor). In circumstances when personal data is sent to the United States or another country where privacy protection is not recognized as adequate, the data subject must be informed about the general level of protection afforded by the receiving country.[119]

Although the Directive requires a consent be given "unambiguously," it does not require that the data subject provide a written consent. Nonetheless, because the informed consent must comply with applicable national laws and international guidelines (e.g., the ICH GCP guidelines), a data controller should obtain a written consent from each data subject. This should not pose additional burdens, given that the informed consent form for clinical trial participation must be provided in writing and signed by the trial participant.

According to the ICH GCP guidelines, the EU Data Protection Directive requirements regarding consent may be incorporated into the data subject's consent to participate in the clinical trial. Nevertheless, the consent to transfer data to an "unsafe" third country should be clearly distinguishable from the trial participation language. This could be accomplished by providing the EU Data Protection Directive language in bold type away from the other required language.

The consent to transfer should be obtained prior to the collection of data. While some EU member states, such as the United Kingdom and Belgium, permit a retroactive consent, other members do not. In any case, failing to obtain written consent before data is collected can have significant regulatory implications, including fines and cessation of future data collection.

The unambiguous informed consent is a logical method for transferring data from the EU to the United States in clinical trials. This is because most national laws and the ICH GCP require an informed consent prior to enrolling a subject for clinical trials. The first step would be to combine the language required by the EU Data Protection Directive (and relevant member state law) with the language required by the FDA, the ICH GCP, and HIPAA into a unified informed consent. The likelihood is small that the Directive language stating that the information may be transferred to the United States, a country deemed to have inadequate laws, will dissuade the data subject from signing the consent. Sponsors and CROs should consider compliance with the Safe Harbor Principles and adding a statement of such compliance to counter any concerns in this area.

Binding Corporate Rules for International Data Transfers

The newest option that is being considered by the Working Party is to use "Binding Corporate Rules" to demonstrate adequate privacy controls.[120] Under this method, legally binding and enforceable corporate rules may provide the legal basis for adequacy. To be eligible, the corporate rules must apply generally throughout the corporate group, irrespective of where the corporate presence is located or the nationality of the data subjects whose personal data is being processed.

Under this exemption, data subjects covered by the scope of Binding Corporate Rules become third-party beneficiaries through

- the legally enforceable corporate rules to protect personal data;
- intercompany contracts entered into by the members of the corporate group; and
- intracompany contracts that guarantee internal compliance with binding corporate rules.[121]

Combining the three elements may be sufficient for U.S. companies to properly receive personal information from EEA countries. To accomplish this, the company would document the management of its transborder data flows in a corporate compliance plan. The compliance plan would describe many of the aspects of its system of personal data management through internal policies and procedures, rules, and other management and technical mechanisms to protect the personal information it processes and discloses.

This documentation would be very similar to that required under the U.S. Safe Harbor Principles and for entities required to comply with HIPAA. They would include documenting the steps taken by a company's management to fulfill its privacy protection objectives, including security measures, staff training programs, and audit programs, and third-party contracting procedures for data transfers outside of the company.

This method arises from a Working Party recommendation and has not yet received the full approval of the EU. Nevertheless, the method may be approved today by the DPA in a member state. In the long term, it may provide U.S. corporations with a method to conduct intracompany transfers of personal information without having to certify its voluntary compliance with the U.S. Department of Commerce. Binding corporate rules provide additional incentives for a corporation to integrate mandatory privacy and security compliance programs under U.S. laws with its international obligations to protect to privacy and security of personal information.

Unified Approach to Compliance

Given the complexity of complying with the growing number of laws and regulations addressing privacy, organizations will be well-served to plan ahead when conducting international clinical trials. Creation of a program that attains compliance with all the laws under which the trials will be conducted will free international researchers to concentrate on conducting the trials, rather than the nuances of compliance in each country. In this final section of the chapter, we provide an outline of a unified approach to privacy compliance that will assist international researchers in anticipating and complying with the privacy laws we have discussed. The goal of the unified approach is to fully comply with all of the regulations in a way that is seamless and integrated into the international clinical trial process. The process begins with a legal analysis, includes a risk analysis, and concludes with policies and procedures to guide researchers in their international research activities.

Legal Analysis: Identification of the Applicable Laws and Regulations

The first step is to determine the laws, regulations, and guidelines applicable to the international clinical trials your organization will be conducting. This chapter introduces the reader to some of these, but it will be necessary to review the laws and regulations in each country where a particular clinical trial will be conducted. The information gathered in this step will provide a clear understanding of the privacy rules that must be complied with and also assist in assessing the manner in which the compliance requirements can be harmonized.

To complete this analysis, a chart should be prepared comparing informed consent, authorization, data subject consents, and other requirements for obtaining, processing, and disclosing PHI and other personal information in the clinical trials process. This chart will be used to prepare documents, policies, and procedures and establish harmonized practices for gathering and using clinical trial information.

Risk Assessment and Analysis: Identifying Safeguards to Protect PHI and Other Personal Information in the Clinical Trial Process

Sponsors, CROs, investigators, and other entities involved in the clinical trial process will conduct a risk assessment and analysis to determine whether the proper safeguards have been implemented to protect PHI and other personal information collected and used in the clinical trial process.

The results of the risk analysis will be documented in a risk analysis report. The report lists identified threats and vulnerabilities, as well as safeguard selection criteria. To demonstrate due diligence, the report will include and reference specific portions of the applicable privacy and security regulations. To maximize effectiveness, the risk analysis report will also contain a plan and schedule for implementing the changes necessary to enhance security and attain compliance with applicable laws and regulations.[122]

Information must be gathered on how PHI and personal information is handled during clinical trials as part of assessment and risk analysis. This information is obtained through document reviews, interviews, and security testing.

Documents to be reviewed include written policies and procedures and other documents evidencing the organization's efforts to protect personal information. These include contracts; informed consents; authorizations; Internet policies and procedures; procedures for assigning, modifying, or removing access rights; password management policies; sanctions; and disciplinary procedures.

Interviews will differ slightly, depending on the state, federal, and international laws and regulations that apply. The areas of inquiry include:

- the individual(s) within the organization responsible for privacy;
- how the privacy is structured within the organization;
- how policies and procedures are to be implemented and integrated with current compliance activities;
- how well departments work together to ensure that privacy practices are uniform;
- what third parties have access to the organization's information system;
- what type of personal information is used and disclosed by the organization;
- what contractors and other organizations receive personal information from the organization;
- what are future plans and proposed budgets to improve compliance within the organization; and
- how change management methodologies can be optimized to implement a comprehensive security privacy compliance program.

Security testing may include vulnerability scanning and configuration analysis, as well as assessment of system policies and network architectures. Physical security may also be reviewed to determine whether measures are in place to protect areas of buildings where this information is stored.

Information and reports may be protected by the attorney-client privilege if counsel is involved. If established correctly, this privilege will protect information identified during the compliance process from being subject to discovery procedures under state and federal rules of evidence. Third parties cannot obtain or use detrimental information in a lawsuit against the organization so long as the attorney-client privilege and/or attorney work product protections are intact. Keeping the privilege intact will require documentation and provision of notice about the privilege to employees during the information-gathering phase.

Compliance Program Implementation

The implementation plan provided in the risk analysis report is put into effect in this step, encompassing all the safeguards identified in the risk analysis. It also includes policies and procedures for protection of PHI and other personal information in the clinical trial process.

At this stage of the compliance process, it is important to integrate measures implemented for privacy and security compliance with other compliance efforts currently underway within the company, including the Sarbaner Oxley Act and other state and federal laws. Integration of compliance programs will ensure uniformity and avoid redundancy. For example, time, money, and other resources may be saved by using existing policies and procedures to comply with the privacy and security regulations. Organizational considerations and third-party contracts should also be integrated into the international clinical trial privacy compliance efforts.

Evaluation/Safe Harbor Principles Certification

The document collection, risk analysis, safeguard selection, and implementation in the foregoing steps should be fully documented to demonstrate due diligence and to track compliance efforts. This documentation can be used to support a legal evaluation of compliance, which will include an opinion that the steps taken by the company, based on the documented evidence prepared during risk analysis and implementation efforts, comply with applicable privacy laws. The evaluation can also be used to support the Safe Harbor Principles certification, should the company decide to pursue it.

Periodic Reviews and Evaluation

Protection of privacy in international clinical trials is an ongoing process. Given the changing nature of technology, companies are required to periodically review whether risk management, selected safeguards, and policies and procedures continue to be effective.[123] If not, the company should modify them by performing periodic risk analyses to validate that safeguard selection and implementation features continue to be reasonable, appropriate, and effective.

Notes and References

1   The number of foreign clinical investigators conducting drug research under Investigational New Drug Applications increased 16-fold in the past decade. In 1990, 271 of these foreign clinical investigators were in FDA's database. By 1999 the number grew to 4,458. FDA inspections of foreign clinical investigators conducting drug research have also increased dramatically, from just 22 in 1990 to 64 in 1999.

2   International Conference on Harmonization of Technical Requirements for Registration of Human Use (ICH), ICH Harmonized Tripartite Guideline—Guideline for Good Clinical Practice (GCP), 62 Fed. Reg. 25,691–25,709 (May 9, 1997) (hereinafter "ICH GCP").

3   ICH GCP §§ 5.1.2, 5.15.1 and 6.10

4   Under the ICH GCP, investigators must provide sponsors, monitors, and regulatory agencies with direct access to "source data/documents" for purposes of monitoring, auditing, Institutional Review Board review, and regulatory inspections. ICH GCP §§ 1.51, 1.52, 5.1.2, 5.15.1, and 6.10.

5   Directive 2001/20/EC of April 4, 2001, on the approximation of the laws, regulations, and administrative provisions of member states relating to the implementation of good clinical practice in the conduct of clinical trials on medicinal products for human use (*O.J.* L121/34, May 1, 2001).

6   *See* Clinical Trials Directive, Recital 17.

7   21 C.F.R. § 312.

8   62 *Fed. Reg.* 25,692- 25,709 (May 9, 1997).

9   *See* ICH GCP, definition No. 1.68.

10 *See,* e.g., 21 C.F.R. Parts 312 (drugs), 600 (biological), or 812 (devices).

11 The final security rule (the "Security Rule") was published on February 20, 2003. It establishes a risk analysis and safeguard implementation process for protection of PHI stored in electronic form. The scope of the Security Rule is beyond the scope of this chapter.

12 45 C.F.R. §§ 160.102 (a), 164.500 (a) (2000).

13 *Id.* The transactions are health care claims, payment and advice, coordination of benefits, claim status, enrollment and disenrollment, plan eligibility, premium payments, referral certification, first report of injury, and claims attachments.

14 *Id.* at § 164.501.

15 *Id.*

16 20 U.S.C. 1232g, as amended.

17 45 C.F.R. § 164.512(b)(1)(iii).

18   45 C.F.R. § 164.508.

19   45 C.F.R. § 164.512(i)(1)(ii).

20   45 C.F.R. § 164.512(i)(1)(iii).

21   45 C.F.R. § 164.514(a)–(c) (De-identified health information is no longer PHI or EPHI and, therefore, not subject to the HIPAA Privacy and Security rules).

22   45 C.F.R. § 164.514(e).

23   45 C.F.R. § 164.532(c).

24   45 C.F.R. § 164.512(i).

25   *Id.*

26   *See* 45 CFR § 160.103. These include legal, actuarial, accounting, consulting, data aggregation, management, administrative, accreditation, or financial services to or for such covered entity or Organized Health Care Arrangements in which the covered entity participates. *Id.*

27   Unless a disclosure for which authorization is not required is related to the clinical trial process, it will not be further described in this chapter. However, readers interested in these regulatorily permitted disclosures may find them at 45 C.F.R. § 164.512.

28   45 C.F.R. § 164.508(c)(3).

29   45 C.F.R. § 164.514(b)(1).

30   45 C.F.R. § 164.532(c)(1)

31   45 C.F.R. § 164.532 (c)(2)

32   45 C.F.R. § 164.532(3)

33   45 C.F.R. § 164.532 (c)

34   The *Federal Policy for the Protection of Human Subjects* (the "Common Rule" was adopted in 1991 by 15 Federal departments and agencies and was published at 50 *Fed. Reg.* 28002–28032 (1991), and subsequently adopted by the Social Security Administration by Statute and the Central Intelligence Agency by Executive Order.

35   45 C.F.R. Part 46 at http://ohrp.osophs.dhhs.gov/humansubjects/guidance/45cfr46.htm.

36   21 C.F.R. Parts 50 and 56. 21 C.F.R. Part 50 can be found at http://www.accessdata.fda.gov/scripts/cdrh/cfdocs/cfcfr/showCFR.cfm?CFRPart=50&showFR=1; Part 56 at http://www.access-data.fda.gov/scripts/cdrh/cfdocs/cfcfr/showCFR.cfm?CFRPart=56&showFR=1. Additional requirements are found in 21 C.F.R. Part 312 at http://www.accessdata.fda.gov/scripts/cdrh/cfdocs/cfcfr/CFRSearch.cfm?CFRPart=312&showFR=1, and Part 812 at http://www.access-data.fda.gov/scripts/cdrh/cfdocs/cfcfr/CFRSearch.cfm?CFRPart=812&showFR=1.

37   1999-2000 S.C. 2000, Ch. 5, Part 1 (Can.).

38   *See* Privacy Act.

39   The CSA is a not-for-profit, membership-based association serving businesses, industry, government, and consumers in Canada and the global marketplace. The CSA's Internet address is http://www/csa/ca (last visited 8/13/04).

40   Second Report of the Standing Committee on Social Affairs, Science and Technology (Dec. 6, 1999); Phillips 1999 Annual Report of Privacy Commissioner.

41   CSA Model Code Principle 1—Accountability; PIPEDA Schedule 1, § 4.1.

42   CSA Model Code Principle 2—Identify Purpose; PIPEDA Schedule 1, § 4.2.

43   CSA Model Code Principle 3—Consent; PIPEDA Schedule 1, § 4.3.

44   CSA Model Code Principle 4—Limiting Collection; PIPEDA Schedule 1, § 4.4.

45   CSA Model Code Principle 5—Limiting Use, Disclosure and Retention; PIPEDA Schedule 1, § 4.5.

46   CSA Model Code Principle 6—Accuracy; PIPEDA Schedule 1, § 4.6.

47   CSA Model Code Principle 7—Security; PIPEDA Schedule 1, § 4.7.

48   CSA Model Code Principle 8—Openness; PIPEDA Schedule 1, § 4.8.

49   CSA Model Code Principle 9—Individual Access; PIPEDA Schedule 1, § 4.9.

50   CSA Model Code Principle 10—Challenging Compliance; PIPEDA Schedule 1, § 4.10.

51   Canadian Medical Association, Listening to our Patient's Concerns: Comments on Bill C-54, submitted to House Standing Committee on Industry (Mar. 18, 1999).

52   PIPEDA § 2(1).

53   PIPEDA § 4(1)(a).

54   Office of the Privacy Commissioner of Canada, Your Privacy Responsibilities: A Guide for Business and Organizations 2 (2001). (Hereinafter "Guide for Business".)

55   PIPEDA § ____.

56   PIPEDA § 2(1).

57   PIPEDA § ____.

58   PIPEDA § 4(2).

59   PIPEDA § 7(2).

60   PIPEDA § 5(3).

61   PIPEDA Schedule 1, § 4.4.1.

62   PIPEDA Schedule 1, § 4.5.3.

63   Guide for Business, *supra*, ____, at 8.

64   *Id.*

65   PIPEDA Schedule 1, § 4.3.7.

66   *See*, e.g., PIPEDA § 7(1) (disclosure clearly in the interest of the individual and organization cannot obtain consent in timely fashion).

67   PIPEDA Schedule 1, § 4.6.1.

68   PIPEDA Schedule 1, § 4.1.4.

69   *See,* e.g., R.S.Q. Ch. P-39.1, An Act Respecting the Protection of Personal Information in the Private Sector (applicable to intra-province disclosures in Quebec).

70   Directive 95/46/EC of the European Parliament and of the Council of 24 October 1995 on the protection of individuals with regard to the processing of personal data and on the free movement of such data. (referred herein as the "Data Directive"). An English language copy of the Directive may be found at http://europa.eu.int/comm/internal_market/privacy/law_en.htm.

71   The EAA, includes the European Union—Austria, Belgium, Czech Republic, Denmark, Estonia, Finland, France, Germany, Greece, Hungary, Ireland, Italy, Latvia, Lithuania, Luxembourg, the Netherlands, Poland, Portugal, Slovakia, Slovenia, Spain, Sweden, and United Kingdom—plus Iceland, Lichtenstein, and Norway.

72   Federal Data Protection Act (Bundesdatenschutzgesetz), Bundesgesetzblatt I Nr. 23/2001, page 904 (May 22, 2001). An unofficial English version of this law can be found at http://www.bfd.bund.de/information/bdsg_eng.pdf.

73   Data Protection Act of 1998, 1998 Chapter 29, http://www.hmso.gov.uk/acts/acts1998/19980029.htm.

74   Personal Data Protection Code (Legislative Decree no. 196 of 30 June 2003), entered into force on January 1, 2004. An unofficial version of this law can be found at http://www.garanteprivacy.it/garante/doc.jsp?ID=311113.

75   Act 78-17 of 6 January 1978 on Data Processing, Data Files and Individual Liberties (hereinafter, the French Act). For an English translation of this law, see http://www.bild.net/dataprFr.htm.

76 The term establishment implies the existence of office rooms, but does not specify the legal form of the establishment. *See* EU Data Protection Directive, Recital 19.

77 The EU Data Protection Directive permits a member state's laws to apply when international public law permits it and where a controller not established in the Community Territory uses equipment located in the member state for processing. EU Data Protection Directive Article 4.1 (b) and (c) In addition to the EU Data Protection Directive and related national legislation, there may be specific rules from other areas of law that may stipulate privacy requirements. These can include drug laws and laws pertaining to professional secrecy. Readers are advised to review these laws as well.

78 EU Data Protection Directive, Article 1(2).

79 EU Data Protection Directive, Article 2(a).

80 *Id.*

81 EU Data Protection Directive, Article 2(b).

82 EU Data Protection Directive, Article 2(a). One.

83 EU Data Protection Directive, Article 2(d).

84 EU Data Protection Directive, Article 6(1)(c).

85 Article 10 (a)–(b). These rights are provided to data subjects in accordance with EU Data Protection Directive, Article 12.

86 EU Data Protection Directive, Article 10(c).

87 EU Data Protection Directive, Article 11.

88 Eu Data Protection Directive Article 11(2)

89 EU Data Protection Directive, Article 12(a).

90 EU Data Protection Directive, Article 12(b).

91 14(b).

92 *Id.*

93 Sensitive data is personal data revealing racial or ethnic origin, political opinions, religious or philosophical believes, trade-union membership, and the processing of data concerning health or sex life. EU Data Protection Directive, Article 8(1).

94 *Id.*

95 EU Data Protection Directive, Article 8(3).

96 EU Data Protection Directive, Article 8(2)(a).

97 EU Data Protection Directive, Article 19.

98 See generally http://www.dataprotection.gov.uk. The fee is currently £35. http://www.informationcommissioner.gov.uk/eventual.aspx?id=316#Notification%20Fee.

99 EU Data Protection Directive, Article 25(1).

100 EU Data Protection Directive, Article 25(4).

101 EU Data Protection Directive, Article 25(2).

102 Decision of the Commission C (2003) 1731 of June 30, 2003.

103 Decision of Commission 2002/2/EC of Dec. 20, 2001 (*O.J.* L 2/13, Jan. 4, 2002).

104 Decision of Commission 2002/821/EC of November 21, 2003 (*O.J.* L 308/27, Nov. 25, 2002).

105 Decision of Commission 2000/519/EC of July 26, 2000 (*O.J.* L 215/4, Aug. 25, 2000).

106 Decision of Commission 2000/518/EC of July 26, 2000 (*O.J.* L 215/1, Aug. 25, 2000).

107 Sensitive data is personal data revealing racial or ethnic origin, political opinions, religious or philosophical believes, trade-union membership, and the processing of data concerning health or sex life. EU Data Protection Directive, Article 8(1).

108 NIST 800 Series, http://csrc.nist.gov/.

109 ISO Standard 17799.

110 Eli Lilly & Co (*In re Eli Lilly and Co.,* FTC, No. 0123214, 1/18/02); Microsoft (*In re Microsoft Corp.,* FTC, File No. 012-3240, 8/8/02); Guess? Inc. (*In re Guess? Inc.,* FTC, File No. 022 3260, 6/18/03); *In re MTS Inc.,* FTC, File No. 032-3209, 4/21/04); *In re Gateway Learning Corporation,* FTC File No. 042-3047, 7/7/04).

111 EU Data Protection Directive, Article 26(2).

112 EU Data Protection Directive, Article 26(4).

113 The model contract can be found at http://europa.eu.int/comm/internal_market/privacy/modelcontracts_en.htm.

114 EU Data Protection Directive Article 27(2).

115 *See* Court of Appeal, Civil Division (C.A.): Simon Brown, Aldous and Schiemann LJJ: 21 December 1999 in which the U.K. appeals court stated in review of *Regina v. Department of Health,* Ex Parte Source Informatics Ltd. (Source Informatics case), that if a patient's identity was not disclosed, it is not a breach of confidence for general practitioners and pharmacists to disclose to a third party, without the patient's consent, the information contained in the patient's prescription form for marketing research purposes. This same result would be reached if analyzed under the HIPAA privacy regulations.

116 45 CFR § 164.514.

117 EU Data Protection Directive, Article 26(1)(a).

118 EU Data Protection Directive, Article 2(h).

119 EU Data Protection Directive, Article 29; Working Party Recommendation 2/2001, p. 5.

120 Working Document: Transfers of personal data to third countries: Applying Article 26(2) of the EU Data Protection Directive to Binding Corporate Rules for International Data Transfers, 11639/020EN June 3, 2003.

121 *Id.,* page 18.

122 *See,* e.g., 45 C.F.R. §§ 164.306 (a) and (b).

123 *See,* e.g., 45 C.F.R. § 164.306.

SEVEN

Identifying Applicable Laws and Reducing Key Risks in Nonregistrational, Postmarketing Studies

Judith E. Beach and Nancy Strehlow

Introduction

What is the purpose of "nonregistrational, postmarketing studies," which are studies that are not designed to support applications for significant changes in labeling, indications, or uses, or to gather FDA-required data in support of a New Drug Application (NDA), and what are the key U.S. laws and regulations that apply to them?

Which of those laws and regulations pose the most serious legal risks to sponsors, clinical research organizations (CROs), and clinical investigators, and what practical steps can be taken to reduce those risks?

Of the laws and regulations that apply to postmarketing studies (including nonregistrational, postmarketing studies), the Antikickback Statute and the False Claims Act (FCA) give rise to the most serious legal risks to pharmaceutical companies and clinical investigators, and potentially to CROs. How those risks arise in postmarketing studies and practical steps to reduce those risks are discussed in this chapter.

Nonregistration, postmarketing studies are needed to gather important information beyond the data that is collected to support pharmaceutical companies' marketing applications and label changes. In a nonregistrational, postmarketing study, determining which laws and regulations apply can be complex. This chapter discusses the key laws and regulations that apply to nonregistrational studies, as well as distinguishing clinical trial regulations that do not apply to nonregistrational, postmarketing studies.

The Increasing Need for Nonregistrational, Postmarketing Studies

In clinical studies involving medicinal products (drugs, medical devices, and biologics) that have not yet been approved for marketing, the object of the studies is almost always to gather safety and efficacy data for use in support of an application to the U.S. Food and Drug Administration (FDA) for approval to market or sell the product. In clinical studies involving a product that already has been approved for marketing, however, the studies may have a number of different purposes, and those purposes are critical in determining which laws and regulations apply to the study. In a significant percentage of cases, the FDA will require that a sponsor gather additional data about the drug, (usually long-term safety data) as a condition of its approval of the product. In such an FDA-ordered safety study, all regulations governing studies that are conducted for the purpose of obtaining FDA approval will apply, including virtually all 21 of the Code of Federal Regulations (CFR) Part 312. Similarly, if the manufacturer of a product wants to apply to the FDA for approval to market the product for additional uses (referred to as a "label change," because the product's "label" includes a description of the approved uses), then any studies it conducts in support of such an application for a label change also would have to comply with virtually all of the regulations in 21 CFR Part 312.

Once a medical product has been approved, however, there is often a need for information about the product beyond what was gathered in the premarketing studies. Increasingly, doctors, patients, and payors are faced with numerous choices for treating any given indication. Due to the high cost of obtaining approval of a new drug or device, however, the data currently collected for FDA applications tend to be limited to provide only the information specifically required by FDA to make an approval decision. Moreover, these premarket data are typically derived from controlled clinical studies, which may not present the same compliance problems, comorbidities, variety of patient populations, or other pertinent conditions that physicians actually encounter in their practice. Premarket clinical studies also typically do not address product cost comparisons and cost-effectiveness issues that payors face.

There is, therefore, an increasing need for the collection of additional data to supplement the information provided in FDA applications. For instance, two influenza drugs may both have met all FDA approval standards, but one might prove to be generally more cost-effective because it reduces symptoms more quickly, whereas the other might be a preferable course of treatment for the pediatric population, because they find it tastes less bitter. Similarly, two asthma treatments might be equally effective, but one might be used more consistently due to the more comfortable design of its applicator. As another example, one postanesthesia nausea drug may cost more per dose than its competitors, but it may actually be more cost-effective because it controls nausea so quickly that it significantly reduces the time spent in high-cost intensive care units.

As the number of available drugs increases, the focus of the health care industry is turning less toward trying to find new drugs to deal with specific diseases, and more toward determining which already-available drug is best for particular groups of patients. For that reason, health-care providers and payors need increasing amounts of data about approved, prescribed products to enable them to make the best choices among therapies. As companies conduct greater numbers of postmarketing studies, there is an increasing need for information as to exactly what laws and regulations apply to "nonregistrational" versus "registrational" studies, and how sponsors, clinical research organizations and investigative sites can reduce the legal risks arising from those laws and regulations.

Key Laws and Regulations Applicable to Nonregistrational, Postmarketing Studies

The following laws and regulations generally apply to postmarketing, nonregistrational studies:

- The Antikickback Statute
- The False Claims Act (courts are split)
- Debarment
- Reporting Postmarketing Adverse Drug Experiences and Unanticipated Adverse Device Effects

- HIPAA (in some circumstances)
- The Common Rule (in some circumstances)
- The Federal Acquisition Regulations (if the study is federally funded) Promotion and Charging for Investigational Medical Products
- Food and Drug Administration Modernization Act (FDAMA) (in some circumstances)

Each of these laws and regulations is discussed in the following sections.

Section 312.2(b) Studies

Under 21 CFR § 312.3(b), the use of a marketed drug in the course of medical practice does not meet the FDA's definition of a clinical investigation, and so is not required to comply with the requirements of § 312.2. Although this includes situations where a physician—using his or her medical judgment, in the course of medical practice—changes patients from one marketed medical product to another or puts patients on a marketed medical product, some CROs and sponsors voluntarily treat these types of studies as clinical investigations as set forth in § 312.2(b), and for the purposes of these studies adhere to the requirements listed below, which are discussed later in this chapter.

- Part 50
- Disqualification
- ICH GCP
- Part 56

Laws and Regulations That Generally Do Not Apply to Nonregistrational, Postmarketing Studies

The following laws and regulations generally do not apply to nonregistrational, postmarketing studies:

- 21 CFR Part 54 (Financial Disclosure)
- 21 CFR Part 11 (Electronic Records)
- 21 CFR Part 312 (IND Requirements)
- Stark Anti-Referral Law

Identifying the Highest Risk Statutes

Of the statutes and regulations listed previously, the two that create the most serious legal risks to sponsors, investigators, and CROs in postmarketing studies are the Antikickback Statute and the False Claims Act. For this reason, although each of the applicable statutes or regulations are described below, these two statutes are covered in the greatest detail.

The Antikickback Statute

Of the statutes that apply to postmarketing studies, including nonregistrational studies, the one that poses the highest risks in such studies is the Antikickback Statute (AKS). The application of this statute to postmarketing studies is fairly complex, and the consequences for errors are grave, so it is extremely important for sponsors, CROs, and investigative sites to understand it.

Overview of the Antikickback Statute

The federal health care program Antikickback Statute, 42 U.S.C. § 1320a-7b(b) provides for criminal penalties and civil monetary penalties for persons who pay or receive payments or remuneration in connection with supplies or services that are reimbursable under federally funded health care programs, including Medicare. This statute has implications for studies involving approved drugs and devices, because those items are reimbursable under federal programs.

Statutory Language

For studies involving marketed products, the key sections of the AKS are as follows:

1.   whoever knowingly and willfully solicits or receives any remuneration . . . directly or indirectly . . . in cash or in kind . . . in return for purchasing, . . . ordering, or arranging for or recommending purchasing . . . or ordering any good, . . . service, or item for which payment may be made in whole or in part under a Federal health care program . . . shall be guilty of a felony and upon conviction thereof, shall be fined not more than $25,000 or imprisoned for not more than five years, or both.

2.   whoever knowingly and willfully offers or pays any remuneration . . . directly or indirectly... in cash or in kind to any person to induce such person . . . to purchase

. . . order or arrange for or recommend purchasing, . . . or ordering any good, . . . service or item for which payment may be made in whole or in part under a Federal health care program, shall be guilty of a felony and upon conviction thereof, shall be fined not more than $25,000 or imprisoned for not more than five years, or both.

Additional Criminal Penalties

In addition to the criminal penalties listed above in the AKS (imprisonment and $25,000 per violation), the fines listed in 18 U.S.C. § 3571(b)(3) and 18 U.S.C. § 3571(b)(3) also apply, because AKS violations are felonies. Those sections provide that for individuals, the fines for each violation will be the greater of the fine stated in the statute or $250,000, and for corporations, the greater of the fine stated in the statute or $500,000. Because the $25,000 fine in the statute is a per-occurrence fine, a single, illegal payment made to 1,000 investigative sites possibly might be considered 1,000 violations, thereby resulting in a fine of $25,000,000. Therefore, it is important to note that the criminal fines are not "capped" at $250,000 or $500,000.

Civil Monetary Damages

In addition to the criminal fines set forth in the AKS and 18 U.S.C § 3571 (b)(3), civil monetary damages also can be incurred for a violation of the AKS. For civil monetary damages, the government would not be required to meet the "beyond a reasonable doubt" standard required for criminal convictions, but would only have to show by a "preponderance of the evidence" that a violation occurred. "The burden of showing something by a preponderance of evidence . . . simply requires the trier of fact to believe that the existence of a fact is more probable than its nonexistence...." *Concrete Pipe & Products of Cal., Inc. v. Construction Laborers Pension Trust for Southern Cal.,* 508 U.S. 602, 622 (1993).

For the criminal fines and penalties, the government must show a violation "beyond a reasonable doubt." The civil monetary damages are $50,000 for each act in violation of the AKS, plus "three times the total remuneration offered, paid, solicited, or received, without regard to whether a portion of such remuneration was offered, paid, solicited, or received for a lawful purpose," 42 U.S.C. § 1320a-7a(7).

Exclusion from Federal Programs

In addition to criminal fines, civil monetary penalties and possible imprisonment, violating the AKS can result in exclusion from all state and federal health care programs,

42 U.S.C. § 1320a-7a. This exclusion is for the person or corporation that committed the violation, not the product that was involved in the violation. For that reason, a corporation that violates the AKS in a study involving a single drug could, in theory, have all of its products banned from participation in federal and state health care programs, including Medicare and Medicaid, which would effectively be the equivalent of the death penalty for that corporation. The government, however, tends to leverage this provision to force the company to settle for larger fines based on other violations, such as "off-label promotion violations" because patients taking the companies' products also would suffer should the companies' products be banned from federal and state health care programs.

Antikickback Statute Safe Harbor Provisions

The AKS permits the Secretary of the Department of Health and Human Services (DHHS) to promulgate regulations that identify specific practices that might appear to come under the statute, but that do not violate the statute. Those regulations, which are referred to as "safe harbors," are found at 42 CFR § 1001.952. If the requirements of a safe harbor are met, then the individuals and entities are insulated from prosecution for conduct that otherwise would violate the Antikickback Statute. Currently, there is no safe harbor for research on marketed products, although a proposal for such a safe harbor is pending before the Office of the Inspector General (OIG).

The only existing safe harbor provision that is potentially applicable in studies involving marketed products is the one for "personal services and management contracts," 42 CFR § 1001.952(d), which exempts payments made as compensation for services, as long as the following seven criteria are met:

(a)   The agreement is set out in writing and signed by the parties;

(b)   The agreement specifies the services to be provided, and covers all of the services the agent provides to the principal during the term;

(c)   If the agent is to provide services on a periodic or part time basis, then the agreement specifies the exact schedule of such intervals, their precise length, and the exact charge for such intervals;

(d)   The term of the agreement is for not less than one year;

(e)   The aggregate compensation: (i) is set in advance; (ii) is consistent with fair market value; and (iii) is not determined in a manner that takes into consideration the volume or value of any referrals or business otherwise generated between the parties for which payment may be made under Medicare or a state health care program;

(f)   The services do not involve the counseling or promotion of a business arrangement or other activity that violates any state or federal law; and

(g)   The services contracted for do not exceed those that are reasonably necessary to accomplish the commercially reasonable business purpose of the services.

Antikickback Issues and Risks in Postmarketing Studies

In conducting clinical trials, the relevant data generally needs to be collected by health care providers, and those providers generally must be compensated for their services. In a study involving marketed products, therefore, sponsors generally pay, and health care providers generally receive, remuneration in connection with products for which reimbursement can be made under federal health care statutes, which raises potential AKS implications.[1] Under the broad language of the AKS and certain court rulings, a payment to a health care provider violates the statute if "one purpose" of the payment is to induce a health care provider to prescribe a reimbursable product. Thus, if the sponsor makes a payment to a doctor in the course of the study, and "one purpose" of the payment is to compensate the doctor for his or her time, but a secondary purpose is to induce the doctor to prescribe the sponsor's product more frequently, then both the sponsor and the doctor may be guilty of a felony. *See United States v. Greber,* 760 F.2d 68, 71 (3rd Cir.), *cert. denied,* 474 U.S. 988 (1985). In addition, if a CRO proposed or encouraged such payments, they might be guilty of the crime of aiding and abetting a felony, or conspiring to commit a felony.

It is reasonable to interpret the "one purpose" rule, however, as applying to the purpose of the *payment,* rather than the purpose of the *clinical trial.* In any clinical trial conducted by a pharmaceutical company, one underlying motivation is almost always to collect data that it hopes will encourage the more frequent prescription of its products. The critical factor in the AKS analysis, however, is whether the purpose of the *payment* is to induce prescriptions, rather than to simply compensate the investigators for their time. Thus, if investigators should reasonably be paid $500 for their time in conducting a study, but they are paid $2,000, the implication will be that the other $1,500 was for some other purpose, and the OIG may well conclude that the purpose was to provide an incentive to prescribe the product.

Under the AKS, the only legitimate purpose for a payment to a health care provider in connection with a clinical trial involving marketed products is reasonable compensation for the services performed. Obviously, the amount of the payment in relation to the time and expertise spent by the investigator is critical in determining if the purpose of the payment was solely to compensate the investigator for his or her time. The OIG, however, also looks at the source of the payment and the way in which payees were selected in determining the purpose of the payment. Research that originates or is directed by sales or marketing groups is considered "particularly suspect." *See* "OIG Compliance Program Guidance for Pharmaceutical Manufacturers," (hereafter, "OIG Guidance") 68 Fed. Reg. 23731, 23738 (May 5, 2003). For instance, if the selection of the investigators and the conduct of the study is controlled by a sponsor's promotion or marketing departments, it may appear that the research is being "used as a pretense to promote product," which is a major concern of the OIG and raises serious AKS implications. *Id.*

Practical Steps to Reduce Antikickback Risks

The following are practical steps that can be taken to reduce the risk of AKS violations in clinical trials involving marketed products. The steps are grouped into three areas: (a) compliance with the basic AKS requirements; (b) additional requirements of the personal services safe harbor; and (c) additional Office of the Inspector General ("OIG") compliance requirements. Each step is discussed in more detail in the following sections.

Compliance with Basic Antikickback Statute Requirements

Based on the AKS and comments, together with the OIG Guidance, the following practical steps can be taken to reduce the risk of AKS violations in clinical trials involving marketed products:

- Pay reasonable compensation
- Keep payments consistent
- Provide compensation only
- State a clear scientific purpose
- Design the protocol carefully
- Conduct the study strictly as research
- Select investigators based on research needs
- Establish a reasonable study size

Each step is outlined below.

(1) Pay Reasonable Compensation

Payments to investigators in a study involving marketed products must be limited to reasonable compensation for services performed. Prior to beginning the study, the sponsor or CRO should estimate the amount of time that investigators and staff generally will spend in conducting the clinical trial. The sponsor or CRO should then estimate the fair market value of the investigator's and the staff's time—based on what investigators generally earn in their practices and the amount of compensation needed to make the services worth their time—and set the payment structure based on the reasonable value of that time.

(2) Keep Payments Consistent

Payment criteria and amounts need to be consistent among sites. It may be reasonable, however, to vary compensation based on actual differences in practice costs. For instance, if a study involves both general practitioners and neurosurgeons, it may take a higher compensation to make it worth the neurosurgeons' time than the general practitioners' time. Similarly, study cost may be higher for investigators that are in large cities or part of academic medical centers than for those in individual practices in small towns, so "reasonable compensation" may vary among those groups. Individual variations in payments, however, raise potential AKS implications, especially if the higher payments are made to higher prescribers. Similarly, bonus payments in reasonable amounts for early deliver of data generally are justifiable if they are administered consistently among sites, but bonuses for sites that enroll a higher number of patients may raise AKS concerns.

(3) Provide Compensation Only

Any remuneration to an investigator in a clinical trial for marketed products that is not compensation for services is suspect under the AKS. Gifts, even in the types and amounts that meet the other applicable practice guidelines or codes, raise AKS implications. All remuneration (including small items such as textbooks and stethoscopes that meet other practice guidelines or codes) must be solely for the purpose of providing fair compensation for the services provided. For that reason, it is not advisable to label any remuneration to an investigator as a "gift" or an "honorarium" (even though many investigators prefer that term), or anything other than "compensation."

(4) State a Clear Scientific Purpose
The sponsor must be able to articulate a legitimate scientific research purpose for the study, or it will be suspect as a pretext for promotion. Prior to designing the protocol, the sponsor should specifically identify the data it intends to collect and the reason it needs that data, and document those factors. It is clear based on the comments and guidance of the OIG that it considers the previously prevalent industry practice of conducting studies for the purpose of "seeding" the market with a product to be a signal for potential AKS violations. The need for the data must be real, and if data is collected but never analyzed or used by the sponsor, the clinical trial will be suspect under the AKS. *See* OIG Guidance at 23738.

(5) Design the Protocol Carefully
The clinical trial must have a written protocol, which should be designed as independently as possible from the sponsor's promotion and marketing departments. The protocol must identify the scientific purpose of the clinical trial and specify how the investigators' services are needed to accomplish that purpose. If clinical trials are designed and conducted by the sponsor's marketing or promotion departments, the OIG considers that a strong indication that the primary purpose of the trials is promotion, which raises AKS implications. *See* OIG Guidance at 23738.

(6) Conduct the Study Strictly as Research
The clinical trial must be conducted under research study criteria and conducted as independently as possible from the sponsor's promotion and marketing departments, or it will be suspect under the AKS. Informed consents and HIPAA authorizations must be obtained where necessary. Further, review by an Institutional Review Board (IRB), although generally not legally required in a nonregistrational postmarketing study, is highly recommended as a factor for AKS compliance purposes. If the conduct of the study is overseen by the sponsor's marketing or promotion departments, it again raises questions as to whether the purpose of the clinical trial is really promotional. *Id.* Where sponsors' budgets and structures are set up such that postmarketing research is under the auspices of their promotion or marketing departments, they should reorganize those departments if possible, or outsource the conduct of the trial to a CRO with a strong AKS compliance program.

(7) Select Investigators Based on Research Needs

Prior to the start of the study, the sponsor or CRO should establish rational criteria for selecting investigators that are based on the research purpose and needs, not on marketing or promotion factors, and not the investigators' prescribing of the products. *Id* at 23736. For instance, selecting investigators based on their experience in a particular therapeutic area or with a particular type of patient would be legitimate, but selecting investigators because they are "high prescribers" of the sponsor's product could implicate AKS factors. *Id.* Because there may be a fair amount of overlap between those two groups ("experienced in the area" and "high prescribers"), the criteria for selection must be clearly articulated and documented. Once the criteria are established, the selection of investigators should be done by either the sponsor's research personnel, or by a CRO with expertise in AKS compliance, rather than by the company's sales or marketing personnel.

(8) Establish a Reasonable Study Size

Prior to commencing the clinical trial, the sponsor should establish the size of the study based on the research purpose of the study and the type of data that will be collected. If the sponsor could reasonably collect all of the data it needed from 500 sites, and it included 5,000 sites in the study, the OIG might view the clinical trial as an impermissible "seeding study" that is "unnecessarily duplicative or is not needed by the manufacturer for any purpose other than the generation of business." *See* OIG Guidance at 23738. The sponsor, therefore, should carefully assess and identify the data it needs to accomplish its research purposes. For instance, if a sponsor wanted to assess how much influence secondary factors, such as the taste of its drug, influence compliance with doctors' instructions, it would require a larger number of sites if it intended to do a comparison of older patients versus younger patients, male versus female, and ethnicity versus ethnicity, rather than just doing a simple analysis of the overall influence of taste.

Additional Requirements of the Personal Services Safe Harbor

The personal services safe harbor requirements are listed below. Detailed discussions of each requirement follow.

- Sign written agreements with investigators
- Set a one-year investigator agreement term
- Ensure the Investigator Agreement covers all services
- Preset the payments for each site service

- Do not set different payments for higher prescribers
- Do not promote or condone illegal activities

Several of the requirements of the AKS services safe harbor are already covered by the basic AKS requirements set forth above: (a) "the aggregate compensation . . . is consistent with fair market value; and (b) The services contracted for do not exceed those that are reasonably necessary to accomplish the commercially reasonable business purpose of the services." *See* 42 CFR Sec.1001.952 (d)(5) and (7). *See also* sections 7.3.4(b) 1 and 8 above. The personal services safe harbor, however, also sets forth additional requirements, which are addressed below. If a company is in compliance with the basic requirements of the AKS, its actions should not be in violation of the AKS, even if it does not meet all the requirements of a safe harbor. Nonetheless, the AKS is vague enough, and the consequences are dire enough, that prudent sponsors and investigative sites will come as close as possible to meeting the requirements of the personal services safe harbor, as set forth below. *See* OIG Guidance at 23735.

(1) Sign Written Agreements with Investigators

There must be a written agreement signed by the investigative site and either the sponsor or CRO that specifies the services to be provided. Informal agreements with investigators that are oral or are not signed by both parties are unacceptable under the personal services safe harbor. *See* 42 CFR Sec.1001.952 (d)(1).

(2) Set a One-Year Investigator Agreement Term

The personal services safe harbor requires that the agreement be for a term of not less than one year. On its face, this requirement appears to be a challenge in clinical trials, since the length of each trial is variable, and many postmarketing studies last less a full year. It is reasonable to interpret this requirement, however, as applying to the term of the *agreement,* rather than the length of the *services*, so that if a provision is included in the investigator agreement stating that the contract will be for a term of one year, or until completion of the services, whichever is longer, that should be helpful in addressing this requirement. *See* 42 CFR Sec.1001.952 (d)(4).

(3) Ensure the Investigator Agreement Covers All Services

The personal services safe harbor also requires that the contract "covers all of the services the agent [2] provides to the principal during the term." *See* 42 CFR Sec.1001.952 (d)(2). The wording of this requirement raises issues in clinical trials, since large investigative sites often conduct more than one study for a sponsor at any given time.

Given the purpose of the AKS and the safe harbor, however, it is reasonable to interpret this requirement as a ban on "side" agreements for the same services (which would allow a sponsor to give more money to sites that are frequent prescribers), rather than a ban on investigative sites performing multiple clinical trials for a single sponsor, or a ban on contract amendments (which are not uncommon in clinical trials). Thus, a sponsor cannot have two different agreements for the same services by a single investigative site if it wants to come within the personal services safe harbor.

(4) Preset the Payments for Each Site Service

Under the personal services safe harbor, if a person "is to provide services on a periodic or part-time basis, then the agreement specifies the exact schedule of such intervals, their precise length, and the exact charge for such intervals" and the "aggregate amount" of the payments must be set in advance." *See* 42 CFR Sec.1001.952 (d)(3) and (5). Since investigators' services often involve patient visits that have not been scheduled at the time the agreement is signed, and the total amount paid will vary depending on the number of patient visits, this requirement can be perplexing in a clinical trial setting. Given that some of the primary goals in AKS compliance are to establish reasonable compensation for specified services and avoid special benefits for high prescribers, this requirement can be interpreted as requiring that each type of service (e.g., each screening or patient visit) have a consistent, preset charge. If this section is strictly construed as requiring the sponsor to specify in advance the date that each patient visit will take place and exactly how long such visits will last, it would be highly unlikely that sponsors and sites could comply with it. Nevertheless, it is still worthwhile for the parties to comply with as many of the safe harbor criteria as possible. *See* OIG Guidance at 23735.

(5) Do Not Set Different Payments for Higher Prescribers

The personal services safe harbor also requires that the payment amount "is not determined in a manner that takes into consideration the volume or value of any referrals or business otherwise generated between the parties for which payment may be made under Medicare or a State health care program." *See* 42 CFR Sec.1001.952 (d)(5). If this requirement is interpreted as a ban on basing a site's total compensation on the total number of patients seen, then this requirement would be practically impossible to fulfill in a clinical trial setting. Because the AKS requires sponsors to base payments on the amount of actual services rendered, however, and because the only fair way to do so generally is to tie the payments to the number of patient screenings and visits, it seems reasonable to conclude that if all payments are the same for each service, and high-volume prescribers are not given special benefits or bonuses, such consistent payments should satisfy this requirement.

(6) Do Not Promote or Condone Illegal Activities
The personal services safe harbor also requires that "the services do not involve the counseling or promotion of a business arrangement or other activity that violates any State or Federal law." *See* 42 CFR. Sec.1001.952 (d)(6). If all of the other AKS requirements are followed, however, this requirement should be easily satisfied in a clinical trial setting.

Additional OIG Compliance Requirements
In addition to the specific AKS compliance steps listed, the OIG has also issued general compliance standards that it expects all companies to meet. Each requirement is listed below, followed by brief discussions of each.

- Create and follow a formal compliance program
- Identify a compliance officer/committee
- Describe and document the training received
- Convey the OIG's risk areas
- Provide an accessible, readable written policies manual
- Provide an accessible corporate hotline
- Demonstrate endorsement of compliance by senior management
- Exemplify compliance training as a competency evaluation item

(1) Create and Follow a Formal Compliance Program
The OIG has indicated that if it is investigating possible AKS violations, one of the factors it will consider is whether the company has established a formal compliance program that covers this statute. Compliance with this statute is not considered intuitive, and the OIG will presume that if formal program is not in place, violations may be occurring.

(2) Identify a Compliance Officer/Committee
Under the OIG guidance, a specific individual or specific individuals must be identified as having responsibility for compliance with this statute.

(3) Describe and Document the Training Received
A company must be able to describe, and show documentation of, its training of all relevant personnel, and the training should be systematic, comprehensive, and widespread.

(4) Convey the OIG's Risk Areas
The training must specifically identify the relevant risk areas discussed in the OIG's guidance to be considered effective.

(5) Provide an Accessible, Readable Written Policies Manual
AKS policies should be documented in a policy manual that is accessible by all relevant personnel.

(6) Provide an Accessible Corporate Hotline
A corporate hotline to report compliance violations should be provided and publicized.

(7) Demonstrate Endorsement of Compliance by Senior Management
Personnel should be made aware that the compliance program is supported by senior management.

(8) Exemplify Compliance Training as a Competency Evaluation Item
Policies should require tracking of training received and provide consequences in evaluations for failure to take the required training or to follow compliance policies. *See* OIG Guidance at 23739–23742

The False Claims Act

Overview of the False Claims Act

The False Claims Act, 31 U.S.C. § 3729 provides for criminal penalties and civil monetary penalties for persons who make, or cause to be made, false claims to the government. Some courts have held that payments to investigators that violate the AKS by wrongfully inducing the investigators to prescribe drugs or devices also cause the filing of false claims for reimbursements to Medicare and Medicare in violation of the FCA. *See U.S. ex rel. Kneepkins v. Gambro Healthcare, Inc.* 115 F. Supp. 2d 35 (D. Mass. 2000) (holding that AKS violations can form the basis for FCA claims); *U.S. ex rel. Roy v. Anthony,* 914 F. Supp. 1504 (S.D. Ohio 1994) (holding that a violation of the AKS can support a FCA claim if the illegal payments "tainted" the Medicare claims). Sponsors and CROs generally do not submit claims to Medicare or Medicaid, but some courts have ruled that violations of the AKS by sponsors can "cause" the filing of false claims for Medicare or Medicaid reimbursement, thereby making them indirectly liable under the FCA. Other courts, however, have held that FCA cannot be "piggybacked" on AKS violations. *See U.S. ex rel. Franklin v. Parke-Davis,* 147 F. Supp. 2d 39 (D. Mass 2001) (holding that payments for sham studies in violation of the AKS did not state a FCA violation under the circumstances of the case); *U.S. ex rel. Barmak v. Sutter Corp.,* No. 95 CV 7637, 2002 U.S. Dist. LEXIS 8509 (S.D.N.Y May 14, 2002) The OIG Guidance endorses the position that "a violation of the anti-kickback statute may give rise to liability under the False Claims Act," 68 Fed. Reg. at 23734.

In addition to FCA liability through AKS violations, investigators also can be directly liable under the FCA if they falsely or fraudulently bill Medicare or Medicaid for study products or services. Also, although the FCA risks during clinical trials generally arise through AKS violations or false billings for study products or services, sponsors, CROs, and investigators also should be aware that FCA claims may be based on off-label promotion of products. *See United States of America v. Warner-Lambert Company LLC,* U.S.D.C. D. Mass, May 13, 2004, Settlement Agreement (in which Warner-Lambert agreed to pay over $150 million to the settle FCA claims based on off-label promotion of the drug Neurontin). Similarly, sponsors and CROs should be aware that inaccurate reimbursement advice also can form the basis for FCA violations. *See* Settlement Agreement between U.S. and Abbott Laboratories Ross Products Division, June 2003. In addition, investigators who conduct studies funded by the National Institute of Health or other federal bodies should be aware that at least one prominent prosecutor has indicated that failure to obtain a sufficient informed consent may be grounds for prosecution under the FCA. [3]

FCA Statutory Language

The section of the False Claims Act potentially applicable to clinical trials states as follows:

(a) Liability for Certain Acts. Any person who:

(1) knowingly presents, or causes to be presented, to an officer or employee of the United States Government . . . a false or fraudulent claim for payment or approval;

(2) knowingly makes, uses, or causes to be made or used, a false record or statement to get a false or fraudulent claim paid or approved by the Government;

. . . is liable to the United States Government for a civil penalty. . . . *31 U.S.C. § 3729*

Penalties for Violating the FCA

The penalty for a violation of the FCA is "not less than $5,000 and not more than $10,000, plus 3 times the amount of damages which the Government sustains because of the act of that person."

There is a reduced penalty of two times the amount of damages for people who self-report violations within 30 days of learning of the violation and cooperate with the government investigations. *See 31 U.S.C. § 3729(a).* FCA penalties are civil, not criminal, penalties, which means that a violation will not result in a prison sentence, but only a "preponderance of the evidence" is required to find a violation.

Whistleblower Provision in the FCA

The FCA, unlike the AKS, contains a *qui tam* or "whistleblower" provision. *See 31 U.S.C. § 3730.* Lawsuits for violations of governmental laws and regulations normally only can be brought by governmental agencies, but a *qui tam* provision allows an individual, in certain circumstances, to sue on behalf of himself or herself, as well as the government. This provision allows an individual, who is referred to as a "relator," to collect a portion of any award or settlement in certain circumstances, even if he or she has not been personally damaged by the FCA violation. The relator must notify the government of the *qui tam* lawsuit, and the government may decide to take over the conduct of the lawsuit. The relators usually are current or former employees of the company against which the FCA is being made.

FCA Risks and Issues in Clinical Trials

FCA Liability for AKS Violations

Under some court decisions, sponsors, CROs, and investigators can become liable for FCA violations due to AKS violations. The courts are divided on this issue, but some courts have ruled that if a sponsor makes a payments to investigators as part of a study involving marketed products, and those payments are intended to induce the investigators to write more prescriptions for the product (which is an AKS violation), those payments "cause" a false claim to be filed when the investigator or patient seeks reimbursement for the product from a governmental agency. Sponsors that make the payments would be liable for "causing" the false claim for reimbursement, and if a CRO persuaded the sponsor to make the payments, the CRO might also be found to have "caused" the filing of the reimbursement claim. The investigators who violated the AKS by accepting the illegal payments also could be found to have committed an AKS violation via the FCA.

FCA Liability for Billing for Free Products

If an investigative site receives free medical products from the sponsor as part of a study, but files reimbursement claims with a governmental agency for those products, those claims may directly violate the FCA. In addition, if a sponsor or CRO expects or encourages an investigator to bill Medicare for the free samples or products, then the sponsor or CRO may potentially be liable for FCA violations. In 2001, TAP Pharmaceuticals paid $875 million to settle a variety of claims, including a claim that TAP had provided a large number of free samples of a cancer drug to doctors and expected or encouraged them to bill Medicare for the samples. *See* Complaint, *Porter v. TAP Pharmaceuticals*, 01CV1086RGS, D. Mass, May 18, 2001.

FCA Liability for Double-Billing for Study Services

An investigative site similarly could incur FCA liability for inappropriately billing Medicare or Medicaid for study services that are reimbursed by the sponsor, and a sponsor or CRO could potentially be liable for condoning or encouraging such billing. For example, if a sponsor paid an investigator for a service that was performed specifically for the study—such as the collection of a extra blood sample to take a study measurement—and the investigator billed Medicare for that service, that claim potentially could violate the FCA. Because many studies involve a mix of standard care for which a doctor may be entitled to government reimbursement and procedures required by the study, it may be difficult to determine which services may be billed to Medicare. In general, if a procedure or visit would not have been required if the patient were not in the study, then that procedure or visit is not part of the standard of care and should not be billed to Medicare or Medicaid (or any private insurer, although billing to a private insurer would not constitute a FCA violation).

For instance, if a patient on dialysis normally would visit the doctor and have blood drawn and tested every three weeks, but to satisfy the study goals the patient is seen and blood is drawn every week, the extra visits cannot be billed to Medicare,

Medicaid, or other insurers. Instead, the sponsor and investigator should ensure that the sponsor adequately compensates the investigator for the extra visits and procedures required by the study. A sponsor or CRO that encouraged claims for such procedures or visits could be found to have violated the FCA by "causing" the false claims to be followed.

Knowledge Required for a FCA Violation

For sponsors, CROs, and investigators, it is important to note that the government is *not* required to show a specific intent to defraud the government in order to prove a FCA violation. The FCA does require that the violation be "knowing," but the term "knowing" is defined in the FCA to include acting with "reckless disregard" or in "deliberate ignorance." *Id.* at 3729(b)(2) and (3). Thus, a reckless billing error potentially could be enough to create liability.

Practical Steps to Reduce FCA Risks

The following are practical steps that can be taken to reduce the risk of FCA violations in clinical trials involving marketed products.

- Avoid any AKS violations
- Prohibit billing for free products
- Do not encourage or condone billing for free products
- Include a "no billing for free products" provision
- Don't double-bill for study services
- Prohibit double-billing
- Include a "no double billing" provision

Each of these recommendations is discussed in more detail below.

Avoid Any AKS Violations

Although it may seem that the risk of prison, fines, and potential exclusion from Medicare would be reason enough to avoid violating the AKS, the threat that AKS violations could be used as a basis for FCA violations really does provide additional, serious incentives to comply with the AKS. Besides adding potentially large damage payments, the FCA *qui tam* provisions provide a lucrative incentive for disgruntled existing and former employees to divulge potential AKS violations. In making decisions with AKS implications, therefore, companies should proceed as though every meeting is being held and every decision is being made with a representative of the OIG sitting in the room and listening to what is said, because that may indeed become the case.

Prohibit Billing for Free Products

This advice should seem self-evident, but some sites apparently consider that they are somehow entitled to bill Medicare or other insurers for products they received for free. Given the magnitude of the financial incentives for employees to report activities under the FCA *qui tam* provisions, the likelihood that such activities will be reported to the authorities is very high, and the damages ($10,000 per reimbursement claim submitted, plus 3 times the amount that was paid on those claims) is very significant.

Do Not Encourage or Condone Billing for Free Products

Similarly, some sales representatives and other corporate representative allegedly have encouraged investigators to file reimbursement claims for free products. For that reason, it is essential that entire staffs, not just upper management, receive training in the AKS and FCA, so that everyone understands the consequences of such unlawful suggestions.

Include a "No Billing for Free Products" Provision

To ensure that sites are aware that they cannot bill for free products, and to ensure that, if a rogue sales rep makes inappropriate suggestions, the site will know they are not endorsed by the sponsor or CRO, the parties to an investigator agreement involving marketed product should include a "no billing for free products" provision in the agreement. Some suggested language is as follows:

> "If the Sponsor or CRO provides any free products for use in the Study, you agree that you will not bill any governmental or insurance agency, or any other third party, for such free products."

Do Not Double-Bill for Study Services

As discussed above, many studies involve both standard visits and procedures for which a doctor is entitled to reimbursement, and study-specific visits and procedures for which compensation is provided by the sponsor. In preparing the study budget, the sponsor and CRO should verify that the sites are compensated by the sponsor for all procedures and visits required by the protocol that are not part of the normal standard of care for patient treatment. The investigators should ensure that they understand and identify which services are specific to the study and are compensated by the sponsor, and which services are part of the standard of care for the patient's treatment and thus are a legitimate basis for reimbursement claims. When in doubt, the investigator should ask the sponsor to identify which services are being compensated by the study budget, and if a service that is not part of the standard patient care is not included in that list, the investigator should insist on inclusion before signing the agreement.

Prohibit Double Billing

Similarly, all of the sponsor and CRO staff who come into contact with investigators should be trained so that they do not encourage the investigator to bill Medicare, Medicaid, or other third parties for visits or procedures that are specific to the study.

Include a "No Double Billing" Provision

Some suggested language is as follows:

> "You agree that the payments specified in the budget will cover all of the extra time and expenses you will incur in conducting the Study and collecting the specified data. You agree that you will not bill any patient, insurer, or governmental agency for any visits, services, or expenses incurred during the Study that you would not ordinarily perform in providing care for the patient, because those visits, services, and costs are already covered by the payments you will receive from the Sponsor or CRO."

Debarment

Another statutory provision that applies to postmarketing studies, including nonregistrational studies, is the section of the Generic Drug Enforcement Act of 1992 that gives the FDA authority to forbid people and firms convicted of certain crimes from participating in the drug industry. Individuals and firms that have been convicted of such crimes are placed on the FDA's "debarment list." Persons on the FDA debarment list cannot be employed in any capacity by investigative sites, sponsors, and CROs or by sites performing study services, including for work on postmarketing, nonregistrational studies.

Compliance with this statute is critical, but it is not as complex as compliance with the AKS or FCA. To comply, sponsors, CROs, and investigative sites should take three primary compliance steps. First, they should ask every employment applicant whether they have been debarred or convicted of crimes that are grounds for debarment. Second, they should check for each applicant's name on the FDA debarment list, which currently can be found at http://www.fda.gov/ora/compliance_ref/debar/. Third, they should insert a clause into every contract with any company or individual who will be providing study services requiring that company or individual has not been debarred.

Reporting Postmarketing Adverse Drug Experiences and Unanticipated Adverse Device Effects

Another key legal requirement in postmarketing studies, including nonregistrational postmarketing studies, is compliance with 21 CFR § 314.80, which requires the submission of serious and unexpected adverse drug experiences, and 21 CFR § 812.150(b), which requires the submission of unanticipated adverse device effects, on an expedited basis regardless of the source. Investigators and CROs must notify the applicant (study sponsor) as soon as possible of any adverse drug experience that is both serious and unexpected, or unanticipated adverse device effects that investigators and CROs become aware of in the course of providing services, so that the applicant can meet its reporting obligation under §§ 314.80 and 812.150. The applicant will then need to make a determination whether it is reasonably possible that the drug or device was the cause, and if so, report this to the FDA.

Health Insurance Portability and Accountability Act (sometimes applies)

The Health Insurance Portability and Accountability Act of 1996 (HIPAA) Privacy Regulations, 45 CFR Parts 160 and 164, which establish standards for the protection of individually identifiable health information, apply to virtually all investigators and sites in all studies, including nonregistrational, postmarketing studies, but it generally does not apply to sponsors or CROs, as they do not meet the HIPAA definition for "covered entities." The exception for CROs and sponsors would be for medical institutions or practices that also act as CROs or sponsor (for instance, some academic medial centers, in addition to serving as investigative sites, also offer CRO-type services and sponsor clinical trials).

The HIPAA Privacy Regulation came out of the Health Insurance Portability and Accountability Act of 1996 with a compliance date of April 14, 2003. Under the

regulations, in general, investigators/investigator sites are considered "covered entities" and as such have a new set of privacy requirements to meet. For instance, an
investigator/investigator site as a covered entity must provide patients with a Notice
of Privacy Practices (NPP) that explains patients rights and mentions the site's uses
and disclosures of protected health information, designate, a privacy officer or privacy contact, and provides privacy awareness training for the site's workforce.

Further, with certain exceptions, investigator sites are allowed to disclose the
health information about the research subject to CROs or study sponsors only
with an authorization from the research subject for use and disclosure of health
information for research purposes, or a waiver of such authorization by an IRB.
This authorization can be a stand-alone document or combined with the research
study informed consent. A copy of the signed document must be provided to the
research participant.

The Common Rule (sometimes applies)

The Common Rule, 45 CFR Part 46, requires IRB review and approval and informed
consent for all research involving human subjects conducted, supported, or otherwise
subject to regulation by any federal department or agency. Nonregistrational studies,
which do not meet the definition of "clinical investigation" in 21 CFR § 312.3(b), and
therefore fall entirely outside of the regulatory coverage of Part 312, therefore generally are also outside of the coverage of the Common Rule. The Common Rule
would apply if the customer is a federal department or agency, or if the study is otherwise federally funded. Despite this seemingly narrow application of the Common
Rule, many institutions participating in studies as sites may have commitments related
to their receipt of federal funding or may have given "Assurances" to the government (meaning a Multiple Project Assurance or Federal-wide Assurance) so that it
is obligated legally or through its Assurance respectively to follow the Common
Rule. If the Common Rule applies, then as a practical matter, complying with Parts
50 and 56 could be used as the means for meeting most if not all of the Common Rule
requirements for those studies. The following provisions are instructive in determining, on a study by study basis, whether the Common Rule applies.

§ 46.101 To what does this policy apply?
   Except as provided in paragraph (b) *[listing exceptions]* of this section,
   this policy applies to all research involving human subjects conducted,

supported, or otherwise subject to regulation by a federal department or agency which takes appropriate administrative action to make the policy applicable to such research.

§ 46.122. Use of Federal Funds

Federal funds administered by a department or agency may not be expended for research involving human subjects unless the requirements of this policy have been satisfied.

§ 46.102. Definitions

(d) Research means a systematic investigation, including research development, testing, and evaluation, designed to develop or contribute to generalizable knowledge. Activities which meet this definition constitute research for purposes of this policy, whether or not they are conducted or supported under a program which is considered research for other purposes.

(e) Research subject to regulation, and similar terms, are intended to encompass those research activities for which a federal department or agency has specific responsibility for regulating as a research activity (for example, IND requirements administered by FDA). It does not include research activities which are incidentally regulated by a federal department or agency solely as part of the department's or agency's broader responsibility to regulate certain types of activities whether research or nonresearch in nature (for example, Wage and Hour requirements administered by the Department of Labor).

(f) Human subject means a living individual about whom an investigator (whether professional or student) conducting research obtains

(1) Data through intervention or interaction with the individual, or

(2) Identifiable private information.

Intervention includes both physical procedures by which data are gathered (for example, venipuncture) and manipulations of the subject or the subject's environment that are performed for research purposes. Interaction includes communication or interpersonal contact between investigator and subject.

Private information includes information about behavior that occurs in a context in which an individual can reasonably expect that no observation or recording is taking place, and information which has been provided for specific purposes by an individual and which the individual can reasonably expect will not be made public (for example, a medical record). Private information must be individually identifiable (i.e., the identity of the subject is or may readily be ascertained by the investigator or associated with the information) in order for obtaining the information to constitute research involving human subjects.

Federal Acquisition Regulations (sometimes applies)

When performing a study for the federal government or agency that is federally funded (collectively, "federal studies"), certain Federal Acquisition Regulations (FARs) will apply in addition to other federal laws and regulations, depending on the requirement in the request for proposal or solicitation for the particular study. Many of the FARs impose contractual requirements, particularly tracking, hiring, and certifications requirements, that are not commonly found in nongovernmental contracts. Before entering into an agreement to perform any federal study, investigators, sponsors, and CROs need to carefully review the applicable FARs and ensure that they have the ability to comply with these regulations.

Promotion and Charging for Investigational Medical Products

Provisions 21 CFR § 312.7 (for drugs) and 21 CFR § 812.7 (for medical devices) strictly regulate any promotional or marketing claims relating to marketed products and charges for investigational, medicinal products. Any promotional or marketing claims would be prohibited from being part of a research study, including a post-marketing, nonregistrational study, so investigators, sponsors, and CROs need to understand this regulation and train their staffs under it.

Food and Drug Administration Modernization Act (FDAMA) (sometimes applies)

Section 21 CFR Part 201 of FDAMA governs labeling, advertising, promotional, and educational activities. The Division of Drug Marketing, Advertising & Communications (DDMAC) is the unit of FDA administering these regulations. In 1995, DDMAC issued draft guidelines for pharmaco-economic claims. Although later abandoned by DDMAC, these guidelines continue to be the unofficial regulatory approach for pharmaco-economic claims directed to physicians. For that reason, sponsors, CROs, and investigator sites that participate in postmarketing studies involving pharmaco-economics need to become familiar with these guidelines. The guidelines set the preferred clinical standard of "substantial evidence typically demonstrated by two adequate and well-controlled studies," and discouraged the use of economic modeling, except in cases where it was impractical or impossible to gather data through adequate and well-controlled studies. For pharmaco-economic claims directed to formularies, Section 114 of FDAMA applies the slightly looser standard of "competent and reliable scientific evidence."

21 CFR Part 50 (Informed Consent) (sometimes applies)

21 CFR Part 50, Protection of Human Subjects, is applicable to pre-approval studies, and whether it applies to postmarketing studies depends on the type of study. If the postmarketing study is a clinical investigation (meaning an experiment involving the use of any drug in humans, except for the use of a marketed drug in the course of medical practice, then Part 50 applies (see 21 CFR § 312.2(b)(1)(iv) and 21 CFR § 312.3(b)). If the postmarketing study is observational (meaning that a marketed drug is prescribed in the course of medical practice and the prescription decision is independent from the decision to enroll the patient in the study) then the study is outside the 21 CFR § 312.3 (b) definition of "clinical investigation," and therefore entirely outside of both Parts 312 and 50.

Disqualification (sometimes applies)

The disqualification provisions, 21 CFR § 312.70 (for drugs) and 21 CFR § 812.119 (for medical devices) give the FDA authority to disqualify a clinical investigator. Although some nonregistrational studies come within the exemption to the provisions of 21 CFR Parts 312 and 812, 21 CFR §§ 312.70 and 812.119 nonetheless allow the FDA to disqualify an investigator for failing to comply with the requirements of Part 50, relating to the protection of human subjects, and Part 56, relating to institutional review boards, which apply to some sponsors and CROs nonregistrational studies.

ICH GCP (sometimes applies)

The International Conference on Harmonization of Technical Requirements for Registration of Pharmaceuticals for Human Use (ICH) Good Clinical Practice (GCP) guidance has been published in the United States by the FDA as a guidance document, applicable to drug and biological products. FDA guidance documents represent the FDA's current thinking, and do not create or confer any rights for or on any person and do not operate to bind the FDA or the public. Although compliance with ICH GCP is not legally required in the United States, [4] compliance with it is treated a "best practice" at many companies, and contracts between sponsors, CROs, and investigative sites sometimes require ICH GCP compliance.

21 CFR Part 56 (IRB Review) (sometimes applies)

21 CFR Part 56, Institutional Review Boards, is generally applicable to studies initiated prior to NDA approval. Whether Part 56 applies to postmarketing studies depends on the type of study. If a postmarketing study is a clinical investigation (meaning an experiment involving the use of any drug in humans, except for the use of a marketed drug in the course of medical practice) then Part 50 applies (see 21 CFR § 312.2(b)(1)(iv) and 21 CFR § 312.3(b)). If the postmarketing study is observational (meaning that a marketed drug is prescribed in the course of medical practice and the prescription decision is independent from the decision to enroll the patient in the study) then the study generally is outside the 21 CFR § 312.3 (b) definition of "clinical investigation" and therefore not covered by Part 56.

Most nonregistrational, postmarketing studies are observational, and thus the IRB reviews detailed in Part 56 would not be required. Some nonregistrational, postmarketing studies, however, may not be purely observational, in which case IRB review is required. In addition, many sponsors and CROs obtain IRB reviews in nonregistrational, postmarketing studies as a matter of "best practice," even if it is not required by the regulation. Obtaining IRB review also can help ensure that the scientific purposes of the study are clearly understandable, which assists in meeting Antikickback Statute requirements.

Laws and Regulations That Generally Do Not Apply to Nonregistrational, Postmarketing Studies

The laws and regulations discussed below generally relate to clinical trials but do not apply to nonregistrational, postmarketing studies.

21 CFR Part 54 (Financial Disclosure)

21 CFR Part 54, which requires the disclosure to the FDA of certain financial arrangements between the sponsors and the clinical investigators, as well as certain interests of the clinical investigators in the product under study or in the sponsor of the study, generally does not apply to nonregistrational studies. The Financial Disclosure regulation applies only to "covered studies," which are defined as studies that "the applicant or the FDA relies on to show that the product is effective . . . or. . . in which a single investigator makes a significant demonstration of safety." *21 CFR § 54(e)*. Because nonregistrational studies do not collect data that will be submitted to the FDA to show safety or efficacy in support of an application, this regulation generally does not apply in nonregistrational, postmarketing studies.

21 CFR Part 11 (Electronic Records)

Nonregistrational, postmarketing studies generally are outside of the scope of 21 CFR Part 11, Electronic Records; Electronic Signatures, because they do not contain records required by regulation to be submitted to the FDA.

Section 11.1 Scope, states in part:

> (b) this part applies to records in electronic form that are created, modified, maintained, archived, retrieved, or transmitted under any records requirements set forth in agency regulation. This part also applies to electronic records submitted to the agency under requirements of the Federal Food, Drug, and Cosmetic Act and the Public Health and Service Act, even if such records are not specifically identified in agency regulations. However, this part does not apply to paper records that are, or have been, transmitted by electronic means.

21 CFR Part 312
(Investigational New Drug Application Requirements)

21 CFR Part 312, Investigational New Drug (IND), generally does not apply to non-registrational, postmarketing studies, because these studies generally either fall within the exemption in § 312.2 (set forth below); or fall entirely outside of Part 312 as not meeting the definitions of "clinical investigation," and "investigator."

§ 312.2 Applicability, states in part:

(a) Applicability.

Except as provided in this section, this part *[meaning Part 312]* applies to all clinical investigations of products that are subject to section 505 of the Federal Food, Drug, and Cosmetic Act *[governing new drugs and providing for the IND and abbreviated IND approval process]* or to the licensing provision of the Public Health Service Act (58 Stat. 632, as amended (42 U.S.C. § 201 et. seq.) *[governing biological products]*.

(b) Exemptions.

(1) The clinical investigation of a drug product that is lawfully marketed in the United States is exempt from the requirements of this part if all the following apply:

(i) The investigation is not intended to be reported to FDA as a well-controlled study in support of a new indication for the use nor intended to be used to support any other significant change in the labeling of the drug;

(ii) If the drug that is undergoing investigation is lawfully marketed as a prescription drug product, the investigation is not intended to support a significant change in the advertising for the product;

(iii) The investigation does not involve a route of administration or dosage level or use in a patient population or other factor that significantly increases the risks (or decreases the acceptability of the risks) associated with the use of the drug product;

(iv) The investigation is conducted in compliance with the requirements for institutional review set forth in Part 56 *[21 CFR Part 56—Institutional Review Boards]* and with the requirements for informed consent set forth in Part 50 *[21 CFR Part 50—Protection of Human Subjects]*; and

(v) The investigation is conducted in compliance with the requirements of § 312.7 [Promotion and Charging for Investigational Drugs].

21 CFR Part 812 (IDE Requirements)

21 CFR Part 812, Investigational Device Exemptions, generally does not apply to non-registrational, postmarketing studies.

§ 812.2 Applicability, states in part:

(a)   General. This part applies to all clinical investigations of devices to determine safety and effectiveness....

§ 812.3 Definitions, states in part:

(h)   Investigation means a clinical investigation or research involving one or more subjects to determine the safety or effectiveness of a device.

§ 812.2 (c) lists the following clinical investigations of medical devices that need not comply with Part 812:

- Legally marketed devices that are being investigated in accordance with the indications in the labeling
- Certain conditions involving diagnostic devices
- Consumer preference testing
- Devices intended solely for veterinary use
- Custom devices

Studies on approved, marketed medical devices prescribed in the course of medical practice are not subject to regulation by Part 812, and thus this regulation generally does not apply to nonregistrational, postmarketing studies.

Stark Anti-Referral Law

The Stark Anti-Referral Law ("Stark"), 42 U.S.C. § 1395, prohibits physicians from referring Medicare and Medicaid patients to an entity in which the physician or family member has a financial relationship. The Centers for Medicare and Medicaid Services (CMS), however, have not construed Stark to apply to clinical trials. The preamble to the January 2001 final rule states that drug manufacturers are not entities that furnish designated services to patients, and therefore the ordering or prescribing of a drug generally does not constitute a "referral" in violation of Stark, even if the physician or his or her family has a financial relationship with the drug manufacturer. 66 Fed. Reg. 856,872 and 920 (Jan. 9, 2001).[5]

Conclusion

Although there is an increasing need for information about marketed products beyond the safety and efficacy data gathered to support applications for marketing approval and label changes, it can be very complex to determine which laws and regulations apply to those types of nonregistrational, postmarketing studies. In addition, several of the laws that apply to postmarketing studies, including nonregistrational, postmarketing studies, are laws that carry extremely high legal and compliance risks. For those reasons, this chapter has set forth a brief summary of the laws and regulations applicable to nonregistrational, postmarketing studies, analyzing the high-risk statutes and providing practical steps to reduce the legal risks in those statutes.

Glossary of Terms

Clinical Research Organizations (CROs): CROs are companies that provide various research services and other services to pharmaceutical companies, and to which sponsors outsource various aspects of clinical trials.

Clinical trials: In the United States, clinical trials generally are research studies involving drugs, devices, or biologics that involve human participants. (Note that in the European Union the term has a more specialized meaning.)

Investigators and investigational sites: Investigators are the health care professionals that actually conduct the clinical trials and oversee the administration of the drugs, devices, or products to human subjects. Investigational sites are the hospitals, medical offices, or academic institutions at which the clinical trials are conducted.

Label: The description of the uses, populations, and indications for which a marketed product has been approved is called the product's "label."

Label change: If a product's manufacturer wants to get approval to market a drug for a different use, population, or indication, it needs to apply to the FDA for a "label change."

Marketed products: Drugs, devices, or biologics that have received market registration or marketing authorization from the relevant regulatory authority.

Nonregistrational studies: Any study that is not intended to support a New Drug Application (NDA), a Premarket Approval (PMA), or a label change.

Registrational studies: Well-controlled studies for submission to FDA in support of an NDA, PMA, or a label change. They include studies involving marketed products that (i) are intended to support new indications, (ii) are intended to support significant changes in labeling or advertising, (iii) involve a change in the route of administration, dosage level, or other factor that significantly increases the risks associated with the use of the product as determined by an institutional review board or ethics committee.

New Drug Application: The application to the FDA for approval to market a medicinal product.

Office of the Inspector General (OIG): The governmental branch that is responsible for enforcement of various statutes, including the Antikickback Statute.

Sponsors: The persons or companies that design and fund the clinical study. The sponsor is usually the manufacturer of the product being studied, but sometimes it can be a joint-venturer or licensee of the manufacturer, or it can be an academic medical center that is conducting the study for research and publication purposes.

Additional Resources

Statutes and Regulations: One of the best sources for the texts of statutes and regulations is the web site maintained by Cornell University School of Law, which is found at http://www4.law.cornell.edu.

Antikickback Statute: http://www4.law.cornell.edu/uscode/42/1320a-7b.html.

False Claims Act: http://www4.law.cornell.edu/uscode/31/3729.html.

Fraud and Abuse Summary: For an outline of all key health care fraud and abuse laws, see the "Application of Health Care Fraud and Abuse Laws to Pharmaceutical Marketing," by Alan M. Kirschenbaum and Jeffery N. Wasserstein. (For information contact Alan Kirschenbaum at AMK@hpm.com.)

Safe Harbor Regulation Comments:

http://oig.hhs.gov/fraud/docs/safeharborregulations/getdoc1.pdf.

Notes and References

1 It is important to note that investigational medical products are not products for which reimbursement is provided by federal programs, so the AKS generally does not apply to premarketing studies.

2 Although the personal services safe harbor refers to "agents," the OIG has clarified that the term does not refer to a party's legal agent and an agent is "any person, other than a bona fide employee of the principal, who has an agreement to perform services for, on behalf of, the principal." 42 CFR § 952(d).

3 David R. Hoffman, Assistant U.S. Attorney for the Eastern District of Pennsylvania stated in an April 21, 2004, presentation to the Fourth Annual Medical Research Summit that the "absence of elements relating to consent" could give rise to FCA liability in federally funded studies because the federal government would not have paid for the study if it had known that valid consents were not being obtained. *See Medical Research Law and Policy Report*, Vol. 3, page 347, May 5, 2004. Hoffman stated, however, that he was not aware of any such case. *Id.*

4   It is important to note, however, that for studies conducted in the European Economic Area that meet the definition of an Interventional Clinical Trial, ICH GCP now is a legal requirement in conducting those studies.

5   If a drug manufacturer also owned a retail pharmacy, or provided health care services to patients, however, it might become, through them, an entity that provides designated services to patients, and a prescription might constitute a referral in that situation. *Id.*

EIGHT

Key Compliance Issues for Institutional Review Boards

Michael J. Meehan and Marleina Thomas Davis

Introduction

This chapter will address the key compliance issues that should be considered by members of an Institutional Review Board (IRB), IRB staff members, and compliance officials who are responsible for the compliance oversight of IRB activities. There are excellent resources available that provide a more comprehensive background and analysis of the IRB system itself.[1] This chapter will focus on critical areas where IRBs have been challenged by oversight agencies and others for failure to comply with regulatory requirements. We will also explore other areas, including more recent trends, that are fertile for compliance mishaps.

From time to time we will refer to the Belmont Report,[2] the Common Rule and other governing laws,[3] additional regulatory requirements for certain vulnerable subject populations,[4] and the major compliance findings and guidance published by the Office for Human Research Protection (OHRP) of the Department of Health and Human Services (DHHS).[5] These resources should serve as the primary tools—although not the exclusive tools—of any IRB compliance initiatives.

Four key areas of potential compliance activity will be evaluated: the research review process, the investigators, obtaining consent from subjects, and the IRB staff and records. We will also explore the topics of privacy and financial conflicts of interest as emerging areas for compliance review.

Research Review Process

Institutions that perform human-subjects research that is funded by the Department of Health and Human Services must provide a written Assurance of Compliance that is satisfactory to the Office for Human Research Protection.[6] Institutions that conduct human-subjects research that is supported by the Department of Health and Human Services must provide a certification to the applicable government agency that the research has been reviewed and approved by an Institutional Review Board designated under an Assurance of Compliance.[7] Nearly all institutions provide a written Assurance that promises to apply the DHHS Human Subjects Regulations to all human-subjects research, regardless of the financial sponsor. These regulations are discussed in the next section.

The typical IRB meeting involves protocol reviews of primarily two types: initial review and continuing review. IRBs will also receive reports about research protocols that were approved administratively through an "expedited review" process. Administrators and compliance officials should also understand the criteria for when certain research is exempt from IRB review.

Is It Really Research?

The Federal Policy for the Protection of Human Subjects[8] obligates IRBs to review and approve "research" involving "human subjects." "Research" generally means a systematic investigation—including research development, testing, and evaluation—designed to develop or contribute to generalizable knowledge.[9] "Human subjects" are living individuals about whom investigators (whether professional or student) conducting research obtain data through intervention or interaction with the individuals, or identifiable private information.[10]

Reduced to its essence, "research" requires the following four characteristics:

- Systematic—more than one data element
- Investigation—testing a hypothesis
- Designed to develop or contribute—prospective intent
- Generalizable knowledge—the scientific community

In the vast majority of cases, "research" proposals are submitted to IRBs that clearly satisfy these elements. That is, the proposals describe the aims of the study, the scientific design, inclusion and exclusion criteria, subject recruitment methods, research procedures, etc. Occasionally, however, the IRB will be presented with a treatment protocol or regimen that seemingly omits one or more of the defining characteristics of research. For example, many IRB members and administrators do not believe that a "case report" in which a single case is described in a publication constitutes research, because it fails to be "systematic." Case reports are also usually retrospective in nature, and arguably were not "designed" in advance.[11] Similarly, institutional quality improvement projects that are designed only to improve quality within an institution often lack the element of "generalizable knowledge," unless publication outside the institution is anticipated in advance.[12]

Perhaps the most challenging dilemma occurs when physicians engage in an innovative technique or procedure in treating their patients—query: When does the innovation become an "investigation"? Physicians have the legal right to engage in the practice of medicine, as conferred upon them by state licensing authorities. Federal policy applies only when the innovative procedure or treatment crosses the line and becomes an investigation, e.g., when the physician performs the procedure with the prospective intent of experimenting to determine whether the procedure is safe or effective. When that line is crossed, the physician becomes an investigator testing a hypothesis. The mere collection of patient-identifiable data relating to innovative treatment strongly suggests that a prospective intent exists to publish the data and, while the procedure may be nonresearch, the data collection itself may constitute a research database.

IRBs should have procedures or mechanisms in place to determine who decides whether a particular treatment procedure is "research" that is subject to IRB review. IRBs (or other knowledgeable institutional officials) are expected to be the final institutional authority on whether various institutional activities constitute research; these decisions should not be left to investigators. The Belmont Report suggested that radically new procedures should be discussed in practice committees and converted to formal protocols as soon as practicable.[13]

Initial Review

Institutional Review Boards must review and approve (or modify, disapprove, or otherwise act on, as the case may be) all research activities covered by their institutional assurances of compliance. An IRB's first consideration of a research proposal is referred to as the initial review. Subsequent reviews of the same protocol are called continuing reviews and are discussed in the next section. State-of-the-art IRBs process their initial reviews by using administrative forms. At a minimum these forms should include a protocol application, and often IRBs use a reviewer work sheet. Many IRBs use different types of protocol applications, depending on the nature of the proposed research, e.g., new study applications, registry and database research applications, and continuing review applications. Protocol applications enable the IRBs to obtain relevant information from investigators in a consistent format. For example, a new study application could typically request information about the following topics:

- Study title
- Sponsor protocol number (if applicable)
- Study staff, including the principal investigator and study coordinator
- Study sponsor
- Aims of the study, including primary and secondary objectives
- Summary of the protocol (a copy of the complete protocol should be attached)
- Research procedures, including clinical tests, drugs, devices, and patient information materials to be used in the research (questionnaires and cover letters should be attached)
- Description of prior related research, particularly evidencing that the proposed research is not unnecessarily duplicative of previous studies
- Study sample size justification
- Study recruitment methodology, including how informed consent will be obtained
- Nature of subject population, identifying any normal healthy volunteers, and vulnerable subjects such as minors, non-English speaking persons, pregnant women, fetuses and in vitro-fertilization, institutional employees, cognitively or mentally impaired individuals, and prisoners
- Risk vs. benefit analysis, including how risk will be minimized
- Privacy and confidentiality
- Data and safety monitoring methods
- Subject compensation, if any

- Informed consent, identifying whether a waiver or alteration of consent is being requested (any proposed informed consent form should be attached)
- Identification of any investigational drugs
- Identification of any investigational devices
- Whether an exception to the usual IND/IDE requirements is being requested, e.g., "off-label" investigational use
- Radiation safety considerations
- Bio-safety considerations, such as radioactive tests or materials being proposed
- Bio-safety considerations, such as infectious agents, rDNA, gene testing, or biohazards
- Special institutional scientific review approvals, if applicable
- Tissue procurement issues
- Patient billing and third-party payor information
- Conflicts of interest (a disclosure statement could be required from all study investigators and study coordinators for commercially sponsored research)
- Certification statement, in which the principal investigator acknowledges and accepts certain delineated responsibilities (outlined in the section entitled "The Investigators")
- Acknowledgement of human-subjects training required at the institution (a training certificate could be attached for each member of the research team)
- Signatures of principal investigators with dates (ideally, department chairs should also sign to validate that adequate departmental resources are available to conduct the research properly)
- Listing by name of all co-investigators and study coordinators (a separate signed application could be required from each co-investigator and study coordinator acknowledging their responsibilities and financial disclosures and providing evidence of human-subjects training)

Principal investigators should certify that they will notify the IRB of any changes in personnel after the initial submission, and a separate change form could be available for that purpose.

Most IRBs use a "primary reviewer" system. Under this approach, each research proposal is assigned in advance to a specific IRB member called the primary reviewer who reviews the application, protocol, informed consent form, financial disclosure documents, patient information forms, investigator brochure, and any other pertinent information supplied by the investigator in advance, and presents a summary of the material at the IRB meeting. When a primary reviewer system is used, the other

IRB members should receive and review at least a detailed protocol summary. Many IRBs suggest or require their primary reviewers to use a "review worksheet" to facilitate their analysis and presentation. Reviewer worksheets may be made part of the IRB file. Reviewer worksheets guide the primary reviewer through a proper analysis of the proposed research. A reviewer worksheet may contain the following items:

- Clear study goals
- Adequate animal studies or other data
- Appropriate scientific design
- Achievability of study goals within reasonable time
- Appropriate inclusion and exclusion criteria
- Clearly described recruiting methods
- Skill of individual doing the recruitment
- Distinction between research and standard care
- Informing subjects of results afterward
- IND/IDE requirement, if applicable
- Significant risk device, if applicable
- Adequate statistical and data monitoring methods
- End points, safety stops, and data safety monitoring boards
- Acceptable risk-benefit ratio
- Minimization of potential risks
- Additional safeguards for vulnerable subjects
- Special risk/benefit categories for pediatric research
- Reasonable noncoercive compensation, if any
- Privacy protections, including privacy plans for off-site storage
- Next review date

IRBs should have a thoughtful and meaningful discussion of each initial protocol submission at a convened meeting where a quorum is present. A nonscientific member must be present for the IRB to convene any meeting.[14] IRBs that appear to lack sufficient information to approve research have been cited as noncompliant. IRBs frequently approve protocols subject to certain modifications. The OHRP has recommended that IRBs "defer" further action, including approval, when substantive clarifications or modifications are necessary. In those cases, the IRB should revisit the protocol at a future meeting. If the changes or modifications are not substantive, i.e., when the IRB merely requests the investigator's concurrence to an IRB request, then the IRB chair or IRB member-designate may subsequently approve the revision under the expedited review procedure discussed later in this chapter.[15] The next review (continuing review) must occur within one year; it should occur sooner if the research risks warrant a more frequent review.

Since many IRB members are investigators themselves, it is common that they may be principal investigators or co-investigators on research submitted to the IRB. No IRB member may participate in the IRB's initial or continuing review of research in which that member has a conflicting interest, except to provide requested information.[16] The OHRP has recommended that IRB members physically leave the meeting room when the IRB reviews conflicted research and that the IRB have a corresponding reference in the meeting's minutes.[17]

The quorum for IRB meetings is a majority of the IRB's voting members, at least one of whom must have primary interests in a nonscientific area, e.g., an attorney or a bioethicist who does not possess a science degree or certification. Research should be approved by a majority of those present at the meeting. If a quorum is lacking—whether due to recusal of conflicted members, early departures, or otherwise—the IRB may not approve research or exercise any other regulatory power.[18]

Sometimes you will be asked whether human-subjects research may be conducted in an emergency without IRB review and approval. The OHRP has clarified that patients may not be considered research subjects under such circumstances, and any data regarding such care may not be included in any report of a prospectively conceived research activity.[19] If the emergency care involves investigational drugs, devices, or biologics, you should refer to the FDA Information Sheet entitled "Emergency Use of an Investigational Drug or Biologic."[20] Research conducted in emergency settings is discussed further later in this chapter.

Continuing Review

IRBs must have written procedures for reviewing research that it has previously approved and for determining which projects require more than annual reviews.[21] IRBs must review approved research at intervals appropriate for the risk involved, but at least once per year.[22] Many IRBs use the "primary reviewer" system to conduct continuing reviews. In any event, research being reviewed after the initial approval must be done so at a convened IRB meeting. The quorum rules described above apply for continuing review as well as initial review.

Where a primary reviewer system is used, the primary reviewer should receive a copy of the complete protocol. Proper compliance requires that all IRB members should receive and review at least a summary of the protocol and a status report, including:

- Number of subjects approved, and the number enrolled
- Adverse events, unanticipated problems, withdrawals of subjects, and complaints about the research, and significant changes in the risk vs. benefit ratio
- Recent literature, interim findings, and protocol amendments
- Multicenter trial reports, data safety monitoring board reports, and interim analyses (if applicable)
- Current informed consent documents (ICD), and if applicable, revised proposed ICD[23]

At the meeting, the IRB should ensure that the consent documents are still accurate and complete and that significant new findings are provided to future subjects if they may relate to a subject's willingness to continue to participate. The IRB's minutes should document, on a project-by-project basis, the continuing reviews conducted by the IRB, as well as the votes taken, recusals, etc. The IRB chair or member-designate should receive and review these materials, as well as the complete protocol, when reviewing research under the expedited review procedure described in the following section. For research that is permanently closed to new enrollment, even when subjects have completed all research-related interventions, an IRB must still conduct continuing review on a periodic basis while the research project remains active. This is true even if the research activities are limited to only data analysis.[24]

Expedited Review

IRBs are not expected to comprehensively discuss and review every research protocol at a convened meeting. Certain types of research may be reviewed either by the IRB chairperson or an experienced IRB member designated by the chairperson. Two types of research may be reviewed under an "expedited review" procedure:

- Research involving no more than "minimal risk," as identified on the list shown below
- Minor changes in IRB-approved research[25]

Expedited reviewers may not disapprove research, but otherwise may exercise the full powers of the IRB. IRB members must be advised of research approved by expedited review.[26]

Periodically the Department of Health and Human Services publishes the listing for which the expedited review procedure may be used as long as the research involves no more than "minimal risk." As defined in the DHHS regulations, "minimal risk" means "that the probability and magnitude of harm or discomfort anticipated in the research are not greater in and of themselves than those ordinarily encountered in daily life or during the performance of routine physical or psychological examinations or tests."[27] The most recent listing was published in the Federal Register[28] in 1998 and includes research summarized as follows:

- Drug and device studies for which no investigational new drug or new device applications are required
- Collection of very small amounts of blood
- Prospective collection of hair clippings and other biological specimens by noninvasive means
- Collection of data through most noninvasive procedures
- Research involving data, documents, and other materials that have been previously collected, or will be collected solely for nonresearch purposes
- Collection of data from voice, video, digital, or image recordings
- Research on individual or group characteristics or behavior, including surveys, interviews, quality assurance, and similar methodologies
- Continuing review (as previously discussed) of research that is closed to new enrollment, and all subjects have completed the research-related interventions, and the research remains active only for long-term follow-up; or where no subjects have been enrolled and no additional risks identified; or where the remaining research activities are limited to data analysis
- Continuing review (as previously discussed) not conducted under an IND or IDE involving no greater than minimal risk

Continuing review must occur within one year (or a shorter time interval determined by the IRB) of the convened IRB meeting at which the IRB reviewed and approved the protocol. If the approval is contingent upon specific minor changes subsequently verified by the IRB chair, the one-year clock begins to run on the date of the IRB meeting at which the full IRB gave its contingent approval. If the IRB, after its initial review, requires substantive changes which are made at a subsequent IRB meeting, then the one-year period starts on the date of the subsequent meeting when final approval was given.[29]

Be careful not to confuse all minimal-risk research with minimal-risk research that qualifies for expedited review. IRBs that apply the expedited review procedures to research that involves *greater* than minimal risk are not in compliance with federal regulations (unless the review relates to minor changes in previously approved research as described previously). Institutions should adopt policies describing the types of minor changes in previously approved research that can be approved by the expedited review procedures.[30]

Exempt Research

Six categories of research are "exempt" from review by IRBs.[31] Generally speaking, they are as follows:

1. Research conducted in established or commonly accepted educational settings, involving normal educational practices
2. Research involving the use of educational tests, survey procedures, interview procedures or observation of public behavior, unless (i) information that is obtained is recorded such that human subjects can be identified and (ii) disclosure of responses outside the research could reasonably place the subjects at risk for criminal or civil liability or be damaging to their financial standing, employability, or reputation
3. Research involving educational tests not exempt under paragraph (2), if the subjects are public officials or candidates or federal law will protect the human subjects' confidentiality
4. Research involving the collection or studying of existing data, documents, records, pathological specimens, or diagnostic specimens, if these sources are publicly available or recorded in a nonidentifiable manner
5. Research and demonstration projects of the federal government that examine public benefit or service programs
6. Taste and food quality evaluation and consumer acceptance studies if wholesome food without additives is consumed or if the food consumed is otherwise considered safe by the Food and Drug Administration, the Environmental Protection Agency, or the Food Safety and Inspection Service of the U.S. Department of Agriculture.

You should ensure that your institution has a clear policy defining who shall determine what research is "exempt." Persons with that authority should be well acquainted with applicable regulations and the exemptions allowed by law. Investigators should not have the authority to make an independent determination that research is exempt. Investigators should consult the IRB when in doubt. Be careful not to confuse exempt research with research eligible for expedited review.

Some institutions may decide that *all* research, including exempt research, should be reviewed by their IRBs. In such cases, it is perfectly acceptable to require that exempt research be reviewed through the expedited review procedure. Compliance officials should ensure that IRB policies clearly define how this process would occur. No legal requirement exists, however, for institutions or IRBs to review exempt research.[32]

The Investigators

Primary responsibility for protecting the rights and welfare of research participants should be that of the principal investigators. Co-investigators have secondary responsibility for ensuring this protection. All investigators must be familiar with the ethical principles of human subject protections, the requirements of DHHS and FDA regulations, and the IRB policies and procedures of their institutions.

Investigators are responsible for conducting their research in accordance with IRB-approved protocols and in compliance with all IRB determinations. They should ensure that each potential research subject understands the nature of the research and voluntarily agrees to participate. Investigators should maintain copies of their study records and signed consent documents for as long as institutional policy requires. They should promptly report to the IRB and others if required by institutional policy any protocol amendments or proposed revisions to the consent documents, except where necessary to eliminate apparent immediate hazards to the research subjects.

Investigators should provide annual (or more frequent) renewal reports to the IRB in a timely manner within the IRB approval period. They are obligated to report any unanticipated problems involving risks to subjects and any serious adverse events that are unexpected and associated with the research. It is critical that investigators employ knowledgeable research support personnel who are appropriately trained in human-subjects protections and IRB procedures. Many institutions require that all persons involved in consenting subjects and/or analyzing data complete training programs. Completion of such training programs should be documented in the IRB Office.

Adverse Events and Unanticipated Problems

DHHS regulations require that investigators report unanticipated problems involving risks to subjects or others to appropriate institutional officials, to the IRB, to OHRP, and, if applicable, the head of the sponsoring federal department or agency.[33] FDA regulations require that an IRB review reports of adverse reactions and unexpected events involving risks to subjects or others as part of its continuing review responsibilities. The timing of these reports may depend on the seriousness of the event and whether the event is anticipated in the written research protocol and/or consent document. IRB procedures should explain when the reports should be submitted and whether a specific form should be used. It is a good idea for IRBs to remind investigators at the time of initial approval and at the time of the continuing review that they have the duty to report unanticipated problems and adverse events. Many drug protocols contain defined reporting obligations (different than FDA requirements); investigators for those protocols should become familiar with these requirements.

IRBs may need to reconsider their approvals of research protocols after reviewing these types of reports. IRBs should consider whether it is appropriate to add the adverse events or unanticipated problems that are reported to the informed consent documents. IRBs should also ensure that reports of unanticipated problems involving risks to human subjects or others are reported to the FDA in drug and device trials.[34] This type of reporting is usually accomplished by investigator reports to the sponsors, which in turn notify the FDA.

Obtaining Consent

Obtaining informed consent from research subjects is at the heart of the protections that are in place for human subjects. The following four sections describe the requirements for consent, the prohibition against exculpatory language, when an IRB may waive or alter the consent requirements, and when the special waiver rules for emergency research apply. IRB administrators and compliance officials should ensure that complete documentation is maintained regarding the consent provisions for each research project, the consent forms, any waivers or alterations approved by the IRB, and the "findings" (identified in the next four sections) that IRBs must make in certain circumstances.

Consent Requirements

With the rare exceptions discussed in this chapter, investigators may not involve humans as research subjects without obtaining the legally effective informed consent of the subject or the subject's legally authorized representative. Who qualifies as a legal representative is defined by state law. The information given to the subject should be in language understandable to the subject. Ideally IRBs should strive to achieve eighth-grade reading level in informed consent documents. For non-English speaking research subjects, compliance officials are referred to guidance issued by the OHRP.[35] Informed consent information, whether written or oral, may not include any exculpatory language through which the subject waives legal rights (as discussed in the following section).

Research subjects must be provided with at least the following information:

- Statement that the study involves research, an explanation of the research, and a description of the procedures to be followed
- Reasonably foreseeable risks or discomforts
- Reasonably expected benefits to the subject or others
- Appropriate alternative procedures or courses of treatment
- Extent of confidentiality to be afforded to the subject's records
- Whether any compensation and medical treatments are available if injury occurs, what they consist of, or where any further information may be obtained
- Contact information for questions about the research and research-related injuries
- Statement that participation is voluntary and refusal to participate involves no penalty or loss of benefits, and that the subject may discontinue participation at any time

In addition to the required elements of informed consent listed above, the following elements of informed consent should also be provided to research subjects when appropriate:

- Existence of research risks that are currently unforeseeable
- Participation that may be terminated by the investigator without the subject's consent

- Any additional cost to the research subject
- Consequences of the subject's decision to withdraw, and the procedures for orderly termination of participation
- Significant new findings discovered during the research
- Approximate number of subjects in the study

These elements are usually provided in a written informed consent document. As noted later in this chapter, the IRB may alter some of these requirements or even waive them completely. The IRB may also modify the informed consent document or waive its use completely if certain conditions are met.

Informed consent should be *prospectively* obtained. "Deferred consent" or "ratification" of consent in a retroactive manner is not legally effective informed consent under federal regulations for the protection of human research subjects.[36]

IRBs must be mindful that informed consent is a process—not just a form. The information identified above should be presented in a manner that will enable research subjects to voluntarily decide whether or not they want to be involved in a clinical trial. Using the first person, (e.g., "I understand that . . .") may be suggestive and constitute a coercive influence over a subject. It is better to write informed consent forms in the second person referring to the research subject as "you" and the investigators or institution as "we" or "us." OHRP has provided helpful guidance[37] to assist in the writing of informed consent forms. Compliance officials or IRB administrators should have procedures in place to ensure that a copy of every IRB-approved consent form is on file.

Exculpatory Language

You may not use wording in an informed consent form that exonerates the investigators or hospital in advance from blame, fault, or liability. This wording is called exculpatory language. No informed consent documents or discussion may include any exculpatory language by which the research subject waives legal rights, or even appears to waive them. Investigators and hospitals cannot use informed consent forms or consent discussions to release themselves, the research sponsors, or their agents from liability for negligence.[38]

Many people confuse informed consent forms with releases. They are not synonymous. An informed consent form explains a procedure, its risks, its benefits, its alternatives, and the consequences of not having the procedure. It also provides other information about the procedure and contains words of consent and understanding. A release, on the other hand, is a document through which one party legally exonerates the other party in advance. You will frequently see release language contained in consent forms, such as for school field trips, fitness center memberships, youth sports programs, and rental agreements. Many if not most state laws, however, render waiver language that exonerates professionals to be legally ineffective. In the case of human-subjects research, such language is absolutely prohibited. If exculpatory language is used, it would have no legal effect in most jurisdictions. In remote circumstances the entire consent may be nullified.

The following are examples of improper exculpatory language.

- *By agreeing to serve as a research subject I give up any and all rights to compensation for any injuries that I may incur.*
- *I hereby waive any interest and rights that I may have in any commercial products developed with the use of my tissue samples or bodily fluids.*
- *You should understand that you will relinquish all rights and opportunities for personal benefit from the commercial development of these substances.*

Although investigators must refrain from using exculpatory language, they have an obligation to inform research subjects of material considerations that would affect the subjects' decisions to participate in research. Thus it is entirely appropriate for an informed consent form to state that the institution has no plans to provide financial compensation for research-related injuries. Other examples of acceptable language are:

- *We make no commitment to provide payment or medical care for poor outcomes resulting from your involvement in this research.*
- *This institution's policy would enable your tissue to be used to establish a cell line that could be licensed or patented. There are no plans to compensate you if this happens.*
- *By signing this form, you are authorizing the use of your tissue samples for research and possible commercial development.*
- *In the event of a research-related injury, medical services will be offered at the usual charge but free medical care or other compensation is not available.*

Effective compliance oversight may involve a sampling of informed consent documents to identify potentially offensive language of the nature described above.

Waiving and Altering the Consent Requirements

IRBs may waive or alter the informed consent requirements outlined in the prior section under certain circumstances. Proper compliance oversight requires careful documentation when these circumstances are present.

An IRB may approve a consent procedure that alters or even completely waives the requirement to obtain informed consent if the IRB finds *and documents* all of the following:

- The research involves no more than minimal risk[39] to the subjects.
- The waiver or alteration will not adversely affect the rights and welfare of the subjects.
- The research could not practicably be carried out without the waiver or alteration.
- Whenever appropriate, the subjects will be provided with additional pertinent information after participation.[40]

An IRB has the ability to modify or waive some or all of the elements of informed consent. In such cases, the IRB may exercise this authority if the research could not practicably be carried out without the waiver or alteration.[41]

IRBs may also waive the requirements for investigators to obtain a signed consent form for some or all of the subjects if it finds either of the following conditions:

- The only record linking the subject and the research would be the consent document, and the principal risk would be potential harm resulting from a breach of confidentiality. In such a case, subjects should be asked whether they want documentation linking themselves with the research, and their wishes should govern.
- The research presents no more than minimal risk.[42]

If the IRB is simultaneously functioning as a Privacy Board under HIPAA, the IRB must also review and document that certain privacy protections are in place whenever it waives or alters the informed consent requirements. This is addressed in the section on privacy. When an IRB waives the documentation requirement, it may require that subjects be provided with a written statement or information sheet about the research. Effective compliance would mandate that the findings and any such information sheets be clearly documented in the IRB's records.

Emergency Research

Research that is contemplated in emergency departments or in other emergent circumstances brings with it a number of problems. As described earlier in this chapter, IRBs and research investigators must follow certain rules for obtaining informed consent and documenting informed consent.[43] IRBs have historically had the authority to alter or waive the informed consent requirements in certain circumstances.[44] By the mid-1990s, however, it was clear that high-quality research in emergency circumstances was being hampered by these regulatory restrictions. In October 1996, DHHS and the FDA jointly announced a new narrow exception to the requirement for obtaining and documenting informed consent for certain emergency medical interventions.[45] These provisions are recognized by both the OHRP and the FDA.[46]

Under this "Emergency Research Consent Waiver" an IRB may waive the general requirements for informed consent if it finds *and documents* each of the following:

1. the human subjects are in a life-threatening situation, available treatments are unproven or unsatisfactory, and the collection of valid scientific evidence is necessary to determine safety and efficacy;
2. obtaining informed consent is not feasible;
3. direct benefit may inure to the research subjects;
4. the research could not practicably be carried out without the waiver;
5. the proposed research provides a certain time period during which each subject's legal representative, if any, could be contacted;
6. the IRB has reviewed and approved an informed consent procedure and document to be used when feasible; and
7. additional protections will be provided, including consultation with local communities, public disclosure to the communities both before and after the research, establishment of independent data monitoring committees, and contacting family members in the absence of a legal representative.[47]

The IRB must also find *and document* whether or not the research is subject to FDA regulation and, if so, whether the research activity will be carried out under either an FDA Investigational New Drug (IND) Application or an FDA Investigational Device Exemption (IDE). The application for the IND or the IDE must clearly identify that the protocols would include subjects who are unable to consent. The IRB must also have procedures to inform the research subjects of the research at the earliest feasible opportunity. Other requirements are provided as well. It is critical from a compliance standpoint that the IRB records (e.g., the meeting minutes) reflect the specific findings made by the IRB when altering or waiving the usual informed consent requirements.

IRB Staff, Policies, and Records

Federal regulations require that institutions provide written assurance to the Department of Health and Human Services that their Institutional Review Boards have meeting space and sufficient staff to support the IRBs' review and recordkeeping duties.[48] Each IRB should have written procedures that it will follow. At a minimum the IRB's procedures must address the following areas:

- Conducting the initial and continuing review of research and reporting IRB actions back to the investigators and the institution
- Determining which projects require review more often than annually and which projects need verification from noninvestigators that no material changes have occurred since the last IRB review
- Ensuring prompt reporting to the IRB of proposed changes in research activities and ensuring that changes in approved research will not be initiated without IRB approval[49]

IRBs should also have procedures that ensure prompt reporting of unanticipated problems involving risks to subjects, serious or continuing noncompliance with IRB determinations, and suspensions or terminations of IRB approval.[50]

The OHRP has issued helpful guidance regarding what should be covered by the IRB's policies.[51] We encourage you to read this document because it provides many useful details. In general, however, IRB procedures should include the following important operational details:

1. A description of any "primary reviewer system" that is used for reviews conducted by the IRB. A strong policy would include when and how the system is used in the following different scenarios: initial review, continuing review,

review of protocol changes, review of unanticipated event reports, and review of serious or continuing noncompliance.

2. Lists of specific documents given to the primary reviewers (when a primary reviewer system is used) and to other IRB members, categorized by initial review, continuing review, etc.

3. A description of any process that the IRB uses to supplement its own review process, such as subcommittees or consultants.

4. How soon documents are delivered to IRB members prior to meetings.

5. The range of possible actions that the IRB might take, e.g., approval, denial, tabled, deferred, referred for additional information.

6. How expedited review is conducted and how those actions are communicated to all IRB members.

7. How the IRB communicates its actions back to investigators and how the IRB processes investigators' responses.

8. Which institutional officials are notified of IRB findings and actions and how that is done.

9. Whether any institutional officials must review and approve research protocols after they receive IRB approval.

10. How the IRB determines which protocols require continuing review that is less frequent than annual and how this is determined.

11. How the IRB determines which projects need verification from noninvestigators that no material changes have occurred since the prior IRB review.

12. What steps ensure that investigators do not implement protocol changes without IRB approval.

13. Who in the institution is responsible for promptly reporting to the IRB, appropriate institutional officials, and government authorities any:
    - unanticipated problems involving risks to subjects or others
    - serious or continuing noncompliance with federal regulations or IRB determinations
    - suspensions or termination of IRB approval

14. The time frame for the reporting outlined above.

15. The range of possible actions taken by the IRB in responding to reports of unanticipated problems involving research risks or of noncompliance.

In addition to written policies, IRBs should also have detailed records of the research projects that they review and approve, the IRB meeting minutes, the documentation of IRB findings, and the time period for which the research is approved. All of these documents, and the others discussed further below, must be retained for at least three years from the end of the research (and for six years if the informed consent documents include HIPAA privacy authorizations). Records relating to specific research studies must be retained for three years after the completion of the research.[52] Your records should be accessible for inspection and copying by OHRP and FDA representatives when they ask for them in a reasonable time and manner.

You should keep copies of all research protocols, scientific evaluations that accompany the protocols, approved sample consent documents, progress reports submitted by the investigators, and reports of any injuries of subjects, whether at your institution or elsewhere. You should also keep records of continuing review activities and copies of all correspondence between the IRB and the investigators. Statements of significant new findings that are provided to subjects should also be maintained.

The minutes of the IRB meetings should be in sufficient detail to show attendance at the meeting, the actions taken by the IRB, the votes for each protocol undergoing initial and continuing review (identifying the number of members voting for, against, and abstaining), IRB members with conflicts of interest, the basis for requiring changes in or disapproving any of the research projects, and a written summary of controversial deliberations and their resolution. The OHRP recommends that votes be recorded in minutes using the following format: Total = 15; Vote: For—14, Opposed—0, Abstained—1 (name of person abstaining).[53]

Whenever your IRB approves a consent procedure that modifies or omits some or all of the required elements of informed consent, you should document that the four findings required for such a waiver or alteration are present.[54] The discussion of these four findings should include *protocol-specific* information that justifies each finding. IRB administrators and chairs should be sufficiently familiar with federal regulations to know when "specific findings" must be made by the IRB when approving certain research protocols. Other examples of research approvals requiring specific findings include research involving pregnant women, human fetuses, or neonates;[55] research involving prisoners;[56] and research involving children.[57] Similarly, research reviewed through an expedited review procedure should also have documentation affirming why the research qualified for an expedited review. This is best done by the IRB chairperson or designate who performs the expedited reviews.

Privacy

Several bodies of law impose restrictions on the disclosure of a subject's health care information. These protections have evolved from the core concept of physician–patient confidentiality. Federal and state laws and regulations, as well as the ethical standards of professional associations such as the American Medical Association, have been established to protect the physician–patient relationship and outline the circumstances under which it is appropriate to disclose medical information. This section will focus on the privacy protections for research and medical information as established by federal law, mainly the rules promulgated under the Health Insurance Portability and Accountability Act of 1996 (the "Privacy Rule").[58] Unlike most federal legislation, the Privacy Rule does not always preempt state laws,[59] so you should check with local counsel to ensure that your program conforms to state as well as federal law.

HIPAA Privacy Rule

The Privacy Rule has specific regulations pertaining to the uses and disclosures of "protected health information" that "covered entities" may make, including for research purposes.[60] "Covered entities" are defined as health care providers, health plans, and health care clearinghouses.[61] Hospitals and academic medical centers that perform human subject research are considered "health care providers" under the Privacy Rule. "Protected health information"[62] or "PHI" is essentially the medical or research information created or received by a covered entity that identifies the individual or contains information that would lead to identification of the individual. This includes research records that identify the subject's name or are coded in a manner that uses an identifiable code (e.g., a subject's social security number). This does not include research records that are de-identified in accordance with the Privacy Rule standards, discussed in detail below.

The Privacy Rule regulates how and when covered entities may use and disclose PHI. Generally speaking, covered entities may use and disclose PHI without the individual's written authorization under the following circumstances: (1) the use or disclosure is made for treatment, payment, or health care operations purposes[63] or (2) the use or disclosure is specifically excepted from the written authorization requirement.[64] Research is not considered a treatment, payment, or health care operations function; however, one of the specific exceptions referenced above does pertain to research. Therefore, prior to using or disclosing PHI, the IRB is charged with ensuring that either obtain the subject's written authorization or use or disclosure PHI in a manner that meets one of the enumerated exceptions.

Uses and Disclosures with a Subject's Written Authorization

For an authorization to be valid, the Privacy Rule sets a general set of requirements for all authorizations as well as additional provisions for authorizations used for research purposes. The general requirements entail the following:[65]

- A specific description of the PHI to be used or disclosed (e.g., "your research information" or the "information recorded about you during your participation in this study");
- An affirmative statement that the covered entity is permitted to make the use or disclosure;
- The "name or other specific identification of the person(s) or class of persons" that may make the disclosure (e.g., the investigators or the name of the research institution);
- The "name or other specific identification of the person(s) or class of persons" to whom the covered entity is going to make the disclosure (e.g., the research sponsor or the Food and Drug Administration);
- A description of the purpose(s) for the disclosure;
- An expiration or date of expiration (for research only, this may be listed as "none" or "the end of the research study");
- A statement that the individual may revoke the authorization at any time;
- A description of how the individual may revoke the authorization (e.g., must be in writing to the principal investigator);
- A statement that the revocation will not apply to disclosures made prior to the revocation; and
- Signature of the individual[66] and the date.

In most circumstances, the Privacy Rule does not allow a covered entity to condition "treatment, payment, enrollment, or eligibility for benefits" on the execution of an authorization.[67] However, there is an exception for research purposes.[68] The authorization should therefore contain a statement that the individual will not be enrolled in the study unless he or she signs the authorization. Another exception specific to research pertains to the form of the authorization. Except in limited circumstances,[69] the authorization must be a stand-alone document. One of the limited circumstances in which the authorization may be combined with another document is an authorization for research purposes. The Privacy Rule permits this type of authorization to be combined with "any other type of written permission for the same research study, including . . . a consent to participate in such research."[70] Either way is permissible: you can have a separate HIPAA authorization for disclosure of the research records, or you can combine the prior language into the informed consent document discussed previously.

Uses and Disclosures without a Subject's Written Authorization

IRBs may approve the use and disclosure of PHI for research purposes without requiring the investigator to obtain a written authorization from every subject. The Privacy Rule sets forth certain criteria that the IRB[71] must evaluate for these types of requests. These criteria are in addition to those set forth in the Common Rule and discussed previously. There are also provisions related to uses and disclosures preparatory to research and research related solely to decedents. Finally, IRBs may allow uses and disclosures of "Limited Data Sets" and de-identified information.

Criteria for Evaluation Waiver/Alteration of Authorization Requests

The Privacy Rule sets forth additional criteria that must be met for the IRB to approve a request for a waiver or alteration of the authorization requirement:[72]

- the investigators need access to PHI in order to conduct the research;
- the research "could not practicably be conducted without the waiver or alteration" (e.g., a retrospective review of charts); and
- there is no more than minimal risk to the privacy of the subjects.

To demonstrate the last criterion, the protocol must contain an "adequate plan" to protect identifying information from "improper" use and disclosure and destroy all identifying information at the earliest practical time.[73] The protocol must also contain written assurances that the investigators will not reuse or disclose the PHI unless required by law, for institutional or government oversight of the research, or for other research that would fit this same criteria.[74]

Researcher Certification: Reviews Preparatory to Research

One of the research activities that the Privacy Rule recognizes would be burdened by the authorization process is a review preparatory to research. This usually entails a review of medical charts for individuals treated by the covered entity. This is done for a variety of reasons, such as determining potential subject population size, potential subjects, or adequacy of medical or other criteria in the protocol. While the main goal is to protect patient privacy, the Privacy Rule also aims to ensure that "researchers continue to have access to medical information necessary to conduct vital research."[75]

It would be difficult for most researchers to obtain written authorization during the preparation stages because they most likely have not had any interaction with the potential subjects yet, or cannot finalize their protocols without reviewing patient records. Therefore, the Privacy Rule contains a provision that allows IRBs to approve this type of activity without written authorization. To do so, the investigators must certify that the use and disclosure of the PHI is necessary "to prepare a research protocol" or similar purposes, the PHI will not be removed from the covered entity's premises, and access to the PHI is "necessary for research purposes."[76]

Researcher Certification: Research on Decedents
Throughout the Privacy Rule provisions regarding research, it states that reviews may be done by either the IRB or a Privacy Board.[77] Since the Common Rule does not regulate research on decedents, most IRBs did not review protocols that pertained to this type of research prior to the enactment of the Privacy Rule. Even today, they do not technically have jurisdiction over research on decedents unless specifically charged by the institution. These protocols must have a level of review, however, so a Privacy Board must review this type of research. A simple solution is to have your institution's IRB also sit as the Privacy Board and review applications related to research on decedents.

Again, a certification from the investigators that complies with the Privacy Rule requirements is sufficient for a Privacy Board, or an IRB sitting as the Privacy Board, to approve this type of research. The certification must contain representations that the research is using PHI solely derived from decedents and use of this PHI is necessary for the research.[78] The Privacy Board may also request documentation of the death of each individual whose PHI is going to be accessed.[79] This documentation is usually obtained by accessing the Social Security Death Index.[80]

De-Identification
Information that does not meet the definition of "Protected Health Information" is not regulated by the Privacy Rule. Therefore, IRBs can approve uses and disclosures of research information that does not identify the individual and for which there is no "reasonable basis to believe that the information can be used to identify the individual."[81]

De-identification can be achieved through one of two methods: using a statistician to develop a method to de-identify the information that poses a "very small" risk of identification;[82] or removing the identifiers enumerated in the Privacy Rule. These identifiers include but are not limited to:[83]

- Names
- All geographic subdivisions smaller than a state (although zip codes may be used in certain circumstances)[84]
- All elements of dates (except year) for dates directly related to an individual, including birth date, admission date, discharge date, date of death; and all ages over 89 and all elements of dates (including year) indicative of such age, except that such ages and elements may be aggregated into a single category of age 90 or older
- Numbers related to the individual telephone and fax numbers, social security numbers, account or medical record numbers, health plan subscriber number, etc.
- E-mail addresses
- Device identifiers and serial numbers
- Biometric identifiers, including finger and voice prints
- Full-face photographic images and any comparable images

IRBs may approve the use and disclosure of PHI that includes a code assigned by the covered entity or the investigators. This is a common practice so that the investigators can maintain appropriate documentation and audit their findings on a periodic basis. This code (or the mechanism for developing the code) may not be disclosed outside the covered entity for the information to remain de-identified. Further, the code must be derived in a manner that does not use any of the identifiers listed above (e.g., using social security numbers would not be acceptable).[85]

Limited Data Sets and Data Use Agreements

If the PHI cannot be de-identified in the manner discussed above, the Privacy Rule does allow disclosures of "Limited Data Sets" to outside parties pursuant to a "Data Use Agreement." A Limited Data Set is a data set that excludes most of the identifiers listed above, however it may include the following: towns, cities, and full zip codes; dates and all ages; and unique identifying numbers, characteristics, and codes.[86] The IRB may approve disclosures of Limited Data Sets to outside researchers so long as the disclosure is being done for research, public health, or health care operations purposes,[87] and the parties have entered into a Data Use Agreement. For a Data Use Agreement to be compliant with the Privacy Rule, it must:[88]

- Establish the permitted uses and disclosures by the recipient, including a statement that the recipient cannot use or disclose the Limited Data Set in a manner that would violate the Privacy Rule if done by the covered entity

- Identify who may receive the information
- Provide that the recipient may not identify the individuals or contact the individuals whose information is contained in the Limited Data Set
- Provide that the recipient will not further use or disclose the Limited Data Set; implement appropriate safeguards to prevent unauthorized uses and disclosures; report any unauthorized uses and disclosures; and require any subcontractors or agents to agree to the same terms and restrictions

Several agencies and institutions have published their Data Use Agreements online, including the Centers for Medicare and Medicaid Services (CMS). To view an example, go to http://www.cms.hhs.gov/data/requests/cmsldsdua.pdf, which contains CMS's template Data Use Agreement.

Other HIPAA Considerations
Reporting to the FDA or the OHRP
IRBs may continue to report events as they deem necessary to the FDA and the OHRP without an individual's written authorization.[89] If a report is made that identifies the individual, an accounting of this disclosure must be included in any accounting requests made by the individual (the accounting process is discussed below).

Access and Accounting Rights under HIPAA
In addition to regulating how covered entities can use and disclose PHI, the Privacy Rule establishes new federal patient rights. Most states also have laws and regulations that set forth similar rights, but HIPAA marks the first time these rights have been established by the federal government. You should check with legal counsel to determine if your state's laws provide for broader patient rights than those afforded by the Privacy Rule. In the event they do, the state law will not be preempted by HIPAA, so you may have additional requirements.

Two of these rights have a direct impact on research activities: a patient's right to access his or her medical information and the right to an accounting of all disclosures of the information.

- **Access**
  The Privacy Rule provides that individuals have the right to access their medical records.[90] However, if an individual is enrolled in a research study, access to his or her medical records could jeopardize the integrity of the study and the data being collected (e.g., if the study contains a placebo, the subject must

be unaware of whether he or she received a placebo). The Privacy Rule, therefore, permits covered entities to deny access to research records (or the portion of the medical record containing research information) for the duration of the study.[91] To be afforded this exception, the informed consent document must inform the individual that access will not be permitted, and access must be reinstated at the completion of the study.[92]

- **Accounting**

  The Privacy Rule requires covered entities to provide, upon an individual's request, an accounting of all disclosures made by the covered entity that included the individual's PHI.[93] Not all disclosures have to be included in the accounting,[94] and two of these exceptions are worth noting. First, covered entities do not have to account for disclosures that were authorized by the individual in writing. So if a HIPAA authorization was obtained from the subjects (by being embodied in the informed consent or a separate document), the authorized disclosures are not subject to the accounting requirement. Second, if the disclosure was for research purposes and involved the disclosure of PHI related to 50 or more individuals, the Privacy Rule has established a simplified accounting process. The covered entity may "provide individuals with a list of all protocols for which the patient's [PHI] may have been disclosed . . . as well as the researcher's name and contact information."[95] Additional requirements for this simplified process can be found in 45 CFR § 164.528(b)(4).

As mentioned above, one class of disclosures that would have to be included in an accounting would be disclosures to health oversight agencies, such as the FDA and the OHRP.

Almost all aspects of the Privacy Rule touch on research in some way or another because they affect the overall conduct of the covered entities in general. IRBs should be knowledgeable in this area and review their policies to ensure compliance with the Privacy Rule.

Certificates of Confidentiality

Certificates of Confidentiality are another mechanism by which the federal government protects identifiable research information. The Public Health Services Act[96] permits the Department of Health and Human Services to authorize individuals "engaged in biomedical, behavioral, clinical, or other research (including research on mental health and research on the use and effect of alcohol and other psychoactive drugs)" to afford extra protections to research information. The Department of Health and Human Services has delegated this authority to the National Institutes of Health (NIH). The NIH issues Certificates of Confidentiality to researchers in these fields. The holder of a Certificate of Confidentiality is authorized to "withhold from all persons not connected with the conduct of such research the names or other identifying characteristics of such individuals." This means that they can "refuse to disclose identifying information in any civil, criminal, administrative, legislative, or other proceeding, whether at the federal, state, or local level."[97]

These Certificates of Confidentiality offer more protection than those put in place under the HIPAA Privacy Rule, which allows for disclosure of protected health information in the course of judicial or administrative proceedings.[98] Because they are so restrictive, they are reserved for research that includes sensitive information. The NIH considers "sensitive information" to mean information which, if disclosed, could have "adverse consequences for subjects or damage their financial standing, employability, insurability, or reputation."[99] On its web site, the NIH lists the following examples of research that involves sensitive information:

- Collecting genetic information
- Collecting information on psychological well-being of subjects
- Collecting information on subjects' sexual attitudes, preferences, or practices
- Collecting data on substance abuse or other illegal risk behaviors
- Studies where subjects may be involved in litigation related to exposures under the study (e.g., breast implants, environmental or occupational exposures)[100]

The Certificate's restrictions, however, do not extend to certain limited disclosures. Researchers are still obligated to disclose information to the Department of Health and Human Services in response to an audit or evaluation, and to the Food and Drug Administration as required under the Federal Food, Drug and Cosmetic Act.[101]

Certificates of Confidentiality are not issued in a blanket manner; rather, they are issued for a "single, well-defined" research protocol.[102] If the protocol is designed as a multicenter study, the coordinating center can apply for a Certificate on behalf of all study sites. The IRB should ensure that the coordinating center has obtained a Certificate of Confidentiality before allowing investigators to share the research information with other study sites. If your institution is the coordinating center, or if the study involves only your site, the principal investigator must apply for the Certificate of Confidentiality. The application requires that the study have IRB approval, so your IRB will have to review the protocol first. The IRB can grant approval, conditional upon a Certificate of Confidentiality being issued.

Both the principal investigator and the research institution are required to sign the application for a Certificate of Confidentiality. This is to bind both to the assurances required by the NIH in the application. Following are the assurances listed on the application that have to be agreed upon by the institution and the investigator:[103]

This institution agrees to use the Certificate of Confidentiality to protect against the compelled disclosure of personally identifiable information and to support and defend the authority of the Certificate against legal challenges.

The institution and personnel involved in the conduct of the research will comply with the applicable Federal regulation for the protection of human subjects or, if no such Federal regulation is otherwise applicable, they will comply with 45 CFR Part 46.

This Certificate of Confidentiality will not be represented as an endorsement of the project by the DHHS or NIH or used to coerce individuals to participate in the research project.

All subjects will be informed that a Certificate has been issued, and they will be given a description of the protection provided by the Certificate.

Any research participant entering the project after expiration or termination of the Certificate will be informed that the protection afforded by the Certificate does not apply to them.

Whether a single or multicenter study, the IRB should also require that the informed consent state that a Certificate has been issued, explain what the Certificate means, and identify the various institutions (if any) that are participating in the study and which may receive this information. The institution applying for the Certificate must include a copy of the informed consent document with the application. The NIH requires this information be included in the informed consent document. The NIH offers example language that can be included in the informed consent document that would satisfy this requirement. You can find this sample language at the NIH's web site at http://grants2.nih.gov/grants/policy/coc/appl_extramural.htm.

Conflicts of Interest

A number of concerns has arisen in recent years that investigators in clinical trials may be biased—or appear to be biased—in their research due to financial or reputational conflicts of interest. A more involved discussion of conflicts of interest in human subjects research is covered in another chapter of this book. From an IRB compliance perspective, you should know that OHRP issued final guidance in May 2004 urging institutions, IRBs, and investigators to consider the impact of real and apparent conflicts of interest in clinical research and to address them appropriately.

We must always remember that an IRB, in addition to its regular duties, may always require that additional information be given to subjects when, in the IRB's judgement, the information would "meaningfully add to [the] protection of the rights and welfare of subjects."[104] When investigator or institutional conflicts of interest surface in clinical trials, IRBs should consider whether disclosure of this information would add meaningfully to the rights and welfare of the potential research subjects. OHRP's guidance document[105] on conflicts of interest addresses specific points for consideration by institutions, IRB operations, IRB review, and investigators.

- **Institutions**

  OHRP suggests a dozen or so actions that institutions should consider in establishing a disclosure and management review process of real and apparent conflicts of interest. Institutions are urged to consider establishing firewalls between institutional responsibility for research activities and the management of the institution's financial interest. The establishment of Conflict of Interest Committees (COICs) should be considered to address investigator and institutional financial interests in research. Institutions should enable clear and direct communication channels between COICs and IRBs.

- **IRB Operations**

  As noted earlier IRB members with conflicting interests in a research project may not participate in an IRB's initial or continuing review of that project. The only exception is to provide information that is requested by the IRB. We suggest that IRB members with conflicts of interest physically leave the IRB meeting during votes. OHRP encourages IRBs to constantly remind their members of Conflict of Interest policies at each meeting and to document any actions taken regarding IRB member conflicts. IRBs are also encouraged to develop educational materials for their members to ensure awareness of federal regulations and institutional policies regarding financial interests in research.

- **IRB Review**

  IRBs should consider taking certain extra actions whenever they review human-subjects research that involves financial interests held by investigators or the institution. The IRB should:
  - consider whether the conflict management methods proposed by the investigator or the institution adequately protect the rights and welfare of human subjects
  - determine whether other actions are necessary to minimize risks to subjects, and
  - determine what information should be provided to research subjects regarding the source of funding and other financial interests of the parties involved in the research.

- **Investigators**
  - Investigators can assist IRBs by considering whether additional information should be placed in the informed consent document regarding the source of funding and any other funding arrangements involved in the research. Research subjects may also be better informed by knowing about the financial arrangements of an institution or an investigator with a research sponsor and how it is being managed. Investigators, as well as IRBs, should also consider whether disclosure of financial interests in the informed consent document alone is adequate. In some cases, special measures may be advisable as a supplement to the informed consent form, e.g., having a nonconflicted individual involved in the consent process or using independent monitoring of the research.

Any steps taken by the IRB to ensure disclosure, monitoring, and management of real or apparent conflicts of interest should be clearly documented in the IRB records.

Conclusion

Strong compliance programs begin with written documentation of policies, actions, and educational efforts. Effective IRB management and operations require the commitment of individuals who are scientifically astute and who also possess a knowledge of applicable law and regulatory guidance. A compliance official's most valuable allies are competent IRB members and a knowledgeable IRB office staff. Effective IRB compliance initiatives require competent personnel, on the IRB and in the IRB Office, and adequate maintenance of all of the documents referred to in this chapter.

Notes and References

1   *Institutional Review Board: Management and Function;* Amdur and Bankert, Ed., Jones and Bartlett Publishers, 2002. *Institutional Review Board: Member Handbook;* Amdur, Ed., Jones and Bartlett Publishers, 2003. *Protecting Study Volunteers in Research: A Manual for Investigative Sites,* 2d Ed. Dunn and Chadwick, Centerwatch Publisher, 2002. *Study Guide for the Institutional Review Board: Management and Function;* Kornetsky, Jones and Bartlett Publishers, 2003.

2   National Commission for the Protection of Human Subjects of Biomedical and Behavorial Research. T*he Belmont Report: Ethical Principles and Guidelines for the Protection of Human Subjects of* Research. (DHEW (OS) 78-0013 and (OS) 78-0014.4). Washington DC: U.S. Government Printing Office 18 Apr 1979. Access date 22 Mar 2001.

3   45 C.F.R. 46, 21 C.F.R. 50, 21 C.F.R. 56.

4   45 C.F.R. 46.

5   OHRP Compliance Activities: Common Findings and Guidance (web site: http://OHRP.osophs. gov/compovr.htm).

6   45 C.F.R. 46.103(a).

7   45 C.F.R. 46.103(f).

8   45 C.F.R. 46. The regulations promulgated by the Food and Drug Administration at 21 C.F.R. 50 and 56 provide that Institutional Review Boards should also review clinical investigations and experiments regulated by the FDA that involve any of the following for human use: a drug, biological product, medical device, human food or color additive, electronic product, and any other regulated test article. The complete text of the FDA regulations pertaining to IRBs is contained in *Information Sheets: Guidance for Institutional Review Boards and Clinical Investigators,* Food and Drug Administration, Office of Health Affairs (1998 Update). A useful self-evaluation checklist for IRBs is also available in this document, along with helpful information on a variety of relevant topics.

9   45 C.F.R. 46.102(d).

10 45 C.F.R. 46.102(f). "Private information" includes individually identifiable information about behavior that occurs in a context in which there is a reasonable expectation of privacy.

11 This interpretation represents an area of concern. The responsible federal oversight agency may interpret the actual writing of the case report as a prospective act of "designing" research if patient identifiers are recorded anywhere by the author, whether in the case report or in the author's files.

12 Guidance is available on the OHRP web site to provide assistance regarding quality improvement activities (web site: http:\\OHRP.osophs.gov).

13 National Commission for the Protection of Human Subjects of Biomedical and Behavorial Research. T*he Belmont Report: Ethical Principles and Guidelines for the Protection of Human Subjects of* Research. (DHEW (OS) 78-0013 and (OS) 78-0014.4). Washington DC: U.S. Government Printing Office 18 Apr 1979. Access date 22 Mar 2001. The Office of Human Research Protections (OHRP) has published decision charts that provide graphic aids to help determine if an activity is "research" that must be reviewed by an IRB. The charts also address whether the review may be performed by expedited procedures and whether informed consent or its documentation may be waived (web site: http://www.hhs.gov/ohrp/humansubjects/guidance/decisioncharts.htm).

14 45 C.F.R. 46.108(b), OHRP Compliance Activities: Common Findings and Guidance (web site: http://OHRP.osophs.gov/compovr.htm), Item (11).

15 OHRP Compliance Activities: Common Findings and Guidance (web site: http://OHRP.osophs.gov/compovr.htm), Item (5).

16 45 C.F.R. 46.107(e).

17 OHRP Compliance Activities: Common Findings and Guidance (web site: http://OHRP.osophs.gov/compovr.htm), Item (10).

18 OHRP Compliance Activities: Common Findings and Guidance (web site: http://OHRP.osophs.gov/compovr.htm), Item (12).

19 OHRP Compliance Activities: Common Findings and Guidance (web site: http://OHRP.osophs.gov/compovr.htm), Item (13).

20 *Information Sheets: Guidance for Institutional Review Boards and Clinical Investigators;* Food and Drug Administration, 1998 Update.

21 45 C.F.R. 46.103(b)(4).

22 45 C.F.R. 46.109(e).

23 Guidance on Continuing Review. Office for Human Research Protections, Department of Health and Human Services (July 11, 2002) (web site: http:\\OHRP.osophs.gov).

24 OHRP Compliance Activities: Common Findings and Guidance (web site: http://OHRP.osophs.gov/compovr.htm), Item (16).

25 45 C.F.R. 46.110(b). The Office for Human Research Protections (OHRP) has published decision charts that provide graphic aids to help address whether the review may be performed by expedited procedures. The charts also help determine if an activity is "research" that must be reviewed by an IRB and address whether informed consent or its documentation may be waived (web site: http://www.hhs.gov/ohrp/humansubjects/guidance/decisioncharts.htm).

26 45 C.F.R. 46.110(c).

27 45 C.F.R. 46.102(i).

28 63 Fed. Reg. 60364-60367 (Nov. 9, 1998). *See also* Categories of Research That May Be Reviewed by the Institutional Review Board (IRB) through an Expedited Review Procedure (web site: http:\\OHRP.osophs.gov).

29 Guidance on Continuing Review. Office for Human Research Protections, Department of Health and Human Services (July 11, 2002) (web site: http:\\OHRP.osophs.gov).

30 OHRP Compliance Activities: Common Findings and Guidance (web site: http://OHRP.osophs.gov/compovr.htm), Item (21).

31 45 C.F.R. 46.101(b)(1)–(6).

32 OPRR Reports: Exempt research and research that may undergo expedited review (NO 95-02; May 5, 1995) (web site: http:\\OHRP.osophs.gov).

33 45 C.F.R. 46.103(b)(5).

34 21 C.F.R. 56.108(b)(1).

35 OHRP Guidance. Subject: Obtaining and documenting informed consent of subjects who do not speak English. (Nov. 9, 1995) (web site: http:\\OHRP.osophs.gov).

36 OPRR Reports, No. 93-3. Subject: Informed consent—legally effective and prospectively obtained (Aug. 12, 1993) (web site: http:\\OHRP.osophs.gov).

37 Office for Protection from Research Risks. Tips on Informed Consent (Sept. 30, 1998) (web site: http:\\OHRP.osophs.gov).

38 45 C.F.R. 46.116.

39 "Minimal risk" means that the probability and magnitude of harm or discomfort anticipated in the research are not greater in and of themselves than those ordinarily encountered in daily life or during the performance of routine physical or psychological examinations or tests. 45 C.F.R. 46.102(i).

40 45 C.F.R. 46.116(d).

41 45 C.F.R. 46.116(c).

42 See note 41. The Office for Human Research Protections (OHRP) has published decision charts that provide graphic aids to help address whether informed consent or its documentation may be waived. The charts also help determine if an activity is "research" that must be reviewed by an IRB and address whether the review may be performed by expedited procedures. (web site: www.hhs.gov/ohrp/humansubjects/guidance/decisioncharts.htm).

43 45 C.F.R. 46.116 and 45 C.F.R. 46.117.

44 45 C.F.R. 46.116(c)–(d).

45 Federal Register, Vol. 61, pp. 51531–51533 (Oct. 2, 1996) and Federal Register, Vol. 61, pp. 51498-51531 (Oct. 2, 1996).

46 The waiver applies to basic HHS policy for Protection of Human Research Subjects, (Subpart A of 45 C.F.R. Part 46) and to research involving children (Subpart D of 45 C.F.R. Part 46). The waiver is inapplicable to research involving fetuses, pregnant women, and human in vitro fertilization (Sub Part B of 45 C.F.R. 46) and research involving prisoners (Subpart C of 45 C.F.R. 46) because of special regulatory limitations.

47 21 C.F.R. Section 50.24 and OPRR Reports, Subject: Informed consent requirements in emergency research (Oct. 31, 1996) (web site: http:\\OHRP.osophs.gov).

48 45 C.F.R. 46.103(b)(2).

49 45 C.F.R. 46.103(b)4.

50 45 C.F.R. 46.103(b)5.

51 Guidance on Continuing Review. Office for Human Research Protections, Department of Health and Human Services (July 11, 2002) (web site: http:\\OHRP.osophs.gov).

52 45 C.F.R. 46.115(b).

53 45 C.F.R. 46.108(b), OHRP Compliance Activities: Common Findings and Guidance (web site: http://OHRP.osophs.gov/compovr.htm), Item (68).

54 45 C.F.R. 46.116(d). The IRB must find and document that: (1) the research involves no more than minimal risks to the subjects; (2) the waiver or alteration will not adversely affect the rights and welfare of the subjects; (3) the research could not practicably be carried out without the waiver or alteration; and (4) whenever appropriate, these subjects will be provided with additional pertinent information after participation.

55 45 C.F.R. 46.204-207.

56 45 C.F.R. 46.305-306.

57 45 C.F.R. 46.404-407.

58 45 CFR Parts 160 and 164.

59 45 CFR § 160.203.

60 45 CFR § 164.512(i).

61 45 CFR § 160.103.

62 For the full definition of "protected health information," see the definitions of "health information" and "individually identifiably information" at 45 CFR § 160.103, and "protected health information" in 45 CFR § 164.501.

63 For the full definitions of "treatment," "payment," and "health care operations," see 45 CFR § 164.501. Also, you should check your state law regarding general principles of patient consent as they may require a written authorization for treatment, payment, or health care operations purposes. If the state law is more restrictive than the Privacy Rule, the state law will still apply.

64 To review all of the referenced exceptions, see 45 CFR § 164.512 (e.g., disclosures for law enforcement purposes or the reporting of communicable diseases as mandated by state law).

65 45 CFR § 164.508(c).

66 If the individual is a minor, incapacitated or otherwise unable to sign, the individual's "personal representative" may sign this authorization. For more information, see 45 CFR § 164.502(g).

67 45 CFR § 164.508(b)(4).

68 45 CFR § 164.508(b)(4)(i).

69 45 CFR § 164.508(b)(3).

70 45 CFR § 164.508(b)(3)(i).

71 The Privacy Rule also establishes a body for review referred to as a "Privacy Board." These reviews may be done by either the IRB or a Privacy Board. The membership of a "Privacy Board" is similar to that of an IRB: (1) the members must have "varying backgrounds and appropriate professional competency as necessary to review the effect of the research protocol on the individual's privacy rights and related interests;" (2) it must include "at least one member who is not affiliated with the covered entity, not affiliated with any entity conducting or sponsoring the research, and not related to any person who is affiliated with any of such entities;" and (3) the board "does not have any member participating in a review of any project in which the member has a conflict of interest." 45 CFR § 164.512(i)(1)(i)(B).

72 45 CFR § 164.512(i)(2)(ii).

73 45 CFR § 164.512(i)(2)(ii)(B)–(C).

74 45 CFR § 164.512(i)(2)(ii)(A).

75 Office for Civil Rights, Department of Health and Human Services, "OCR Guidance Explaining Significant Aspects of the Privacy Rule," 31-35 (as revised on April 3, 2003).

76 45 CFR § 164.512(i)(ii).

77 For the definition and membership of a "Privacy Board," see Note 12, above.

78 45 CFR § 164.512(i)(iii)(A)&(C).

79 45 CFR § 164.512(i)(iii)(B).

80 This can be accessed online through a variety of genealogy-based web sites.

81 45 CFR § 164.514(a).

82 45 CFR § 164.514(b)(1).

83 For the complete list, see 45 CFR § 164.514(b)(2)(i).

84 See 45 CFR § 164.514(b)(2)(i)(B)(1)–(2).

85 45 CFR § 164.514(c).

86 45 CFR § 164.514(e)(1).

87 45 CFR § 164.514(e)(3).

88 45 CFR § 164.514(e)(4)(ii).

89 45 CFR § 164.512(b).

90 45 CFR § 164.524.

91 45 CFR § 164.524(a)(2)(iii).

92 *Id.*

93 45 CFR § 164.528.

94 45 CFR § 164.528(a)(1).

95 Office for Civil Rights, Department of Health and Human Services, "OCR Guidance Explaining Significant Aspects of the Privacy Rule," p. 35 (as revised on April 3, 2003).

96 42 USC 241(d).

97 "Certificates of Confidentiality: Background Information." Office of Extramural Research, NIH, found at http://grants.nih.gov/grants/policy/coc/background.htm.

98 45 CFR 164.512(e).

99 "Certificates of Confidentiality: Background Information." Office of Extramural Research, NIH, found at http://grants.nih.gov/grants/policy/coc/background.htm.

100 *Id.*

101 *Id.*

102 *Id.*

103 "Detailed Application Instructions for Certificate of Confidentiality: Extramural Research Projects." Office of Extramural Research, NIH, found at http://grants2.nih.gov/grants/policy/coc/appl_extramural.htm (updated March 15, 2002).

104 45 C.F.R. 46.109(b), 21 C.F.R. 56.109(b).

105 Department of Health and Human Services. Final Guidance Document: Financial Relationships and Interests in Research Involving Human Subjects: Guidance for Human Subject Protection (May 5, 2004) (web site: http:\\ OHRP.osophs.gov).

NINE

Conflicts of Interest in Biomedical Research—Avoiding Bias

Kendra Dimond and Joseph B. Clamon

Introduction

There is a common understanding in the research community that the privilege of being allowed to conduct human-subjects research imposes a specific obligation on investigators and institutions to prevent, eliminate, or manage financial or personal considerations that might cause bias or compromise the judgment of the researcher. This obligation is owed to research subjects, students, the government, donors, benefactors, and society.[1] We call these considerations "conflicts of interest."

The problem of conflicts of interest is not new. However, the growth in collaboration between private enterprises and nonprofit entities engaged in biomedical research (e.g., universities, hospitals, research institutes), often promoted in the form of technology transfer, and the opportunity under the Bayh-Dole Act for research institutions to profit from federally-funded research[2] have heightened awareness of the issues surrounding conflicts of interest. This push to transform innovations into commercially viable products creates a substantially larger burden on institutions to avoid conflicts of interest. It also creates new liability risks if institutions fail to implement policies and procedures that prevent conflicts of interest. In response, investigators and institutions must strive to understand the existing regulatory requirements as well as the potential legal risks (such as increased exposure to lawsuits) that arise if conflicts of interest are not recognized and reduced, eliminated, or managed appropriately.

Transformation of Biomedical Research: Increase in Academic–Government–Industry Collaboration

Commercial sponsorship of biomedical research and technology transfer was largely unknown in the United States until the expansive growth of biomedical innovations in the early twentieth century.[3] Before then, many researchers and research institutions considered commercialization of discoveries and inventions outside, and perhaps even antithetical to, their mission as disinterested repositories and expanders of publicly held knowledge. The growth of biomedical research that began in the twentieth century caused universities to begin to explore how and whether to transform these new ideas, such as antibiotics and vitamins, into commercial products that could be beneficial to the general public.[4] One of the most prevalent methods to achieve their goal became commercial research sponsorship or technology transfer, the process by which universities cooperate with private industry in research to transform basic science discoveries and inventions into marketable products.

Along with the growth of biomedical research and technology, collaboration between government, universities, and private industry grew in response to economic pressures to enhance technology capabilities while simultaneously cutting the ever-growing overhead costs.[5] Government also viewed collaboration, especially through technology transfer, as a means of enhancing the industrial capabilities and competitiveness of the United States.[6] Yet prior to 1980, the federal government restricted the commercialization of technology developed using federal funds.[7] Although no uniform policy on technology transfer existed for all federal agencies, it was common for the government to retain title to patents arising from federally-funded research, regardless of whether or not the work was conducted in a government laboratory or in a university setting.[8] With little clear direction regarding the ownership of intellectual property rights, collaboration to bring basic science innovations to market was sharply curtailed. It was theoretically possible to obtain a nonexclusive license to discoveries made in government or university laboratories, but these were rarely granted by the funding agency.[9] These conditions gave clinical researchers and commercial research sponsors less incentive to collaborate on developing technologies. However, beginning in 1980, the government made significant changes to federal research and patent policies to help stimulate collaboration among universities, government, industry, and nonprofit entities engaged in biomedical research (e.g., academic medical centers).

In 1980 the Bayh-Dole Act was enacted, which authorized recipients of federal dollars, such as small businesses and nonprofits including universities and hospitals, to retain title to inventions made under federally-funded research programs and license them to other entities for commercial use.[10] The Bayh-Dole Act allows federally-funded institutions to obtain and transfer patents to promote and market inventions created under federally-funded research.[11] In exchange, institutions must provide the government with a permanent royalty-free license to the invention, must share some of the licensing proceeds with the inventor(s), and must reinvest licensing proceeds in the organization.[12] The Stevenson-Wydler Technology Innovation Act, enacted at the same time as the Bayh-Dole Act, authorizes federal laboratories to transfer technology developed in laboratories to nonfederal entities.[13]

The government continued its push to encourage collaboration between industry and academia in 1986 with the passage of the Federal Technology Transfer Act, which amended the Stevenson-Wydler Technology Innovation Act and authorized government laboratories to enter into Cooperative Research and Development Agreements (CRADAs) with private industry.[14] The Technology Transfer Act gives companies, regardless of their size, the right to retain title to intellectual property created in collaboration with government laboratories.[15] The National Competitiveness Technology Transfer Act of 1989 further enhanced the government's efforts to encourage collaboration by extending the right to retain title to intellectual property developed in contractor-operated labs.[16] The Technology Transfer Commercialization Act of 2000 also encouraged collaboration by increasing the ability of federal agencies to retain license to their own inventions developed in cooperation with private industry, when appropriate.[17]

Put together, these laws served as catalysts for government, universities, and private industry to work together. Simultaneously, they created an environment in which the public's perception of the biomedical research enterprise has been altered. Commercialization of publicly-funded research may have had an unintended negative effect on public confidence because it fostered the perception that the medical community is concerned with its own financial interests first and human subjects' well-being second. As Dr. Robert Kelch, Executive Vice-President for Medical Affairs at the University of Michigan and member of the Association of American Medical Colleges' Task Force on Financial Conflicts of Interest in Clinical Research, wrote, "what was once seen as a social good is now considered a purchasable commodity."[18] This questioning of researchers' motives, combined with several well-publicized tragic outcomes from clinical trials where financial conflicts of interest may have been present, has had a negative effect on the public's confidence in the ability of the medical community to monitor itself.

Conflicts of Interest: A Threat to Collaboration

Conflicts of interest, both actual and potential, can pose some of the greatest threats to the integrity of research and the public's confidence in the purposes and outcomes of biomedical research. Perhaps the greatest challenge to addressing problems of conflicts of interest is identifying the conflict. To begin to understand the potential harm caused by conflicts, including compromising data and placing human subjects in physical jeopardy, and to contemplate the appropriate corrective actions, it is necessary to first determine what a conflict of interest is and under what conditions it exists.

Defining Conflicts of Interest

The term "conflict of interest," as it is used in everyday parlance, actually incorporates two distinct concepts: conflicts of interests and conflicts of commitment.[19] Conflicts of commitment generally refer to an investigator's distribution of effort between the obligations of an academic appointment and a commitment to outside activities.[20] Conflicts of commitment can be created by pressures to publish; pressures to serve entities other than the institution; rivalries between institutions, within institutions, between institutions and businesses; and by pressures to maintain the secrecy of proprietary information. Although these pressures are significant, they present concerns that are different from conflicts of interests as discussed in this chapter.

In contrast, conflicts of interest as discussed here involve personal gain, most frequently financial gain, and thereby create the potential for bias. This conflict occurs when one person's personal gain, whether money or power, can only be advanced at the expense of another person. In the context of biomedical research, the exact definition of what threshold facts constitute a conflict of interest is unclear. The federal regulations that govern clinical research do not articulate a uniform definition. Instead, each regulatory body (e.g., the Public Health Service or the Food and Drug Administration), individual institutions, and associations have each developed their own definitions.[21] Nevertheless, most of these definitions are similar to the extent that they tend to focus almost exclusively on financial incentives and the possible effect of those incentives on the objectivity of the researcher or the institution.

For example, the American Association of Medical Colleges (AAMC) has defined conflicts of interest as "situations in which financial or other personal considerations may compromise, or have the appearance of compromising an investigator's professional judgment in conducting or reporting research."[22]

Harvard Medical School defines conflicts of interest as follows:

A Faculty Member is considered to have a conflict of interest when he/she, any of his/her Family, or any Associated Entity possesses a Financial Interest in an activity which involves his/her responsibilities as a member of the Faculty of Medicine. Included in these responsibilities are all activities in which the Faculty Member is engaged in the areas of teaching, research, patient care, and administration.[23]

The definition of conflicts of interest may be different for institutions than for investigators. The Association of American Universities has defined financial conflict of interest for institutions as:

[W]hen the institution, any of its senior management or trustees, or a department, school, or other subunit, or an affiliated foundation or organization has an external relationship or financial interest in a company that itself has a financial interest in a faculty research project. Senior managers or trustees may also have conflicts when they serve on the board of (or otherwise have an official relationship with) organizations that have significant commercial transactions with the university. The existence (or appearance) of such conflicts can lead to actual bias, or suspicion about possible bias, in the review or conduct of research at the [institution].[24]

AAMC has published a similar definition for its institutional members.[25]

These current definitions of conflict of interest focus primarily on actual, existing conflicts but also recognize the issue of potential conflicts, which can be an equally important concern. An existing financial relationship may create potential for bias, but it is not possible to be certain that such a result will occur. Furthermore, an interest that may appear insignificant now may change its value or significance later. For instance, an investigator may possess a 10% share in a start-up pharmaceutical with little or no current marker value. While this may not constitute a conflict at the time, the analysis may shift if the new drug being investigated works for its indicated purposes (e.g., cures a form of cancer). Thus, any definition of conflict of interest must address both actual and potential conflicts held by investigators, institutions, or both.

Types of Conflicts of Interest

Conflicts of interest come in many different forms and can be created by an array of different relationships. Perhaps the most common sources of conflicts are individual investments by investigators, their spouses, or their dependents in commercial entities sponsoring research. In particular, stock ownership or equity interests in commercial research sponsors, stock options, or royalties may lead to actual or potential conflicts of interest. Fees and honoraria from sponsors, such as from lectures, represent another type of potential conflict, as they may create significant pressures on the investigator to report research results that reflect favorably on the company with whom the financial relationship exists. Consequently, these payments, although made for legitimate purposes, may cause investigators to conduct or report their results in a less objective fashion. Similarly, consulting fees, salaries and retainers, and retention of intellectual property rights by researchers produce a situation in which researchers could benefit financially from reporting research results favorable to the commercial research sponsor. This opportunity for financial benefit creates a possibility that the researcher will experience partiality or bias in the design, conduct, and reporting of the research.

Another type of possible conflict is payment for patient referral into clinical trials, enrollment bonuses, or milestone incentive payments. These types of payments create an incentive to place patients on research protocols when it is in the financial interest of the researcher, but perhaps not in the best interest of the patient.

Payments coupled to trial results can create similar problems. These types of payments to researchers, conditioned on achieving or reporting particular results, place tremendous power in the hands of commercial research sponsors and threaten to compromise the objectivity of the research results.

Finally, any type of unrestricted bonuses, gifts, gifts to spouses or dependents, or coverage of "travel" expense for investigators, spouses, or dependents can create a substantial conflict by creating a sense of indebtedness to the commercial sponsor. These types of payments reduce objectivity by escalating the researcher's dependence on the sponsor, instead of the interests of the human subject. Additionally, such activities should be highly scrutinized because they may run afoul of federal or state anti-kickback laws.[26]

Most importantly, financial benefits may create a scenario in which an investigator may not have a research subject's safety as his or her principal concern. This can be the most dangerous result of a conflict of interest. If a financial relationship exists that rewards a successful experiment, then any injury to human subjects may be examined for evidence that it was caused by compromised judgment. Was the researcher too eager to achieve good results that he overlooked or ignored evidence to the contrary? Were inclusion criteria altered so that more subjects could be entered into a trial when payment was made per subject? These and similar questions have been raised in litigation brought by individuals injured in clinical trials.

Not all financial relationships present a conflict of interest. Fair market value payment for the time, effort, and expertise to conduct a study does not in itself create a bias on the part of the researcher or institution. However, when the researcher is also receiving other income from the research sponsor, such as consulting fees, the potential for bias is heightened. The determination must be made as to whether or not the various relationships, when viewed together, may compromise or appear to compromise the researcher's professional judgment and independence in the design, conduct, or reporting of research.

Who Can Have a Conflict of Interest

Conflicts of interest have many forms and are held by several categories of persons, as well as institutions. The issue is particularly relevant to clinical investigators, study coordinators, research technicians, and people involved in technology transfer. Conflict of interest scenarios for an institution often pose an indirect threat to data integrity and human research subjects. These scenarios include any decision-making processes that involve the financial holdings of the institution (e.g., a university's endowment) or that include allocation of institutional resources for research. For example, if a vice-president has control or influence over both how the university's endowment is invested and also controls what projects get financial support or laboratory space, the institution (and that vice-president) can have a conflict of interest because there may be pressure to provide financial support to projects sponsored by contributors to the university's endowment. This example is only one of many ways in which institutions can have less obvious conflicts. Other conflicts for an institution can be of a more traditional nature, such as holding an equity interest in a product under development.

Regardless of who is involved or the type of conflict posed by the interest, conflicts arise when career and personal advancement desires or institutional enhancement interfere, or appear to interfere, with research objectives. Different governing bodies may mandate different thresholds at which an interest is declared a conflict. Professional organizations have made different recommendations to remedy the situation. Nonetheless, all of the laws, regulations, and guidelines articulate the concept that "conflicts of interest" means financial or other personal incentives that may jeopardize objectivity and professional judgment in the design, conduct, or reporting of research such that it would compromise the welfare of human subjects, the integrity of the research, and the public's welfare and trust.

Ramifications of Conflicts of Interest

The actual and potential ramifications for investigators and research institutions that fail to address problems of conflicts of interest can be quite serious. First and foremost, conflicts of interest may jeopardize human subjects' safety by causing the investigator to put financial interests ahead of the subject's welfare. Knowledge of a conflict may jeopardize the research subject's faith in the investigator and or lead the subject to question whether the investigator is acting in the subject's best interest or using the subject as a vehicle to enhance the investigator's career or financial status. Third, conflicts of interest may reduce the public's willingness to participate in future studies. The knowledge or suspicion that conflicts of interest have influenced research in the past may inhibit future discoveries by causing people not to participate in or be willing to support research. Moreover, any real or perceived conflict may increase the potential liability of investigators and institutions for breach of fiduciary duty, fraud, negligence, unjust enrichment, violation of specific state laws, or other more novel causes of action.[27]

Moore v. Regents of the University of California

In one of the seminal cases regarding failing to inform patients of actual and potential conflicts of interest, John Moore, a patient at the UCLA Medical Center, sued his physician, a university researcher, and the university, among others, for failing to disclose to him and obtain his permission for the use of his cells for scientific research and commercial development.[28] The case proceeded to court. According to the California Supreme Court opinion, the following events occurred: Moore was a leukemia patient whose physician recommended that his spleen be removed. Portions of his spleen and other body fluid samples were then given to a group of investigators, which included his own physician, to use in researching blood products, in particular to study the lymphokines produced by Moore's T-lymphocytes.[29] Moore's T-lymphocytes were interesting to researchers because they overproduced certain lymphokines. The genetic code for lymphokines does not vary from person to person, but it is difficult to locate the gene responsible for a particular lymphokine. Moore's overproduction made the identification of certain genetic material easier.[30]

Moore was not informed of, nor did he consent to, the research use.[31] From the removed spleen, Moore's physician and the researchers established a cell line from his T-lymphoctes and the Regents of the University patented the line. Moore's physician, with the collaboration of the university, also negotiated agreements for commercial development of the cell line and products derived from it.[32] In his suit, Moore attempted to state thirteen causes of action, including conversion, lack of informed consent, breach of fiduciary duty, fraud and deceit, unjust enrichment, quasi-contract, bad-faith breach of implied covenant of good faith and fair dealing, intentional infliction of emotional distress, negligent misrepresentation, intentional interference with prospective advantageous economic relationships, slander of title, accounting, and declaratory relief.[33] Eventually, the California Supreme Court held that no cause of action for conversion could prevail because Moore did not retain an ownership interest in cells following their removal. The court stated that statutory law substantially limited Moore's control over excised cells, and that the patented cell line was distinct from the cells taken from his body and thus was not his property.[34] However, the court did hold that the allegations stated a cause of action against the physician under California state law for invading a legally protected interest of his patient. The court declared that the doctor is a fiduciary to the patient, and as such has an obligation to act with a duty of care and loyalty.[35] The court concluded that this fiduciary relationship must be expressed through the informed consent process, and that under California law disclosure of personal interests unrelated to the patient's health that may affect medical judgment is included in that process. This case is a significant illustration of the importance of state law regarding financial relationships that may apply in research scenarios.

Gelsinger v. Trustees of the University of Pennsylvania

One of the most publicized cases regarding conflicts of interest in clinical studies began when the parents of Jesse Gelsinger, an 18-year-old suffering from a rare liver disorder who participated in a gene therapy study, sought to hold the University of Pennsylvania and others liable after their son died.[36] The Gelsinger family sued the University of Pennsylvania, the Institute for Human Gene Therapy, the Institute's researchers, the medical centers involved in the clinical trials, the head of the University's Center for Bioethics, and a related research corporation, alleging negligence and fraud in the recruitment of their son to participate in the study as a volunteer because he did not meet the eligibility criteria.[37] The family alleged that the defendants fraudulently failed to disclose the extent to which the principal researcher and the University had a financial interest in the study, and the extent to which the principal researcher and the former dean of the medical school had patents on aspects of the procedure.[38] They also asserted that the principal researcher controlled up to 30% of Genovo stock and the University of Pennsylvania possessed a 5% equity interest in the company.[39] Moreover, they claimed that the contract between the company and the University of Pennsylvania gave the company rights to gene research discoveries at the Institute in exchange for financial support.[40] Finally, the plaintiffs maintained that the university's standing committee on conflicts of interest was aware of the possible conflict, created by the financial relationship between the researcher and the company, but allowed the study to continue without informing the human subjects.[41] The suit was resolved quickly in a confidential settlement.[42] However, the case received national publicity and illustrated how the informed consent process can be attacked as being significantly flawed.

The Fred Hutchinson Cancer Center Cases

The Gelsinger case became a model for personal injury litigation involving human-subjects research. A series of lawsuits were filed in Seattle, Washington, beginning in 2001 on behalf of research subjects who participated in clinical trials at the Fred Hutchinson Cancer Center under a protocol that involved T-cell depletion during bone marrow transplants.[43] The suits alleged that the researchers failed to adequately disclose the risks involved in the studies as well as the researchers' and the institution's financial interest in the company that developed the experimental method of T-cell depletion.[44] The plaintiffs made several claims including a failure to disclose the conflicts of interest, failure to give adequate informed consent, common law fraud, intentional misrepresentation, assault and battery, and violations of the Washington Consumer Protection Act. Cases were consolidated, and a trial was held in

March 2004. The court dismissed the conflict of interest allegation citing a lack of evidence, and the defendants were acquitted by the jury on allegations of lack of informed consent. However, even though no nexus between the financial relationships held by investigators and the institution was proved, the allegations themselves resulted in enormous adverse publicity both locally and nationally that threatened to damage the institution and the investigators' reputations.

Quinn v. Abiomed, Inc.

Another recent case illustrates the need to examine all relationships in the research setting that may become targets for accusations of conflict of interest. The widow of a participant in an artificial heart experiment sued Abiomed, the maker of the artificial heart, as well as Hahnemann University Hospital, Tenet Healthcare Corp (owner of Hahnemann Hospital), and the patient advocate for the study from the University of Pennsylvania.[45] The suit alleged that each of the defendants failed to inform the research subject, James Quinn, of all of the risks involved in the experiment. It also alleged that the commercial research sponsor was funding the patient advocate who served as Quinn's advocate in the study, creating either a conflict, or at the very least the appearance of a conflict, between the advocate's duty to the patient and the temptation to encourage participation in the study funded by the company. The case was settled, but not until after it had received much attention by the media.

These cases illustrate the significant liability that institutions face and potential harm posed to human research subjects if conflicts of interest are not properly prevented, managed, or eliminated. Allegations of financial conflicts of interest make headlines in the press. As the publicity surrounding cases involving clinical research increases, there is growing concern that the public's willingness either to participate in or support future research will decrease.

Additionally, the existence of financial interests between sponsors and investigators or institutions can violate federal law. A false disclosure to the FDA by a sponsor regarding the financial interests of investigators or a false disclosure by federally-funded investigators to the National Institutes of Health (NIH) could be prosecuted as a false statement to a federal agency under federal law.[46] In addition, a false or misleading statement to the FDA may result in delays in the agency's review of an application, or even a refusal by the FDA to accept research data regarding the drug or device that was the subject of the clinical trials, thus rendering the time, work, and expenses associated with the trial useless. Payments such as gifts, stipends, or consulting fees by sponsors to investigators, institutions, or anyone in a position to influence research decisions may violate the Medicare/Medicaid

Anti-Kickback Statute and state anti-kickback statutes.[47] Today many United States Attorneys' offices are focusing on research matters and have active investigations into these issues.

Government Oversight

Defining conflicts of interest is not always easy in the current framework of laws, regulations, and professional guidelines. Government definitions, published as part of oversight of federally-funded or regulated research, have been created in regulations and policies by the Department of Health and Human Services (HHS).[48]

HHS Public Health Service Regulations

The current Public Health Service (PHS) regulations require that all PHS-funded institutions, such as the NIH, "[m]aintain an appropriate written, enforced policy on conflict of interest . . . and inform each Investigator of that policy, the Investigator's reporting responsibilities, and of these regulations."[49] The regulations require investigators to disclose to an institutional official any significant financial interests in entities whose financial interests might be affected by the research.[50] A significant financial interest is defined as income of an investigator, investigator's spouse, or dependent child exceeding $10,000 over 12 months or equity interests exceeding $10,000 or 5% ownership of a company.[51] Under this definition, institutions are largely responsible for determining which significant financial interests constitute a conflict. If an institution determines that a conflict is present, it must report the conflict to the PHS awarding component and "take such actions as necessary to ensure that such conflicting interests will be managed, reduced, or eliminated."[52] The government may take further "corrective action," if it is deemed necessary.[53]

In May 2004, HHS issued guidance recommending consideration of approaches and methods for dealing with issues of financial interests as related to the HHS human-subjects protection regulations at 45 CFR Part 46 and 21 CFR Parts 50 and 56. This guidance does not address the regulatory requirements discussed above, which were designed to enhance data integrity and objectivity in research. Instead, the guidance, which is further discussed later in this chapter, is aimed at protection of human subjects who may be placed at risk due to financial conflicts of interest.[54]

The National Institutes of Health, which is governed by the PHS regulations, requires institutions to work to address conflicts of interest.[55] The NIH has notified its grantees that exploitation of opportunities for personal gain by investigators is "intrinsically unacceptable."[56] NIH grant applications require institutions to certify that they have a written administrative process to identify and manage, reduce, or eliminate financial conflicts of interest regarding NIH-funded research. The NIH advises that IRBs, despite the lack of any clear regulatory directive for their participation in conflicts of interest management other than for their IRB members, should consider issues of conflicts when reviewing investigators' protocol submissions in light of their role in protecting of human subjects.[57] In handling conflicts, the NIH proposes in its Grant Policy Statement that any conflicts might be handled using one or more of the following techniques:

1. public disclosure of significant financial interests;
2. monitoring of research by independent reviewers;
3. modification of the research plan;
4. disqualification from participation in all or part of the research;
5. divestiture of the significant financial interest; or
6. severance of relationships that create actual or potential conflicts.[58]

Beyond requiring a written policy and proposing these management techniques, the NIH reserves the right to request future reports from its grantees regarding mitigation of conflicts of interest.

HHS Food and Drug Administration Regulations
The Food and Drug Administration evaluates clinical studies submitted in marketing applications for new drugs, biologics, and medical devices. In doing so, the FDA may consider clinical studies inadequate if appropriate steps have not been taken to minimize bias in the design, conduct, report, and analysis of the studies.[59] The FDA has identified potential sources of bias in clinical studies. One is a financial interest of the clinical investigator in the outcome of the study because of the method of payment, for example, by way of a royalty. Another identified source of potential bias is an investigator's proprietary interest in the product, such as a patent, or an equity interest in the sponsor of the covered study.[60]

Because of these concerns, the FDA requires the applicant to disclose certain financial arrangements between the sponsor of the covered studies and the clinical investigations, and also to disclose certain interests of the investigators in the product under study or in the sponsor.[61] The FDA uses this information in its assessment of the reliability of the data submitted in the marketing application. These interests include the following:

1. any financial arrangement entered into between the sponsor of the study and the investigator involved in the conduct of a covered trial, where the value of the compensation to the investigator for conducting the study could be influenced by the outcome of the study;

2. any significant payments of other sorts from the sponsor of the study, such as a grant to fund ongoing research, compensation in the form of equipment, retain for ongoing consultation, or honoraria;

3. any proprietary interest in the tested product held by any investigator involved in a study;

4. any significant equity interest in the sponsor of the study held by any investigator involved in any study.[62]

The applicant provides the information to the FDA either in a disclosure statement (Form FDA 3455) or in a certification that no such interests exist (FDA Form 3454).[63]

HHS Human-Subjects Protection

A noted earlier, the HHS regulations for protection of human research subjects apply to research performed or funded by HHS.[64] These regulations require that any member of an institution's Institutional Review Board (IRB) refrain from participating in review of projects in which the member has a conflicting interest.[65] FDA regulations contain the same prohibition.[66] However, there is no provision in the criteria for IRB approval of research or in the requirement for informed consent that specifically requires disclosure of financial interests or other potential conflicts of interest to potential human subjects by the investigator or institutions conducting the research under IRB review. [67]

This gap was partially addressed by the Department of Health and Human Services in its guidance document issued in May 2004 entitled "Financial Relationships in Research Involving Human Subjects: Guidance for Human Subject Protection."[68] The guidance applies to human-subjects research conducted or supported by PHS agencies or regulated by the FDA, and deals with issues of financial interest in relation to the human-subjects protection regulations at 45 CFR Part 46 and 21 CFR Parts 50 and 56. The overall purpose of these recommendations is to create a research environment that protects the human subject; maintains the integrity of the research; guards the reputation of the institution, the investigator, and the IRB; and enables continued funding from federal sources. It is designed to provide "points to consider" in determining whether or not a financial interest affects the rights and welfare of human subjects. It recommends various approaches and methods to managing interests, including identifying and detecting financial considerations, evaluating financial considerations in order to distinguish between those that create a conflict of interest and those that do not, and developing strategies to manage conflicts where they do or potentially could exist.

When evaluating financial interests, the guidance suggests asking the following questions:

1. Does the research involve financial relationships that could create potential or actual conflicts of interest? How is the research supported or financed? Where and by whom was the study designed? Where and by whom will the resulting data be analyzed?

2. What interests are created by the financial relationships involved in the situation? Do individuals or institutions involved receive any compensation that may be affected by the study outcome? Do individuals or institutions involved in research have any proprietary interests in the product, including patents, trademarks, copyrights, and licensing agreement? Do they have an equity interest in the research sponsor, and if so, is the sponsor a publicly held or nonpublicly held company? Do they receive significant payments of other sorts (e.g., grants, compensation in the form of equipment, retainers for ongoing consultation, or honoraria) or receive payment per participant or incentive payments and are those payments reasonable?

3. Given the financial relationships involved, is the institution an appropriate site for the research?

4. How should financial relationships that potentially create a conflict of interest be managed?

5. Would the rights and welfare of human subjects be better protected by any or a combination of the actions listed below?
   - reduction of the financial interest
   - disclosure of the financial interest to prospective subjects
   - separation of responsibilities for financial decisions and research decisions
   - additional oversight or monitoring of the research
   - an independent data and safety monitoring committee or similar monitoring body

- modification of role(s) of particular research staff or changes in location for certain research activities, e.g., a change of the person who seeks consent, or a change of investigator
- elimination of the financial interest

Through these points, the guidance hopes to help investigators and institutions ask the appropriate clarifying questions that will help direct how an interest should be managed. The guidance emphasizes that institutions and researchers have a duty to human subjects to manage financial relationships that have become increasingly connected to research activities. Where an institution determines that a conflict exists or potentially exists, the institution should develop strategies to manage the conflict and thereby maintain the integrity of the research and the reputations of the institution, the investigator, and the IRB. These strategies will also help ensure continued funding from federal sources, and most importantly, will protect the welfare of human subjects.

Other Guidance

Beyond direct regulation and government guidance, additional insight has come from several professional associations. Many professional associations have worked to address the problem of conflicts of interest by encouraging self-policing as opposed to greater government oversight. These associations have made recommendations on ways to combat the problems caused by the existence of bias in clinical research.

The Association of American Medical Colleges Task Force Recommendations

In two reports published in 2001 and 2002, the Association of American Medical Colleges (AAMC) examined how to manage investigator and institution conflicts. The AAMC's recommendations regarding dealing with investigator conflicts of interest included each institution creating a definition or policy that stipulates what constitutes a conflict of interest, and making efforts to ensure that investigators are aware of the policy.[69] To enforce the policy and determine how to manage conflicts, AAMC recommended that institutions should establish a conflict of interest committee and conflict of interest official. This committee and official would review reports of all individual financial interests prior to final IRB approval of the research. The AAMC also recommended that institutions adopt a rebuttable presumption that financially interested individuals may not conduct human-subjects research. The main instrument for dealing with conflicts in the AAMC proposal is disclosure with sanctions for noncompliance. In addition, it proposed prohibiting payments to researchers or institutions that are conditioned on production of results that are favorable to the commercial research sponsor. It also listed ways to implement its proposals, such as through increased education.

The AAMC's report on institutional conflicts recommended separation of those who make financial decisions for the institution from those who make research decisions.[70] While encouraging establishment of this type of decision-making "firewall," the report acknowledges that it is not possible at the highest levels to completely remove the potential for bias. Following its earlier proposal for investigators, the AAMC's next report advocated creation of an institutional conflict of interest committee, and reporting to that committee by the institution of such potential conflicts as licensing agreements, royalties, other contractual arrangements, and institutional officers' interests. The report also urges institutions to address issues arising from multicenter trials, where different academic medical centers working on a project may have different thresholds for conflicts of interest or different policies regarding the management of conflicts. For example, in situations where one institution favors divestiture and another disclosure, dealing with these discrepancies may be difficult.

Beyond addressing the problems of institutions and institutional officials, the AAMC advises that conflicts of interest held by IRB members must be addressed. Finally, the second report urges the use of recusal as a technique for addressing conflicts. It states that the committee that reviews financial interests should have the authority to recommend recusal from any matters or decisions that might reasonably appear to affect research, when an official holds a significant financial interest in the product under investigation or in an entity sponsoring human-subjects research. It also proposes that officials should recuse themselves temporarily if a possible conflict exists, until the committee is able to review the situation and reach a decision. However, under the AAMC's recommendations, recusal is not appropriate when recusal would prevent the official from fulfilling the responsibilities of his or her position. If sufficiently serious, the AAMC suggests in these situations that the official either divest from the interest or vacate his or her position.

The Pharmaceutical Research and Manufacturers of America

The Pharmaceutical Research and Manufacturers of America (PhRMA), as part of its *Principles on Conduct of Clinical Trials*, offered guidance to its members on how to handle potential conflicts of interest.[71] The organization encourages investigators and institutions to disclose whether or not the investigator or the institution, or both, are being paid to conduct the clinical trial.[72] The guidance also recommends that payment to investigators or their institutions should not exceed what is reasonable for the work performed, and should not be for other considerations.[73] PhRMA suggests that to ensure that payments are appropriate, a written budget agreement should be part of the contract, specifying the nature and basis for payments.[74] PhRMA recommended that payments should not be tied to the outcome of clinical trials, and that investigators, their spouses, or their dependents should not have direct ownership interest in the specific pharmaceutical product being studied.[75] Furthermore, the guidance states that investigators and institutions should not be compensated in company stock or stock options for work performed on individual clinical trials.[76]

On the other hand, PhRMA would permit "reasonable" enrollment bonuses to compensate investigators or institutions for "extra recruiting efforts" when finding subjects is "particularly challenging."[77] Also, the guidance notes that investigators and their staff should be permitted to be compensated for travel, lodging, and meal expenses associated with meetings held in conjunction with the clinical trial, and that the venue and circumstances should be "appropriate for the purposes of the meeting."[78]

Managing Conflicts of Interest

An institution's efforts to address the problems of actual and potential conflicts of interest should have three objectives. The first objective is to protect those who volunteer to participate in the research. The second is to protect the integrity of the research. The final objective is to protect the institution.

The first element in any institution's effort should involve creating a precise definition as to what constitutes a conflict of interest. The institution must determine what standard will be used in evaluating what should be done with a conflict, such as whether there should be a rebuttable presumption against doing the research if there is an interest, or whether the standard should be that the research is only done under compelling circumstances. The definition should give both a broad definition of what a conflict is, and articulate what specifically is and is not allowed with respect to investments, fees and honoraria, consulting fees, payments coupled to results, enrollment bonuses, gifts, stipends, travel expenses, intellectual property rights, or payments to spouses or dependents, or any other incentives. Along with an unambiguous definition, an institution must establish enforcement mechanisms and sanctions for noncompliance by both investigators and the institution itself.

To manage conflicts of interest and enforce the policy, institutions should establish a standing conflict of interest committee composed of persons both affiliated and unaffiliated with the institution, including researchers, clinicians, attorneys, ethicists, research subject advocates, and community members. The committee should be responsible for reviewing any financial interests that may pose a conflict and determine whether disclosure, management, elimination, or another course of action is appropriate. The committee should carefully document its decisions, and it should develop an oversight mechanism to ensure that their decisions are implemented. The committee should also monitor procedures and conditions surrounding research involving a financially interested individual. Finally, as part of its oversight and management, the committee should be in regular communication with the IRB, and the committee should consider whether it will develop a process by which its decisions or related IRB decisions may be appealed.

Records should be kept throughout this entire process. The institution should designate an official to obtain and review disclosure statements, and it should allocate resources for maintenance of records of investigator and institution disclosures, conflict of interest committee decisions, and IRB decisions.

Other important aspects of dealing with conflicts of interest include ensuring representation of the public on committees, creating and maintaining educational programs for researchers, data managers, IRB members, and institutional officials with financial decision-making responsibilities. The institution should, as much as possible, create a firewall between offices responsible for financial decisions and those responsible for research decisions, with the overall goal of minimizing the scope of severity of any conflicts.

Within these guidelines, tremendous variation may still exist. A comparison of Harvard Medical School (HMS) and Stanford Medical School (SMS) conflict of interest policies as posted on the institutions' web sites illustrates this range.[79] Harvard Medical School's policy consists of a general policy statement, specific guidelines for conflicts of interest, key definitions, and implementation policies.[80] The HMS policy applies to faculty members only, and defines a conflict of interest as "when he/she, any of his/her Family, or any Associated Entity possesses a Financial Interest in an activity which involves his/her responsibility as a member of the Faculty of Medicine."[81] Beyond this broad statement, the policy divides treatment of interest into specific categories. For example, category 1(a) addresses stock or similar issues of ownership and royalties involving human subjects.[82] The policy creates a *de minimis* threshold for conflicts of this type of fees.[83] This threshold does not apply to nonpublicly traded equity interests, which might include biomedical startups. If the interest the investigator possesses is below this threshold and was acquired at arms' length (i.e., acquired before the research, as a gift, as part of an inheritance, etc.), then the investigator may conduct the research while still holding the interest.

Category 1(b) describes stock, ownership, or royalties regarding research that does not involve human subjects.[84] Category 2 governs conflicts other than those in categories 1(a) and (b), which are conflicts that are ordinarily permissible following disclosure. HMS's policy contains separate provisions on licensing and licensing derived stock.[85]

In contrast, Stanford Medical School's policy is broader. One explanation for this difference may be that the HMS policy applies only to the medical school, whereas SMS operates under Stanford's general conflict policy in the university's Research Policy Handbook, which applies to more than just SMS faculty. The difference in approaches may exist because Stanford has a more unified organizational structure under which the medical school, hospital, and clinics exist as one single, large institution. HMS, by comparison, has a less integrated organizational structure involving HMS and many hospitals including Massachusetts General Hospital and Brigham & Women's Hospital, and institutions such as the Dana Farber Cancer Institute.

Beyond the difference in scope, the two policies also differ in their definition of what constitutes a conflict of interest. SMS's policy defines a conflict of interest to be ownership interests in an equity amounting to at least one-half percent of the company's equity or at least $10,000 in ownership interests (except when the ownership is managed by a third party such as a mutual fund).[86] Disclosure of an equity interest in a private company is required, regardless of the amount. However, clinical research by a faculty member who possesses a financial interest is not explicitly prohibited at SMS.[87] Rather, SMS may require assignment of an oversight group while still permitting the investigator to proceed with the research on human subjects.[88] The policy does not state who is in this "oversight group," nor does it explicitly describe the group's powers.

The SMS policy also contains four transactions that automatically trigger disclosure and require review: (1) unrestricted gifts; (2) technology licensing agreements; (3) sponsored research; and (4) procurement of materials or services where the faculty member is employed by, consults for, or possesses a significant financial interest in the outside entity.[89] Thus, in practice, Stanford's policy amounts to a case-by-case method.

A comparison of the two policies reveals that both policies rely on disclosure as the principal management technique. However, the two schools have different approaches to resolving conflicts. HMS's strategy is to outline a broad purpose statement with specific requirements that must be met, while Stanford's tactic is to have only a broader statement and to decide how to handle situations on a case-by-case basis. Also, the two institutions have different disclosure thresholds and different levels of guidance. The differences between these two policies illustrate a number of the fundamental approaches that exist regarding how to address problems of conflicts of interest at the institution and investigator level.

Conclusion

The growth of opportunities for biomedical research and the increasing number of high-profile incidents involving conflicts of interest and the harm they may pose to human subjects has brought the issue of how to address the problem into sharp relief. The issue is now receiving greater attention than ever before from Congress, administrative agencies, and professional associations. The issue likely will continue to be a problem for the biomedical community as investigators, academic medical centers, private industry, and government continue to emphasize the transformation of basic science research into commercially viable products. The growth in opportunities for technology transfer has overlapped with the trend toward greater government enforcement activities in health care, including congressional hearings on the issues of conflict of interest in the House and the Senate, as well as individuals enforcing the law through personal injury litigation or derivatively through the False Claims Act. The increased attention and greater liability exposure risk heighten the need for researchers and institutions to be sensitive to existing laws and regulations.

This attention underscores the need to strive for a more precise definition of what constitutes a conflict of interest and to address any gaps in the law governing how those conflicts are handled. The solution to the problem of conflicts of interest in biomedical research starts with developing a greater understanding of the problem and its scope, and translating that analysis into policies and procedures to prevent and manage conflicts of interest so that they do not threaten the integrity of biomedical research or the public's trust in the research enterprise.

Notes and References

1   Assoc. of Am. Med. Colls. (AAMC) Task Force on Financial Conflicts of Interest in Clinical Research, *Protecting Subjects, Preserving Trust, Promoting Progress II: Principles and Recommendations for Oversight of an Institution's Financial Interests in Human Subjects Research* 1 (Oct. 2002), available at http://www.aamc.org/members/coitf/2002coireport.pdf [hereinafter Institutional Task Force].

2 Bayh Dole Act of Dec. 12, 1980, Pub. L. No. 96-517, §6(a), 94 Stat. 3015, 3019-28 (codified as amended at 35 U.S.C. §§ 200–212 (2000)).

3 Kenneth Sutherlin Dueker, "Biobusiness On Campus: Commercialization of University-Developed Biomedical Technologies," 52 *Food and Drug L. Journal* 453, 456 (1997).

4 *Id.*

5 *Id.*

6 Nat'l Sci. Bd., Science and Engineering Indicators 2002 (Apr. 2002), at 4-35, available at http://www.nsf.gov/sbe/srs/seind02/ c4/c4s3.pdf.

7 Joshua A. Newberg and Richard L. Dunn, "Keeping Secrets in the Campus Lab: Law, Values, and Rules of Engagement for Industry-University R&D Partnerships," 39 *Am. Bus. L.J.* 187, 194 (2002).

8 *Id.*

9 *Id.*

10 *See supra* note 2.

11 35 U.S.C. §§ 200-212 (2000).

12 35 U.S.C. § 209.

13 15 U.S.C. §§ 3701–3714 (2000).

14 Federal Technology Transfer Act of 1986, 99-502, 100 Stat. 1785, 15 U.S.C. §§ 3710–3714 (2000).

15 15 U.S.C. §§ 3710–3710d.

16 National Competitiveness Technology Transfer Act of 1989, Pub. L. No. 101-189, 103 Stat. 1674, 15 U.S.C. §§ 3701 and 3710a.

17 Technology Transfer Commercialization Act of 2000, Pub. L. No. 106-404, 114 Stat. 1742 (codified as amended in scattered sections of 15 U.S.C., 35 U.S.C., and 42 U.S.C.).

18 Robert Kelch, "Maintaining the Public Trust in Clinical Research," 346 *New Eng. J. Med.* 285, 285 (2002).

19 Peter Harrington, "Faculty Conflicts of Interest in an Age of Academic Entrepreneurialism: An Analysis of the Problem, the Law, and Selected University Policies," 27 *J.C. & U.L.* 775, 775 (2001) (articulating a similar definition of conflict of interest). *See also* Harvard Medical School, Policy on Conflicts of Interest and Commitment, available at http://www.hms.-harvard.edu/ visited integrity/conf.html (last visited May 21, 2004).

20 *Id.*

21 *See,* e.g., 21 CFR § 54.2; 42 CFR § 50.603 (2004) (defining conflicts of interest for the FDA and the PHS).

22 AAMC, "Guidelines for Dealing with Faculty Conflicts of Commitment and Conflicts of Interest in Research," 65 *Acad. Med.* 487, 490–91 (1990) [hereinafter AAMC]. *See also* Association of American Medical Colleges (AAMC) Task Force on Financial Conflicts of Interest in Clinical Research, *Protecting Subjects, Preserving Trust, Promoting Progress—Policy and Guidelines for the Oversight of Individual Financial Interests in Human Subjects Research* 1, 4 (Dec. 2001), available at http://www.aamc.org/members /coitf/firstreprot.pdf.

23 Harvard Medical School, Policy on Conflicts of Interest and Commitment, available at http://www.hms.harvard.edu/integrity/conf.html (last visited May 21, 2004). For another example, see Stanford University, Faculty Policy on Conflicts of Commitment and Interest (RPH 4.1), available at http://www.stanford.edu/dept/DOR/rph/401.html (last visited May 21, 2004).

24 Association of American Universities Task Force on Research Accountability, *Report on Individual and Institutional Financial Conflict of Interest,* available at http://www.aau.edu/research/COI.01.pdf14 (Oct. 2001).

25 Institutional Task Force, *supra* note 1, at 2-3. AAMC's definition states "An institution may have a conflict of interest in human subjects research whenever the financial interest of the institution, or of an institutional officer acting within his or her authority on behalf of the institution, might affect – or reasonably appear to affect—institutional processes for the conduct, review, or oversight of human subjects research." *Id.*

26 *See* 42 U.S.C. § 1320a -7b

27 *See Greenberg v. Miami Children's Hospital Research Institute,* 264 F. Supp. 2d 1064 (2003).

28 *Moore v. Regents of the University of California,* 793 P.2d 479 (1990).

29 *Id.*

30 *Id.* at 482 n. 2.

31 *Id.* at 481.

32 *Id.* at 482.

33 *Id.* at 483 n. 4.

34 *Id.* at 488–489.

35 *Id.* at 485, citing Cal. Bus. & Professional §§ 654.1, 654.2; Cal. Health & Safety Code §§ 24170, 24173, 24176.

36 *Gelsinger v. Trs. of the Univ. of Pa.,* No. 000901885 (Pa. Dist. Ct. filed Sept. 18, 2000) (settled Nov. 2, 2000).

37 Complaint of John Gelsinger as Administrator and Personal Representative of the Estate of Jesse Gelsinger and Paul Gelsinger, No. 000901885 (Pa. Dist. Ct. filed Sept. 18, 2000) [hereinafter *Gelsinger Complaint*]. D. Nelson and R. Weiss, "Penn Ends Gene Trials on Humans," *Washington Post,* May 25, 2000 at A1; B. Gose, "U. of Pennsylvania, Doctors, and Ethicist Are Named in Suit Over Gene Therapy Death," *Chronicle of Higher Education,* Sept. 29, 2000, at A34.

38 *Gelsinger Complaint supra* note 37; *see also* Jesse A. Goldner, "Dealing with Conflicts of Interest in Biomedical Research: IRB Oversight as the Next Best Solution the Abolitionist Approach," 28 *J.L. Med. & Ethics* 379 (2000).

39 *Id.*

40 *Gelsinger Complaint supra* note 37.

41 *Id.*

42 *Id.*

43 *See Wright v. The Fred Hutchinson Cancer Research Ctr.,* 2001 WL 1782714, *1 (W.D. Wash. Nov. 19, 2001); *Berman v. The Fred Hutchinson Cancer Research Ctr.,* (W.D. Wash. 2001); *Dagosto v. Fred Hutchinson Cancer Research Center,* (Wash. Super. Ct. 2002). *See also* Duff Wilson and David Heath, "Uniformed Consent: What Patients at 'The Hutch' Weren't Told About the Experiments in Which They Died," *Seattle Times,* Mar. 11, 2001, at A1.

44 *Id.*

45 *Quinn v. Abiomed, Inc.,* Pa. Ct. Com. Pl., No. 001524 (complaint filed Oct. 16, 2002).

46 18 U.S.C. § 1001.

47 42 U.S.C. § 1320a-7b.

48 21 CFR Part 54 (2004); 42 CFR Part 50, subpart F (2004); *see also* United States General Accounting Office, Report to the Ranking Minority Member, Subcommittee on Public Health,

Committee on Health, Education, Labor, and Pensions, U.S. Senate, *Biomedical Research: HHS Direction Needed to Address Financial Conflicts of Interest* 1, 7 (GAO 02-89, Nov. 2001), [hereinafter GAO], available at http://www.gao.gov/new.items/d0289.pdf (last visited Sept. 18, 2003).

49 42 C.F.R. § 50.604(a) (2004).

50 42 C.F.R. § 50.604(c)(1) (2004).

51 42 C.F.R. § 50.603 (2004).

52 42 C.F.R. § 50. 604 (2004).

53 42 C.F.R. § 50.606(b) (2004).

54 Financial Relationships in Research Involving Human Subjects: Guidance for Human Subject Protection, 69 Fed. Reg. 26393-02 (May 12, 2004).

55 National Institutes of Health, *NIH Grants Policy Statement*, available at http://grants.nih.gov/grants/policy/nihgps_2003/NIHGPS_Part4#_Toc54600065 (June 1, 2004).

56 NIH Notice 0D-00-040, *Financial Conflicts of Interest and Research Objectivity: Issues for Investigators and Institutional Review Boards,* June 5, 2000, available at http://grants1.nih.gov/grants/guide/notice-files/NOT-0D-00-040.html.

57 *See supra* note 55.

58 *Id.*

59 21 C.F.R. § 54.1(b) (2004).

60 *Id.* 21 C.F.R. § 54.2(e) states:
A Covered clinical study means any study of a drug or device in humans submitted in a marketing application or reclassification petition subject to this part that the applicant or FDA relies on to establish that the product is effective (including studies that show equivalence to an effective product) or any study in which a single investigator makes a significant contribution to the demonstration of safety. This would, in general, not include phase 1 tolerance studies or pharmacokinetic studies, most clinical pharmacology studies (unless they are critical to an efficacy determination), large open safety studies conducted at multiple sites, treatment protocols, and parallel track protocols. An applicant may consult with FDA as to which clinical studies constitute "covered clinical studies" for purposes of complying with financial disclosure requirements.

61 The definition of "sponsor" as used in 21 C.F.R. Part 54 is "the party supporting a particular study at the time it was carried out."

62 21 C.F.R. § 54.4(a)(3)(i-v) (2004).

63 21 C.F.R. § 54.4(a)(3) (2004).

64 45 C.F.R.§ 46.101 (2004).

65 45 C.F.R. § 46.107(e) (2004).

66 21 C.F.R. § 56.107(e) (2004).

67 45 C.F.R. §§ 46.111, 116 (2004).

68 Financial Relationships in Research Involving Human Subjects: Guidance for Human Subject Protection, 69 Fed. Reg. 26393-02 (May 2004).

69 *See* Individual Task Force, *supra* note 22.

70 Institutional Task Force, *supra* note 1, at 3.

71 Pharmaceutical Research and Manufacturers of America, *Principles on Conduct of Clinical Trials and Communication of Clinical Trial Results* (July 2002).

72 *Id.* at 10

73 *Id.* at 15.

74 *Id.* at 16.

75 *Id.*

76 *Id.*

77 *Id.* at 17.

78 *Id.* at 17.

79 Harvard Medical School, *Policy on Conflicts of Interest and Commitment*, available at http://www.hms.harvard.edu/integrity/conf.html (last visited May 21, 2004). Stanford University, *Faculty Policy on Conflicts of Commitment and Interest* (RPH 4.1), available at http://www.stanford.edu/dept/DOR/rph/401.html (last visited May 21, 2004).

80 Harvard Medical School, *Policy on Conflicts of Interest and Commitment*, available at http://www.hms.harvard.edu/integrity/conf.html (last visited May 21, 2004).

81 *Id.*

82 Harvard Medical School, *Guidelines for Conflicts of Interest*, available at http://www.hms.harvard.edu/integrity/guide.html (last visited May 21, 2004).

83 *Id.*

84 *Id.*

85 *Id.*

86 Stanford University, *Conflict of Commitment and Interest for Academic Staff*, Stanford Research Policy Handbook 4-4, available at http://www.stanford.edu/dept/DoR/rph/4-4.html (last visited May 12, 2004).

87 *Id.*

88 *Id.*

89 *Id.*

TEN

Enhancing Data Quality and Patient Safety through the Use of Technology in Clinical Trials

Jeffrey A. Green and Marc Shlaes

Introduction: Inevitable Advancement of Technology Use in Clinical Trials

Over the past twenty years there have been many attempts to advance the global clinical trials industry beyond manual handling of three-ringed binders of paper as the standard for data collection and management. For an industry that envelopes the sophistication of gene therapy and risks "rolling the dice" with innovative treatment modalities as a daily routine, its hesitancy to advance data collection and review beyond NCR paper, air travel to review information, "yellow stickies," manual "key punching" of data, and the toleration of nine-month lag times for query resolution is difficult to explain.

There are many reasons addressed in this chapter that partially document why this seemingly logical transition toward technology, which took place in other business sectors decades ago, has lagged behind within the international pharmaceutical and medical device industries. Some of the reasons are justified, while others are not. Some excuses merely represent political protectionism within silos of departments by individuals who have delayed such advancements at the expense of their company's product development objectives. In order to avoid repeating the mistakes made by others, one needs to carefully and honestly examine all of these reasons along the road to achieving long-acclaimed goals of positively influencing the quality, time, and cost of getting innovative therapies and devices to market.

Moreover, it should not be forgotten that the most important beneficiary of an increased reliance on technology use in clinical trials is the patient, due to the safety-enhancing capabilities of real-time "data awareness" that are impossible with paper. This topic is dealt with in this chapter after the quantifying information on the value proposition.

Despite the slower-than-expected corporate adoption of EDC (electronic data capture) worldwide as the new standard for collecting, reviewing, and transmitting clinical trial information, this market sector has made significant advancements over the past several years. Specific to our company, the growth rate in contracts has been more than eight-fold in three years. Simply stated, the quest for technology in all aspects of our lives, including clinical trials, means that EDC "will not go away." Successive approximations will continue until the "right process" and the "right technology platform" are found. In this respect, delays are valuable learning experiences for those wise enough to observe. The experiences of pioneering "early adopters" have progressively solved many past limitations, both real and perceived, and are now bringing definable and significant value to their organizations. This chapter will summarize some of the key criteria and steps that have been instrumental in successful EDC deployments in hundreds of clinical trials performed in over 40 countries around the world.

Quantifying the Value Proposition—What Is at Stake?

The three most important criteria to improve in any product development effort are quality, time, and cost. These three metrics have all been significantly impacted through the proper use of EDC. Moreover, these metrics have been substantiated by independent sources—the hallmark of verifying new concepts.

The initial public study of metrics with EDC was done by Banik et al.[1] while at Bayer Pharmaceuticals in 1998. These results are depicted in Figure 10-1.

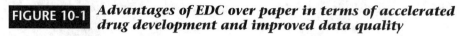

FIGURE 10-1 *Advantages of EDC over paper in terms of accelerated drug development and improved data quality*

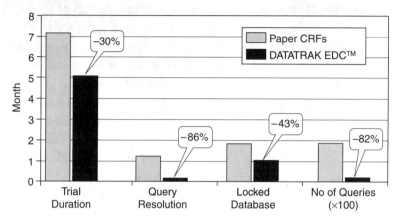

The long-stated, but rarely realized goal of accelerating clinical development was shown to be an impressive 30% improvement over paper methods. Outsourcing, simply to another party, as with a Contract Research Organization (CRO), has not produced such results, since a *change in process* is required, not simply a different group deploying identical procedures.

Equally impressive were dramatic reductions in queries (82%) and query rates (86%), through use of immediate edit checks that are not possible with paper, and a significant reduction in the time to database lock (43%).

It is difficult to imagine any changes that can be made internally at a pharmaceutical company, outside of enhanced drug discovery efforts, that can have such an important impact on product development metrics and eventual speed to market.

The metrics representing quality and time have been reproduced by the data management department at Gilead Sciences by Mr. Adrian Hsing in 2002.[2] Their data, derived independently four years after Banik's findings, was virtually superimposable, with a 75% reduction in query rates and a 45% reduction in the time to database lock.

In order to quantify the economic value proposition of EDC versus manual methods, two other independent sources have produced surprisingly similar results concerning this parameter. Green[3] utilized the foundational data of Banik[1] and The Center for Drug Development and Research[4] to create a financial model for the use of EDC in an entire drug development program. Cost savings alone versus paper methodologies with EDC was calculated to be greater than $60,000,000 per drug.

In 2003, Novartis Pharmaceuticals documented actual savings of $65,000,000 in substituting EDC for outsourced paper methodologies, previously done with CROs.[5] This would have to be a minimum figure for savings with more modern deployment strategies, as the relatively outdated platform of required hardware deployment at every site used by Novartis continues to be burdened by accompanying logistics and excessive costs representing significant scalability and expense questions. Some have estimated such additional costs of a distributed model to be as much as $15,000 per site.

Neither of these economic assessments included augmented revenue from a faster speed to market due to accelerated development, nor did these assessments include savings resulting from the ability to cancel ineffective products based upon superior and timelier results. To accurately assess the full value of EDC, such figures would be additive. And, related to the topic of patient safety following this economic assessment, as some recent product companies have realized, not protecting patient safety to the maximum extent possible has a significant price tag associated with that as well.

Though it is stated by some that "we can't afford to do EDC," upon an examination of the data above, one should rephrase this statement to "how can you afford *not* to do EDC"?

It's All about Process

The organizations that are optimizing success with EDC have two major approaches in common: (1) they have selected the correct technology and (2) they are gradually changing their process in moving to EDC. They are not simply "automating paper" and forcing future process to be driven solely by decisions made years ago on systems for manually handling data.

A poignant example relates to some companies that use EDC to simply feed into traditional "back-end" systems for the resolution of queries exactly as is done with paper. This "process" mitigates one of the major advantages of EDC and is classified by some as "getting your garbage faster." Under this scenario the massive reduction in query workload and accompanying economic and speed benefits do not exist.

Figure 10-2 summarizes graphically how the clinical trial process changes with EDC. One can see how accelerating the drug development process by 30% can be achieved and explained, step by step.

Steps to Success with Global EDC Implementations

Vendors often have an advantage because of exposure to competitive intelligence from each customer. This can accumulate into a great deal of information. Close interactions with the rank and file almost always gravitate to comparisons of competitive companies within a sector. While maintaining confidentiality, a vendor can learn which products and/or companies are good or bad and their reasons for such classifications, based upon previous experiences. What is never discussed publicly is often elaborated upon privately.

As a result of this learning process—which has intensified over the past several years as EDC has advanced—one can summarize factors that have been consistently predictive of success and can also explain why some companies have had to revisit

FIGURE 10-2 *Process steps involved with managing data from paper methods and what is improved with the use of EDC*

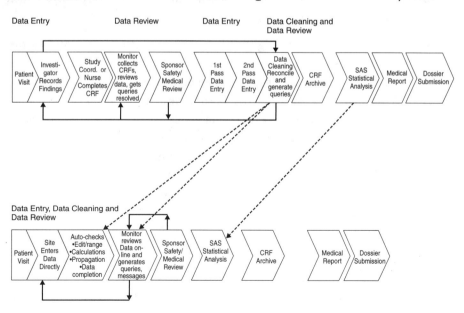

initial decisions on a specific technology platform that were once thought correct. Understanding these paths already taken can be very valuable to companies currently considering EDC.

Predictive Factors of Success

Listed below are the top seven factors predictive of success with EDC, accumulated from over 25 customers and data collected in more than 50,000 patients around the world. Reasons related to each factor are briefly described. It is assumed that the most important factor of regulatory compliance with 21 CFR Part 11 can be ascertained by customer audits and is not itemized. Factors listed are those that apparently are not obvious, as many customers have changed paths based upon initial choices of technologies that were incorrect.

1. Experience in Global Implementations and an Approval Pedigree

Clinical trials are often international. It makes little sense to standardize on only a single-continent solution. Bringing a product to market is the ultimate goal. Thus, a successful regulatory approval where a software suite was used seems important. Additionally, since modifying processes is critical, experience of the vendor can help in creating new "e-SOPs"—electronic standard operating procedures—for clinical trials. Take advantage of their experiences.

2. System Performance at Investigative Sites Worldwide at Low Bandwidths

System performance is one factor involved with user acceptance. This can be evaluated easily via dial-up connections on independent laptops without the assistance of caching downloads during product demonstrations. Unwillingness of a vendor to do this is a tell-tale sign. This has been a common mistake of customers who selected product suites after presentations from C-drives instead of demanding live performance via the Internet—the medium that would ultimately be used by their sites. Fancy marketing programs do not change the laws of physics. Subsequent performance problems, therefore, are not surprising. Remedies to compensate for these inadequacies cause increased customer expense such as hardware deployments or high-speed line placements.

3. User Acceptance

This topic includes system performance, workflow, and user interfaces, and has been the main reason for EDC failures of the past. All vendors should supply independent assessments of user acceptance to customers. There must be a balancing of priorities between "back-end" needs of data managers and "front-end" acceptance by investigative personnel. When one need takes precedence inappropriately, process becomes unproductive.

4. Diligent, Field-Based Audit Trail

EDC audit trails should be superior to those with paper. Though many EDC systems are compliant today with audit trail tracking as in 21 CFR Part 11, many believe that diligence in audit trails will increase in future revisions[6]. This is proving to be the case with the new draft language from the federal Food and Drug Administration (FDA) stating that *all* changes to the case report form should be tracked in the audit trail, not just the last one that was entered before "submit page" was selected in standard HTML-based web solutions.

5. Transparent Business Model

Data with EDC are more easily tracked. The same should be true with the financial aspects of software use in clinical trials. "Bait and switch" tactics should be minimized, as there is less room for cost fluctuation compared to manual processes of surprise expenses. Transparency allows for multiyear projections for entire programs of development. Beware of license models or fixed monthly payments where costs are not directly proportional to the amount of work performed in a clinical trial.

6. Service Levels (Hosting, Help Desk, Problem Solving, etc.)

Technology is a necessary but not sufficient factor for success—this remains a service business. With EDC, service is now extended to investigative personnel worldwide (Internet connections, help desk, etc.) and not just the clinical trial sponsor. EDC is a very uniquely delivered software application because the majority of the users (i.e., investigative staff) are not the paying customer and the minority of the customer personnel (i.e., clinical trial sponsors) are not actual users. Virtually no other software application has such characteristics.

7. Software Ease of Use

EDC is inevitable, just as e-mail and Internet use has expanded worldwide. As comfort levels rise, sponsors will take more tasks in-house, much in the same way the functionalities of Excel™ and PowerPoint™ have been internalized instead of outsourced. Therefore, ease of use and technology transfer will become a critical decision factor in the selection of a product.

EDC and Patient Safety in Clinical Trials

The Issue—Suboptimal "Data Awareness"

Usually, It's Better to Know Than Not to Know

Virtually everyone will agree in most situations in life that it's better to know rather than the alternative. This statement is unquestionable when knowing or not knowing can affect someone else for whom you are responsible.

The Patient Is Paramount

It is indisputable that the patient is the most important aspect of clinical trials. The objective of safety in clinical investigation is irreproachable; satisfying it is priceless. This goal is the undeniable primary mission of investigative staff, pharmaceutical and medical device companies, Institutional Review Boards (IRBs), and the federal government. The FDA is officially charged with serving the public on the *safety* and *efficacy* of new drugs and devices. Notice that safety is *always* listed first. If you have ever been a patient, you are interested in safety. If you have ever received investigational drugs, your interest in safety is even greater.

Unfortunately, either because of technological advancements being ahead of a willingness to change behavior, or because of a selfish focus by many who don't want their "cheese moved" or their business practices altered, or because of a complacency that often results in extremely successful industries, there exists a disproportionate lack of urgency in pursuit of maximal protection of patient safety in clinical trials.

What substantiates this strong statement?

First, in hundreds of meetings regarding EDC use in clinical trials, this concept has never arisen in any discussions. Databases are always discussed. Technology platforms are always discussed. Price is always discussed—multiple times. But never once has anyone brought up the patient and the expedient surveillance of information as an advantage of technology. The patient is the most important issue, but unfortunately is often the least discussed.

This statement is also supported by the fact that greater than 90% of all global clinical trials remain paper-based in 2004, despite the availability of technologies that have been proven to increase the ability to know what is transpiring day-to-day. Therefore, with regards to data in patients receiving investigational drugs, the choice today by most is to "know" later rather than sooner. The ability of EDC to provide instantaneous information is not conjecture—it is fact. It is impossible to have equal "data awareness" capabilities with paper-based clinical trials.

Though obvious, it needs to be stated that the ability to know has a direct impact upon the ability to react—and delays in the ability to react have the potential to impact patient safety. In the absence of using EDC, a sponsor is left with manual pickup, review, transportation, and transformation methodologies (from papyrus to digital formats) in order to provide an accurate data awareness. Paper produces insurmountable delays in "informational visibility" extending six to nine months in multicenter clinical trials.

How do we know that this is true?

Those experienced in clinical trials know that paper-based monitoring can be delayed two to six months after data is collected from a patient. Following the monitoring visit, the paper forms must be transported to a central location where the information is "double-punched" from paper into a database. Given these manual steps, usually performed by different sets of people, the six- to nine-month delay to accurate data awareness or the ability to survey subliminal safety issues is apparent.

Figure 10-3 shows metrics obtained from a global EDC clinical trial where as much as four to six months passed from the time of data entry at the site to the point of review by the monitor or Clinical Research Associate (CRA). The information in the graph was collected easily from automatic audit trails that are date-, time- and identity-stamped with EDC every time one logs into the system. Without traversing through multiple travel records of multiple monitors at multiple Contract Research Organizations in multiple countries, one is easily able to receive such a summary report as an inherent capability of EDC. This report proves that absent the proper use of technology in clinical trials, the administration of investigational drugs are subject to delays in data awareness of six or more months, because a clinical trial is only as fast as its slowest step.

In the paper model this delay can be justified because there is no ability to quickly review data manually, especially in large multicenter trials. (Whether or not it is appropriate to wait so long to review such data on an investigational agent is a separate question.)

In paper-based models of clinical trials, such time delays are the norm—and, by definition, is the current "standard of practice." When few groups "raise the bar," the majority are therefore in compliance. Peer competitive pressures occur when certain companies in an industry strive for excellence more aggressively. With paper, the situation depicted in this graph can be mitigated in its importance or somewhat disguised because there is no involuntary audit trail tracking behavior. And there are always many reasons why manual pickups are delayed (i.e., travel problems, weather, personal schedules, etc.). Many of these reasons disappear or become unjustifiable when EDC is used, allowing for instantaneous access to a central, live database from anywhere in the world as long as an Internet connection is available.

From this information it is obvious that there is a gap in data awareness or informational visibility in clinical trials when either paper is deployed or when technology is improperly utilized. One cannot be "aware" of what they don't know—and if they don't look at the information, it is impossible to know anything about it.

The sharp declines shown in the figure or improvements in the "awareness scale" resulted from the sponsor viewing these reports and understanding the poor quality of monitoring being done by certain CROs. Such reports can be used as a grading scale to remove inefficient monitoring. Improvements were not self-generated but were forced by the sponsor. Responsible CROs were terminated from the project.

This information was obtained with EDC. Doesn't this show it can't solve the problem?

It is true that EDC was used in this case, as this is how such detailed information was obtained. However, if one elects not to use the advantages of technology, it is likely that it won't be able to help you. Delays that occurred here were "allowed" because human behavior simply placed manual workflow on top of technology, thereby completely preventing the benefits from being realized for the sponsor, but most importantly, for the patients. Once again, one is only as fast as the slowest step. The CRAs could have remotely reviewed the data any time after entry (within minutes, if they so chose), but instead they elected only to log on to the database when they were physically at the site during the next scheduled visit. Inexplicably, there was no change whatsoever in behavior with the use of technology. Lack of time is certainly not an excuse, because monitoring can be much more efficient with fewer resources through the use of EDC compared to hopping from one airport to another. The cynic would conclude that behavior was not advanced because the CRO wanted to justify payment for a physical visit, just as with paper. This is not the only case example of this behavior. There are many more similar examples.

Sadly, this case shows that such awareness was possible within minutes of data entry, but the delays were actually "elected" based upon a refusal to transition human behavior from a paper to a technology process. Awareness of the patient information

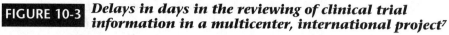

FIGURE 10-3 *Delays in days in the reviewing of clinical trial information in a multicenter, international project[7]*

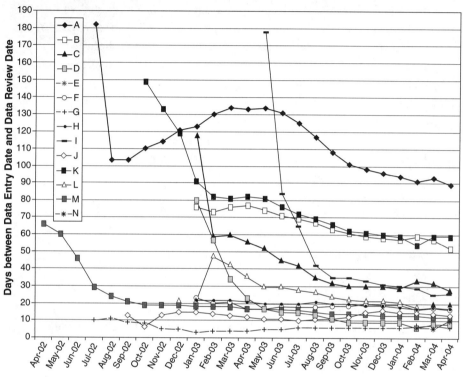

was clearly a secondary consideration to logging a certain number of monitoring visits, because the information was not even viewed until a physical visit occurred. This is going on every day with thousands of paper-based clinical trials, because there is little augmentation in awareness that can occur simply because the manual transmission of information is riddled with process complications, necessary personnel-laden steps, and excessive costs in order to achieve the same level of awareness as can be achieved with technology in a matter of seconds to minutes.

Who else has recognized this as an issue other than an EDC company? Dr. Mark McClellan, former Commissioner of the FDA, realizes it.

Faced with rapid changes, the nation's healthcare system has fallen short of its ability to translate information into knowledge that can be used in practice, and to apply new technology safely and appropriately. The results are exactly what you would expect. Everyone who uses the current system constantly confronts large *information gaps*, whether it's at the doctor's office, on the hospital ward, or at government agencies charged with protecting the public health. That goes for the FDA—we're no exception. You can still find medical reviewers huddled in their offices between the 15 boxes that it took to ship a new drug application. There's still too much paper at the FDA—we're a fire hazard. This [paper situation] is bad for FDA, it's bad for many of your businesses and most importantly, *it's bad for patients*. We need to fix it. The kinds of *information bottlenecks* created by poorly accessible paper records are *dangerous*, inefficient and expensive, whether it's our own evaluation of a new drug application, or a doctor's evaluation of their patient.

The remainder of this chapter will provide evidence on how EDC could augment patient safety. The goal is to stimulate improvement and discussion about the way in which we currently manage information in clinical trials.

Current Status

It is inconsistent that a sophisticated discipline represented by the clinical testing of investigational drugs and devices remains decades behind other industries in information processing. Support for this statement is provided by the general reluctance and hesitancy with which this sector has moved toward the Internet for the cost-efficient transmission of its clinical trial data. Even if it were true that the Internet is an "unproven communication medium," such an over-exaggerated fear of leveraging technology would be contradictory to the exploratory nature and inherent pioneering spirit of clinical trials themselves. It seems hypocritical to encourage patients to absorb risks of taking a new drug while the sponsor avoids "risks" of the Internet. Society worldwide has certainly not delayed in explosively adopting the Internet over the past few years for any number of uses, and even the pharmaceutical industry leverages this platform for accentuation of its commerce.

In the clinical trial industry there is an inappropriate hesitancy to leverage the benefits of technology in order to create an environment of real-time data awareness. This delay is shrouded in many excuses that all, more-or-less, fit into the category of an unwillingness to timely change human behavior and the status quo. It is an understandable aspect of the human condition to be hesitant toward changing habits, especially when those behaviors have been proven. However, it is not justifiable to use the reluctance to change behavior as a shield against what might be beneficial for someone else, such as the patient enrolled in a clinical trial.

The main focus of this position is on the patient and highlights the belief that the inability to access real-time data awareness is not maximally protecting their interests because you cannot offer protection from that of which you are unaware.

To justify the previous statement, consider the following scenario that could be present in hundreds of clinical trials ongoing worldwide at this time.

Imagine patients are being enrolled in a clinical trial where a subliminal adverse event is developing. The data is being processed using paper methods. This adverse event is not immediately serious; therefore, the required calls within 24 hours are not necessary. As such, this adverse event accumulates "under the radar screen."

From past "real life" examples, these effects could be cardiac valve abnormalities, liver dysfunction, clotting disorders, angina, or transient ischemic attacks. In-and-of-themselves and on an isolated basis, they go relatively unrecognized in the totality of the clinical trial, since the individual physician-investigator has no ability or responsibility to be aware of the accumulation of data across multiple locations. They are only responsible for the patients directly under their care. The "cumulative data awareness" responsibility lies with the product development company and with the FDA as the governing body safeguarding public health. As such, each investigator continues to enroll patients.

The adverse event, of course, exists and is appropriately recorded—but, the data sits in paper files for weeks to months before it is in a form to allow credible review, as was emphasized by the previous case study. Patients continue to be enrolled throughout this time at multiple locations.

Six months after the event began to appear, the clinical trial is discontinued. A patient who was enrolled one month prior to discontinuation suffers from the adverse event. The family, knowing that the trial was discontinued, wonders how long this event was known to have the potential to occur.

If the full truth were known, the characterization of this adverse event was residing in files of paper waiting to be picked up and undergo double data entry. The patient who was recently entered in the clinical trial and who suffered the adverse event possibly could have been prevented from entering if real-time data awareness allowed quicker evaluation, by either the product development company or the safety committee.

Is the justification of an unwillingness to change behavior moving from paper to technology going to be a satisfactory explanation for that family?

If one believes such a scenario is not possible, consider the morbidity and mortality problems with anticholesterol and anticancer medications recently released into the marketplace. These have been widely publicized. Is it possible that deficiencies of a current "awareness system" that is not real time could have exacerbated such "surprises"?

In an Associated Press article regarding an anticancer drug that is producing heart ailments, the spokesperson for the manufacturer stated, "I don't have the data."[8] In 2004, this is problematic. This individual is to be commended for honesty—in a paper-based data collection process, or in a voluntary reporting program for post-marketed drugs or devices, it is truly impossible for the manufacturer to "have the data" in a timely fashion. We all must evaluate whether or not lack of such awareness is a legitimate excuse in 2004 for any product that is felt to potentially cause unacceptable risk or harm to patients. Products predisposed to such adverse events should be tracked continuously and on an electronic basis so that unbiased safety committees can make informed, scientific decisions, and, if necessary, institute immediate halts or cautions to usage to appropriate clinicians instead of waiting for occurrence to rise up and slap you in the face.

The Clinical Care Parallel—Accentuating Timeliness

Are there parallel examples that indicate we're behind with information processing in clinical trials? Consider the situation of a blood sample being obtained from a patient who has been complaining of being tired. If the physician waited three months for paper to work its way through the system, as occurs in paper-based clinical trials, and the results indicated leukemia, the physician could be sued for the delay of an appropriate and timely action. The standard of practice in clinical care suggests that a delay of only hours to just a few days could be viewed as the standard of practice in such a situation.

Why, then, do we tolerate as much as six to nine months in cumulatively reviewing information on investigational drug exposure to patients where far more uncertainty exists than with a routine blood sample? It is ironic that we are more demanding in forcing routine and proven tests to adhere to a rigid, diligent time schedule than we are for less predictable and more risky, investigational information. It could be argued that these situations should be in the reverse, or at least, the stance taken that investigational data have no less of an expectation of surveillance than the clinical parallel, accepted to be hours to a few days following the performance of the tests in question. It appears that the "standard of care" today for investigational data is to wait for the paper to work its way through the system.

Speaking from past experiences as an investigator on more than 90 projects, patients enrolled in a clinical trial were always followed more closely compared to routine care situations because of respect for the unknown. In fact, by virtue of this activity being clinical research, the exact purpose was to track and record information expeditiously.

The clinical care parallel brings to light a disturbing reality that there is actually less diligence in managing investigational information collected in research subjects than what is expected in normal health care practice. This could be accepted when mechanisms were not available to physically review such information faster, but with technology advancements, this is no longer true. The fixation of many individuals on demanding paper in clinical trials, for whatever "justifiable" reason, is responsible for promoting a gap in data awareness that is not in patients' best interests, as referred to in Dr. McClellan's quote.

The EKG Parallel—Accentuating Accuracy

Several years ago the Cardio-Renal Advisory Panel at the FDA determined that digital EKGs were more accurate than their paper counterparts. This topic became prominent secondary to life-threatening arrhythmias that could be drug-induced from relatively "innocuous" compounds such as antihistamines. It was decided that in the performance of clinical trials, more exact information was necessary on EKG interval changes induced by these compounds. There appeared to be little justification in the Committee's thinking for the toleration of inexact information when a superior option was available.

The identical analogy of using the most unambiguous information possible also applies to EDC. Though the vagaries of handwriting are probably overemphasized when directed only to physicians, those familiar with clinical research know all too well the ambiguities and mistakes possible with handwriting. One can only imagine the problems that manual handwriting can produce when data needs to be reviewed after being stored in boxes of NCR (no carbon required) paper for years in warehouses.

Pursuit of accuracy, of which handwriting is only one component, is the exact reason why double data entry is required in the clinical data management process when paper is used, under the belief that two people manually entering a variable twice, ensures that the correct answer survives—well, at least it ensures that the interpretations are consistent.

With EDC, ambiguities do not exist in an Electronic Case Report Form (eCRF) since the information is typed, and like the EKG parallel, stored in digital format. Moreover, "smart" eCRFs can be programmed so that inappropriate or boundary-limited answers alert users for clarification. Paper is silent, requiring months of processing time before achieving the same goal that is achieved with EDC in seconds. Therefore, EDC follows the identical digital EKG pathway by presenting the most accurate information possible. Digital EKGs are now required in clinical trials— EDC is not.

The Governmental Parallel—Accentuating Universality

Several years ago the Securities and Exchange Commission (SEC) mandated that electronic filing of documents for publicly traded companies replace paper. The system developed is called EDGAR and has been very successful bringing convenience, timeliness, and fairness to the process by which voluminous information is examined involving matters of corporate health.

EDGAR was initiated broadly, across a massive industry, in only a few months. This example serves as substantial evidence to those who believe that similar efforts could not be successful from the FDA, if desired. Today, any investor can access a central database about any company and immediately receive posted information from which to make investment decisions. Today, without EDC, no one can access a live database and review clinical information entered ten minutes previous and thousands of miles away at an investigational site.

The ability to access timely financial information about public securities unquestionably has a higher priority for modern functionality than accessing worldwide information on the adverse effects of a new drug or device given to society.

Regarding the concept of data awareness, EDGAR put an end to inherent delays in the equitable availability of financial information. Prior to EDGAR, in order to receive such information investors had to call the company and have the information individually mailed—akin to sending CRFs via the mail, except that the expense of plane fights, rental cars, or hotel stays were not necessary, as is usually the case in the acquisition of clinical trial data.

The institution of EDGAR for all publicly traded companies was a massive undertaking enacted with little pain. Score one for the business folks over the scientific arena—both of which live in challenging regulatory environments—so this cannot be an excuse for delay on the part of the FDA-mandated industries. Though it can be attempted, it will probably not be a successful argument to state that instituting an electronic system by the SEC is any less challenging than attempting the same task with a similar governmental arm, the FDA. In fact, it can be speculated that the cost and efficiency advantages for the FDA exceed those of the SEC from the use of technology in this analogy. It can also be conceptualized that the societal impact of rapid availability of information on a new drug or device supercedes the importance of an investment decision. It is presumed that all parties would agree with this statement, as we all have the potential to be patients.

The need, direction, and justification for the clinical trials industry to adopt a technology paradigm shift is apparent. With all of the recent interest in publicly posting the results of clinical trials, the use of technology in the investigational process is the next logical step for the betterment of patient welfare.

Critic's Corner on Safety Concerns

This section contains expected counterarguments taking the stance that current processes utilizing paper in clinical trials are not deficient.

1. *There is a requirement for a 24-hour notification of any serious adverse event in a clinical trial, and how will technology improve this? I don't think that any serious issues are being missed by not using EDC.*

As stated earlier, the serious adverse events are not the most important, because products that develop such problems receive immediate attention and do not get approval anyway. The recent problems with Vioxx and Avastin were accumulated from drugs *already on the market.* There is nothing necessarily deficient about the 24-hour notification period. Nonetheless, with the capabilities of technology one could argue that 24 hours is too slow.

The situations that need improvement are the subliminal, nonserious adverse events that accumulate under the radar screen and go unnoticed until massive exposure causes problems to manifest. Most of the drugs removed from the market for deleterious effects such as valvular problems, liver abnormalities, clotting disorders, and cardiac syndromes fit into this category. It remains unknown whether or not closer and continuous examination of a growing database of information would have provided signals that might have been predictive, or if these events are merely statistical in nature resulting from increased exposure to the public.

As a case in point, in March 2004 the National Institutes of Health discontinued a project involving 11,000 female patients treated with estrogen in order to reduce hip fracture rates. The drug was effective but carried an increased incidence of stroke. The clinical trial was discontinued a year early. This clinical trial was performed using paper.

To evaluate what impact EDC might have had on patient safety in this project, it would be valuable to know how long the information about the stroke incidence resided in stacks of paper before being summarized to the safety committee for their decision. Considering normal practice, anywhere from two to six months would not be out of the question. If this is the case, how many additional patients in the interim were enrolled and exposed to potentially harmful effects of estrogen treatment? In this type of situation, hours to days could be significant as the onset of risk and duration of exposure required for stroke to manifest is likely unknown.

With EDC, results could be remotely examined by a safety committee in a real-time database minute by minute, if desired. What possibly could be the justification for not having the most timely and accurate information immediately available?

Cancellation of this NIH project provides an excellent example pertaining to this topic. The antagonists of EDC would say that one would never know if a live database would have made a difference in the timing of this study cancellation. That is exactly the point—in all trials such as this one does not know but has the capability to know immediate information and most continue to choose not to deploy the most advanced process as possible. What one doesn't know, one cannot react to. In the marketplace we have experienced almost hostile resistance to EDC by individuals and companies with a self-interest aligned with paper. Yes, it could be said that this author has a self-interest aligned with EDC, and that is true. It is for both of these prejudices that the focus of a discussion such as this must always be on the *patient*. Is the achievement of accelerated decisions either approving a good drug or killing a bad drug to the benefit of the *patient?* Is lower cost for the development of a drug or device to the benefit of the *patient?* Is immediate access to the safety statistics about a drug or device to the benefit of the *patient?*

2.   *Following up on adverse events is what investigators are hired to do.*

This statement is true; however, investigators can only be responsible for the patients under their direct care. They have no access to a cumulative database obtained throughout a multicenter study. Therefore, any categorical decisions about continuing or discontinuing a multicenter clinical trial reside with the clinical trial sponsor or a safety committee and not with the individual investigator. In fact, the investigator must trust that the clinical trial sponsor is providing them with as up-to-date information as possible on an experimental medication across all locations.

Moreover, from the standpoint of liability protection of any safety committee, one has to believe that these groups should increasingly demand immediate availability of global information in order to best fulfill their mission of being patient advocates.

3.   *Since the total adverse event picture is included in a submission to the FDA, having such data earlier would not have prevented the ultimate withdrawals from the market of recent drugs, thereby indicating that these occurrences were not from oversights but from statistical effects of increased exposure.*

It is possible that this description is true, but why risk less-than-immediate availability of data throughout the trial? From the corporate world one could also wait for yearly revenue figures—yet quarterly financial information is hotly anticipated. Boards and management usually track monthly or even weekly financial performance. Once again, financial data appears to have a higher priority of timeliness than clinical trial information. EDC is less expensive, improves fraud detection, and accelerates clinical development. The benefits greatly exceed the risks of having to restructure the activities of a clinical or data management department.

However, it's possible that this scenario is not true. The submission process is many times a hurried event, compiling data quickly, locking databases, and hitting corporate projections for "getting in line" with the FDA. It is also possible that in such situations the desire for speed exceeds diligence in data examination. Consider the thalidomide history. Taking the time for careful examination of the facts prevented this tragedy in the United States, but effectiveness of the drug's intended actions overshadowed a similar evaluation that produced tragic results in Europe. Scientists will acknowledge that one often sees previously obscured relationships that exist and "have always been there" the longer you are able to "live with your data." Having the time to "twist and turn" your data can lead one to ask additional questions and, quite possibly, to reach different conclusions. Having improved data awareness provides the opportunity to collect additional information during a clinical trial that could possibly clarify suspicions of untoward actions of a drug before such agents reach the magnitude of public exposure. In other words, prevention is better than reaction and all efforts to do the former are to be encouraged.

4.   *Having data immediately available can produce bias.*

This is a legitimate scientific concern that exists with almost any clinical trial endeavor when the treatment arms are prematurely revealed. This concern can be easily protected while still allowing for the advantages of EDC to be realized. Much more so than with paper methods, the use of EDC allows for members of a Safety Committee to have effortless access in a "read-only" mode to the live database of any clinical trial. Such an approach would be prohibitive and much more risky in paper-based studies, because too many "hands" would have to touch the information in order to make it available in a summarized form. With EDC, no hands, other than the investigative staff at each site, need touch the data. No double data entry is necessary and no data management staffs need to be exposed to the information.

However, there is also another form of bias that exists if EDC is not used—that is the bias against the patient from the inability to access real-time information that could potentially be for their benefit. One bias is controllable through Safety Committee access and the other bias can harm the exact people who are intended to be helped by new therapies.

5.   *To prove EDC enhances safety, this needs to be compared to paper methods.*

In the purest scientific sense this statement is correct. This comparison over several actual clinical trials would be easy to perform—some trials could be managed with paper and some trials could be managed with EDC. Comparisons could be done where the timing of data awareness on actual side effects could be catalogued.

However, consider the hypothesis. Is it not obvious what the conclusions will be before this is attempted? It could be unethical placing patients in the control group where one knows that information will be delayed. There is no need to run a comparative study to prove that information can be processed faster and broader over the Internet versus manually picking up paper by hand.

There are probably a number of counterarguments against EDC that can be offered. Over the past six years we have heard many reluctances such as security, need for metrics, quantifying the value proposition, investigator acceptance, waiting for electronic patient medical records, integration with other systems, the FDA's inability to accept electronic data, and standardization to name a few. Interestingly, most of these concerns have been satisfied from a growing body of experience and advancement, yet adoption rates continue to be lower than what one would expect in 2004.

Any critics of EDC deployment need to keep in mind these challenging questions:

- "What is the logical stance against a greater access to clinical data at lower costs, which also is proven to accelerate clinical development?"
- "Do you want to see your data in nine months or nine seconds?"
- "Why are you choosing not to know, rather than to know?"
- "Are the methods you are choosing to deploy in the best interest of the patient?"

What Is Needed?

Since society worldwide is affected by drug and device development, direction for change should come from regulators that govern this area. This would be preferable to direction provided by litigators. The information gaps are clear and technology can rectify such data awareness issues. We are fortunate that these changes afforded by EDC come at reduced expense and also possess revenue benefits. Most regulatory mandates do not arrive with such advantages.

Nonetheless, there are inappropriate delays in internal adoption of EDC and, unlike other industries, the pure competitive advantages of this technology are not enough to accelerate changes in behavior because the business model for patented products allows economic inefficiencies to be passed onto the consumer. Therefore, change must be initiated outside these organizations.

Though there are economic pressures on the pharmaceutical industry, as they exist for any corporate endeavor, these pressures are obviously not strong enough to encourage an alteration in human behavior in order to pursue proven benefits of accelerating product development, reducing costs, providing for greater protection against fraud, enhancing data quality, or generating more diligence in patient surveillance. Moreover, it is doubtful that the pharmaceutical industry is under the identical magnitude of competition as manufacturing industries, leading one to agree with Mr. Fauntleroy of the FDA who stated, "You are too comfortable with paper."[9]

The purest rationale for enforcing technology adoption in clinical trials is for the assurance of patient safety to the highest degree possible. If we all have the *patient* as the focal point, it will make an unwillingness to change behavior an inadequate justification and quite visible in public forums. Not only does changing behavior need to be justified with many endeavors but, sometimes, reasons for keeping current behavior needs to also be honestly assessed from time to time.

Conclusion

The advantages of EDC are numerous, if the correct product is chosen. Some excuses not to use EDC will persist by select groups, but these will gradually dissipate with continued successful implementations. The value of reference checking cannot be overemphasized as one attempts to bring competitive advantages to their product development company through the strength of technology.

This chapter reflects upon the current state of information management in the clinical trials industry in 2004. The current standard of practice is rooted in a manual paper process that provides no complete real-time data awareness of investigational drug and device exposure to subjects and patients. Paper-based processes provide for limited informational visibility.

It is disappointing that proven business reasons such as accelerating drug development at a lower cost (commonly touted as the goal of these industries) has been relatively ineffective as an impetus to cause drug and device manufacturers to aggressively substitute paper with technology in their clinical research and development efforts.

The inability to have immediately available information about patients being exposed to investigational drugs and devices in worldwide clinical trials is difficult to support given the availability of technology today. It is virtually impossible to take a position against enhanced patient surveillance as resultant safety issues that may develop are priceless when the goal is prevention instead of reaction.

The new standard of practice in clinical trials should be real-time data awareness. This new standard has additional proven benefits of significantly decreased costs, improvement in the quality of the data collected, and, furthermore, accelerates the availability of innovative products to our global society. From many different viewpoints, "justifications" of continuing to use paper as the transport medium in clinical product development should be seriously questioned as a conflict of interest to the maximal benefit of the patient.

A blueprint for implementation exists with the enactment of EDGAR by the SEC and digital EKG requirements by the FDA several years ago. There is no substantive reason why "EDGARization" of clinical trials cannot be pursued.

Such recommendations in 2005 are not radical—they are responsible.

Notes and References

1   Banik, N. "Evaluation of EDC versus Paper in a Multinational Asthma Trial." Presented at the DIA European Data Management Meeting, Berlin. October 1998.

2   *Personal Communication*. October 2002.

3   Green, J. A. "The EDC Value Proposition to the Pharmaceutical Industry." White Paper. July 2001.

4   Tufts Center for Drug Development Research. 2001.

5   Dodge, J. "Successful EDC requires true grit first, technology second." *Bio-IT World*. Volume 2; 14: 2003.

6   Green, J. A. "Benefits of eCRF and EDC versus Paper—Does Your EDC Product Complete Its Case Report Form in Pencil?" White Paper. 2002.

7   Klein, J. and Kenvin, L. Using EDC to Improve Monitoring Practices Worldwide." Presented at the Society of Clinical Data Management Meeting, Toronto. October 5, 2004.

8   Associated Press, Avastin Story, *The Cleveland Plain Dealer,* August 2004.

9   Fauntleroy, M. Presentation on EDC at the Annual Drug Information Association Meeting. San Antonio, Texas. June 2003.

ELEVEN

Legal Issues in the Conduct of Multinational Clinical Trials by U.S. Entities

Jan E. Murray

Introduction

Clinical trials in support of investigational new drug applications (INDs) undertaken by U.S. pharmaceutical and biotechnology companies are often designed as multinational in scope. The reasons for the growth in multinational trials include the desire to secure marketing approval in several jurisdictions, and the need to find sufficient numbers of eligible subjects. Consequently, "since 1990, the scope of global research has grown from 28 to 79 countries and the number of investigators conducting FDA research worldwide has multiplied 16-fold."[1] Sponsoring multinational trials increases the number of challenges inherent in conducting clinical trials. This chapter will describe in broad terms the legal framework for conducting multinational trials from the standpoint of a company applying for marketing approval in the United States. This legal framework will draw heavily from the guidelines of the International Conference on Harmonization of Technical Requirements for the Registration of Pharmaceuticals for Human Use (ICH), because these guidelines have been adopted by countries representing the world's wealthiest markets and have profoundly influenced the setting of standards in other countries.[2, 3]

This chapter will focus primarily on clinical trials conducted pursuant to INDs or new drug applications (NDAs) because most trials are conducted in support of these applications. References to INDs or NDAs can be read to include Biologic License Applications (BLAs) that are required for approval of vaccines and a few other biologicals. Companies manufacturing medical devices may be required to conduct clinical trials to demonstrate safety and effectiveness under an Investigational Device Exemption (IDE); differences in regulation of these trials are noted.

Commencing Clinical Trials

Clinical investigations of new drugs manufactured by U.S. companies that are intended for marketing in the United States can only commence after an IND has been filed with the U.S. Food and Drug Administration (FDA).[4] The IND sets forth information about the composition of the drug, its manufacture, and the results of studies on animal models. The sponsor must also provide a description of the investigational plan to test the safety and efficacy of the drug. The investigational plan will include the clinical trial protocols as well as investigator brochures. A clinical trial protocol describes the design of the trial, its risks and benefits, clinical endpoints, and data collection and analysis methodology.[5] The sponsor must also identify the investigators who will actually conduct the trial. If foreign sites are included in the IND, then the data generated by those sites in accord with the protocol described in the IND will become part of the NDA that is filed upon completion of the clinical trials. The NDA is the document that presents the clinical trial results for review by the FDA for its determination of whether to permit the drug to be marketed and how it should be labeled.

The growth in multinational trials is reflected in the increasing number of NDAs using foreign data. From 1995 through 1999 the number grew three-fold from 7% to 22%.[6] Corresponding to that growth is the dramatic increase in human subjects participating in NDA trials from countries outside the United States: In 1995 the number was around 4,000 and by 1999 the number jumped to 400,000.[7]

The introduction of medical devices into the market is very different from the introduction of new chemical entities. The level of regulation imposed on the device before and after its introduction into the marketplace depends upon the classification of the device. In the United States a device is classified as a Class I, II, or III device, with a Class III device subjected to the strictest regulation. A Class I or II device may be marketed only after the manufacturer has filed a 510(k) or premarket notification with the FDA, unless the device is exempt from this requirement. Ninety percent of 510(k)'s do not require the collection of data from clinical trials. Those that do generally are required to produce clinical data to demonstrate that the device is "substantially equivalent" to a previously marketed device. Class III devices by contrast require the submission of a Premarket Approval (PMA) application. PMAs must include clinical data demonstrating the safety and effectiveness of the device. Clinical studies that are conducted to demonstrate safety and effectiveness must conform to the requirements of the IDE regulation, 21 CFR Part 812. The IDE regulation imposes many of the same requirements imposed on clinical trials conducted pursuant to an IND: formulation of a well-designed and controlled trial; use of qualified investigators to conduct the trial; review, approval, and monitoring of the trial by a qualified IRB; monitoring of the conduct of the trial; and reporting of certain events and the results of the clinical trial.[8] Although the concepts are the same as the GCPs, the GCPs were developed particularly for the conduct of clinical trials involving pharmaceutical products. However, both the IDE regulations and the GCPs conform to the general principles of the Declaration of Helsinki that is discussed in greater detail later.

Use of Data from Foreign Trials

A sponsor may also include in an NDA data generated in foreign clinical trials from sites that were not included in the IND if certain conditions are met.[9] These data may also be used to support clinical investigations in the United States if the studies meet these requirements. The sponsor must submit certain information about foreign trials including description of the investigator's qualifications and the research facilities where the studies were conducted; a detailed description of the protocol and results of the study; a description of the drug substance and drug product used in the study; and, if the study is to be used in support of an NDA, assurance that the study is adequate and well-controlled in accordance with 21 CFR § 314.126. In addition, foreign clinical trials are required to have been conducted in accordance with the ethical principles set forth in the Declaration of Helsinki (1989 version stated in full in the body of the regulation) and the sponsor must show how the trial was conducted in accordance with these principles. The sponsor must also provide information about any independent review of the trial by an independent review committee (e.g., Institutional Review Board or Ethics Committee).

The Declaration of Helsinki was formulated by the World Medical Association (WMA) at its meeting in Helsinki, Finland, in June 1964 and has been amended several times since then.[10] The WMA drafted the document to provide guidance to physicians who participate in medical research involving human subjects. The Declaration states that the "health of my patient will be my first consideration." The document also notes that it is the duty of the physician to "promote and safeguard the health" of the community—goals that are often advanced by medical research.

In order to provide a framework for a physician to conduct research while honoring his or her commitment to the patient, the Declaration sets forth "basic principles" for all medical research that include the following. First, the physician must protect the life, health, privacy, and dignity of the subject. The research must be based on generally accepted scientific principles and the design and performance of the research must be clearly formulated in a protocol that is reviewed by an independent committee. The research should be conducted only by scientifically trained persons under the supervision of a competent "medical person." The risks of the experiment should be clearly understood and stated, and physicians should abstain from participation in any research that poses undue risks to patients. The Declaration also requires that the subject be well informed about the nature and risks of the research and the research should not proceed until the subject has freely given their consent to participate "preferably in writing." Consideration is given in the Declaration for subjects who are unable to give consent. The Declaration also provides guidance to the physician on combining medical care with research and also addresses certain special concerns related to the use of a treatment placebo, a common feature in research.

At the time of the writing of this chapter, the FDA has proposed to revise this rule and require instead that sites conform to the ICH *Good Clinical Practices: Consolidated Guideline* (GCPs).[11] The FDA offered several reasons for revising the regulation. First, the FDA noted the need to update the standards reflected in the rule; the Declaration version incorporated into the rule reflects the 1989 amendments and has been amended several times, and several organizations including the ICH have developed other more detailed standards. Second, the FDA seeks to ensure that quality data are generated by these trials. It notes that although the Declaration addresses these issues, it does not provide any detail on how to achieve this objective. By contrast, the GCPs provide considerable guidance on data quality including monitoring of data collection. Finally, the FDA proposes to eliminate reference to the Declaration because it may be amended by the WMA, an organization that is independent of the FDA.

The GCPs reflect the U.S. regulatory scheme codified at 21 CFR Parts 312, 50, and 56 and were adopted as guidance for industry by the FDA in 1997.[12] The proposed rule defines the GCPs as

> a standard for the design, conduct, performance, monitoring, auditing, recording, analysis, and reporting of clinical trials in a way that provides assurance that the data and reported results are credible and accurate and that the rights, safety, and well-being of trial subjects are protected.[13]

Other aspects of the GCPs are incorporated into other industry guidance published by the FDA including *Structure and Content of Clinical Study Reports, Clinical Investigations of Medicinal Products in the Pediatric Population* and *Choice of Control Group and Related Issues in Clinical Trials.*[14] The GCPs are described in detail later in this chapter.

The new rule establishes the GCPs as the standard that foreign clinical trials must meet, and highlights certain aspects including advance review and monitoring of the trial by an Independent Ethics Committee (IEC) and securing informed consent from a participant or his or her legal representative. Therefore, the sponsor will be required to submit more information about how the studies will be conducted in addition to the information that was required under the rule that will be revised. This information includes a summary of the IEC decision, a description of how informed consent was obtained and any incentives offered to study subjects, a description of monitoring practices, and a description of how investigators were trained to comply with the GCPs. Additionally, the proposed rule establishes a second condition that must be present for the data to be acceptable: The FDA must be able to validate the data through on-site inspection if the agency deems it necessary.

The FDA has also promulgated rules that govern the acceptance of data that has only been generated in foreign trials at 21 CFR § 314.106. This regulation allows for acceptance of applications and abbreviated applications based solely on foreign data if the data are applicable to U.S. populations and medical practice; the trials were conducted by clinical investigators of recognized competence; and the data appear to be valid or could be validated by an on-site inspection.

The ICH has also promulgated a guideline designed to permit the use of data generated in foreign clinical trials entitled "Ethnic Factors in the Acceptability of Foreign Clinical Data."[15] The objectives are to provide guidance in evaluating the effect of ethnic factors on a medicine's effect and reducing duplication of trials for pharmaceutical products. The guideline also suggests the use of bridging studies where indicated to validate the applicability of the data on the population served by the regulatory authority considering the data.

The FDA has also promulgated a rule governing the use of data generated in foreign trials in support of a PMA for a medical device.[16] For PMAs that are conducted under an IDE, the rule provides that the FDA will accept data from studies conducted outside the United States that were begun on or after November 19, 1986 (Effective Date), if the data are "valid" and performed in accordance with the Declaration of Helsinki or the laws of the country in which the study is performed, if those laws afford greater protection to the subjects. The applicant is required to explain the difference between the Declaration and the laws and explain why the laws offer greater protection. If the research was conducted before the Effective Date, the data may be accepted if the FDA is satisfied that the data are "scientifically valid" and the "rights, safety, and welfare of human subjects have not been violated." Data from foreign clinical studies in support of PMA that is not conducted pursuant to an IDE are acceptable if they meet the applicable criteria. The criteria that are applied to data submitted in support of a PMA that are drawn solely from foreign studies are very similar to those imposed on INDs or NDAs: The foreign data must be applicable to U.S. populations and medical practice; the investigators must be of recognized competence; and the data must be considered valid without on-site inspections or can be validated with on-site inspections.

Conducting Global Clinical Trials

Formulation of Good Clinical Practices

Clinical trials that are included as part of investigational plans set forth in INDs at foreign sites must meet the requirements of 21 CFR Parts 312, 50, and 56. Under the proposed rule, data from foreign trials that are not included as sites in the investigational plan in these applications may also be considered in support of these applications if the trials are conducted in accordance with the GCPs. Moreover, many countries have adopted the GCPs as the basis for their own regulatory approach to review of marketing applications for pharmaceutical and biotechnology products, or as a basis for permitting the conduct of clinical trials in those countries. Finally, the GCPs are offered as guidance to industry by the FDA in conforming to the regulatory requirements set forth in the Code of Federal Regulations on the conduct of clinical trials.[17]

The ICH was established in 1990 in response to the growing globalization of the pharmaceutical industry and the increasing complexity of regulations governing the approval for marketing of pharmaceuticals. Because most new drugs are developed and tested in the United States, Japan, and Western Europe, the ICH founding members were industry and government representatives of the European Commission, United States, and Japan. The ICH is based on a model of equal collaboration between the government regulators and industry and, therefore, the ICH is comprised of representatives of U.S. FDA; Ministry of Health, Labour, and Welfare of Japan; European Federation of Pharmaceutical Industries and Associations; European Commission; Pharmaceutical Research and Manufacturers of America; and the Japan Pharmaceutical Manufacturers Association, referred to as the "Six Parties."[18] In addition to the founding members or Six Parties, there are observers from Canada, the European Free Trade Area, and the World Health Organization. The ICH organizes its work by reference to three topics: safety, quality, and efficacy—the pillars of regulatory approval in many jurisdictions. Expert Working Groups (EWGs) were created to work on issues falling within the purview of the three topics. Some of the significant projects undertaken and completed by the EWGs include MeDRA, the medical terminology dictionary for reporting adverse events, GCPs, and the Common Technical Document or CTD. The CTD is the basis of regulatory submissions to the authorities of the founding members because it will include all of the elements common to regulatory application submissions in these jurisdictions. The document can be submitted in electronic form, referred to as e-CTD.

The GCPs were prepared by the EWG (Efficacy) and endorsed by the ICH Steering Committee in April 1996. At this point in the ICH process the EWG product is referred to the regulatory authorities of the founding members for adoption. By proposing the GCPs as guidance, the FDA signals to the industry that these guidelines reflect its current thinking on meeting regulatory guidelines but do not bind the agency or preclude the use of alternatives to conform to regulatory mandates.

Standards of Good Clinical Practices

The GCPs incorporate many of the principles enunciated in the Declaration of Helsinki but provide far greater detail and guidance to assist in implementing the principles. The GCPs also establish certain principles that are explicitly drawn from the Declaration, including:

- identifying and weighing the risks against the anticipated benefits

- the primacy of the rights, safety, and well-being of the individual over the interests of science and society
- the necessity for a scientifically sound design reduced to writing in a clear, detailed protocol
- IRB or Ethics Committee review
- use of qualified investigators to conduct the trial and qualified persons to provide medical care
- importance of freely given informed consent
- accurate and verifiable recording and reporting of clinical trial information
- preservation of subjects' confidentiality
- observation of Good Manufacturing Practices in manufacturing, handling, and storage of the drug and administration of the drug in accordance with the protocol[19]

These principles are further fleshed out in the six sections that follow Section 2 of the Standards of Good Clinical Practices:

- Institutional Review Board/Independent Ethics Committee (IRB/IEC) (Section 3)
- Investigator (Section 4)
- Sponsor (Section 5)
- Clinical Trial Protocol (Section 6)
- Investigator's Brochure (Section 7)
- Essential Documents for the Conduct of a Clinical Trial (Section 8)

The version that will be used to describe the GCPs in this text is the version promulgated as guidance in the United States because the focus of this chapter is global trials conducted by U.S. companies. The U.S. version did not vary much from the version developed by the ICH EWG.

Institutional Review Board/Independent Ethics Committee (Section 3)
Section 3 outlines the scope of review by an IRB or IEC, including specific documents that should be reviewed including: protocol, written informed consent form, subject recruitment procedures, written information to be provided to the subjects, Investigator's Brochure, available safety information, information about compensation and payments to subjects, investigator's qualifications, and any other information deemed appropriate by the IRB or IEC. Section 3 states that this panel may then move to approve the trial, modify it prior to approval, disapprove the trial, or terminate or suspend any prior approval based on general considerations outlined in the Section.

This section also outlines the "composition, functions, and operations" of these review panels. Among the important procedures described in Section 3 is the requirement for a written procedure whereby the IRB or IEC would be informed prior to protocol amendment or upon deviation from the protocol.

Investigator (Section 4)

Section 4 describes the necessary qualifications of the investigator and the requirement to document his or her qualifications. The investigator is also charged with the obligation to be familiar with the Investigator's Brochure, the GCPs, and applicable regulatory requirements. The investigator should be able to demonstrate that he or she has access to the facilities, staff, time, and other resources to run the trial and must ensure that persons involved in conducting the trial are adequately informed about the protocol, investigational products, and duties in conducting the trial. The investigator and the institution in which the trial is conducted are charged with ensuring that adequate medical care is available to subjects including access to treatment for trial-related injuries. The investigator is also charged with serving as the primary person responsible for communicating with the IRB or IEC and must be prepared to secure IRB or IEC approval prior to commencing a trial. Ensuring compliance with the protocol in conducting the trial is a primary responsibility of the investigator. He or she should not deviate from the protocol without prior review by the IRB or IEC, unless it is determined necessary to eliminate an immediate hazard to trial subjects.

Section 4 also imposes on the investigator and institution the responsibility for ensuring that the investigational product is stored and administered properly and accounted for throughout the trial. The GCPs permit an institution to assign this responsibility to a properly trained pharmacist.

The investigator is also responsible for ensuring that the trial is conducted according to the randomization procedures designed for the trial and that the code is only broken in accordance with the protocol.

The responsibility to provide clinical trial subjects with all of the information that they need to make a truly informed, free decision to participate in the trial is one of the key responsibilities of the investigator. An ancillary obligation includes keeping the informed consent information current and subjects advised of changes that could affect their decision to participate in the trial. The investigator must ensure that the consents are secured from the subjects in a manner that is noncoercive and that elicits questions and discussion of subjects' concerns. This section provides considerable detail on the requirements for the content of a written informed consent as well as the process of securing the consent and the acceptability of the consent of legal representatives in lieu of the subject's personal consent.

Section 4 also covers the investigator's responsibility for preparing records and reports about the progress of the trial and about the occurrence of adverse events.

Sponsor (Section 5)

The sponsor's obligations in conducting a clinical trial are delineated in Section 5 and include the responsibility to formulate Standard Operating Procedures to assure that the trials are conducted and data generated in accordance with the GCPs. The sponsor is also required to secure written agreements with the investigator and institution and others involved with the trial to ensure that these parties adhere to their responsibilities in the trial. Section 5 also specifies that a sponsor may transfer its responsibilities to a CRO but must do so specifically in writing and remains responsible for the quality and integrity of the trial data.

Section 5 requires the sponsor to utilize the services of qualified medical professionals to advise on trial-related medical problems and also to utilize qualified professionals in the design of the trial and at all stages of the trial as it is conducted. The sponsor is primarily responsible for the overall trial management as well as the management of data generated through the trial and analysis of the data. Section 5 includes considerable detail about maintenance of trial documents including retention periods in instances where marketing approval is granted or a trial is discontinued.

Another key sponsor responsibility is the selection of qualified investigators. If a trial is a multicenter trial, the sponsor is obligated to ensure coordination among the centers. Financing of a clinical trial is also addressed in Section 5; these provisions include requirements for indemnity or insurance where mandated by law and description of sponsor's policies related to handling of a trial-related injury. The sponsor is also obligated to ensure that regulatory requirements are met in all jurisdictions before beginning trials and that the approval of an IRB/IEC has been obtained.

Section 5 also outlines the sponsor's responsibilities in the manufacturing, labeling, and coding of the investigational product as well as supplying the investigational product to the site. Prior to supplying the investigational product, the sponsor is required to verify that the site can and will follow written instructions prepared by the sponsor to store, retrieve, and account for the investigational drug. The sponsor is also required to ensure that it has complied with regulations of the receiving country regarding import of the investigational product.

The sponsor is also required to ensure that the site has agreed to permit access to the trials and that each subject provides consent to access his or her medical records for trial-related marketing. The growing complexity of privacy regulation, discussed later in this text, is increasing the challenge inherent in meeting these obligations. The mandate for ongoing safety evaluation of the trial and timely reporting of adverse drug reactions (ADRs) also falls to the sponsor under Section 5. This also involves notifying all regulatory authorities that require notification of ADRs.

Sponsor duties in monitoring the trials are also described in Section 5. The objectives of clinical trial monitoring include ensuring that the trial is conducted in such a way that the rights and well-being of the trial subjects are protected; that the trial data is complete, accurate, and verified; and that the conduct of the trial accords with the protocol, GCPs, and other regulatory requirements. The sponsor is charged with appointing qualified monitors, who are appropriately trained and thoroughly familiar with the investigational product and clinical trial documents. Section 5 also describes the monitor's responsibilities in considerable detail, as this task is central to ensuring that the trial is run accountably and that the data that is collected is verifiable and accurate. If and when a sponsor audits a trial, a task separate from ongoing monitoring, Section 5 also details the qualifications of auditors and the procedures that should be followed in conducting an effective audit. The duty of the sponsor to promptly respond to noncompliance by a site, including termination of a site for serious noncompliance, is also set forth in Section 5.

The sponsor is also required to notify authorities of any suspension or termination of a trial and to generate reports upon the conclusion of a trial. In addition, Section 5 details responsibilities of sponsors who are conducting multicenter sites. These include ensuring coordination and communication among the sites, clearly identifying the responsibility of a coordinating investigator(s), and designing case report forms (CRFs) to capture all the data at the sites.

Clinical Trial Protocol (Section 6) and Investigator's Brochure (Section 7)

Sections 6 and 7 detail the content and structure of the clinical trial protocol and the investigator's brochure (IB)—the cornerstone documents of a clinical trial. All of the content described in these two sections must be documented in the protocol, the IB, or written agreements with the sites and investigators. It is important for legal staff who are documenting the trial to be familiar with these documents and ensure that the documents work together to comprehensively address all relevant matters.

The protocol sets forth the background for the trial and, most importantly, the actual trial design including its objectives and purpose, the primary and secondary endpoints, the actual design (e.g., double-blind), the trial treatment (dosage, etc.), and the identification of data to be recorded on CRFs, among other items. Subject selection is also detailed in the protocol, including inclusion and exclusion criteria. In addition to these basic clinical details, the protocol also includes information about the statistical methods to be employed, data handling and reporting, quality control and assurance, and ethical considerations. Other issues that must be addressed in the protocol or through separate agreements include financing of the trial, insurance, and publication policies. These types of issues are usually covered in separate clinical trial agreements (CTAs) with the sites and investigators.

The IB is a compilation of clinical and nonclinical data about the study drug that are relevant to an investigator conducting the trial. The objective of the IB is to ensure that the investigator has sufficient background to understand the trial design and treatment indications as well as clinical management of the study subjects. The IB would include detailed information about the pharmaceutical properties of the drug and about all prior clinical and nonclinical studies done with the substance related to pharmacological, toxicological, metabolic, and pharmacokinetic properties. Detailed safety and efficacy data should also be provided. The IB should also describe any experience with the product if it has been marketed elsewhere.

Essential Documents (Section 8)

Section 8 lists pages of essential clinical trial documents required before, during, and upon conclusion of a clinical trial. This describes the construct of the trial master file maintained at the sponsor's office and investigator's site and how these files are developed over the course of the trial.

Adoption of the GCPs

Seventeen of the world's wealthiest countries (represented by the ICH founding members) have adopted the GCPs as a framework for regulating clinical trials, albeit with modifications based on each jurisdiction's requirements. The regulatory authorities of the founding members of the ICH adopted the guidelines as guidance within their respective jurisdictions. The Committee for Proprietary Medicines (CPMP) of the European Agency for the Evaluation of Medicinal Products (EMEA) approved the guidelines July 17, 1997. [20] In the United States, the FDA published the GCPs as industry guidance May 9, 1997. In Japan, the GCPs were published in March 1997 by the Ministry of Health, Labour, and Welfare as "Japanese Technical Requirements for New Drug Registration 1997." [21] Australia, through its Therapeutic Goods

Administration, has also adopted a modified version of the GCPs as guidance.[22] Similarly, Canada's Therapeutics Products Directorate has adopted the GCPs.

As indicated earlier, the number of clinical trials that are being conducted outside of Western industrialized nations is growing dramatically. These regions, sometimes referred to as the "ascending markets," include Eastern Europe, Latin America, and Asia. According to one author, CenterWatch data showed that 20% to 30% of clinical trials are now being conducted in the ascending markets.[23] These regions and their regulatory schemes adherence to the principles incorporated into the GCPs are discussed below.

Asia has tremendous potential for clinical trials because of the size of the treatment-naïve population and, even though behind the European Union (EU) in regulatory advances, the region shows real evidence of creating a favorable framework for trials. For example, organizations such as the Association of South-East Asian Nations (ASEAN) have used many of the guidelines developed by the ICH to inform the harmonization efforts of its member countries. The member countries of ASEAN support a total population of 500 million and a combined gross domestic product of USD 737 billion.[24] Singapore, Hong Kong, and Taiwan have very sophisticated clinical facilities and personnel and their national guidelines follow the GCPs; in fact, Singapore has established the Asia Pacific Economic Co-operation Coordinating Centre for Good Clinical Practice to provide a platform for GCP training in the region.[25] The medical faculty of the National University of Singapore has also entered into a joint venture with Quintiles to advance training in the GCPs and conduct of clinical trials.[26] Malaysia has adopted the GCPs as well.[27] Nonetheless, some commentators have rated this region as "fair to poor" on GCP experience, although that is likely to change as the programs described here achieve their missions.[28]

Seven of the eight eastern European "accession countries" that joined the EU on May 1, 2004, had harmonized national legislation with the EU Clinical Trial Directive. The Clinical Trial Directive (2001/20/EC of 4 April 2001) harmonized requirements relating to the conduct of clinical trials in the EU.[29] EU member states were obligated to implement the Directive by May 1, 2003, and to apply implementing legislation by May 1, 2004, at the latest, although as of the drafting of this chapter several member states had failed to do so but were actively considering legislation to satisfy this obligation. Although the EMEA has adopted the GCPs as guidance, it is important to note that the European Commission as yet has not adopted the GCPs in the form of a directive accompanied by further detailed guidance. A directive obligates the Member States to adopt national implementing legislation and therefore is not mere guidance. The EU Clinical Trial Directive that does harmonize many other aspects of clinical trial regulation is discussed in more detail later in this chapter.[30] As these legal developments indicate, however, the countries of Eastern Europe and Russia have well-established frameworks for conducting clinical trials and, according to one study, "ethical care and compliance with Good Clinical Practice guidelines is at least as good as anywhere else."[31]

Argentina, Mexico, and Brazil host most clinical research in Latin America.[32] From 1991 to 1993, Argentina hosted six U.S. clinical trials while hosting 271 in 1997–1999. Brazil's trial numbers grew from 16 to 187 during the same period and Mexico's from 29 to 187.[33] Peru, Costa Rica, and Chile also provide clinical trial sites. Although countries in this region have generally adopted GCPs, their regulatory processes remain more cumbersome and complex.[34] The FDA has also undertaken harmonization efforts in the Americas through the Pan American Health Organization (PAHO) and has convened conferences among drug regulatory agencies in the Americas for this purpose. A report on these activities also detailed other regional harmonization efforts including the Mercado Comun del Sur (MERCOSUR) that was established by Argentina, Brazil, Uruguay, and Paraguay in 1991.[35] One of the aims of PAHO is the creation of a "mechanism to follow-up on implementation of GCP."[36]

The ICH also established in 1999 the Global Cooperation Group whose specific objective is to expand the use of the ICH recommendations to non-ICH countries. This effort has not been without controversy as described in a report authored by a committee of the WHO that examined the effect of the dissemination of ICH standards to non-ICH countries.[37] Some of the concerns include the exclusion of non-ICH nations in the formulation process, lack of sufficient consultation with the academic sector, the appropriateness of using an industry organization as the secretariat, the capacity of developing nations to implement the standards, and the public health implications of adopting the standards in non-ICH countries.

Other Regulatory Considerations

Brazil, Latin America's largest and most populous country and the region's leading economic power, poses the most problematic regulatory environment in Latin America. Customs laws in Brazil are complex, and importing/exporting is costly.[38]

Other Clinical Trial Regulations

The GCPs provide the framework for conducting clinical trials at specific sites in a country. However, national laws impose other specific legal mandates on sponsors of clinical trials. While it is impossible to even summarize all of the potential types of regulations that may be brought to bear on the conduct of clinical trials in jurisdictions throughout the world, this section of the chapter will highlight a few categories of regulation that are most likely to arise in the conduct of trials.

These can be generally divided into three segments: those dealing with the import of drugs into a country; other sponsor qualifications and obligations; and official notification requirements before, during, and at the conclusion of clinical trials. These requirements vary from jurisdiction to jurisdiction. For example, as indicated earlier, Brazil's import laws are complex and costly. With respect to sponsor qualifications, Australia requires that any sponsor of a pharmaceutical clinical trial in that country must be a legal entity organized in that country. The EU Clinical Trial Directive requires that a sponsor be present in the EU or appoint a legal representative established in any of the EU member states to act in the name and on behalf of the sponsor in conducting the clinical trial.[39] The Directive details many sponsor responsibilities but provides little clarification about the nature of the liabilities associated with the status of the legal representative. Some countries require that a sponsor indemnify clinical trial subjects and maintain certain insurance coverage against injuries arising from the trials.

Notification of authorities prior to the commencement of clinical trials is a very common feature of the regulatory scheme in most jurisdictions. For example, in Australia the sponsor of a clinical trial must submit a Clinical Trial Exemption (CTX) or Clinical Trials Notification (CTN) to the Therapeutic Goods Administration. In the EU, member states have regulatory agencies—or Competent Authorities (CA) in the parlance of the Clinical Trial Directive—overseeing clinical trials research that require notification prior to the commencement of a trial.[40] The EU Clinical Trial Directive standardized notification to the CAs as well as their review process and timelines.[41] Moreover, the EU Clinical Trial Directive established a central database of investigational trials conducted in the EU called EUDRACT.[42] The purpose of EUDRACT is to provide the European Commission and CAs of the Member States information on all clinical trials in the EU. Therefore, each clinical trial must have a unique EUDRACT number that is obtained upon registration. EUDRACT is linked to the reporting of serious unexpected adverse events (SUSAR) for incorporation into a database.[43]

Another important result of the passage of the Clinical Trial Directive is the requirement for notification of a Member State CA before commencement of Phase I trials; prior to the Directive, such notice was not necessary.[44] Another significant change implemented by the Clinical Trial Directive regarding commencement of clinical trials is the streamlined ethics committee review process. As a result of the Directive, sponsors are required to seek only one Ethics Committee opinion rather than an opinion from each site. The application for the Ethics Committee is also set forth in the detailed guidance as well as information about when amendments to protocols are required to be reported to CAs and Ethics Committees.[45]

The laws of many nations require notification prior to importing an investigational product or commencing clinical trials. While a compilation of these laws is beyond the scope of this chapter, it is important for sponsors to be aware of the laws in each jurisdiction or to have engaged consultants and CROs that have expertise in the regulatory requirements of the jurisdictions where the trial will be conducted.

Medical Privacy Protection

Medical privacy laws also affect the conduct of clinical trials. The United States enacted a medical privacy law that, among other things, details the content and format for securing consent from clinical trial subjects in order to access their personal health information. Canada adopted privacy legislation that set standards for provincial legislation to incorporate in enacting provincial privacy legislation. The EU adopted a sweeping directive regarding protection of personal privacy, including data that pertains to a person's medical condition.[46] Personal data concerning health is considered as being particularly sensitive, and its processing is generally prohibited except in specific cases, and subject to more rigorous precautions, which are identified in the Directive.[47] U.S. companies conducting clinical trials become subject to the Directive because they may have entities or offices established in the EU or, even if a company has no European presence, because it uses equipment located in the EU for the purpose of processing data. "Data controllers" are those entities that control the purpose ("why") and means ("how") of the data processing. Sponsors of clinical trials do not automatically qualify as data controllers, but often do perform activities that result in their being considered as such.[48] The Directive enunciates a body of principles that determine when the processing of data is lawful. For example, the Directive requires the communication of detailed information to a subject for the purpose of securing unambiguous consent to the processing of medical data. The subject also has certain rights regarding access to the data and to correct or block processing of data. Data must be gathered and stored securely to prevent unauthorized access. For the purposes of this chapter, a requirement of note is the prohibition of transfer of data outside the EU except to other jurisdictions that ensure "an adequate level of protection" of the data.

The United States can be viewed by the EU authorities as providing an adequate level of protection to the extent that U.S. entities receiving the data comply with certain principles set forth in the Directive. One of the ways that a company can demonstrate compliance is to adhere to a Safe Harbor Agreement program that is supervised by the U.S. Federal Trade Commission and originally negotiated by the U.S. Department of Commerce.[49] The program enshrines the principles formulated in the Directive and, although entering the program is voluntary, if a company does not adhere to the principles, it may be charged with committing a deceptive trade practice and subject to further enforcement action, including fines. It may also be disqualified from continued participation in the Safe Harbor program.

If a U.S. company does not conduct trials in the EU in a manner that complies with the Directive, several consequences can accrue. Depending on the specific jurisdiction, sites and other contractors may be forbidden to permit access to data and both criminal sanctions and monetary fines may be imposed.

Intellectual Property

Although Intellectual Property (IP) laws are beyond the scope of this chapter, it is important to note that local IP laws can affect how discoveries are treated in the context of a multinational clinical trial. Generally, innovations or discoveries are not made in the course of conducting a clinical trial—these are much more likely to happen in earlier research phases. Nonetheless, innovations or discoveries are not outside the realm of possibility and ownership of the resulting IP rights is typically covered in the CTA.

Drugs and devices are typically patented and the patent (or license as the case may be) is typically held by the manufacturer or sponsor. A number of international treaties and conventions attempt to harmonize or coordinate the filing and processing of patent applications of many nations.[50] Of note for this discussion are the laws of certain countries that, first, govern payment to employees that make discoveries and, second, create "moral rights." With respect to the first category, some national laws require that an employer pay an employee a reasonable sum for any invention they may discover in the course of their employment. Thus, for example, Germany requires that a hospital pay its employee-investigator the value of his or her invention. The concept of moral rights was developed in Europe and has only been applied in the most limited manner in the United States. Moral rights are separate from the economic rights of authors and creators and generally embrace three distinct rights: the right of attribution of a literary or other work, the right not to have the work mutilated or modified by another, and the right not to have a work falsely attributed to an author or creator.[51] For the purposes of this discussion, it is important to note that these issues can be raised in negotiating clinical trial agreements in countries outside the United States. In countries where an employer may be obligated to pay an employee, the sponsor may be asked to indemnify the hospital against claims by its employee where the sponsor insists on ownership of all IP flowing from discoveries made about the study drug, or which arise in the course of conducting the trial. Second, it may be important in countries that have enacted laws protecting moral rights that investigators be asked to waive moral rights, particularly as it relates to other clauses about publication of the study results. These clauses should be coordinated.

Legal Tasks

> A medical director of a U.S. pharmaceutical company based in China stated that it is difficult to obtain memberships, meeting schedules, and minutes of Chinese institutional review boards. . . . An employee of a Russian-based contract research organization reported that she had frequently encountered problems with lack of full disclosure to potential subjects about the side effects of drugs.[52]

In conducting multinational trials, legal, regulatory, and clinical staffs must be aware of the requirements imposed by each jurisdiction where the trial will be conducted, and have the capacity either internally or through outsourcing for complying with regulations. Legal, clinical, and regulatory staff also need to be concerned about some of the risks inherent in conducting trials in countries with little experience or infrastructure. Moreover, the burden to comply with regulations and ensure that compliance responsibilities flow through to key legal documents falls within the bailiwick of these staffs or their outsourced contractors.

In a study entitled *The Globalization of Clinical Trials: A Growing Challenge in Protecting Human Subjects,* the Office of Inspector General (OIG) of the U.S. Department of Health and Human Services identified several problematic trends arising from increasing use of foreign clinical trial sites (referred to as "Globalization"). First, the FDA relies heavily on review of clinical trials by IRBs or ECs, to ensure that the trials are conducted so that the rights of human subjects are protected. In the United States, the FDA inspects IRBs to ensure that they are operating in a manner that complies with the law.[53] However, the FDA does not have the authority to inspect foreign IRBs or ECs and the OIG found evidence that many foreign IRBs or ECs lack the expertise and resources necessary to effectively monitor trials.[54] The World Health Organization in 1999 uncovered significant deficiencies in the ethical review systems for clinical trials in Asia, Africa, and the Western Pacific and published guidelines entitled *Operational Guidelines for Ethics Committees That Review Biomedical Research.*[55]

The second risk area relates to the use of investigators that lack experience in conducting trials and protecting the rights of human subjects enrolled in the trial. The FDA can and does inspect clinical trial sites and investigators in foreign countries and has stepped up this effort in view of the growth of clinical trials according to the OIG in *Globalization.* However, the agency's resources are far outstripped by the growth in clinical trials. Another deficiency cited in *Globalization* is the lack of a requirement for investigator attestations for foreign trials that are not included in the IND.[56]

Thus prior to considering specific legal contractual issues, sponsors should review the problems likely to be encountered in each country where the trials will be conducted and take action to resolve these problems. Sponsors should understand the strengths and weaknesses of the country's ethical review system and take ameliorative actions before the trial starts. In addition, sponsors should choose investigators carefully and ensure that the chosen investigators are well-trained in human-subjects protection and are required to attest to their commitment to fulfilling their responsibilities. Finally, trial design should always reflect the highest ethical standards no matter where the trial is to be undertaken.

Outsourcing Regulatory/Legal Tasks in the Conduct of Trials

Even the largest pharmaceutical and biotechnology companies outsource certain responsibilities in conducting multinational trials. These are usually outsourced to CROs, although narrower responsibilities may also be contracted to individual contractors or entities such as site management organizations (SMOs). The trend among

CROs has been growth through merger or acquisition in order to provide the global coverage required by their life science clients in the conduct of multinational trials. According to Arthur D. Little, pharmaceutical outsourcing in the United States is a $30 billion business that is projected to grow to $48 billion by 2008.[57] The reasons for the growth in outsourcing include the dramatic increase in the costs of conducting trials as well as the increasing sophistication in regulation of the conduct of clinical trials worldwide. According to one author "the average cost of developing a drug is growing at a compounded annual rate of 7.3% (from $138 million in 1975 to $318 million in 1987 and $897 million in 2003), according to a Tufts Center for the Study of Drug Development Report."[58]

As CROs have grown more sophisticated, they have been able to reduce the costs of conducting trials accounting for their increasing popularity even among large, well-staffed companies. According to one estimation, CROs are able to "shorten testing times by as much as 30%" which is a very significant reduction in overall drug costs.[59] The same report notes that one of the critical challenges facing CROs is "regulator scrutiny" as well as consolidation of the pharmaceutical industry itself.

Several CROs have positioned themselves to handle global clinical trials. As one author noted:

> The largest contract research companies maintain worldwide networks of 30 or more offices. Many, however, are expanding their presence in Europe and Asia through alliances with and acquisition of local providers. This is an important way of quickly establishing local expertise and relationships, which may otherwise take years to establish.[60]

Obviously, local regulatory expertise is critical as are experts in the culture and language of local trial sites. Some CROs have particular strength in certain geographic regions and, while offering coverage in all or other regions, do not boast the same level of strength across the board. Other CROs tend to be stronger in certain therapeutic areas than in others. It is critical to ferret out these strengths and weaknesses prior to contracting with a CRO.

Important tasks for legal representatives of companies conducting clinical trials are the preparation and negotiation of contracts with CROs or other entities that a company may use to assist in conducting a multinational clinical trial. As indicated, a critical first step is conducting a due diligence process to determine whether the

CRO has the capabilities in the right geographic area to assist in the trial. Their services can range from trial design through final data analysis—in other words, all of the key sponsor tasks set forth in the GCPs. Many companies conduct due diligence in the course of a more formal bidding process and some companies rely on long-term working relationships with select CROs. The task of gaining in-depth information and insight into the quality of a CRO's services is critical to a successful matching of needs and services.

The contract between CRO and company should achieve the same goals as other commercial contracts and should establish the identity of the parties, respective obligations of the parties, performance standards, indemnification and insurance requirements, term and termination of the agreement, and remedies in the event of poor performance. However, there are unique industry spins that apply to these standard commercial contract clauses. These are identified below:

- *Identification of the parties*—State clearly whether a CRO can subcontract or further outsource the obligations imposed by the contract and whether all of the affiliates that it may use are identified in the contract. To extend their global reach, many CROs own or contract with local affiliates. The contract should include a process whereby the sponsor approves use of these affiliates to meet contract obligations.
- *Defining obligations*—The contract must also identify those specific sponsor duties that are delegated to the CRO in accordance with the GCP standards and applicable law in many jurisdictions. Often, these agreements are drafted as "master" agreements whereby scope-of-work changes and additions can be accommodated.
- *Performance standards*—These clauses should incorporate obligations to conduct the CRO duties in accordance with GCP standards as well as other applicable law. Key personnel should be identified prior to contracting and the CRO should be obligated to use them on the project. The company should receive assurances that no personnel, including investigators if the CRO is responsible for recruiting these, should be disqualified or debarred due to regulatory violations. Moreover, the CRO should be able to warrant that all investigators are fully qualified to undertake the trials, not only from a technical scientific standpoint but from an ethical standpoint as well.
- *Indemnification and insurance requirements*—Most CROs will seek to be indemnified by the sponsor for any claims that arise out of conducting the study, and also will require that sponsors carry adequate clinical trials

insurance. Many jurisdictions require proof of this type of insurance and the GCPs require descriptions of sponsor policies regarding reimbursement of clinical trial subjects in the event of a study injury. Sponsors also generally look to CROs for evidence of insurance coverage over claims that arise in the course of conducting CRO responsibilities (e.g., professional liability, errors and omissions). Increasingly, CROs are including limitation of liability clauses in agreements. These may be reasonable if mutual and if they provide for payment of direct damages by either party to the other for its respective negligence or misconduct.

- *Other*—Clauses addressing ownership of study protocol, drug, and other special proprietary information should be addressed. Strict obligations regarding return of study data also should be included, as well as clauses regarding each other's obligation in the event of early termination of a clinical trial. In that event, due regard should be given to ensuring the safety of participants and complying with applicable law. Finally, many companies are crafting risk/reward or penalty/incentive programs to insure that goals are met. These need to be carefully drafted to ensure that these formulations work as each company intends.

Clinical Trial Agreements in the Context of Multinational Trials

The other important set of agreements for a multinational clinical trial are those that are required to be entered into among the key players—sponsors (or CROs), and investigators and their institutions. These clinical trial agreements (CTA) are important not only in conforming to the GCP guidance but also in raising and resolving issues that are particularly important with foreign sites in regions where investigators and institutions do not have extensive experience with GCPs. As with all legal documents, CTAs also serve to memorialize important aspects of the agreements between the parties, although often in a manner that is culturally jarring when drafted by U.S. companies for use in countries outside of the United States. American legal documents tend to address more issues with far greater detail than is typically seen in contracts from other countries. In the past, in both the United States and other countries, these agreements were often signed by the investigator without negotiation, but this practice has changed. The legal or contract staff of academic medical centers in many countries now review and extensively negotiate these agreements and execution of CTAs is becoming far more time consuming and laborious.

CTAs are binding legal documents that reflect the responsibilities of the sponsor, investigator, and institution. While these agreements are considered in more detail in Chapter __, some of the features that are particularly important in CTAs that will be used in non-U.S. sites are described below, by reference to common contract features.

- *Identification of the parties*—Is the manufacturer the "sponsor" in a jurisdiction that requires an in-country sponsor? Consider whether the sponsor ought to be defined to include the CRO that will be conducting sponsor duties in the country.
- *Defining obligations*—The investigator's obligation to conduct the study in accordance with the protocol, applicable law, and GCPs should be clearly stated, as should the investigator's and institution's responsibility in handling and accounting for the study drug in accord with GCPs and national law. The agreement should also obligate the investigator and institution to ensure, before commencement of the study, that the trial is approved by an independent ethics committee that operates in conformity with the GCPs. Another issue that should be addressed in a CTA as an obligation is approval of an informed consent document that complies with local privacy laws. Typically sponsors provide an informed consent template that includes confidentiality language, including permission to review patient records. The investigator and institution should ensure that the language will permit them to lawfully release both original patient data to the monitors and also coded patient data to the sponsors on the CRFs. Moreover, it is important to secure whatever consent is necessary to permit the FDA and other regulatory agencies to review the records of the study. If the language is deemed inadequate or if the independent ethics committee wishes to modify that language, the sponsor should include language so that they are advised in advance before changes to the template are made.
- *Insurance and indemnification*—The sponsor should state that it carries all insurance that it is required to carry in that jurisdiction. It is also helpful to include in the CTA a summary of the sponsor's policies regarding payment for treatment of study-related injuries.
- *Other*—The CTA should include affirmations by both the institution and the investigator confirming the investigator's qualifications and stating that they have not been disqualified by regulatory agencies.

Conclusion

Multinational clinical trials are both the present reality and the wave of the future. Increasing harmonization is paving the way for continued expansion of multinational trials that can produce meaningful data for drug development and approval. This can be a positive development if sponsors, investigators, and regulators undertake the tasks necessary to ensure that trials are rigorously conducted to produce reliable, meaningful data and protect the rights of those who participate as subjects in the trials.

Notes and References

1   Stober, Mary, "Multinational Clinical Trials: Breaking Language and Cultural Barriers," *Applied Clinical Trials*, May 28, 2004.

2   A similar harmonization initiative has been undertaken for medical devices with the creation of the Global Harmonization Task Force (GHTF) in 1992. GHTF has not formulated separate clinical trial standards. The GHTF approach will be identified where it diverges from the ICH standards.

3   *See*, e.g., "The Impact of Implementation of ICH Guidelines in Non-ICH Countries: Report of a WHO Meeting," World Health Organization, Geneva, Switzerland, 13–15 September 2001.

4   See section 505 of the Federal Food Drug and Cosmetic Act and 21 CFR Part 312.

5   An IND may be submitted for one or all phases of a clinical trial.

6   Frances Crawley, presentation at European Forum for GCP, Washington, D.C., 26–29 January 2004.

7   *Ibid.*

8   In addition to its primary responsibility to approve and monitor these trials, the IRB must also decide whether the device is a "significant risk device" and if so, the FDA must be informed of the determination and approve commencement of the clinical trial. 21 CFR § 812.66.

9   21 CFR § 312.120.

10   www.wma.net/e/policy/b3.htm.

11   69 FR 32467, June 10, 2004.

12   62 FR 25629, May 9, 1997.

13   69 FR 32469.

14   See discussion at 69 FR 32468 and http://frwebgate.access.gpo.gov for guidance documents.

15   ICH Harmonised Tripartite Guideline, "Ethnic Factors in the Acceptability of Foreign Clinical Data E5," Step 4, 5 February 1998.

16   21 CFR § 814.15.

17   The guidance was published in 62 FR 25692 (May 9, 1997) by the FDA to provide guidance to industry on good clinical practices.

18   http://www.ich.org.

19   *Guidance for Industry, E6 Good Clinical Practice: Consolidated Guidance*, 62 FR 25692, May 9, 1997; Section 2. Descriptions in this text will be drawn from this version of the GCPs and the references will be to sections and subsections in this version.

20   European Agency for the Evaluation of Medicinal Products, "Explanatory Note and Comments to the ICH Harmonised Tripartite Guideline E6: Note for Guidance on Good Clinical Practice (CPMP/ICH/135/95)," September 8, 1997.

21   http://www.mhlw.go.jp/english/org/policy/p13-14.html.

22   Introductory Comments of the TGA

23   Lamberti, Mary Jo, "Going Global," *Applied Clinical Trials,* June 1, 2004

24   ASEAN web page www.state.gov/p/eap/regional/asean.

25   http://www.biomed-singapore.com/bms/sg/en_uk/index/about_biomedical_sciences/clinical_development.html.

26   www.med.nus.edu.sq.

27   "Guidelines for Application to Conduct Drug-Related Clinical Trials in Malaysia," Ministry of Health of Malaysia, 2d Edition, 2000.

28   Lamberti, Mary Jo, *op.cit.* 18.

29   In general and subject to exceptions, the provisions of EC Directives are not directly enforceable in the EC Member States but need to be "transposed" through the passage of national law in the Member States.

30   The Clinical Trial Directive applies only to medicinal products and not to medical devices. Medical devices are regulated in the EU in accordance with (among other Directives) 92/42/EEC as well as the law of the Member States.

31   *Int J Clin Pharmacol Ther.* 2003 Jul;41(7):277–80 Clinical trials in Russia and Eastern Europe: Recruitment and Quality. Platonov P. Lund University, Lund, Sweden. Pyotr.Platonov-@evidence-cpr.com.

32   "The Globalization of Clinical Trials: A Growing Challenge in Protecting Human Subjects," Office of Inspector General, U.S. Department of Health And Human Services, Washington, D.C, September 2001, p. 10.

33   *Ibid.,* p. 10.

34   Lamberti, Mary Jo, *op.cit,* 18.

35   Pharmaceutical Regulatory Hamonization in the Americas, Pan American Health Organization/World Health Organization, 42nd Directing Council, 52nd Session of the Regional Committee, September 2000, p. 5.

36   *Ibid.,* Annex A.

37   *op.cit.* Note 3.

38   Stober, M., Multinational Clinical Trials: Breaking Language and Cultural Barriers, *Applied Clinical Trials*, May 28, 2004.

39   For a compilation of all EU directives governing marketing authorization, conduct of clinical trials, and related matters, see http://pharmacos.eudra.org/F2/eudralex/vol-1/home.htm.

40   See Detailed Guidance for the Request for Authorisation of a Clinical Trial on a Medicinal Product for Human Use to the Competent Authorities, Notification of Substantial Amendments and Declaration of the End of the Trial, European Commission Enterprise Directorate General.

41   With certain exceptions, a CA has sixty days to review an application to commence a trial.

42   Detailed Guidance on the European Clinical Trials Database (EUDRACT Database), European Commission Enterprise Directorate General.

43   Detailed Guidance on the Collection, Verification, and Presentation of Adverse Reaction Reports Arising from Clinical Trials on Medicinal Products for Human Use, European Commission Enterprise Directorate General.

44 *See,* e.g., Description of the Medicines for Human Use (Clinical Trials) Regulations 2004, published by the Medicines and Healthcare Products Regulatory Agency, United Kingdom and 2001/20/EC of April 4, 2001.

45 *See* note 27.

46 95/46/EC, October 24, 1995.

47 It is also important to note that the EU Data Protection Working Party, a EC consultative body composed of representative from EC Member States and from the European Commission established under the Data Protection Directive, has recently issued a document on genetic data, stressing the particularly acute data protection problems raised by the processing of such data, also in the framework of clinical trials, and calling for increased regulatory attention. See "Working Document on Genetic Data" of March 17, 2004, 12178/03/EN – WP 91.

48 The Italian Data Protection Authority issued an opinion in 2000 where it noted that if in the framework of a clinical trial the sponsor merely cooperates to a processing activity that is performed by the site, then only the site, and not the sponsor qualify as "data controller." This would be the case if the site decided the purpose and means of the processing and allowed the sponsor to access and handle such information only according to precise instructions and limitations independently and exclusively decided by the site. In contrast, the sponsor would qualify as "data controller" if it identified the purpose and means of any processing in a way independent from the instructions of the site. Both the site and the sponsor could be considered concurrently "data controllers" to the extent that they independently performed separate processing activities in connection with a same trial. See Opinion of Garante per la Protezione dei Dati Personali of May 18, 2000.

49 http://www.export.gov/safeharbor/sh_overview.html.

50 For a discussion of international IP laws and treaties as it relates to biotechnology, see Michael Malinowski, *Biotechnology: Law, Business and Regulation,* Aspen Publishers, 2004 Supp., Chapter 2, Patent Protection.

51 Caslon Analytics, Intellectual Property Guide, July 2004, www.caslon.com.au/ipguide17.htm.

52 *Globalization, op.cit.,* p. 15.

53 Regulations governing IRBs appear at 21 CFR Part 56. To strengthen its monitoring of these bodies, the FDA proposed a rule requiring registration of IRBs and their FDA-regulated trials, 69 FR 40556, July 6, 2004.

54 *Globalization, op. cit.,* p.16.

55 World Health Organization, *Operational Guidelines for Ethics Committees in Biomedical Research,* Geneva, 2000, cited in *Globalization, op cit.,* p. 16.

56 Investigators in clinical trials are required to sign an attestation about how they will conduct the trial including assuring protection of the subjects rights. This attestation also known as Form 1572 is not required if the trial is not conducted as part of the investigational plan described in the IND, *Globalization, op. cit.,* p. 13.

57 Cited in Sangita Viswanathan, "Are You Moving Out?" *Pharmaceutical Formulation and Quality Magazine,* May 2004, www.pharmaquality.com/Cover%20Story6.htm.

58 *Ibid.*

59 Frost and Sullivan, "World Contract Research Organizations (CROs) Market: Poised for Strong Growth Despite Challenges," September 15, 2003, pharmiweb.com, www.pharmiweb.com/pressreleases/pressre.asp?ROW_ID=287.

60 *Ibid. Also see* Grant Coren, "Emotional Relationships—Marriage vs. 'Holiday Romances:' The Ongoing Dalliance Between the Wealthy Pharmaceutical Company and the Service-Oriented Clinical CRO," April 11, 2003, InPharm.com.

TWELVE

Clinical Research Trials in the Courtroom

Andrew Agati

Introduction

By definition, litigation involves a dispute of some kind that consumes time, energy, and financial expense, all of which interferes with the effort to achieve medical advancements, the goal of clinical research trials.

Ultimately, however, litigation is inevitable. As such, this chapter will discuss the types of lawsuits that may emerge from a clinical research trial, with the primary focus on personal injury litigation that arises when a research volunteer alleges a physical injury as a result of his or her participation in the trial. Related topics include the typical individuals or entities who are named as defendants, theories of liability, emerging themes, and the defenses that can be prepared. In this respect, an effort has been made to collect and summarize a number of representative court decisions. Finally, other practical considerations will be discussed, including the nature and extent of discovery, cost considerations, media coverage, and the growing negative perception of clinical research trials.

411

The Type of Lawsuits That Emerge from Clinical Research Trials

Clinical research trials are not unlike any other industry when it comes to litigation. A whole host of different types of lawsuits can arise. For example, a publicly traded company sponsoring a research trial could be subject to securities litigation for violating SEC reporting obligations if the safety and efficacy of a new drug or device cannot be shown during a clinical trial. Intellectual property disputes could arise. A former employee may have stolen confidential trade secret information, thereby necessitating litigation to respond to such theft. A professor at a university subject to an internal research misconduct inquiry could bring suit for defamation or, ultimately, a wrongful termination action for any adverse employment decision. Or breach of contract actions might be necessary against a contract research organization, for example, for that company's failure to perform its contractual obligations. A participant may sue his or her insurance company in order to receive coverage for costs of participating in a clinical trial. A participant may attempt to claim a property interest in his or her own blood or genes. Less glamorously, collection action by the research site may be necessary to obtain payment for any services rendered.

In short, many situations may arise that can result in litigation. However, it is the lawsuit brought by a research volunteer for claimed injuries sustained in a clinical trial that usually garners the most attention and concern. Aside from losing time and money spent investing in the new drug or device, federal funding could be taken away, all research trials, and not just the one from which the allegation emanated from, could be stopped, and both civil and criminal fines and penalties are possible. Individual, corporate, and/or institutional reputations can be sullied, if not ruined.

While the rogue researcher, institution, or sponsor should be held accountable, the fact is that even when something goes not so terribly wrong and questionable allegations are made, negative repercussions are likely. Moreover, it is often not the "rogue" researcher, institution, or sponsor who has been accused. Well-known and well-respected organizations such as The Johns Hopkins University, Duke University, University of Pennsylvania, University of Rochester, University of Cincinnati, Children's Hospital of Pittsburgh, Baylor College of Medicine in Houston, St. Jude's Children Research Hospital of South Florida, The Ohio State University, Rush Hospital in Chicago, and Pfizer, Inc., to name a few, have had to respond to allegations of wrongdoing. Accordingly, the focus of this chapter is on personal injury litigation.

Personal Injury Litigation

Before addressing the "nuts and bolts" of personal injury lawsuits, one must first have a general understanding of the history and regulatory framework under which clinical trials typically operate.

This history starts with *United States v. Brandt, Trials of War Criminal Before the Nuremburg Military Tribunals under Control Council Law No. 10* (1949), which is more commonly called the Nazi Doctors Trial. The defendants, including twenty physicians, were tried for conducting medical "experiments," which were nothing more than grotesque, inhumane atrocities conducted during World War II. At the conclusion of the trial, a number of the defendants were found guilty and the court issued a set of ethical standards for conducting experiments on humans. These standards have become known as the Nuremberg Code. *See generally* National Bioethics Advisory Commission Report, Volume I, Appendix C (August 20, 2001).

In the late 1950s and early 1960s, the thalidomide situation came to light. While the Food and Drug Administration (FDA) had not approved of this drug, it had been approved for use as a sedative in Europe. The drug was then supplied to physicians. These physicians were paid to study the safety and efficacy of the drug in humans. It was later learned that the drug could seriously damage a fetus if taken by a woman during her first trimester. Congressional hearings established that many who had been given the drug in the United States were not told about the drug's experimental nature and had not been asked to give consent. As a result, the 1962 Kefauver-Harris Amendments were added to the then-existing FDA statute, requiring researchers to disclose the experimental nature of a drug and to obtain a volunteer's prior consent. *Id.*

In 1964, the World Medical Association promulgated the Declaration of Helsinki. In 1966, Dr. Henry K. Beecher published his expose, *Ethics and Clinical Research*, in *The New England Journal of Medicine.* This article highlighted ethical shortcomings in various studies, including one study where live cancer cells were injected into patients without their consent. In another study, mentally disabled children were deliberately infected with isolated strains of hepatitis for the purpose of developing a hepatitis vaccine. *Id.*

In 1972, the Tuskegee Syphilis scandal was exposed. This study, which was conducted by the U.S. Public Health Service (n/k/a the Centers for Disease Control and Prevention), lasted for 40 years, during which time black males with syphilis were studied to determine the effects of untreated syphilis. The problem was that these individuals did not know they had syphilis and when penicillin became an accepted form of treating syphilis and was widely available to the public, these individuals were not given penicillin. This practice continued for nearly three decades. *Id.*

Because of the Tuskegee scandal, Congress passed the National Research Act in 1974. This act created the National Commission for the Protection of Human Subjects of Biomedical and Behavioral Research and required the implementation of regulations setting forth informed consent requirements and requiring the creation of institutional review boards (IRBs) for the purpose of reviewing research studies. In 1974, the then Department of Health, Education and Welfare (HEW) (n/k/a Department of Health and Human Services) published regulations at 45 CFR Part 46 governing the protection of human volunteers in research. These regulations, however, applied only to research sponsored by HEW. *Id.*

In 1979, the National Commission for the Protection of Human Subjects of Biomedical and Behavioral Research issued the Belmont Report. In 1981, based on the Belmont Report, the FDA and the Department of Health and Human Services revised their respective regulations. Not all governmental departments or agencies did so at that time. After a ten-year process, fifteen federal departments and agencies agreed on a set of standards, i.e., those appearing in the Department of Health and Human Services' regulations at 45 CFR Part 46, Subpart A. Hence, this regulation is known as "the Common Rule" and covers all research sponsored or conducted by those who adopt it.[1]

It must be noted that not all research is covered by the various federal regulations, generally, and the Common Rule, more specifically. The federal regulations apply only when research is conducted or funded by a particular federal agency or when the research is being conducted for FDA approval. The general rule, then, is that privately funded research is not subject to federal oversight. There is one caveat to this general rule: Many research institutions will voluntarily agree to abide by the Common Rule with respect to all research conducted at their institutions regardless of funding source.[2]

The Typical Defendants

Perhaps it is a misnomer to title this heading the "typical" defendants. No one case is typical, as each case turns on its own unique sets of circumstances. The more appropriate question is "who can be sued?" The answer is, in a single word, everybody. For instance, in *Robertson v. McGee*, Case No. 01-CV-60 (N.D. Ok. 2001), virtually every conceivable participant in a clinical research trial: the consultant, the sponsoring corporation, the principal investigator, the head of the university's Office of Research

Administration, the institutional review board, and even its individual members, as well as the university's president, were named as defendants. Even a "patient advocate," the person representing the interests of the volunteer and a more recent advent in the clinical trial field, was named in a lawsuit for malpractice. *See* Complaint in *Quinn, et al. v. Abiomed, Inc.*, Case No. 001524 (PA Common Pleas 2002).

There are tactical reasons for casting such a wide net. The more defendants, the greater the chance each defendant will "point the finger" at the other. Once that happens, it is much easier for a claim to be successful. Thus, in a multidefendant case it becomes critical for all defendants to coordinate a united defense, if possible.

Theories of Liability

In a sense, the actual theory of liability is not that important—it is merely the means by which to achieve an ultimate end, such as a favorable settlement or a large jury verdict. Instead, it is the underlying facts of the case that must be understood and that will ultimately play the most important role. Nonetheless, it is useful to know what type of claims will likely be asserted.

Typical claims, not all of which necessarily have merit and not all of which have been treated consistently by the courts, include:

- Claims under 42 U.S.C. § 1983, titled Civil Action for Deprivation of Rights (for state actor defendants, such as a state university or VA hospitals), premised on one or more of the following alleged constitutional violations:
  - Breach of the right to be treated with dignity based on the Nuremberg Code and the Declaration of Helsinki
  - Breach of the right to privacy
  - Breach of the right to bodily integrity
  - Breach of the right to be free from unlawful searches and seizures under the Fourth Amendment
  - Breach of the right to access to courts
  - Deprivation of property without due process
- Violation of applicable federal regulations, including 21 CFR §§ 210, 211, 601, and 610, which relate to the manufacture and control of investigational biological drugs for clinical use, as well as 45 CFR § 46, Subpart A
- Third-party beneficiary breach of contract claims for violating Multiple Project Assurances (MPAs) (now Federal Wide Assurances or FWAs), which may also incorporate the Belmont Report

- Breach of contract, based on the informed consent document, although some states treat informed consent claims as a tort, as opposed to a breach of contract claim
- Common law fraud/intentional misrepresentation
- Breach of express and/or implied warranties
- Assault and battery based on the lack of informed consent
- Breach of fiduciary duty
- Products liability claims, such as failure to warn
- Violation of applicable state consumer protection acts
- Intentional and negligent infliction of emotional distress
- Negligence
- Fraud on the FDA
- Punitive damages

It is not the purpose of this chapter to address the specific elements of each of the claims described, although the nature of many of these claims can be determined by reviewing the representative cases outlined later in this chapter. However, to the extent a single generality can be stated that captures the essence of all claims, it is the lack of informed consent, not only at the time the participant initially decides to enter a clinical research trial, but even after the initial consent, such as when new risks (i.e., adverse events) come to light during the course of the clinical research trial.

The requirement of informed consent is not unlike that required for medically-necessary procedures, but it is the scope of disclosure that is different. The reason for this is because the relationship between a researcher/investigator and a human volunteer is not the typical doctor–patient relationship. As stated by the National Bioethics Advisory Commission in its Summary Report: "It is essential that participants and investigators not be led to believe that participating in research is tantamount to being in a traditional therapeutic relationship." The case of *Whitlock v. Duke Univ., et al.,* 637 F. Supp. 1463 (M.D.N.C. 1986), *aff'd,* 829 F.2d 1340 (4th Cir. 1987) is instructive on this point.

In *Whitlock,* the court made a distinction between therapeutic experimentation and nontherapeutic experimentation "where the researcher does not have as an objective to benefit the subject." *Id.* at 1468. In making this distinction, the *Whitlock* court refused to apply the applicable North Carolina statute regarding "health care treatment" performed without informed consent. Instead, the court found that the Nuremberg Code and the Declaration of Helsinki provided persuasive guidance for the applicable standard of care and ultimately concluded that the applicable standard of care would be consistent with that set forth in the Common Rule. *Id.* at 1470–1471.

In so ruling, the *Whitlock* court made the following observation:

> Two important differences to note between the Nuremberg Code and [the North Carolina statute] are that the subjective consent of the subject is always required under the Nuremberg Code whereas under [the North Carolina statute] a health care provider may escape liability if a reasonable person would have consented if the proper disclosure of information had been made; and more importantly for the purposes of this case, *the Nuremberg Code requires the researcher to make known to the subject all hazards reasonably to be expected and the possible effects upon the health and person of the subject whereas [the North Carolina statute] only requires the health care provider to apprise the patient of the "usual and most frequent risks and hazards" of the procedure.*
>
> *Id.* at 1471 (emphasis added).

A number of other cases follow this distinction in clinical trial litigation. In essence, the proposition *Whitlock* and cases like it stand for is that the research subject is entitled to know all risks, apparently regardless of the remoteness of an actual occurrence. The underlying rationale is that the research volunteer does not need to participate in a clinical trial for his or her health. In fact, informed consent documents state virtually universally that the volunteer can expect to receive no benefits from participating in the clinical trial. Bluntly stated, the research volunteer does not need the clinical trial; it is the clinical trial that needs the research volunteer. In this scenario, then, a 1 in 10,000 risk may not be significant but, ultimately, it is the volunteer's choice to make. This is precisely why merely informing the volunteer, as in *Whitlock*, of the "usual and most frequent risks and hazards" will not suffice.

Emerging Themes

Every first-year law student takes a criminal law class and is taught that for the elements of a crime to be proven, the prosecution does not have to prove motive. Yet, no popular TV show, book, or even real-life prosecutor ignores the importance of motive. It provides the "why" a jury craves.

This is no different in the civil litigation context, including clinical research trials. The elements of negligence or even fraud claims are, in and of themselves, quite dry. For negligence, one must show a duty, breach of that duty, that the breach was the proximate cause of harm, and damages as a result of that breach. Therefore, as in any case, a "motive," a "why," will be advanced.

In litigation involving clinical research trials, the motive or theme commonly advanced is conflict of interest, especially of the financial kind. Many of the lawsuits that have been filed are premised on the very theory that risks were not disclosed or were otherwise seriously downplayed because of financial conflicts of interest. Indeed, the FDA itself has concluded that "[o]ne potential source of *bias* in clinical studies is a financial interest of the clinical investigator in the outcome of the study because of the way payment is arranged (e.g., a royalty) or because the investigator has a proprietary interest in the product (e.g., a patent) or because the investigator has an equity interest in the sponsor of the covered study." 21 CFR § 54.1(b).

An instructive case on this issue is *Moore v. The Regents of the Univ. of California*, 51 Cal. 3d 120 (S. Ct. 1990), *cert denied*, 499 U.S. 936, 113 L.Ed.2d 444, 111 S. Ct. 1388 (1991). In *Moore*, the court held that a defendant doctor's failure to disclose his financial/research interest in the plaintiff's cells gave rise to a cause of action for lack of informed consent and/or breach of fiduciary duty. *Id.* at 132–133. Specifically, the *Moore* court stated:

It is important to note that no law prohibits a physician from conducting research in the same area in which he practices. Progress in medicine often depends upon physicians, such as those practicing at the university hospital where Moore received treatment, who conduct research while caring for their patients. *Yet a physician who treats a patient in whom he also has a research interest has potentially conflicting loyalties.* This is because medical treatment decisions are made on the basis of proportionality—weighing the benefits to the patient against the risks to the patient. . . . *A physician who adds his own research interests to this balance may be tempted to order a scientifically useful procedure or test that offers marginal, or no, benefits to the patient. The possibility that an interest extraneous to the patient's health has affected the physician's judgment is something that a reasonable patient would want to know in deciding whether to consent to a proposed course of treatment. It is material to the patient's decision and, thus, a prerequisite to informed consent. . . .* Accordingly, we hold that a physician who is seeking a patient's consent for a medical procedure must, in order to satisfy his fiduciary duty and to obtain the patient's informed consent, disclose personal interests unrelated to the patient's health, whether *research or economic, that may* affect his medical judgment.

Id. at 130–131 (emphasis added).

Currently, no federal regulation requires that financial interests be disclosed to a potential volunteer during the informed consent process. Yet, this will provide little defense to any action.

As an off-shoot of the "financial" conflict of interest, some cases assert a "career" type conflict of interest. That is, risks were not disclosed (or minimized) so that a researcher could publish ground-breaking articles and achieve "prestige." Again, the *Moore* case highlights this conflict, requiring disclosure of "personal interests," whether "research or economic."

Another theme seeks to capitalize on the distinction made by the courts, as in *Whitlock*, that research volunteers are not typical "patients." Increasingly, it is being argued that volunteers are led to believe they would benefit from the clinical trial, notwithstanding language in the informed consent document to the contrary. The name given to this theory is the "therapeutic misconception." Thus, in the complaint filed in *Scheer, et al. v. Burke, et al.*, Case No. 000375 (PA Common Pleas 2003), it was alleged that the informed consent document inappropriately referred to the volunteer as a "patient," a term which is purportedly misleading because it connotes the typical doctor–patient relationship and, therefore, the receipt of a health benefit. It must be noted that in support of this theme the regulations can be cited themselves, which painstakingly make sure that volunteers are not called patients.

By far, however, the most compelling theme is the conflict of interest and, not surprisingly, its appeal resonates. Nowhere is this more evident than in the case of *Grimes v. Kennedy Kreiger Institute, Inc.*, 782 A.2d 87 (Ct. App. Md. 2001), where the court made statements such as:

The "for profit" nature of some research may well increase the duties of researchers to insure the safety of research subjects, and may well increase researchers' or an institution's susceptibility for damages in respect to any injuries incurred by research subjects; and there is always a potential substantial conflict of interest on the part of researchers as between them and the human subjects used in their research. If participants in the study withdraw from the research study prior to its completion, then the results of the study could be rendered meaningless. There is thus an inherent reason for not conveying information to subjects as it arises, that might cause the subjects to leave the research project. That conflict dictates a stronger reason for full and continuous disclosure.

Id. (For a more detailed description of the *Grimes* case, please see the representative cases section.)

Defending the Lawsuit—After It Has Been Filed

The burden of proving a claim is always on the party bringing that claim, i.e., the plaintiff, or in the case of clinical trial litigation, the research volunteer. In reality, the defendant will have to "disprove" each argument advanced. Because each case has its own peculiarities, it is impossible to provide a comprehensive explanation of each and every potential defense, although the representative cases highlighted later provide some insight.

There are, however, a number of stock defenses, more typically referred to as "affirmative" defenses. Affirmative defenses are those which state that even if all allegations are true, the plaintiff is not entitled to relief. Affirmative defenses are waived if not raised timely. An example is the statute of limitations, which means that the claim was not timely filed. The applicable statute of limitation will vary from claim to claim and state to state.

One defense of more relevance in clinical trial litigation is the doctrine of federal pre-emption. Federal preemption issues are deserving of their own lengthy chapter and the nuances of federal preemption are not addressed here. As an oversimplification, however, federal preemption precludes certain state claims from being asserted when there exists a federal regulatory scheme that was enacted to address an entire area of law. In FDA-related studies, the cases of *Buckman Co. v. Plaintiffs' Legal Committee*, 531 U.S. 341 (2001) and *Medtronic Inc. v. Lohr*, 518 U.S. 470 (1996) must be reviewed. *Buckman* held that claims for fraud on the FDA are preempted. In *Medtronic*, the U.S. Supreme Court held that the Medical Device Amendments did not *ipso facto* preempt state claims. Instead, for a state law claim to be preempted, a number of different factors had to be met. A number of questions were left unanswered, such as whether injuries caused by investigational devices were preempted, and the various factors listed by the *Medtronic* case have not led to consistent treatment.

Another "defense" that must be discussed applies to all types of civil litigation. That is, where is the case brought? This is referred to as the "venue" of the case. Justice is not necessarily blind. The jurisdiction in which the case is to be heard and even the judge to whom it is assigned will affect a case. If the case is placed in an unfavorable court, a defendant must examine whether there are options to have the case heard elsewhere. A classic example would be removing a lawsuit from state to federal court, assuming the prerequisites for removal are met.

Defending the Lawsuit—Before It Has Been Filed

It is perhaps counterintuitive to think that a lawsuit can be defended before it is filed. Indeed, there are no guarantees that a research volunteer will not file suit. There are proactive measures, however, one can take that will either reduce the risk of a lawsuit being filed or that will place a party in a stronger position to defend a lawsuit once it is filed.

Take, for instance, the conflict of interest issue. There is no federal regulation requiring disclosure of financial or "research" interests. Yet, if in the informed consent document itself the nature and extent of any financial interests are disclosed or there exists even the possibility that matters relating to the research will be published, such disclosure effectively disarms the conflict of interests theme. In addition, it will buttress the counterargument that the allegedly undisclosed risks were, in fact, disclosed.

Similarly, the therapeutic misconception can be addressed up-front by, for example, ensuring that the volunteer does not execute an informed consent form "on the spot." Instead, the volunteer should take the informed consent document home, review it and study it, and should be even encouraged to consult with his or her own treating physician or a "patient advocate" for a second opinion, assuming there are no confidentiality issues.

Representative Cases

As set forth above, each lawsuit presents its own unique set of facts and circumstances and what may apply in one case may not apply in another. Nevertheless, there is a body of case law (i.e., "precedent") involving clinical research trials that provides guidance to courts and those in litigation. Set forth next is a summary of selected cases in this field, arranged in alphabetical order by plaintiff's name.

1. *Abdullahi v. Pfizer, Inc.*, 2002 U.S. Dist. LEXIS 17436 (S.D.N.Y. Sept. 17, 2002): Pfizer was sued under the Alien Tort Claim Act for a clinical trial conducted in Nigeria. The court held that plaintiff stated a claim for relief under the theory that Pfizer acted as a *de facto* state actor because Pfizer conducted the study with assistance of the Nigerian government. The case dismissed, however, on forum *non conveniens* grounds, i.e., that the case would be more appropriately tried and heard in Nigeria.

2. *Acheff v. Hartford Hospital*, 799 A.2d 1067 (Conn. S. Ct. 2002): This case highlights the difference between medical treatment and research. Here, the plaintiff had back surgery, shortly after which he developed an infection. When he was admitted to the hospital for the infection, the hospital found the presence of a potentially life-threatening form of bone infection and, as a result, ordered the administration of an antibiotic without consent. The plaintiff was eventually discharged from the hospital, but later claimed to have suffered adverse side effects from the antibiotic. The lawsuit eventually proceeded to trial, where the jury found in favor of the hospital. The plaintiff's theory was that the administration of the antibiotic was experimental and the hospital was required to obtain his consent before administering same, especially given certain known side effects. In turn, the hospital argued that the administration of the antibiotic was not experimental in the sense that it was not aimed at testing a theory. Instead, the antibiotic was administered as part of therapeutic medical care and safety to counter the plaintiff's infection. In upholding the jury verdict, the court rejected the plaintiff's claim that the trial court's refusal to admit the Belmont Report into evidence constituted reversible error. In so holding, the court stated that the Belmont Report was unfairly prejudicial. More specifically, the court stated:

> First, it [i.e., the Belmont Report] purported to be, for the most part, a statement of basic ethical principles, and not to be a statement of the legal standard for securing informed consent. Moreover, it invited the jury, in deciding whether the hospital's . . . program constituted research or medical practice, to think about the Nuremberg War Crimes Trials and the Nuremburg Code, the substance of which the report did not describe, and thus, implicitly, to compare the hospital's conduct with whatever the jurors may have understood those terms to

mean. It also invited the jury to engage in a highly abstract and philosophical level of inquiry into such subjects as respect for the autonomy of persons, the notion of self-determination, the concept of beneficence, and the various theories of justice. It invited the jury to think about the meaning of the physician's Hippocratic oath, which was neither given in full nor explained in any detail. It invited the jury to compare the hospital's conduct to the infamous Tuskegee study. It invited the jury to compare the hospital's conduct regarding the plaintiff to complexities of securing informed consent from vulnerable groups such as racial minorities, the economically disadvantaged, the very ill, and the institutionalized. We cannot fault the trial court, as the plaintiff would have it, for determining that submitting this material to the jury would unduly arouse its emotions of prejudice, hostility or sympathy, and would tend to confuse the issues and mislead the jury.

3. *Ahern v. Veterans Administration,* 537 F.2d 1098 (10th Cir. 1976): Upholding award for plaintiff on claim that plaintiff was exposed to radiation levels that were entirely experimental. The court stated: "in order for a physician to avoid liability by engaging in drastic or experimental treatment, which exceeds the bounds of established medical standards, his patient must always be fully informed of the experimental nature of the treatment and of the foreseeable consequences of that treatment."

4. *Buckman Co. v. Plaintiffs' Legal Committee,* 531 U.S. 341, 121 S. Ct. 1012, 148 L.Ed. 2d 854 (2001): Relevant to preemption issue. Fraud-on-the-FDA claims are preempted by federal law. The FDA, not private litigants, is to seek recourse. [Note: One should also consult *Medtronic, Inc. v. Lohr,* 518 U.S. 470, 135 L.Ed.2d 700, 116 S. Ct. 2240 (1996) and its progeny for other preemption issues.]

5. *Craft et al. v. Vanderbilt University et al.,* 174 F.R.D. 396 (M.D. Tenn. 1996): Class action lawsuit alleging that hundreds of pregnant women were given radioactive liquid without their consent. A motion to decertify various classes was granted, in part, and denied, in part. Settlement eventually reached for $10 million. *See United States Fire Ins. Co. v. Vanderbilt University et al.,* 82 F. Supp.2d 788 (M.D. Tenn. 2000).

6. *Daum v. Spinecare Medical Group, Inc.*, 61 Cal. Rptr. 2d 260 (Cal. App. 1997): Malpractice suit based on the theory that the patient was not informed that the device implanted was considered investigational or experimental by the FDA and was not told that the patient's surgery was part of an FDA-approved clinical investigation of the subject device. In partially reversing the lower court based on inappropriate jury instructions, the court stated:

> [T]he California Legislature and the FDA, in their wisdom, have decreed that patients participating in clinical trials of investigational devices must be informed in writing . . . of the nature of the trial and the device. Neither physicians nor courts are free to disregard these requirements. . . . Yet, the net effect of [the instructions] was to permit the medical experts alone to control the jury's consideration of what [plaintiff] had to be told about his . . . surgery, and how the disclosure should have been made. Moreover, the special verdict form did not require the jury to determine whether [plaintiff] had been advised his surgery was part of a clinical trial of an investigational device. It only asked whether he was given "all relevant information," and "relevance" was determined by the experts. This procedure eviscerated the statutory and regulatory requirements. . . .

7. *Diaz et al. v. Hillsborough County Hospital Authority,* Case No. 8:90-CV-120-T025B, 2000 U.S. Dist. LEXIS 14061 (M.D. Fl. Aug. 7, 2000): Class action lawsuit alleging that defendants engaged in a policy or practice of conducting randomized medical research studies without obtaining lawful informed consent. Case settled for $3.8 million. In approving the Settlement Agreement and Consent Decree, the court stated:

> The Plaintiffs faced the risk of not prevailing at trial and on appeal with respect to the merits, the class certification order, and this Court's denial of the individual [defendants'] motion for leave to amend their answer to assert the affirmative defense of qualified immunity. Most importantly, Plaintiffs' basic constitutional theory of the case was novel and untested in any other court in the nation so far as is known to class counsel and this Court. That theory was that these Plaintiffs were entitled to damages for dignitary harm resulting from a violation of their liberty interest in bodily integrity *even in the absence of any*

claimed physical harm. Class counsel has advised the Court that to his knowledge, this is the first case which has produced a substantial monetary recovery to a class of human subjects of biomedical research in the absence of any claim of physical injury. (Emphasis added.)

8. *Doe #1 v. Rumsfeld*, 297 F. Supp.2d 119 (D.C. 2003): Unnamed plaintiffs, members of the military and civil contract employees for the Department of Defense, filed suit to enjoin being inoculated with the Anthrax vaccine without their informed consent. At issue, among other things, was 10 U.S.C. § 1107, which prohibits the administration of investigational new drugs or drugs not approved for their intended use to military members without their informed consent, unless there is a Presidential waiver. Chapter 10 U.S.C. § 1107 was enacted in response to concerns that military service men and women were given investigational drugs during the 1991 Gulf War. In so holding, the court stated, "[t]he right to bodily integrity and the importance of complying with legal requirements, even in the face of requirements that may potentially be inconvenient or burdensome, are among the highest public policy concerns one could articulate."

9. *Gregg et al. v. Kane et al.,* 1997 U.S. Dist. LEXIS 14269 (E.D. Pa. Sept. 5, 1997): The plaintiff enrolled in a clinical trial for laser eye surgery. Ultimately, she brought suit against the doctor who performed the surgery, a medical consultant, the hospital where the surgery was conducted, and the sponsor of the clinical trial. The defendants moved for summary judgment and these motions were denied. The doctor purportedly had failed to follow the protocol in a number of respects. More interestingly, the court cited Section 324 of the *Restatement (Second) of Torts* to find that the medical consultant owed a duty to the plaintiff, even though the medical consultant did not perform the surgery at issue and apparently had no direct contact with the plaintiff. Section 324 of the *Restatement* provides:

One who undertakes . . . to render services to another which he should recognize as necessary for the protection of a third person . . . is subject to liability to the third person for physical harm resulting from his failure to exercise reasonable care to protect his undertaking, if (a) his failure to exercise reasonable care increases the risk of such harm, or (b) he has undertaken to perform a duty owed by the other to the third person, or (c) the harm is suffered because of reliance on the other or the third person upon the undertaking. *Restatement (Second) of Torts* § 324A (1965).

As to the hospital, the court found that its IRB was created pursuant to federal guidelines, but that it failed in carrying out its functions, including, in particular, "an independent risk assessment." As to the sponsor, the court apparently assumed a duty existed in the first instance, but perhaps was more persuaded by facts such as the sponsor's failure to timely report adverse events to the FDA. [Note: Plaintiffs were ultimately unsuccessful at trial and lost on appeal. 1998 U.S. Dist. LEXIS 8437 (Jan. 10, 1998); 185 F.3d 861 (1999).]

10. *Grimes v. Kennedy Kreiger Institute, Inc.*, 782 A.2d 807 (Ct. App. Md. 2001): Litigation over a nontherapeutic scientific study involving children to test the efficacy of lead paint abatement. One issue was whether the trial court erred in finding as a matter of law that a "research entity conducting an ongoing, non-therapeutic scientific study does not have a duty to warn a minor volunteer participant and/or his legal guardian regarding dangers present when the researcher has knowledge of the potential for harm to the subject and the subject is unaware of the danger." The court found that the trial court had erred. Another issue was whether "a parent in Maryland . . . can legally consent to placing a child in a nontherapeutic research study that carries with it any risk of harm to the health of the child." The court answered this issue in the negative. In making these rulings, the court made a number of statements:

    a. "We shall hold initially that the very nature of nontherapeutic scientific research on human subjects can, and normally will, create special relationships out of which duties arise." [Note: The court relied, in part, on the federal regulations and the Nuremberg Code for the finding of a special relationship.]

    b. "[T]he Nuremberg Code, at least in significant part, was the result of legal thought and legal principles, as opposed to medical or scientific principles, and thus should be the preferred standard for assessing the legality of scientific research on human subjects."

    c. "Researcher/subject consent in nontherapeutical research can, and in this case did, create a contract. . . . By having appellants sign this Consent Form . . . a bilateral contract between the parties [was created.] At the very least, it suggests that appellants were agreeing . . . to participate in the research study with the expectation that they would be compensated, albeit, more or less, minimally; be informed of all the information necessary for the subject to freely choose whether to participate, and continue to participate; and receive promptly any information that might bear on their willingness to continue to participate in the study. This includes full, detailed, prompt, and continuing warnings as to all the potential risks and hazards inherent in the research or that arise during the research. KKI, in return, . . . was given the right to test the children's blood for lead."

d. "The fact that if such information was furnished it might be difficult to obtain human subjects for the research does not affect the need to supply the information, or alter the ethics of failing to provide such information. A human subject is entitled to *all* material information." (Emphasis in the original.)

e. "Researchers cannot ever be permitted to completely immunize themselves by reliance on consents, especially when the information furnished to the subject, or the party consenting, is incomplete in a material respect. A researcher's duty is not created by, or extinguished by, the consent of a research subject or by IRB approva . . . . Such legal duties, and legal protections, might additionally be warranted because of the likely conflict of interest between the goal of the research experimenter and the health of the human subject, especially, but not exclusively, when such research is commercialized."

f. "We hold that in Maryland a parent, appropriate relative, or other applicable surrogate, cannot consent to the participation of a child or other person under legal disability in nontherapeutic research or studies in which there is any risk of injury or damage to the health of the subject."

11. *Hagy et. al. v. United States of America,* 976 F. Supp. 1373 (W.D. Wash. 1997): The plaintiff sued the United States, Johns Hopkins University School of Medicine, the State of Maryland, Harbor General Hospital, and ten John Doe physicians for the alleged wrongful death of his wife who contracted a fatal neurological disease from contaminated human-growth hormone treatments allegedly from a government-funded program. The United States' motion to dismiss based on the Federal Tort Claim Act was granted.

12. *Halikas v. University of Minnesota et al.,* 856 F. Supp. 1331 (D. Minn. 1994): A medical researcher brought suit against the University of Minnesota, its IRB, and the individual members of the IRB, seeking, among other things, an injunction that would prevent the dissemination of the results of an IRB investigation regarding the medical researcher's alleged wrongdoings in human experiment studies. In rejecting the plaintiff's claim, the court stated, among other things: "The Court finds that a protocol departure, concerning an experimental drug administered to an unknowing human subject, is not an insignificant event."

13. *Heinrich et al. v. Sweet et al.,* 62 F. Supp.2d 282 (D. Mass. 1999): Plaintiffs filed suit alleging that the United States and a number of private defendants, including Massachusetts General Hospital and Massachusetts Institute of Technology, conspired to conduct dangerous medical experiments on 140 terminally ill patients without their consent. The court addressed a number of issues, including: (1) whether private individuals are subject to a Bivens claim (under *Bivens v. Six Unknown Named Agents of Federal Bureau of Narcotics,* 403 U.S. 388, 29 L.Ed. 2d 619, 91 S. Ct. 1999 (1971)); (2) whether private entities are subject to a Bivens claim; and (3) whether the private defendants acted under the color of state law. The court answered all of these issues in the affirmative. The court also addressed whether the plaintiffs' constitutional claims were valid. The plaintiffs asserted that their right to bodily integrity was violated, that their right to access to the courts was violated (because the defendants had allegedly covered-up the alleged wrongdoing), that they suffered a deprivation of property without due process of law (as a result of the dismissal on statute of limitations grounds of certain state law causes of action), that their right of privacy was violated, and that the defendants' conduct constituted an unreasonable search and seizure under the Fourth Amendment. The court rejected the right of privacy and unreasonable search and seizures claims, finding that these claims did not state a cause of action as a matter of law. As to the bodily integrity claim, the court explained:

> The crucial elements of the constitutional violation are that (1) a government actor, (2) without obtaining informed consent and utilizing false pretenses to obtain participation, (3) conducted medical experiments known to have no therapeutic value and indeed known to be

possibly harmful to the subjects. These elements are far more restrictive than the ordinary medical malpractice action for lack of informed consent that only requires the nondisclosure of a material risk of a medical procedure.

The court then rejected the private defendants' qualified immunity defense. In this regard, the court was persuaded by the Nuremberg Code. "Thus, at the very least, the judgment of the Nuremberg Tribunal regarding fundamental legal principles of human subject experimentation served as an explicit international declaration that the conduct alleged in this case 'shocked the conscience. . . .'"

[Note: An earlier opinion of the court dismissed the plaintiffs' strict liability/abnormally dangerous activity claim, where the plaintiffs argued that by merely conducting experimental treatments the defendants were subject to strict liability. 49 F. Supp.2d 27 (1999). The case against the doctor and Massachusetts General Hospital ultimately went to trial, with a jury returning a verdict totaling $3 million in compensatory damages and $3.75 million in punitive damages. 118 F. Supp.2d 73. Post-trial motions reduced the punitive damages verdict. *Id.* The hospital's charitable immunity defense was rejected. *Id.*]

14. *Hoover v. West Virginia Dep't of Health and Human Services*, 984 F. Supp. 978 (S.D. W. Va. 1997), *aff'd w/out opinion*, 129 F.3d 1259 (4th Cir. 1997): The plaintiff brought suit stemming from an investigation that was conducted regarding her alleged over-prescription of narcotics for a patient. One of her claims was premised on the Helsinki Accord. The court rejected the claim, stating, "The Helsinki Accord does not create a private right of action in U.S. federal courts and do [sic] not have the force of law."

15. *In re: Cincinnati Radiation Litigation*, 874 F. Supp. 796 (S.D. Ohio 1995): Lawsuit stemming from radiation experiments performed on unknowing human subjects. Suit was brought against the investigators and the institutions involved in conducting the experiments. The court held that the Nuremberg Code should be applied.

The Nuremberg Code is part of the law of humanity. It may be applied in both civil and criminal cases by the federal court in the United States. . . . It is inconceivable to the Court that the individual and Bivens Defendants, when allegedly planning to perform radiation experiments on unwitting subjects, were not moved to pause or rethink their procedures in light of the forceful dictates of the Nuremberg Tribunal and the several medical organizations. . . . If the Constitution has not clearly established a right under which these Plaintiffs may attempt to prove their case, then a gaping hole in that document has been exposed.

[Note: The parties subsequently entered into a class action settlement. 187 F.R.D. 549 (1999).]

16. *Karp v. Cooley*, 493 F.2d 408 (5th Cir. 1974), *cert. denied*, 419 U.S. 845, 42 L.Ed. 2d 73, 95 S. Ct. 79 (1974): Concluding that the elements of a state law claim for unlawful experimentation would be like that for a traditional malpractice claim, i.e., lack of informed consent and causation and proximate cause, but noting some support for the notion that "the duty to pre-inform is viewed more strictly when a novel or radical medical procedure is involved."

17. *Kernke v. The Menninger Clinic, Inc. et al.*, 173 F Supp.2d 1117 (D. Kan. 2001): In this case, the deceased, suffering from schizophrenia, entered a clinical study after signing an informed consent document. He successfully completed Phase I and then enrolled in Phase II. Three days after entering Phase II, he left the study. He was found dead three months later. The estate sued the sponsor of the study, a pharmaceutical company, the clinic, and the doctors involved in the clinical trial. The estate asserted claims of products liability, failure to warn, and breach of express warranty. The pharmaceutical company moved for, and was granted, summary judgment. As to the failure to warn claim, the pharmaceutical company prevailed on the basis of the learned intermediary doctrine, which generally provides that a drug manufacturer fulfills its legal duty to warn a patient of risks associated with the manufacturer's drugs if the drug manufacturer warns the patient's prescribing physician of the risks. As to the general negligence claim, the court found that the drug manufacturer had no general duty, finding that, under the applicable federal regulations (21 CFR § 312.6 and 21 CFR § 50.20) it was the investigator who owed the duty to obtain valid consent, not the manufacturer-sponsor.

18. *Lenahan v. The University of Chicago et al.*, 2004 Ill. App. LEXIS 328 (Ill. App. Ct. March 31, 2004): The deceased was initially undergoing treatment for cancer when his doctor recommended that he participate in a clinical research trial. The deceased volunteered for the clinical research trial, but died

during the period of enrollment. Subsequently, the estate of the deceased brought a wrongful death action against the University of Chicago, two doctors, a hospital, a biotech company, and a development company. Conspiracy claims were dismissed for lack of specificity. The administrator, however, was allowed to proceed with individual claims against the defendants, including an "institutional negligence" claim and a medical negligence claim against two doctors, i.e., the research director and the principal investigator of the research protocol. The court held that although it is typically a physician's duty to obtain informed consent, as opposed to the hospital or the university where the research is being conducted, the hospital and university defendants could be held liable on the "institutional negligence" claim, which was premised on faulty consent forms. In this respect, the court was persuaded by the fact that the university and the hospital had adopted policies regarding clinical research trials and had established IRBs to ensure that the consent forms complied with governmental regulations. As to the principal investigator, the court found that a special relationship existed between the deceased volunteer and the principal investigator, even though the two had never met. In effect, the mere status of "principal investigator" was sufficient to find the existence of a duty.

19. *Mackey v. Procunier*, 477 F.2d 877 (9th Cir. 1973): A state prisoner brought an action claiming his civil rights were violated when he allegedly underwent shock treatment and experimental drug treatment, described as a "breath-stopping and paralyzing fright drug," without his consent. The Ninth Circuit held that the district court improperly dismissed the complaint. The district court had concluded that allegations in the complaint constituted a state malpractice claim. In contrast, the Ninth Circuit found that "[p]roof of such matters could, in our judgment, raise serious constitutional questions respecting cruel and unusual punishment or impermissible tinkering with the mental processes."

20. *Missert v. Trustees of Boston University et al.*, 73 F. Supp.2d 68 (D. Mass. 1999): The plaintiff brought a 42 U.S.C. § 1983 claim alleging that his termination from Boston University (BU) violated his right to due process and equal protection under the Fourteenth Amendment. Plaintiff asserted that BU was a state actor because federal law required BU to establish IRBs to review and approve research involving humans. The court stated that "[w]hile an IRB's decision may well constitute state action under [the] traditional government

function test," no state action was at issue because the IRB did not make the decision to terminate the plaintiff's employment.

21. *Moore v. The Regents of the University of California,* 51 Cal. 3d 120 (S. Ct. 1990), *cert. denied,* 499 U.S. 936, 113 L.Ed.2d 444, 111 S. Ct. 1388 (1991): Financial interests must be disclosed. A more detailed explanation of *Moore* is set forth earlier. [Note: *Moore* also addressed the issue of whether an individual could claim a proprietary interest in his/her blood/cells. The recognition of such a claim would have given research volunteers an opportunity to claim a financial interest in any product or medical invention developed. The *Moore* court, however, rejected such a claim for a number of reasons, including the fact that "the subject matter of the [defendant's] patent—the patented cell line and the products derived from it—cannot be [plaintiff's] property. This is because the patented cell line is both factually legally distinct from [plaintiff's body."]

22. *Robertson et al. v. McGee et al.,* Case No. 01-CV-60-C, unreported (N.D. Ok. Jan. 28, 2002): Here, the court dismissed the plaintiffs' 42 U.S.C. § 1983 claims finding there was no federal constitutional right to be treated with dignity, as alleged by the plaintiffs. In addition, the court found that federal regulations for the protection of human research volunteers codified in 21 CFR §§ 210 and 211 and 45 CFR Part 46 did not provide plaintiffs with an implied cause of action. The court also rejected the plaintiffs' claim that there was a cause of action under the Declaration of Helsinki and the Nuremberg Code. The court refused to exercise supplemental jurisdiction over the plaintiffs' remaining state law claims.

23. *Schiff v. Prados,* 92 Cal. App. 4th 692 (Ct. App. 2001): The plaintiff brought suit alleging that a doctor failed to inform about experimental studies available in Texas. Expert physicians for plaintiff claimed that such conduct was "morally offensive and unethical." Plaintiff's claim was dismissed because, under California law, the treatment at issue was not available and, in fact, had been banned. The court did not impose a duty on the physician to disclose treatments that would be available elsewhere in other states.

24. *Stadt v. The University of Rochester et al.,* 921 F. Supp. 1023 (W.D.N.Y. 1996): The defendant-doctor had injected plutonium into a human research volunteer to study the effects of radiation. Plaintiff sued, claiming lack of informed

consent. The doctor sought qualified immunity under the theory that he was a government employee being sued in his individual capacity. The doctor's argument was rejected because government employees sued in their individual capacities are entitled to qualified immunity only so long as their actions do not violate clearly-established constitutional or statutory rights, which rights a reasonable person would have known. The court found the plaintiff had a clearly-established right under the plain language of the Fifth Amendment to be free from being injected with plutonium without consent. The court stated: "The Constitution, and more specifically, the due process clause of the 5th Amendment, clearly established the right to be free from non-consensual government experimentation on one's body. . . ." Another relevant quote from this decision includes: "[T]his case . . . involve[s] . . . the right to be free from non-consensual experimentation of one's body—the right to bodily integrity— a right which has been recognized throughout this nation's history."

25. *T.D. v. New York State Office of Mental Health*, 668 N.Y.S. 2d 153 (N.Y. 1997): At issue was the validity of regulations promulgated by the New York State Office of Mental Health. These regulations set out procedures for the participation of adults and children, who were patients or residents of state mental health facilities and who were incapable of giving consent, in nontherapeutic and possibly therapeutic experiments, some of which could have caused serious side effects, including death. The court held that the regulations did not "adequately safeguard and therefore violate[d] the State and Federal constitutional rights to due process, as well as the common-law right to personal autonomy" of the potential participating adults and/or children. In so holding, the court stated:

> The benefits of, and needs for, the medical research at issue are clear and evident; but at what cost in human pain and suffering to those subjects who are not capable of expressing their consent or object to participation? . . . It may very well be that for some categories of greater than minimal risk nontherapeutic experiments, devised to achieve a future benefit, there is at present no constitutionally acceptable protocol for obtaining the participation of incapable individuals who have not, when previously competent, either given specific consent or designated a suitable surrogate from whom such consent may

be obtained. The alternative of allowing such experiments to continue, without proper consent and in violation of the rights of the incapable individuals who participate, is clearly unacceptable.

26. *U.S., ex rel. Chandler v. Cook County,* 277 F.3d 969 (7th Cir. 2002): This case involved a False Claims Act (or *qui tam*) action brought by a whistle blowing doctor alleging violations of a federal grant and federal regulations, including failure to obtain informed consent from study participants. The suit held that Cook County was a "person" under the False Claims Act and, therefore, subject to liability. The False Claims Act is codified at 31 U.S.C. § 3729. Under this act, civil penalties can be asserted against "any person" who "knowingly presents, or causes to be presented, to . . . the United States Government . . . a false or fraudulent claim for payment or approval," or who "conspires to defraud" the United States Government into paying a false or fraudulent claim. A False Claims Act claim can be brought by the Government, or by a private person who must first give the Government sixty days notice. A private person who brings a suit on behalf of himself and the government is called a relator. Typically, when a private person brings such a suit, it is called *qui tam,* an old Latin term meaning "on behalf of the King." A successful claim under the False Claims Act exposes a defendant to treble damages as well.

27. *United States v. Stanley,* 483 U.S. 669, 107 S. Ct. 3054, 97 L.Ed.2d 550 (1987): Stanley had been given LSD as part of a mind-control experiment conducted by the Army. Stanley did not know he had been given LSD and only found out approximately twenty years later, after he received a letter asking for his cooperation in a study regarding the long-term effects of LSD. Stanley's complaint was dismissed and the dismissal was upheld by the Supreme Court under the Feres Doctrine, which provides that a serviceman cannot sue the government for being put in harm's way. The dissents of Justice Brennan and Justice O'Connor are often cited. Justice Brennan stated that "Soldiers ought not be asked to defend a Constitution indifferent to their essential human dignity." Justice O'Connor stated that "No judicially crafted rule should insulate from liability the involuntary and unknowing human experimentation alleged to have occurred in this case."

28. *Whitlock et al. v. Duke University et al.,* 637 F. Supp. 1463, *aff'd,* 829 F.2d 1340 (4th Cir. 1987): Common Rule is the applicable standard of care when

determining whether informed consent given in a nontherapeutic research experiment, even though the research was not federally funded. A more detailed analysis of *Whitlock* appears earlier.

29. *Wright et al. v. The Fred Hutchinson Cancer Research Center et al.*, Case No. 3:01-cv-05217-RSL (W.D. Wash.): A number of decisions from this case have been reported and should be consulted. These appear at 269 F. Supp.2d 1286; 2002 U.S. Dist. LEXIS 26741, 2002 U.S. Dist. LEXIS 26738; and 206 F.R.D. 679. An unreported decision from this case also should be reviewed. This decision, issued on November 19, 2001, addressed plaintiffs' motion to have the case heard as a class action lawsuit. In order for a case to certified as a class action, a number of prerequisites have to be satisfied. The Wright court rejected the motion, finding that common issue of fact did not predominate, that plaintiffs' claims were not typical of each other, that maintaining the litigation as a class action would have been difficult, and that individual plaintiffs had a significant interest in pursuing their claims independently, given the amount of damages allegedly at stake.

Practical Considerations

Some defendants, such as large pharmaceutical companies or research institutions, have experienced litigation. They have been involved in the time-consuming process, know its ebbs and flows and the inherent risks. For others, including individual researchers, litigation may be an entirely foreign concept. More time, then, must be spent educating and supporting those who conduct clinical trials, but who may not know all of its complexities. The author has seen researchers express sincere shock when they are sued. For many of them, they have devoted their entire lives to helping people and to be accused of abusing those whom they seek to help does not make sense to them.

The shock only continues during the course of litigation. The scope of discovery is likely to be very encompassing, requiring the disclosure of all research studies, articles, and even theses statements written by the researcher defendant. Suddenly, everything they have written or everything they have said is subject to discovery and, unfortunately, subject to be taken out of context.

Forces outside of the litigation—namely the media—will also cause pressure and must be addressed, regardless of who the defendant is. It is not the purpose of this chapter to discuss the pros and cons of speaking to the media, or whether any such communication should occur in the first instance. There are many different views in this respect. The important point to understand is that the media will likely publish an article either right before or during the course of the lawsuit. If a lawsuit has not yet been filed, the nature of the media's inquiry must be determined at the onset. Speaking from personal experience, the media may very well ask for information without disclosing the true nature of the story it will seek to report. Then, to everybody's surprise, a negative piece appears in the Sunday newspaper.

The media exposure leads to the most important practical consideration at issue—the current perception of clinical research trials. Media exposure is typically negative. This is best captured by the April 22, 2002, cover of *Time* magazine which is titled "How Medical Testing Has Turned Millions of Us Into . . . Human Guinea Pigs." Together with the financial conflict of interest issue, the public perception of those involved in conducting clinical research trials is skewed. Unfortunately, perception is often more important than reality and cannot be ignored during litigation. Potential juries, even judges, may share preconceived notions about clinical trials that are difficult to know, let alone defend against.

Conclusion

According to www.clinicaltrials.com, which attempts to bring together people who desire to join clinical trials and those conducting such trials, there are countless thousands of clinical trials currently being conducted all over the United States, studying a wide range of problems from abdominal cancer to athlete's foot. (The U.S. National Institutes of Health provides a similar service through www.clincialtrials.gov.) In turn, these clinical trials have a corresponding multitude of volunteers. In short, the sheer number of ongoing clinical trials and volunteers, to say nothing of the perception discussed, suggest that lawsuits will not only continue, but probably will increase in number.

Notes and References

1   The other federal agencies that have adopted the Common Rule include: (1) Department of Agriculture (7 CFR Part 1c); (2) Department of Energy (10 CFR Part 745); (3) NASA (14 CFR Part 1230); (4) Department of Commerce (15 CFR Participating 27); (5) Consumer Product Safety Commission (16 CFR Part 1028); (6) Agency for Int'l Development (22 CFR Part 225); (7) HUD (24 CFR Part 60); (8) Department of Justice (28 CFR Part 46); (9) Department

of Defense (32 CFR Part 219); (10) Department of Education (34 CFR Part 97); (11) Department of Veterans Affairs (38 CFR Part 16); (12) EPA (40 CFR Part 26); (13) National Science Foundation (45 CFR Part 690); and (14) Department of Transportation (49 CFR Part 11). The Common Rule also applies to research conducted or sponsored by the Social Security Administration, through Public Law 296, 103rd Congress, and the CIA, through Executive Order 12333 (46 Fed. Reg. 59941). Some agencies have their own and/or additional rules. These include the following: (1) Bureau of Prisons (28 CFR Part 512); (2) Department of Education (34 CFR Part 97, Subpart D and 34 CFR Part 98); (3) Office of Special Education & Rehabilitative Services (34 CFR § 356.3(c)); (4) Department of Veterans Affairs (38 CFR § 17.85); (5) Department of Health & Human Services (45 CFR Part 46, Subparts B, C, and D); and (6) FDA (21 CFR Part 50 and 21 CFR Part 56).

2   Some states have enacted laws specific to human research generally. For instance, California, New York, and Virginia have passed such laws. *See* California Health & Safety Code § 24170, *et seq.;* New York Public Health Law § 2440, *et seq.;* and Virginia Code § 32.1-162.16, *et seq. See also* Florida Statutes § 381.85 *et seq.* (setting forth procedures for research under the auspices of Florida's Department of Health). Some state statutes focus on a specific type of research or a specific group of potential research subjects such as prisoners or children. *See e.g.,* California Health & Safety Code § 24185, *et seq.* (prohibiting cloning of entire human being but not cloning of human cells, tissues, or organs which would not result in replication of an entire human); Oregon Statutes § 431.805 *et seq.* (genetic research); New Mexico Statutes §§ 24-9A-2 and 24-9A-3 (fetal research); 9 New York Codes, Rules & Regulations § 7651.27 (prisoners); Illinois Administrative Code Title 89 § 432.1, *et seq.* (children). *See also* Michigan Laws § 330.1919[1] (individuals in mental health facilities); Washington Code § 74.42.040 (nursing home residents); Montana Statutes § 53-20-147 (individuals in developmentally disabled facilities). In this respect, some states have enacted complete prohibitions on certain research. Constitutional challenges to such prohibiting statutes can and have been made. *See e.g., Forbes v. Woods,* 71 F. Supp.2d 1015 (D. Ariz. 1999) (Arizona statute outlawing experimentation on human fetuses from induced abortions ruled unconstitutionally vague). Thus, depending on where the research is conducted, different rules may apply.

INDEX